How Did I Get Here From There?

CLAIRE RAYNER

How Did I Get Here From There?

Virago

A *Virago* Book

First published by Virago Press 2003

Copyright © Claire Rayner 2003

Jay Rayner for The *Guardian* © 1993

A CIP catalogue record for this book
is available from the British Library

ISBN 1 86049 999 6

Typeset in Goudy by M Rules
Printed and bound in Great Britain by
Clays Ltd, St Ives plc

Virago Press
An imprint of
Time Warner Books UK
Brettenham House
Lancaster Place
London WC2E 7EN

www.virago.co.uk

For Des.
Who else?

Acknowledgements

With grateful thanks to the superb support system supplied by so many people without whom not only would this book never have been written, but also my life would not have been lived as it was.

People like Beryl, Wendy, Sue and Alla, and many more, who kept my house clean and the laundry done over the past forty years or so.

People like Stella, Gaby and Maggie – who works with me still, after more than a quarter of a century – and Carole, Brenda and Sylvia, and so many more who typed and typed, and typed again, ensuring that readers' letters were answered fast, and that copy for editors was always readable.

People like Maritza, Alice and Ruby who kept me looking tidy, and Del and his colleagues who kept my wheels turning.

And, above all, my family, Des, Amanda, Adam, Jay, Colin, Julie and Pat and the little ones. Without them all I am and would be nothing.

Preface

This is the book I said I would never write.

'Why should I?' I would say when someone suggested it, and many did. 'I prefer to spend my life in the present, or looking forwards to good things rather than backwards at bad ones. And anyway,' I would add, 'what's the point? Why pick the scabs off old wounds to make 'em bleed and hurt again? No. I shall never write my autobiography.'

Yet here you are reading it, my autobiography. What made me change my mind and embark on what could be a mini orgy of scab picking?

First, I was reading about a man I have always thought fascinating, Oliver Cromwell, and found the section reporting the letter he wrote to the General Assembly of the Church of Scotland in 1650. It made me realise that perhaps I ought to reconsider my strongly held belief that looking backwards is always a pointless exercise.

Cromwell, clearly irritated by some intransigence on the part of good men of the Kirk, wrote: 'I beseech you, in the bowels of Christ, think it possible you may be mistaken!'

This powerful reprimand made me stop short and wonder whether my fascination with the present and the future, while it was no bad thing in itself, might be obscuring a past that perhaps had something to tell me, or even memories that might amuse and warm me in addition to those that I knew would be painful.

I thought perhaps I was being cowardly rather than prudent in refusing to take that backward view. It would not of course be possible to pick out only the nice things to remember but it would be childish to refuse to do so for that reason. And then I remembered something said by another clever man: 'The unexamined life is not worth living.' I felt then that Socrates as well as Cromwell was sitting on my shoulders and nagging me to turn round and take another look at what I had left behind.

And it wasn't just male prodding I was getting. Virago, a publishing house I have admired since the day it was launched by a bunch of feisty women, invited me to write this book because they too thought a backward look might be interesting and implied I should stop my havering and get on with it. There are some invitations it is difficult to refuse . . .

Other reasons then bobbed up to add their own pressures. I now have grandchildren, and that does concentrate the mind wonderfully. In my own childhood I longed to know more about my elders. What made them be the way they were? Had their parents done to them the things that mine did to me? Did they feel as frightened as I so often did? What did they do all day in that adult world from which I was so totally excluded? I would like my grandchildren, and indeed any subsequent great-grandchildren come to that, to have answers to such questions as and when they ask them.

And to the questions they might not think to ask. 'What did you do in the war, Grandma?' I certainly want to tell them about that, so that they understand why I am so fiercely opposed to war and all sorts of violence. And what it was like before we had the NHS and poor people who couldn't afford to pay doctors just didn't get medical care, and how important it is for all of us to get involved with the political battle to change such injustices, of which there are still far too many.

Telling them about medical care in the past will give me special pleasure, because I was a nurse in the NHS before it existed, as it were. It has certainly been at the core of my whole working life, which now spans more than fifty years – a thought which makes me rather tired.

And the last of my reasons; I have to face the fact that I am growing old. Not simply older – we do that all our lives – but old in the sense that my body now intrudes far more into my daily life than I wish it to, and in disagreeable ways. Joints ache, muscles weaken, walking-sticks, glasses and hearing aids become an essential part of the gear without which life cannot be properly lived. I once thought that the worst thing that could happen to disturb the happy busyness of my days was to have my computer crash or the phones cut off. Much more disastrous now is to run out of hearing-aid batteries.

But such physical problems aren't the worst things about being launched on my eighth decade. There is the painful fact that all the best experiences must now inevitably be behind me.

The living I still have to do will, I hope, be reasonably serene, tolerably happy, not too painful (those damned joints!) but it is hardly likely to be filled with the excitement of ambitions achieved, which is what has made my life such fun.

I have few personal ambitions left, sadly. I have to admit that I miss that bounding nagging drive that lived somewhere deep in my belly and from sunup to sundown hissed at me about what I ought to do next to push my work forwards, how I should strive to get that exciting new job, whispering notions about how I could persuade people to listen to what I wanted to say. I have lots of ambition for my children and grandchildren, but only in terms of their health and happiness. Social, financial and intellectual ambition is their business and theirs alone. (That, incidentally, is a rule that Es of the T – Elders of the Tribe – must never ever break, if they are to remain on happy terms with their assorted offspring. Remember this Elder's warning!)

But there is a somewhat backhanded advantage for myself in all this. Now I have reached old age – at past seventy I really can't continue to regard myself as being merely in late middle age – looking backwards is likely to be more interesting than looking forwards. I can't, dammit, in the lifetime I have left do a fraction of what I've already done though I'd love to try, in order to do it better.

Every piece of copy I've ever delivered, every book manuscript I've ever sent to my publishers seemed to me to have so many faults in it that when I re-read it on publication I yearned to start all over again and do it better. It comforts me that I share this with a great many other writers and painters and musicians.

Diminished ambition does not mean, however, that I have sunk deeply into slipperdom; far from it. I'm still having a marvellous time. Life at present, despite the disagreeable stigmata of physical ageing, is amazingly good to me. I feel as though I'm at a splendid party with lots of exciting, glamorous guests, the best possible entertainment and food and drink, and that I've just happened to look at the clock and seen it's almost time to say my polite goodbyes and go. I don't want to of course, but when it is time to go, there's no sense in arguing about it.

But before I do, I want to make one more circuit of the room, talk again to the interesting people I've met and remind myself of all the things they've told me and all the fun we've shared.

If I happen to meet again some of the less pleasant people and hurtful things are remembered, well, that's the way life is. I lived through it before, so I suppose I can again.

And that is the point of autobiography, I suppose. To live a life again. And that is why this book is in your hands.

Introduction

Midsummer, 1998

I am sitting in the committee room of the Royal Commission on the Long-term Care of the Elderly, a body set up by the New Labour Government, which came into power just over a year ago and of which great things are expected.

We are to find out what is required by Britain's elderly and often ailing citizens in terms of nursing, social support, housing and, where necessary, residential care, how much it is likely to cost now and in the future and how those costs are to be met. An important and very special task, undoubtedly.

Not that the room speaks of our significance. It is a large, dull, very stuffy, beigy-greyish space equipped with what look like the cheapest of tables and chairs, and smelling of dust, a hint of antiseptic floor-cleaner and sweaty people, in a dismal sixties concrete block over a bingo hall at the Elephant and Castle in London.

It isn't surprising we're sweating. Some of it is due to the summer heat outside in the traffic-roaring streets and the absence of air-conditioning inside, far more to the rising anger in a great many of us.

There are twelve commissioners, including our chair, Sir Stewart

Sutherland, and eleven members of the secretariat. Up to now, some five months or so into our task – which is supposed to be completed by the end of the year, though we doubt that is possible – we have been in pretty good accord.

We have been trying to seek the best forms of care for all our elders, not just for the present but for the future, and though we realise it will be costly to keep the promise of cradle-to-grave care for all, made when the NHS was founded fifty years ago, we believe it can be done.

Or did until now. There have been whispers round the table that one of our number, many of us understand, who has a close working relationship with Number Ten, has been visiting ministers and senior civil servants behind our backs. *If* this is true, it is highly improper because we are supposed to be free of political influence; our brief is to look at the evidence and report accordingly.

Furthermore, he knocks down suggestions from us with a bleat of 'Oh, no, the Treasury wouldn't like that!', and asks many of us quietly to sign the dissenting report he is going to write. Only one agrees. Together we feel he is clearly trying to scupper what we are trying to achieve, we all agree, and that is making us very angry indeed.

I tell colleagues that I suspect he is trying to oil his way into the House of Lords, fancying himself as lord rather than plain mister, which they doubt. In the event, in the first Honours list after he writes his dissenting view to our report, thus giving the Government precisely the lever they need to ignore the most important (if admittedly, costly) of our recommendations, his name appears. So does that of the only commissioner who signed his dissenting paper.

And as I sit there, seething over what I am coming to believe – very painfully, since I have been a Labour supporter all my adult life – is a piece of New Labour and Number Ten politicking I begin to marvel.

Who the hell am I to be sitting here muttering imprecations against Number Ten, rubbing shoulders with the high and the mighty and generally coming on like a right madam? Here I am, occupying a seat very near the upper reaches of the Government, working on what I and most of my colleagues hope will be the basis of changes in the law that will affect the whole population of these islands. My colleagues are great swells: a couple of powerful doctors, one of them a professor in his field, some people who have spent all their working lives in those famous corridors of power, used to dealing with Civil Service mandarins, and money experts, lawyers and university academics – I stick out like a boil on a bald head.

Paul Boateng, the junior health minister who had recruited me, had said something about my 'understanding the views of ordinary people', but all I am is an East End kid who made it into nursing, then into a few other assorted activities from a very inauspicious beginning.

How on earth did I get here from there?

One

I am lying in my cot, seeing the bars soaring away above my head in the dimness and hearing my father's voice, 'Bless her heart, we've woken her up,' and then my mother's, high, thin and peevish, 'I'll bless her if she doesn't go back to sleep.'

I remember telling them long after about that memory and my mother dismissing it as nonsense. 'You stopped sleeping in the cot when Sheila was born, so you can't possibly remember being in it. Much too young. You're making it up.' Perhaps she was right. My sister is just fifteen months my junior.

So maybe my first memory is walking along grey, wet pavements, my arm stretched high above my head so that I can hold my father's hand. When I look up at him I have to squint because he's so tall, so far away.

On the other side of him walks my mother. I can smell her scent, even on this cold damp day, a mixture of the stuff she gets from a bottle, and fish and chicken cooking smells. She's pushing the big pram that I'm not allowed in any more because it's Sheila's. There is a little puddle of water on the cover from the rain and my sister, my silly baby sister, peers over the top to stare at my mother, who is making 'coochie, coochie' noises at her.

My father begins to play games with me as we cross the wet streets. 'Upsadaisy' pulling on my arm till it hurts but in an exciting sort of way, so I don't cry. 'Downabuttercup', pushing me along. I like the game and hold on to his hand tightly so that my fingers hurt too. But it doesn't matter.

He swings me higher with each 'Upsadaisy!' and pushes me down harder with each 'Downabuttercup!' and the excitement rises in me and the feeling is frightening and breathless, and there is a tingle somewhere right inside my belly.

I feel it like water, lifting higher and higher inside me, and I like the feeling, even though it scares me, and I shriek, half laughing, half crying.

He laughs too, bends down, picks me up and hugs me, and now all the feelings are good, not at all frightening. I put my arms round his neck and hold on tight. 'I love you, Daddy,' I say, feeling myself bursting with it. 'I love you. I'm going to marry you when I grow up.'

My mother looks at me, peering round his big shape the way my sister peers over the cover of the pram. 'Oh, no, you're not,' she says. 'You'll go and find your own man, the way I had to.' And she looks at my father and laughs, and he laughs too, looking at her. Then they both turn their heads and look at me and laugh that private laugh again. It is their laugh, not mine, and I am filled with new feelings, thick, bad, angry ones, and I kick my father against his ribs. He smacks my leg with a stinging blow and puts me down on the ground.

That is the whole of that memory. It starts in blankness and ends in a void. But when I contemplate it from this distance of almost seventy years, it seems to offer me some explanations for the uneasiness of my very young years, although there were other factors.

To be born in 1931 was not wise. A worldwide depression, no welfare state in the UK to cushion the poverty; indeed, not wise. To be born to parents aged nineteen and twenty – she an orphan with only what she could earn as an assistant in a shoe-shop, he the son of reasonably well-off middle-class parents who were so appalled by his choice of wife, as well as his apparent inability to stick to any job for more than a few months, that they had nothing but disgust for the pair of them – was even less wise.

Their fecundity didn't help matters with my father's family either. His oldest sister, Bessie, married to a young grocer, Sidney, whose family went on to be part of the great Tesco empire, yearned for children but had stillbirth after stillbirth. And my mother, who produced three healthy babies in as many years, would preen about her success to Bessie, reducing her to floods of tears and prolonged headaches that sent her to lie in darkened rooms for days at a time.

It was a piece of cruelty the family found hard to forgive, especially my grandfather who adored Bessie – she was always his favourite – but however hard they tried to keep their distance from my parents (well, my mother, really) their essential goodheartedness brought them to our aid whenever there was a crisis.

And what a lot of crises there were. My father had never been a person who could make the world work for him. As an adult he lurched from problems to disasters. Not surprisingly, his boyhood had been stormy, and it has to be said that my grandfather's attitude towards his first son might well have had something to do with that.

Grandfather Joe was a small, shy person, with little to say for himself, but industrious and successful. He had a prosperous factory in Farringdon Road, where he employed a sizeable workforce to manufacture women's coats and suits, known in the trade as Ladies' Mantles. He worshipped his masterful wife, Leah, who was large, handsome and self-assured, with a powerful personality and a remarkable ability to get her own way. It was a surprisingly happy union, considering it had been an arranged marriage in the old Jewish tradition, with Joe around nineteen and Leah barely seventeen.

When she gave birth to my father Percy – he changed his name in adult life to Peter, and who could blame him? – Joe was shown this large bawling infant, over whom his wife, the midwives and everyone else in the neighbourhood were cooing excitedly ('A wonderful thing, Mrs Berk, a boy at last – wonderful'), and said, 'So? What's all the fuss about? So it's a boy – I tell you, he'll never come to anything much,' and went stomping back to play with his adored little Bessie and her sister Nancy.

How do I know? Bessie told me the story many years later, to prove to me what a prescient and altogether brilliant man her wonderful father had been. I suggested mildly that maybe he had made a self-fulfilling prophecy. After all, he and Percy had argued furiously all through the boy's growing-up years. Couldn't he have contributed to Percy's difficulties just a little? But she would have none of it. '*Your* father,' she said darkly, 'was no good from the start and *my* father, rest his sweet soul, knew it.'

This was an opinion of Percy held by almost everyone who knew him. For years afterwards, I would meet old people who, when they were told I was 'Percy's girl', would shake their heads and laugh and cry, 'What a *lobbus!*' – an excellent Yiddish word meaning a scoundrel with a charming personality. 'Oh, the tales I could tell you about your father . . .' They would shake their heads and laugh again. And then tell me the tales.

How he ran away from home so often they almost went mad, Joe and Leah. How he would get himself 'converted' by the Salvation Army, who held regular come-and-join-us services at Marble Arch and Piccadilly Circus and, indeed, all over the West End of London, and gave a good supper, a bed for the night, and a shilling to poor homeless creatures who gave themselves to God. He once got himself converted four times in a week, singing Sally Ann hymns lustily, banging the drum for an hour or two on each occasion and generally having a great time. He was enjoying his freedom and his shillings, until they discovered what a gifted liar he was, a Jewish boy to boot, and dragged him home to his parents. He was about fourteen then.

And how he had run off and joined the Army when he was barely sixteen, lying about his age and getting away with it because he was a large, well-fed boy. His parents had to buy him out, although the Army insisted he had to remain on the reserve list, young as he was. Which was why, long after, at the age of almost thirty, with three children and another well on the way, he had to rejoin the Army on 3 September 1939.

It was inevitable that, once married, he and Betty should lurch from crisis to crisis. In response to his absurd optimism and conviction that he could solve all problems by pulling off some scam or other to bring in the readies, she was desperately insecure, had the self-esteem of a gnat, in spite of being so deliciously pretty, and the pugnacious, manipulative bloody-mindedness such a personality all too often displays. She was also a crashing snob, who put on a special 'refained' accent to disguise her basic London twang. It slipped badly when she lost her temper, which was all the time.

She also pretended to read *The Times* newspaper every day, when actually it was the *Daily Mirror*, and would shamelessly tell people with whom she struck up an acquaintance while out shopping in the West End that she lived 'In Kensington, don't you know'. The new acquaintances would glance at each other and try to keep a straight face as she prattled on, with me at her side dying of embarrassment.

Now I understand why she was like that, and can find it in me to pity her, though for years, I can't deny, I hated her, not only for her posing and pretending but also because of her cruelty to me.

Her own childhood had been painful, and I suspect that all through it she had to struggle to find people to like her, and not see her as a burden, which is the traditional role of the orphan. If she felt she was hated because of what she was, poor and parentless, the answer was to pretend to be someone else.

Dammit, I did that myself as a child, the pretending and inner storytelling that created a life so much more real and enjoyable than the one I lived, but even before my age reached double figures I knew it was vital never to let the pretend slip over to the real, knowing at gut level that it would make me look a fool if it did.

Betty, poor thing, never did learn that and hence displayed her inadequacies and self-doubts to a great many strangers who didn't matter in her life, but who could and did display reactions that made her feel lousy about herself – and when we were alone to fly into a rage that ended in wallops for me.

But what other reasons did she have to hit out at me when we were alone and there was no one to pretend to? When other people

were about she was the Perfect Mother, all sweetness and light, and
indeed many years later, when I was an adult and told my aunt
Nancy a little of what my life with my mother had been, she was
amazed. 'She always seemed a wonderful mother to you three, though
I know you were the problem child,' she said, 'but I never knew she
beat you.' And then she remembered days when I visited, bruised and
battered, and told tales about falling down, and she became abject
with guilt. 'I believed her,' she kept saying. 'She said you were clumsy
and I believed her. If I'd known I'd have made her stop.'

I never again spoke about it to Nancy. I couldn't bear to upset her.
But I wanted to in an effort to find out why my mother had made me
the scapegoat of the three of us, as we were until 1940 when my
brother was born.

I don't think my sisters suffered at her hands as much as I did. In
my memory they were forgiven for things that got me a hiding,
though I could be wrong. We all, I suppose, tend to remember our
own pains better than anyone else's.

Was it because I was the eldest, and therefore the one of whom
she expected most? Had she had a painful labour with me but not the
others and developed a dislike accordingly? It can happen, as I was to
learn long after as a midwife. Was it, as I sometimes thought, the
close resemblance I bore to her mother-in-law, whom she hated as
much as my grandmother hated her? Was it even resentment because
I had what she did not, two living parents? But so did my sisters and
they weren't hit as much as I was. I simply didn't know why then and
I still don't.

The simple historical facts about my mother, which I managed to
glean long afterwards from an almost accidental meeting and conversation with one of her sisters, were that her own mother had died
of tuberculosis when she was around two. Her father had died a
couple of years earlier. The small Betty, the youngest of nine, went
first to an orphanage and then to foster parents who were, she
claimed, hateful to her. She never forgave her much older sisters
and brothers for not taking her into their lives but, in all fairness,
none of them had the wherewithal, scraping bare livings through the

tough post-First World War years. Anyway, two of her older brothers had been killed at the Front, so hating them for letting her down was pointless, but still she did it.

Percy and Betty met at a dancehall somewhere in East London where she lived in digs with a girlfriend. He was immediately captivated by this extremely pretty girl. Neither of them talked much about their lives before we arrived, but sometimes they would say things and laugh, or the wireless would play a tune that reminded them of their courting days, and they would say something about it then. One they liked was 'Lover Come Back To Me', which, my mother shouted at him in the course of one of their rows, 'was bloody prophetic'.

He persuaded her to marry him by telling her that his family were rich and would see to it that they had a lovely flat of their own and all they needed. Maybe he believed that. They'd always rescued him before. Why not now, with his pretty wife as a bonus? Like many people who are good at spinning tales to beguile others, Percy believed his own implicitly till they went wrong.

When Percy married her, his family, faced with the inevitable, tried to like her, but it never worked. First of all they had married in a register office and not a synagogue, and even to my moderately religious grandparents, this was anathema. But she refused to have a religious wedding so that was that.

I have no knowledge about why she refused: on the face of it, it seems a bit puzzling. She adored dressing up when she had the money for clothes, and if there had been a 'proper' wedding in my grandparents' terms she would have had all the trimmings that went with it.

I have wondered if she refused just to exercise a little power of her own over these undoubtedly powerful people. If so, it was a success: they backed off and settled down to trying to like this new member of their family. But it was impossible for them. They were not the sort of people to hide their own feelings. Furthermore they couldn't abide her airs and graces, and they let her know it, so she went into great fits of malingering, lying on the floor, writhing and screaming in pretended pain. Not until a doctor, whom Leah had called for the umpteenth time, said loudly, in Betty's hearing, that the only answer was to have her certified and sent to a lunatic asylum did the malingering stop.

Of course, it was a two-sided failure to make a family meld. My grandparents were – well, Leah, anyway – full of rectitude, utterly certain they knew what was best for everyone and with little sympathy for a damaged unhappy young woman and her thoroughly scapegrace spouse. But they were essentially kind, and their other son and daughters encouraged them to be generous, so time after time they 'helped out'.

They found Betty and Percy a flat, after they had started their married life in a couple of rooms over an East End fruit shop. I was born at that time, and to this day the smell of fruit has a powerful effect on me. It fills me with vaguely uncomfortable sensations, the sort you have when you wake up from a dream that leaves behind an unpleasant flavour but offers no shred of true memory to explain why you should feel so uneasy.

As each of us appeared, my grandparents found extra money for us. I can recall overhearing any number of furious rows between my mother and Percy, because she didn't think his parents offered enough. There were even more furious ones between Percy and his parents, when he took me and my sisters to see them (Betty never visited them, to my knowledge) and tried to persuade his mother to cough up more.

There was also the dreadful day when both Leah and Betty discovered that Percy had been skimming something for himself off the top of what the family had been giving him for our welfare. I remember the terror that filled me as they all shrieked at each other till I thought my head would bounce off my shoulders like a rubber ball. I, too, joined in the screaming.

Those were nasty days of which I have these fleeting memories, which seem to exist as patches of gritty light in an otherwise overwhelming darkness, rather like the gaslights that marched along the dark streets of Hackney, the place where my memories first formed themselves.

Two

I say Hackney, but in fact it was Homerton, a London patch that was further east and rather common in the eyes of Hackney residents who, although they had a decent regard for themselves, were looked down on by those who lived in leafy Stoke Newington, a little to the north.

My mother was an eager student of these social niceties, so we were reared to say we lived in Hackney. When I was old enough to join the library, which was almost next door to our tiny block of flats – there was just that heaven of heavens, the picture palace, between us – the librarian corrected me when I said I lived in Hackney, and I told my mother so and I got a stinging wallop on my face and clear instructions to pay no attention to such an ignorant old cow. That was an early lesson: people of whom my mother disapproved bore animal labels, like cow or mare or swine, and those she admired were described as 'aw'ffly naice' or 'refained'.

The flat we lived in was small for five people: two bedrooms, a 'front room', which was strictly for grown-ups and where we were never allowed to go on our own, a kitchen where we did most of our living, and a scullery where cooking was done.

It was also in the scullery that we suffered the agonies of hair-washing in the bathtub every Sunday night. It had a heavy wooden lid over it, which doubled as a work surface when the bath was not in use, and the whole equipage fitted between the boiler – a corner structure that was just a brick enclosure for a large copper tub, with space beneath it for a fire – and the gas-stove. Washing put in the copper was boiled, filling the whole flat with steam and the smell of soap and soda, then hung out on long lines in the yard behind the flats, to which our flat had access via a rickety fire escape.

The yard was also my playground, until the day when I found in an abandoned horsehair-stuffed sofa a cache of very fat, very active blue-bottle maggots. I wanted to keep them for pets, but that just earned me another wallop and an embargo against ever setting foot in the yard again. I was confined to the tiny 'landing' of the fire escape outside the scullery door, not much of a play space on a hot summer day. One thing I liked about it, though, was that from that level I could see into the alley alongside the picture palace where the Saturday-morning queues formed for entry to the Children's Special Matinée.

I was never allowed to go to those. My mother said they were for common people, not us, but watching the lucky children below queuing with their sticky sweets and the price of entry in paper bags – two glass jam jars that could be sold on by the cinema propri-etors – I could have a lovely time dreaming up stories in my head about them all. The nice boys who smiled and waved were the heroes (I was my own heroine, of course) and the ones who stuck their tongues out or, worse still, set their thumbs to their noses and wag-gled their fingers, were very satisfactory villains and, of course, villainesses. Though my mother could be used for that role, of course . . .

I thought my private films were much better than those they dis-appeared to watch, leaving the yard to its puddles and dirt, occasional shards of glass and torn paper bags from dropped jam jars. Indeed, I learned very early that the best things happened inside my own head, and to an extent that is still so, although many of the sto-ries I made up then and, naturally, starred in, have almost come true. But the dreams were better than the reality every time.

Did my sisters daydream as I did? I have no idea because I have never asked them. We shared a bedroom, of course, but although I have such clear memories of the rest of the flat, that bedroom is absent from them.

Did we play games in there? Possibly, although my sisters were still babies then. When I was three, and we moved into number 4, Francis House, Brooksby's Walk, London E9, Sheila was not yet two years old and Maxine, the third of us, was an infant. But we lived there for the next three years, by which time they would have been old enough for me to play with in our bedroom. And yet I simply can't remember that we did or that we played together anywhere, in fact.

And the harder I try to remember, the more impossible it becomes. I have tried to visualise myself in the flat at various times of the day, and the most vivid memories are wrapped around the afternoons when it got dark early – I always seem to remember winters better than summers. Once I learned to read I think I spent all the time I could on the floor in front of the fire behind the diamond-meshed wire of the tall (taller than me) fireguard with its fringe of drying towels and nappies on the brass rail. I can remember sitting at the kitchen table to eat meals, and that is about it. Although I must have spent at least half my life up to that time in that bedroom it lies behind its door in my memory, a complete blank.

One possible reason for the blankness into which that bedroom has disappeared is the Problem. I don't know when I discovered I was a Problem Child but the words, heavy, threatening, ugly, were part of my awareness very early.

For a start, I could not be trained properly. I learned to use a lavatory for what my mother called 'Number Twos'. That was never any worry. But Number Ones, oh dear, oh dear.

Even at this vast time distance from those days, I still feel the shame of it. I would still rather keep it a secret. Isn't that absurd? To carry still the guilt and shame of a three-year-old in my memory? But I do. I wet my knickers and I wet my bed. There, I've said it. I was a *pisher*, a Yiddish word I learned very early indeed. It bore none of the affection of *lobbus*, all of the anger, dislike and disapproval that, it seemed to me, I carried everywhere. I used to think that if people looked closely at me they would see the word *pisher* written on my forehead. When my mother took me shopping with her in Chatsworth Road market, into which our street led, I would watch the stallholders out of the corner of my eye to see if they were looking at my forehead. Not until I had counted three who were not could I relax and enjoy the market.

Which I did, hugely. It was a place of colour, noise and amazing smells: the cats'-meat man, who sold cooked horsemeat in great slabs that smelled rich and toothsome, and the toffee man, who piled his stall with slabs of buttery jawbreaking heaven, which I was allowed to have sometimes, and pink and white Cokernut Ice – that was how it was spelled on the big white cards pinned to the front of the stall – and twisted sticks of sugary peppermint and paregoric and aniseed called Winter Warmers. Bliss, all of it.

My mother would buy her eggs from the egg stall and a chicken from the chicken lady, who sat in a kitchen chair wrapped in what looked like a pile of rags, pulling feathers out of dead chickens whose heads lolled over her broad knees, their glassy eyes wide and startled. I always sneezed when we stopped there. It was part of the pleasure. She bought carrots, onions and celery (what a smell that was!) and there the stallholder, very tall and handsome, I thought, always offered to scrape a big sweet carrot for me to eat, and I always had to say no, thank you, because it was common to eat in the street.

After she'd bought rashers and sausages from the Home and Colonial Stores that dominated the end of the street, she would bend down and thrust her hand under my dress to see if I was wet or dry. If I was dry, she would give me a ha'penny to spend on Cokernut Ice on the way back. If I was wet, she set her mouth in a straight line, looked at me with one eyebrow raised in a way that filled me always with a horrid flat sort of feeling, and walked me home in silence.

The trouble was I never knew when it happened. I would try to concentrate on my knickers, to feel when the pee came out so that I could stop it, but somehow I was always distracted by something else. When I remembered to think again about my knickers it was too late. If I were lucky she wouldn't check until it had dried by itself. I wasn't usually lucky when we were out and that was especially awful. It seemed to me that everyone who saw her put her hand under my dress knew why and were despising me for being a Problem Child who was a *pisher*.

I can remember seeing the sheets from my bed hanging out to dry in the yard, the telltale yellowish stain all too visible, but not what happened when I went to bed or when I got up in the morning. I have to suspect that the mornings were particularly fraught with my mother's fury, accusations of laziness and dirtiness (the usual epithets), and stinging slaps on whichever part of me she could reach. Perhaps that is why I have no memory of the bedroom I shared with my sisters.

Yet it has not erased other times when she hit me. They are all too vivid. As the oldest, I suspect I was hit more than the other two, who were so much smaller. I was always the tallest of the three of us, all through our lives, and I believe that even at three or four I looked a couple or so years older and therefore more culpable when it came to domestic crimes, like breaking things or being untidy, so more suitable for the necessary punishment.

The worst time was during a row she had with my father, who wasn't often there in my recollection. Probably he left for work before our weekdays started and got home after we were put to bed. It was only on Saturdays and Sundays that he was there, and on Sunday afternoons the four of us went to see Grandma – that is, he and we three. They usually had a row on Sunday mornings. On this particular Sunday they were in the scullery and for some reason I was standing between them. The saucepan lid she was holding in one hand as she stirred something on the stove while she shouted at him suddenly landed on top of my head, the sharp metal edge making a sizeable slice in my scalp.

I remember standing there, blinking through the blood that was trickling over my forehead, and wanting to cry but not being able to. I couldn't breathe either, and the air and tears locked up inside me seemed to make the blood flow faster.

She screamed then, dropped the pan lid and picked me up. He shouted, took me from her and began to mop at my head. This released my breath and I started roaring, and my sisters, in the kitchen, joined in. It must have been pretty scary for the neighbours to hear, though maybe they were used to it. A lot of people shouted and screamed in our flats, especially on Friday and Saturday nights, and whenever I asked what the noise was my mother would say, 'None of your business. We don't mix in, you understand? These people who go to pubs and then have fights, it's none of our business.'

Clearly the neighbours didn't mix in either, because no one came knocking and my father took me out, down the stairs, along the street to the chemist and rang the bell because the shop was shut. I had stopped crying by now and felt oddly sleepy, and was quite content. The chemist came from his flat upstairs, took one look at my scalp, then told my father to take me into the shop and sit me on the counter. He would clean my head with some cotton wool and stinging stuff. They told me I was a very brave girl, and a good girl, which was an agreeable thing to be told for a change, and I didn't tell them I wasn't being brave at all but couldn't really feel what he was doing.

He shaved off some of my hair round the cut, and said that it ought to be stitched by rights but he could probably fix it well enough with plaster strips. My father agreed that that would be fine.

I know with hindsight that the real reason my father had knocked up the chemist at a Sunday lunchtime was that the chemist would do what was necessary for a shilling at most, whereas going to a doctor would cost at least five, and who down our way had that sort of money to throw about? Children bashed themselves up all the time. You could spend a fortune on such luxuries if you had it. The chemist was good enough for us.

'What happened?' the chemist asked, when he had finished. I repeated what my father had told me to say as he had carried me there, word for word: 'I was playing on the stairs and I fell over and hit my head on the banisters.'

'Silly girl,' the chemist said kindly. 'You have to be careful. You could have brained yourself, you know! But you're a brave girl,' and he reached under the counter and brought out a piece of barley sugar.

I looked at my father for permission to take it, which my mother always refused because it was common to take sweets from people, but he nodded and suddenly I was having the best Sunday I had had for a long time.

Three

Although those early years were often difficult and painful they were by no means always bad. Yes, I had this Problem Child label to contend with, to the point of being taken to see a specialist in problem children. How they raised the fees for it I don't know. Perhaps Grandma shelled out, as usual.

Anyway I was taken by my mother on the bus – several buses, actually – to a place where there were more trees, grass and flowers than I had ever seen. I can still feel the rough fabric of the bus seat against my legs as I knelt up and stared out of the window for mile after mile, first of ordinary streets like ours in Homerton, then wider ones with bigger houses and shops, and hedges where in our streets there were railings, and small gardens in front of the houses where all we had were doors that opened straight on to the pavement.

It was beautiful to look at, and smelled beautiful too, and I can remember the pure pleasure that filled me. I turned and grinned at my mother and laughed, just because of the pleasure. And, extraordinarily, she grinned back, a wide, pretty smile that made me feel so good inside I could have burst. But then the bus conductor called out something, and my mother jumped up and, pulling me along behind her, hurried off the bus.

The house we arrived at made me get that bursting feeling again, because it, too, was beautiful in a way I had never seen before. Over the front doorway was a most delectable thing: a curtain made of brightly coloured strips of slippery stuff. I stroked it as my mother rang the bell. She pulled my hand away as someone came from the dimness beyond and parted the strips to look out at us: a woman with dark hair in a black dress with a frilled white apron and a frilly white cap that came down to her eyebrows.

Another first for me. Grandma had a maid called Edie, but she wore an ordinary pinafore and stayed in the kitchen mostly. This one looked severely at us, and my mother said something, and then we were taken into the house. The smell of flowers was even stronger and mixed up with the same polish smell and coffee scent Grandma had in her house. I said that to my mother as the maid went away, leaving us in the big cool hall.

No smiles now. She snapped something at me and squeezed my hand so tightly it hurt. I remembered I ought never to say anything to her about Grandma except nasty things, like she made me cry.

The rest is blurred. I can see myself sitting at a table with a little thin lady, smaller than my mother but sharper to look at, with edges and flatness where my mother was rounded.

I had to do things with coloured blocks and bits of wire, and mend a clothes peg that had been taken apart, and say what different words meant, and then I was told to do drawings. One was to show how I would walk in a big field where I had lost something, to make sure I'd find it. I thought this very silly, I remember, as I drew a continuous line, starting from the outside edge and going round and round till I had covered the whole space with a spiral. It was such a silly, easy question.

I had also been asked to draw a picture of myself on what I thought was a very little piece of paper, and I drew the big round head, then put in my curly hair, my eyes, nose and mouth. Then, seeing there was a little space left at the bottom of the paper, I put in a tiny body, legs and arms.

The little thin lady, who talked a bit like Grandma, saying V when she should have said W and making her words come out thick, looked at the picture of me and shook her head. Then she looked at me very sternly.

'You are a naughty girl, are you not?'

'Not,' I said. Wasn't that what she meant? I was not a naughty girl.

'Yes, you are,' she said. 'You see this picture? You have this big head drawn and that means you think only of yourself and not of being a good girl for your mother. You are big-headed and that is a bad thing to be.'

'It was the little paper,' I started, but she didn't listen, just talked a lot about being good and thinking of others. Then my mother took me home again, talking all the way about being good. I said nothing, because I couldn't explain how hard it was to be good and dry, though I wanted to so badly.

Long after, when I was twelve or so, she told me that the thin lady was Anna Freud, the famous daughter of the great Sigmund – neither name meant much to me. (I doubt it really was she, going by the dates, which I've checked. But she had a famous name, so of course my mother used it.) She had done an intelligence test on me and said I was 'in the highest percentile for intelligence'. It was a phrase my mother repeated several times, though I'm not certain she knew what percentile meant. (She told me then, by the way, because I was doing so badly at school. It was proof to her that I was lazy, rather than stupid, just as I had been about bladder control.)

I have to say now, looking back, that I thought Ms Freud, if it were she, was silly at the time and, from my adult standpoint now, I think she was remarkably bad at her job as a child psychologist. To tell a child of three and half, even a precocious one, that she was 'big-headed' on the basis of a drawing and the complaints of a young mother who clearly had problems of her own was, to say the least, unhelpful. But being 'in the highest percentile' had its values. It ensured that I learned to read before I started school.

My favourite person at Grandma's flat was Auntie Nancy, the second oldest of the family. She was in her twenties, single, pretty, full of fun and seemed actually to like being with me. It was she who started teaching me by reading to me, which no one had ever done before, and being pleased and excited when I recognised the words she read aloud and could point to them when she asked me to.

I was sent to stay at Grandma's when I had chicken-pox, and it was Nancy who took care of me, stroking on the calamine lotion and stopping me scratching. I still remember how awful the itching was. She read to me patiently, day after day, and by the time the spots had vanished and I went home to Homerton, I had grasped the basics of fitting letters together and memorising whole words whenever I could.

From then on, I taught myself. The *Daily Mirror* was delivered to the flat and every morning, before anyone else woke up, I would creep out of bed, fetch it from the letterbox, take it to the kitchen and work my way through it. I liked the comic strips best – *Belinda Blue-eyes*, and *Pip, Squeak and Wilfred, Jane* and *Useless Eustace* – but I made myself read all the duller bits too, especially the words in great big letters.

It was my father who came into the kitchen one morning and found me reading. I thought at first he'd be angry because I hadn't had time to fold up the paper and put it back on the floor by the front door. But he wasn't. He stared at me and said, 'Can you read that?'

'Not all of it,' I said, expecting a wallop.

'Show me.' He sat down beside me and I moved close to him, liking the smell of cigarettes, which was always part of him. Clearly there were to be no wallops this morning. I read the headlines to him and he corrected me once because I said the word the wrong way (I read 'Night' as 'Nig-het'). Then, after I'd read *Belinda Blue-eyes* to him, he hugged me very tightly and said, 'Well, well, well! You'll show 'em a thing or two when you start school, won't you, my Berrela?'

I wanted to cry then. I didn't know why at the time, but I do now.

I had been named Claire Berenice. 'Just the sort of airy-fairy names your mother would go in for!' I can hear Auntie Bessie snort when, at my engagement party no less, someone asked me what my full name was, since everybody called me 'Berry', and I told him. For some reason my first name had been abandoned in favour of the second, and a short version of it at that. I was to be teased mercilessly for it at school, and even at this stage of my life, I hated the sound of it. My mother used to shout, 'Berry!' in a particular clipped way that meant I'd done something I shouldn't and was about to be walloped for it. But sometimes, when they were feeling like it, my father especially, they lengthened the diminutive to make it sound much fonder.

From then on, everything was much better. My mother didn't get angry with me quite so often, and brought me American comics from the market on Saturday afternoons. I learned to love *Gasoline Alley* and *The Katzenjammer Kids*, *Tilly the Toiler* and *Blondie and Dagwood* as much as home-grown comic strips. To this day I consider a well-drawn and intelligently written strip one of the crowning glories of literacy rather than fodder for the illiterate. It takes huge skill to get across those complex stories and jokes in so few words and such economical artwork. I wish I was clever enough to write a long-living strip like *Li'l Abner* or *Little Orphan Annie*.

I was not confined to comics for reading pleasure. I asked my mother if I could join the library and she was clearly delighted by this, and her approval gave me all the courage I needed to go and try on my own. My mother was busy doing something for the baby, Maxine, and I couldn't wait to go, and as the building was so close, she let me.

I walked out of the flat, down the stairs, into the street, turned left past the picture palace and there it was: the library, where, I knew, all the books in the world were kept. My mother borrowed books from it all the time, for she was a voracious reader and I now understand that it was my early delight in her own passion that made our shared life a little easier.

The difficulties between my mother and me – again I know with all the crystal clarity that is given us with hindsight – were rooted in her hatred of her mother-in-law, and my grandmother's loathing of her. Betty ached for approval, ached, I suppose, for a mother of her own, but there was no way Grandma would or could take on that role for her, not after those early days when Betty had first come into the family and behaved in so manipulative and unpleasant a way.

And then, within ten months of the marriage my father took off, repeating one of his old tricks of just running away from problems – as usual, for these two, money ones – leaving her high and dry in her rooms over the fruit shop. She, seven months pregnant and unable to go to work (even if a job had been available in those tough times), had no other option but to go, virtually with begging bowl in hand, to her absent husband's family for aid.

They gave it, of course, for they were always generous with money, but accompanied their gift with a few homilies about the proper way to live and behave. Grandma could never resist doing that. Betty must have burned with fury all the way back to the fruit shop. And when her child was born, to the delight of the woman Betty so loathed, and showed a striking physical resemblance before she was twelve months old to that so-hated mother-in-law, it isn't hard to see why Betty had problems with me.

Sheila, who was born a scant fifteen months after me, was a sweet, biddable child – indeed, still is one of the sweetest, nicest people you could hope to meet – and the image of Betty. She gave our mother much more joy than awkward me, constantly on the go, full of questions and curiosity and demands for exciting things to do. Betty preferred Maxine to me, too: she turned out to be lively and very bright, but she was also amazingly pretty and had what the Americans would call a cute little way with her.

But once I learned to read and joined the library, it was different.

For a start, Leah had never learned to read English, or to write it or any other language. She had come as the youngest of an immigrant family to England, fleeing Cossack attacks in their home in the Pale of Settlement, just before the turn of the century. She was the pretty baby sister of four adoring big brothers, who spoiled her outrageously. She had never been taught to read because nice Jewish girls from respectable well-heeled families in the old country never were, that being solely a male activity: being too intellectual could ruin a woman, the old people believed. And although she eventually learned to read Yiddish, that never went beyond newspapers sent from friends in New York's Lower East Side.

So, when I showed clearly that I had inherited something from Betty by learning to read all by myself and that I would be one up on her hateful mother-law in consequence, my stock with my mother went way up. I never told her or my father of Auntie Nancy's early input into my new skill and, for some reason, Nancy never mentioned it either. Did she have some insight into the complex currents of our relationships? It's very likely. Nancy was a sharp and observant person, as well as a kind one.

So, there was the library, and there was I, all of three and a half years old, and I walked in up the steps and across the huge shining expanse of wooden floor to the central desk, feeling both frightened and excited. I was going to get my own books! My books. My *books*.

The smell in the library was wonderful. I didn't know then what it was, though I do now after more years of library membership than I care to count. The major smell was of Jeyes fluid, the same stuff my mother used in the drains outside our flat, but that was a smell that was everywhere, in shops and – well, everywhere. But there was more. Furniture polish like Grandma's again and, yes, coffee, but something more. An old sort of smell that was thick and comforting. Old books, mildewed a little, and it delights me still. I have a few books of my own now that have that original metropolitan-library reek, and I would never part with them. And there were still more scents built in: old shoes, and old men drying out their rain-soaked clothes by the radiators and – so many levels of rich, olfactory pleasures to add to my inner mix of fear and delight.

The woman behind the tall counter leaned over and glared at me. 'Go away,' she whispered loudly.

'I want to join the library,' I whispered back.

'Do you, now?' she hissed. 'You can't read. How old are you?'

'Yes I can.' I was proud and said it loudly and she put a finger to her lips. 'I'm three and a half, almost three and three-quarters. And I *can* read. Ask my mummy. She said I could join.'

The woman came out from behind the counter and looked down at me, then made a funny sort of face, as though she was going to blow bubbles at me. 'All right. We'll see if you can read. Wait a minute.'

She went away and came back with a little book in her hands. Then she bent over, lifted me under the arms and set me down on the top of the counter. Now we were eye to eye. She gave me the book and commanded, 'Read.'

It was called *The Four Winds and the Little Zephyrs.* I looked at it and then at her. She had a smooth look on her face, a sort of you-can't-read-that look. I looked at the title again and began. The and Four and Winds and of course And and The offered no worries. Nor did Little. All easy words that looked the way they sounded. But the last one! And then I remembered being out with Auntie Nancy once and seeing a word on a shop's glass window.

'What does that say?' I had demanded.

'Photographer, darling,' Auntie Nancy had said. 'Whenever you see a P and an H together like that it always sounds like FFF.'

So, I read the last word. 'Zeff—' I got to.

The woman looked at me with quite a different face and laughed. 'You little tinker! You can read! Good girl. Come down now and I'll fill in a form for your tickets. But tell Mummy she has to come in and sign for them.'

And she lifted me down and gave me *The Four Winds and the Little Zephyrs* so that I could read what was on the inside as well as the title while she did the forms.

And I found a chair to sit on while I read, and knew that from now on everything would be lovely, even if I was wet every morning and all day as well.

Four

Everything was, if not lovely, a little easier from then on. I had my problems still, notably the possession of what seemed to me to be a part of my body that did exactly what it wanted and paid me no attention. My bladder was as capricious as ever and seemed to me like a bad fairy that lived in my belly. (My books from the library were educating me thoroughly in the matter of good and bad fairies.) Night after night my sheets blossomed their yellowish blooms, and day after day my legs and bottom were slapped when wet knickers were identified. But there was always a book waiting to be read, and that made everything bearable. For the first time I could remember, there was something nice to look forward to.

When I was almost four I can remember coming home from Grandma's one Sunday filled with the sweets she always gave us (probably more to vex my mother than to please us: Betty didn't approve of sweets, having learned the then modern lesson about the importance of protecting young teeth) and a wonderful present of a book of my own, not one that would have to go back to the library. I was very excited and ran in waving it in the air. It was a copy of *Chicks' Own Annual*, and I can still see the bright picture on the front of assorted animals dressed in school clothes and having glorious fun.

'Look what I've got! Auntie Nancy gave me a book.'

Betty snatched it from my hand and threw it on top of the dresser in the kitchen. I stood there sick with fear. What had I done? I must have done something terrible and I couldn't imagine what.

'Big mouth!' she shouted at me. 'You and your big mouth! Why can't you mind your own business?' She pushed me out of the kitchen into the long narrow hall and slammed the door on me.

I could hear her and my father talking. He and my sisters had got home a little before me, because I had dawdled from the bus-stop, reading my book as I went, and I heard him say, 'Listen, she'll get over it! I told her Berry had it all wrong, that you'd been doing shopping for a neighbour. Give her time. She'll calm down, I know she will.'

'Big mouth,' my mother said again, her voice thick with fury, and I sneaked away down the hall to the lavatory to hide. There was a mirror there, and I stood on tiptoe to look in it, pulling at my mouth with my fingers to make it smaller but finding I couldn't. I stopped trying then, and just stood staring at my face with its huge ugly mouth, feeling horrible.

Later, much later, I discovered from my father what had happened that day. I had told my grandma about shopping in Chatsworth Road market. She had asked me what I liked best about it, and I had told her I liked doing it with my mother. 'All of it,' I said, and went off into a long litany of all the things we saw and bought there. Including the shopping at the Home and Colonial where Betty bought sausages and rashers.

This had enraged my grandmother almost to apoplexy. She might not have been crazily *froom* – deeply observant of all the religious ordinances of Judaism – but this was going too far in wickedness, even for her appalling daughter-in-law. She had sent me out of the room, clearly understanding about the way children pick up adult conversations, and turned on my father, though I could hear perfectly well through the closed door. 'She buys bacon and pork sausages!' Grandma had cried, as my father tried to control his laughter. He found it very funny – or, at least, he did until she sent him away without the usual little bundle of banknotes on which he relied to get through the week.

I never really got over that 'big mouth' epithet. I saw my own face as being slit by a huge mouth, virtually from ear to ear, and every time I passed a mirror or a reflective shop doorway would stop and look and try to pull my mouth smaller.

When she caught me looking my mother would tell me off for being vain. In all fairness to her, vanity in children was considered to be a Bad Habit then, and one that had to be stamped on hard, according to the gurus in the magazines she read so assiduously. And stamp she did. But harder and more cruelly, I think, than was necessary.

'I don't know who you think will ever be interested in looking at *you*! It's more important to be a good girl than a pretty one, you know, so you'd better work harder at being good, hadn't you? Pretty is as pretty does, and that makes you downright ugly sometimes!'

My memory of that conversation is crystal clear. I am standing beside her in a shop lined with mirrors, struggling not to look in them, and I can hear her voice still, every word clear and painful. The resulting conviction that I am unpretty to the point of ugliness has never left me. When I went to school, and the other girls would primp and peer in the mirrors, pushing each other aside for a space, I was terrified of being caught even glancing into one. I could imagine all too easily the jeering if I did.

Similarly it was years after I had grown up before I could bring myself to buy cosmetics from those snooty and glamorous salesgirls in the big stores. I didn't use much but wanted lipstick and powder, just to be the same as other girls. The best I could do was sneak into Boots or Woolworth's and pick them up casually along with other items. Often I pretended I was buying them for someone else.

I was, in fact, almost phobic about anything to do with appearance. I remember being deeply grateful when clothes rationing lingered on after the war, well into my teens. It gave me an excuse to avoid clothes shops, except for things like knickers, bras and stockings, which happily did not fit into my phobia. It was prettifying things that made me go hot and cold at the mere idea of buying them, let alone using them.

Now, when I look at early photographs, or at my daughter who agrees we are very alike – so much so that she once referred to the pair of us as the Clone Rayners – I am sad. I wasn't that bad in my young years *and I didn't know it*. I couldn't imagine any boy ever being remotely interested in me and shied off if one came within yards. I can't help wondering now if one or two of those lads who hung around my friends actually did try to chat me up . . . Ah, well.

Now, large, wrinkled and jowly as I am in my older years, it cannot be denied that I am justified in feeling that costly clothes and makeup are wasted on me – though I have taught myself to waste them with great enthusiasm. Some commentators have compared me with people like Peter Ustinov (that was the theatre critic Jack Tinker, reviewing a play in which Ustinov played a character who 'came on like Claire Rayner solving people's problems, and come to think of it looks like her too') and Benny Hill. But I comforted myself in both cases with the thought that they were both very nice people – and as my mother had said in that shop back in the 1930s, 'Pretty is as pretty does.'

I have to ask myself, did my mother mean to have this effect on me? Or was it just the mores of the time, when you never praised children for fear of making them conceited, and were always offhand about their abilities in their hearing? Except for the 'intelligence test', I never heard her boast about me, which would have made me preen with delight and adoration of her, though she did boast about the achievements and exploits of my sisters. I often heard her do that.

I wonder, did she do the same about me in *their* hearing? Possibly. All I know now is that those ghastly gurus of the time considered it detrimental to let children know they were approved of. It was exhortation and punishment – I know because I've since read their books.

One excellent outcome of such an upbringing has been that it gave me considerable adult insight into other people's anxieties.

When people wrote to me, long after, asking for help with their fears and phobias I had a pretty good notion of where their problems were coming from.

It wasn't long after the big-mouth row that I started school. Rushmore Road Infants School was the nearest and they took children from four into the first class. How Betty persuaded them to take me at three and three-quarters I really don't know, but she did.

From then on I had a whole new set of fears and problems to cope with. I was still wetting my bed, but daytime accidents stopped being so bad because the regime in the First Infants class included an hourly procession of some children, the girls holding the skirt of the child in front, and the boys with a hand on the shoulder of the one in front, being led by the teacher to the lavatories.

It was both a comfort and a shame to me. A comfort because it stopped the problem to a large extent (I often stayed dry all day at school!), a shame because the other children in the class must have known that all of us who made the hourly pilgrimage were *pishers*, I thought.

And then thought again: if all the girls who went to the lavatory with me were *pishers* too, then I wasn't the worst person in the world, after all! It had never before seemed possible to me that I was not unique. Why should it? Both my sisters managed to be dry. I had to be the only one like me in the world. Yet here at school, there *were* others!

I asked our teacher, a small lady who had her grey hair tied in a huge bundle at the back of her head and who wore grey dresses, why only some of us had to go to the lavatory so often.

She smiled and said, 'Well, dear, your mother says you have a little trouble in that area and so do the other children who go there with you. But don't you worry about it. You'll grow out of it.'

That made me think a lot. I knew about growing older. I'd known about that for ever. I was older than my sisters and always would be. And I'd go on getting older, and as soon as I was old enough I wouldn't have to worry about being wet ever again. It was a lovely thought, and from then on I had a good time at school.

There were all sorts of things to enjoy. Masses of toys in our infant class, and books too, but mostly picture books, which were a disappointment because I wanted words. Our teacher, Miss Delight – a name that made us giggle when later she read us the de la Mare poem 'Wynken, Blynken and Nod' who sailed away 'on a sea of misty light', thus introducing us to a pun – saw me looking for books with words and duly supplied them.

There must be, somewhere, a pantheon of superb infant-class teachers, and if Miss Delight isn't there above all the rest, there is no justice in this wicked world.

I have one other memory of her that enchants me today. She was teaching us the Ten Commandments, which were regarded then as the most vital piece of education for all children. It was a list of things that grown-ups said children mustn't do and, used as I was to a constant stream of 'Don't do that!', it just meant another lot of things to forget you'd been told not to do until you'd made a mistake, done whatever it was and been smacked for it. I had some trouble with the notion of coveting oxen, but Miss Delight explained it meant not wanting to play with your best friend's toys but waiting to be invited, and doing a lot of inviting yourself when it was your toy.

But then she went on to the Seventh Commandment. She wrote it on the board carefully. 'Thou Shalt Not Commit Adultery.' 'There,' she said, dusting the chalk off her hands. 'Do you see that last word? Well, if I draw a line here,' and she picked up the chalk again and drew a line before the ery bit of the word, 'it makes *adult*. So this is something grown-ups must never, never do, and you needn't worry about it.' And briskly she cleaned the board, smiled at us and began to talk again about loving God.

I stopped listening – I'd heard all that before and it was dull – and thought of how wonderful it was that there was something grown-ups must never, never do. It wasn't only children who were always getting into trouble.

I'm sure Miss Delight taught me much more before I was moved up into the next class and had to do some much harder work, like proper arithmetic, which I hated, and writing words, which I loved, except for the way the new teacher complained all the time about my handwriting.

But in the new class there was the excitement of doing a Play in which I was chosen to be Mother, 'Because you're the biggest,' the teacher said, and playing the triangle in the class percussion band.

There was also Sports, which meant running about the playground with beanbags and hoops and getting very hot.

There was flag-wagging on Empire Day when we went out into the street to watch a local parade.

There was getting ready for the Coronation, which never actually happened but we didn't mind: we already had our mugs which were a present from the new King, even if he wasn't going to be the new King, after all.

There was Geography, which was mostly admiring how much red there was on the map of the world, which proved all those places belonged to Us. The English. That made me feel quite rich, really.

But then, suddenly, the world fell apart. I came home from school one windy afternoon, all on my own because I was gone five now and perfectly well able to take care of myself, my mother said, to find that all the furniture was gone, the kitchen had big suitcases in it, and my sisters were waiting for me already wearing their best coats.

My mother pulled off my school clothes, pushed them into her bag and gave me my Grandma-visiting clothes, including the best coat that had a hat to match and gaiters to go with it. They needed to be done up with a special hook. Grandma had given them to us because they were smart, like the outfits the Little Princesses wore. 'Are we going to Grandma's?' I asked.

'No,' my mother snapped. 'We're moving. Now, come *on*. We've got a train to catch.'

Five

After that day, and right up to the start of the war, all I have is bursts of memories erupting out of an encircling darkness like fireworks.

We are sitting on the floor in a bare room, the five of us, in the half dark because there are no electric lights yet. 'Tomorrow,' my father says, 'they'll fix them tomorrow,' and I'm suddenly happy because he is back. He'd been away in those last days – or was it weeks? – from the flat in Homerton and now he was back. I lean across and hug him suddenly. He laughs and says, 'Watch it! You're spilling my chips,' and my mother says, 'Berry, for pity's sake stop throwing yourself around like a great lummox.'

The next flash is very odd. There is furniture in the room now, all very new and shiny, and I like looking at it. I am sitting on a sofa with my sisters and that feels funny because we never had a sofa. Grandma did, but not us.

'Say it again,' my mother says. 'One after the other. What's your name? You first, Berry.'

'Berry – um – Brandon,' I say.

'Not like that!' She's annoyed now. 'We've been doing this all morning. Try again and make it ordinary, like you've never been called anything else.'

'Berry Brandon,' I say obediently, and the others follow. 'Sheila Brandon,' and Maxine, lisping because she is still so young, 'Maxine Brandon.'

'All right,' says my mother. 'Now again.' And we do, again and again.

I still don't know what he did or why he was on the run, but clearly he was, and us with him. My father, always looking for the fast answer, the quick money that would solve all his problems and make Betty happy, and let him have a lovely time showing off his largesse to anyone he happened to come across. My father the *lobbus*.

Long after I was told by Auntie Nancy, when I used to spend a lot of time in her home and she told me tales of the old days, that to the best of her knowledge he'd pulled some sort of confidence trick and, in consequence, the people he had cheated and the police were after him.

'I remember they came to our house, the police, to question us about where he'd disappeared to with you all, but we knew nothing and my mother . . .' Auntie Nancy had looked both distressed and a little amused. 'The shock of being questioned by the police put her to bed for a week.' And I had been amused too at the thought of my redoubtable grandma being questioned by a large policeman, whom she would have wanted to throw out of her house for daring to stand on her good carpet in those dreadful boots.

The next snapshot: a hot, sunny afternoon, and I am standing with my father at the side of a road with grassy edges to it, a surprising novelty to me – I had believed hitherto that grass grew only in parks and people's private gardens. There is a big sign there, a wide white one, and written on it in huge black letters is 'BESSES O' THE BARN'. And nearby there is another sign written smaller, but easy to read: 'BURY', it says, and I am convulsed with laughter because I know the word Bury is said as Berry and now here is another sign with my auntie Bessie's name on it.

'If people from London want to find us all they have to do is look at the map and see where Berry is,' I said, and laughed even harder. 'And they'll think Auntie Bessie is here too.'

'God forbid,' said my father and I'm not sure which worried him more: the thought of people from London finding us or Auntie Bessie turning up.

Another time. We are going to the seaside with the people next door, to Morecambe, and my father and the man next door go to get the car they are borrowing. But they don't come back until late in the afternoon and my mother is furiously angry because we have been ready to go since eleven o'clock and Maxine has been moaning and crying when-are-we-going for ages.

But we go to Morecambe and then it starts to rain, though the sun was shining in the morning and the man next door who laughs a lot says, 'Well, that's Manchester for you,' and my mother says nothing, not a word. That is always a bad sign.

When we get to Morecambe all we can see is lots of sand but no sea. It is too far away and hidden in mist. And my mother doesn't say a single word all the way back in the car, and I get more and more frightened of what she will do when we get home. And then I am sick and it comes down my nose as well as out of my mouth, and I cry a lot.

There is a boy of my own age – and I know I am now seven-rising-eight – who also lives in the house next door and he asks me to play with him in his shed. It's his father's, really, of course, but he pretends it's his. I like the shed. It smells deliciously of earth and growing things, and is full of shiny spades and huge forks and other things I don't recognise hanging from hooks on the wall. There is a calendar with pictures of ladies in swimming costumes, and a tray with an old teapot on it, and cups without handles, and a biscuit tin with a picture of a big bridge.

The boy – what *was* his name? Gone completely – shows me a little cupboard under the big shelf that runs all down one side. He opens it and takes out some magazines. I want to look, because books and magazines and comics are the best things in the world, and he laughs, just like his father laughs, and gives them to me, and they are like no magazines I've seen before. There are pictures of naked ladies without even swimming costumes on, and I look at them and I know he is looking at me looking at them.

'They're my dad's, and if you ever tell him I showed you I'll cut your tongue out,' he says, and takes the magazines away. I'm glad because they make me feel funny. I don't know what or why. I just don't feel ordinary.

The boy leans forward suddenly and kisses me on the mouth. I stare at his face so close to mine and feel very odd. But it's an oddness I like and I don't move as delicious feelings from the kiss go all through me as far as my knees. Then we both hear my mother calling me from the garden of our house next door, and he jumps away and pushes the door of the shed open.

'We're in here, Mrs Brandon!' he calls. 'I was showing Berry my mustard and cress. See?' And he picks up a small tray from the shelf and runs out to show her. I follow him, but walking, not running.

She looks at me with the sort of look she puts on when she knows I've been doing something I shouldn't and says, as we go into our house and the boy next door takes his mustard and cress back to his shed, 'And what have *you* been up to?'

'Nothing,' I said, 'just looking at the mustard and cress,' and she makes an odd noise and pushes me into the house. And I know deep inside that I have done something very wicked and very nice, and that if I can I want to do it again.

That memory came back when I got frantic letters from mothers who had discovered their children playing erotic games. Clearly, childish interest in sex is by no means limited to our current relaxed, liberal society. It was part of children's lives, even eight-year-olds, back in the thirties, was before, and still is. I would explain this to my anxious correspondents and push the role of good sex education in rearing their young, and hope they would not fill their children with pointless guilt about it. I have no guilty feelings whatsoever now. I just wish I could remember the boy's name.

We have moved again. I'm not sure where to. Our name is Berk again and I find that quite hard to get used to because it seems to me I've been called Brandon for ages.

We're in a town, a bit like London but not London because the people talk differently here. It's a grey sort of place with trams and dark-coloured buses and without the gardens, grass verges and trees that were at Besses O' The Barn and which I had liked a lot. I think about those days and how, when walking home from school, I would pick the tiny roses that hung over the back fences of the gardens that lined the alleyways I had to go through, and how my mother would be so pleased I'd brought them for her, and put them in a jam jar on the kitchen window-sill. I can't do that in this new place, where there are no flowers anywhere, and I can't understand what people say to me.

Another new place, but I know what this one is called. It is Dublin.

I was past my eighth birthday; I can remember being upset because no one but I had remembered it.

Neither of my parents were very good about presents, though they did remember sometimes to get a card, but usually on the day when I said to them, 'It's my birthday today,' because I had seen the date in the newspaper. Then they would say they were sorry they'd not had time to get a card but I could choose the supper that night to make up.

I always chose fish and chips from the shop, and my mother pretended to think that was common but I knew she quite liked it because it saved her cooking. But that hadn't happened on this birthday.

I remember that, yet I have forgotten the sea journey, which would have been the first ever. I can remember a later one, coming back to England, but not that one. What could possibly have happened on it to make me forget it so thoroughly?

In Dublin we could play in the streets, which we were never allowed to do in Homerton. Perhaps it was because we were older now, or perhaps because all the other children who lived in the house, in which we occupied two rooms on the top floor (and it seemed there were enormous numbers of children of all ages), were allowed to do it.

And I was glad of it. Mostly I didn't play the games with balls or skipping-ropes that the others played all the time, because I wasn't any good at throwing or jumping. Instead I did what I had done in every new place we had gone to; I found the library.

Once I was inside one of those familiar places – and they all looked and smelled just like the one I had first learned to love in Homerton – all was well. I would stay there as long as I could, being very picky over my choices, then walk back with my ration: one story book, two non-fiction. That was the rule. But a kind librarian at Besses O' The Barn had shown me a trick: books of collections of stories, like the Grimm fairy tales or those of Hans Andersen, counted as non-fiction. So did a lot of history books and I discovered, to my huge delight, that some of those were as good as stories, or even better.

Then I would walk back to the street outside the house where the others were playing and sit on a flight of steps and read. A couple of the other girls would try to get me interested in their swapping games – there was a fashion among the children then to collect 'scraps', which were cut-outs of shiny, brilliantly coloured paper depicting soppy-looking ladies and men with great curly moustaches, and puppies and roses and Irish mountains and so forth. I was totally uninterested in them, but I let them spread their treasures around me as long as they didn't put them anywhere near my precious pages.

I was sitting there as usual one Sunday morning. A warm but grey sort of day, it was, with the sun trying to come through, and all the house's windows open. Suddenly my mother leaned out of our window and shouted urgently, telling me to come in at once. I ran up the stairs, my chest knocking with fear. What on earth could I have done? I'd only been reading.

She was standing in the room that was used as the kitchen and in which we three girls slept. It was a big room and she was in the middle, by the big scrubbed table, her hands behind her back, holding her hips, bending backwards slightly. I can see her still and know the reason now. She was five months pregnant.

The wireless was on, rather loudly, and three of the other women who lived in the house were standing by it. They probably didn't own sets: it was a poor part of the city.

'Listen,' my mother said, in a flat sort of voice, 'it's history, this is. You have to know about it.'

I listened and all I heard was one of those voices you always heard on the wireless, with an accent like no one I ever met. I tried to concentrate on what he was saying but it was just words. But then he said, in a slow, thin sort of way, 'and consequently, this country is now at war with Germany.'

My mother looked at me. 'You see?' she said. 'History.'

'Yes,' I said, but it meant nothing to me. War? I'd heard people talking a lot about the war, but they were old people like Grandma and Grandpa and their friends who used to be at their house sometimes when we visited. That was an old war. Was there to be a new one? It sounded interesting, I thought.

'You'll be away home to London, then,' one of the women said, and my mother looked at her.

'I'll have to talk to Percy,' she said. 'I think – maybe we could stay here? It's England that's in the war, not you here in Eire. It could be safer here.'

The woman walked to the door and the other two followed her. She stopped with her hand on the knob and looked back at my mother, then at me and my sisters, who had come up the stairs behind me. 'Ah, well, my dear, that's as may be. But you're Jews, aren't you?' and she nodded and went away down the stairs. We could hear the three of them talking all the way down.

I was confused. Once, long ago at Rushmore Road Infants School, a child had spat at me in the playground and said, 'You're not English, you're not. You're not English,' and I had cried all the way home and asked Betty what she meant, because I liked being English. I liked the red on the map of the world. I liked the flag-waving on Empire Day. I liked the Coronation mug I had with a picture of one king you could peel off to show a different king underneath.

'Of course you're English,' my mother had said. 'You're not a Christian, but that's a religion, like being Jewish. That girl got mixed up. Of course you're English. You were born in the Square Mile, you were. You're a true citizen of Cockaigne.'

I was immediately diverted. 'Cock-where?'

She had laughed. 'Cockaigne, the City of London where Cockneys are born and everyone is rich.'

'Am I rich?'

'From your mouth to God's ears,' she said.

That meant no. I knew that. I went back to the fascinating tale of my birth. 'Where in the City of London was I born? Can I go and see the place?'

'One day,' she said, 'though all you'll see is a railway station. Fenchurch Street station. I couldn't get to Mother Levy's in time and I was in the waiting room and you started to come. They sent for an ambulance but you were born before it came and took us off to Mother Levy's.'

Was it true? It was a tale she repeated to me a few times more, and it always fascinated me. I have wondered whether, while trying to divert a worried child from a complicated question, she was doing her old thing of making up something to glorify herself, like telling strangers she lived 'in Kensington, don't you know'. When I became a midwife and found out how long it can take from the time a baby 'starts to come' to delivery in a first pregnancy, I wondered even more but decided in the end that it was true. She stuck to it so firmly, and I can remember her talking about it when my father was with her and he didn't contradict.

Anyway, I love the idea of being a 'Citizen of Cockaigne' and not merely born within sound of Bow bells, which is the usual marker for a Cockney. And Mother Levy's Nursing Home was in Whitechapel Road, so either way I'm entitled to the label of Cockney. Being a true Londoner is of great significance to me, and always has been.

I was to prove that by what happened after that dull September morning in 1939 in Dublin.

Six

Life seems to speed up now to an amazing degree. If I try to recall it it comes at me like a fast piece of old black-and-white film that I have to squint at to see clearly, for it is jerky, with people moving awkwardly and much too quickly amid sudden gusts of rain.

We are on a ship – this one I *can* remember. It is called the *Ulster* and it is very full of people all in a great hurry to get to England because of the war. They are frightened because a rumour is being repeated by everyone to everyone else that a German U-boat is chasing us across the Irish Sea all the way to England. The ship is bucking up and down, like a demented horse on the dark sea, and it is too dark to see because it is gone ten o'clock at night. I have never been up so late before. All round the bench where my sisters and I are sitting in a row, with my mother on a sort of stool in front of us, people are jerking their way along the deck holding on to the railings at the side or the chairs and benches, only stopping to be sick.

I am deeply shocked because they are sick where they stand, all over the deck and themselves, and my mother has always made it very clear that people *can* get to the lavatory in time if they're feeling sick: it's just a matter of trying. The last time I was sick, in the car on the day of the Morecambe trip, she had told me again that people are supposed to be sick in the right place and had been angry. I had been angry too, because how could I get to the lavatory when there wasn't one in the car and it was going along the road so fast? But I hadn't said that to her, of course.

Now I see all these grown-up people doing what she says we must never do. I turn my head to look at her and say something about it, and she glares at me and says, between her teeth very softly, 'You dare to be sick. You hear me? You dare.' Then she looks at the other two and says it again.

And there we stay all night, on the bench, and we are not sick, not once.

It is still dark and now we are on a train. I am lying on the seat, and it is itchy because of the roughness of the cloth that covers the seat, but I am too sleepy to scratch. I can see across the compartment that both my sisters are asleep on the seats too. I look for my mother and there she is, standing very close to the window, on tiptoe. There is a light with a blue bulb in it over her head, which makes her hair look blue, and that is funny. Even though I am very sleepy I feel myself smile. There is a small place at the top of the window with tiny doors that can be pulled to each side to open them and through that space my mother is kissing my father.

I look through the glass, which is hard to do because it is spotted with dirt, and I can just see him in his yellowish-brown clothes.

'It's not yellow, it's khaki,' my mother had said when we got off the boat and I saw him and said I didn't think men ever wore dark yellowish clothes. 'He's in the Army now, he's a soldier. If anyone asks you anything about your father, you tell them he's in the Army because of the war.'

I thought that was wonderful and looked around at the other people waiting for passengers getting off the *Ulster*. Only one or two wore clothes like my father. I was very proud, and when we went to the station and got on the train with all the other people, so many of them pushing and shoving that Maxine began to cry even though my mother was carrying her, I said loudly to the woman next to me in the crowd, 'My daddy's a soldier. Can you see him through there? He's in the Army because of the war.'

'Is he so?' she said, and sounded very interested. 'Then you'd better be going ahead to catch up with him, poor devil that he is. Fightin' in a war so soon, and him the father of a child. It's terrible, that's what it is, terrible. You go and be with him while you can, you poor wee scrap,' and she made the gesture across her chest that so many of the people in Dublin did that my mother had told me was because of their religion. I thought it must be a kind religion because the lady was very nice. She pushed people aside to get me through to catch up with my father, who had got a whole compartment to himself in spite of the crowds. When anyone tried to get in he said, 'Sorry, mate, reserved for His Majesty's forces,' and they just nodded and went away.

And now he was outside the train we had been on for such a long time, and I thought, just as I slid into sleep once more, He's going away again. She'll be cross. And I felt the train start, then ease into its diddly-dee, diddly-dum, first very slow, then faster and faster.

We are sitting at a table and the grown-ups are drinking tea and looking at the newspapers. Sheila and Maxine aren't there; playing somewhere, I suppose. They like to be together without me and often go off on their own. It happens all the time. I never feel I have a place with them. They have their special games, but I get in the way and am not allowed to play. It is always me and them, but I don't mind. I've always got a book and right now I'm reading *Dr Dolittle*, which I got from the new library in Watney Street yesterday. So I am reading about the Pushmi-Pullyu and enjoying it too much to care about what the women are saying.

All women. Never any men. I never see one anywhere, though the women talk of them a lot so they must be around. I suppose they come home from work too late, after I've gone to bed, for me to see them, then go off in the morning before we get up. Or perhaps they're all in the Army like my father.

'Berry,' my mother says, and it's that voice which tells me it's not the first time. I look up. 'It's the war,' she says, then stops and looks at the newspaper again. The other women, two of them, shake their heads and sigh, and they do it almost at the same moment, which is quite funny and I want to laugh. But my mother's expression is not one that lets me laugh.

'The Germans will probably bomb London,' she says. 'It's going to be dangerous. Very dangerous. You'll have to go away. All the children will.'

'Away? Where?'

'The country.' She looks irritable. 'Away from London.'

'Why?'

'I told you. It's dangerous for children to live here. So you three will have to go away. Soon.'

'Won't you come with us, then?'

We were always going away. Ever since we'd left Homerton all that long, long time ago. I'd forgotten how many different places we'd lived in. It was nothing new to have to go away. Usually it was just the four of us, we three and my mother, though once or twice, like at Besses O' The Barn, my father had been there too. But certainly it was always the four of us.

'You should go, Betty,' one of the women says. 'In your condition you can go. It says so in the paper, mothers of under-fives and mothers-to-be.'

'And Percy comes home on leave and then what? How does he know where we are? No. He brought us here, he knows where I am. I stay here. The girls will go. I'll fix it, they stay together.'

She looked at me then. 'It won't be easy,' she said. 'You'll have to remember to go to the lavatory often, so you don't have accidents in the daytime. The people you'll be living with won't be as careful about changing your knickers all the time as I am. As for nights . . .' She sighed. 'I'll just have to explain to them, I suppose. She's not the only one, is she?' She looked at the other women.

I was sick with shame. I could feel my face hot and sticky with it, felt it all the way down inside me and was suddenly aware that it had happened again, while I was reading probably. I never noticed anything when I was reading. And there I was again, all damp and horrible. I cried. I couldn't help it.

'Oh, God,' my mother said, and pulled a hanky out of her pocket and gave it to me. I would have preferred a hug, I think, but that wasn't her style. Not with me, at any rate. To be fair, I'm not sure it was with the others either, except perhaps Maxine who liked to play 'I am the baby' and would crawl on to Betty's lap and force her to cuddle her.

'Look, it won't be easy for any of us, but there's a war on and we'll just have to get used to it, won't we? There'll be thousands of children with you, thousands. It'll be fun living in the country. The animals and the farms – a bit like going away to those boarding-schools you're always reading about.'

I began to feel a little better. I loved Angela Brazil tales with their titles like *The Madcap of the School*, full of girls with copper curls and blazing blue eyes who were good at Games. I was very bad indeed at beanbag-throwing and running about maypoles and the other things that counted as Games at schools like Rushmore Road, but maybe I could learn.

'So, you'll be evacuated,' my mother said, 'in the next couple of days.' It was the first time I had heard the word. It was to sour my life for the foreseeable future.

The first time was fun, in a peculiar way. I was given a suitcase to carry, a big one, which had all our clothes in, mine and my sisters'. It was awkward to carry, but my mother said she thought I could manage it as long as the other two carried the other things. There was a big bag of sandwiches for all of us, and another smaller bag with sweets in it, which we were to share out after we'd had the sand-wiches.

She tied labels to all of us, with our names on them and where we lived, and made sure we each had our gas-mask. Then it was time to go. The other children from down Antcliff Street were going too, and we fell in with a sort of procession, though it was a very raggedy one: some people, especially the children, were dragging behind.

Most of them were crying, which wasn't surprising because their mothers were crying too. Loud, wet, snuffly crying that made me feel awful when I glanced at them, so I made sure I didn't as the weeping and wailing spread. I walked along, staring at the ground most of the time, though I did look at my mother once, almost against my will, terrified I'd see her crying too. That would have been impossible for me to deal with. I knew that.

But her face was stiff and her mouth was in a straight line across it. She caught my glance and said, 'Don't you dare cry.' I remembered the *Ulster* and how I wasn't sick. I didn't cry. Neither did my sisters. We'd all learned our lesson about what constituted good behaviour in our mother's eyes.

I look back across the vast chasm of over sixty years and I wonder if, as implied by any number of critics of East End mothers, she was glad to get rid of us.

She had her own ways of dealing with pain, and weeping wasn't one of them. All my life I've tried to stop it being mine, but in spite of her tough early training, it isn't easy. These days, I can all too easily dissolve into tears when I see pain on display, but she was never like that. She always managed to put on a face and hide what she really felt to such an extent that, to this day, I can't be sure she loved me and didn't want me to go away. I'm sure she grieved at leaving my sisters, though.

She loved the others, I knew that, because she was different with them. They never seemed to make her as angry as I did. I have wondered in my adulthood whether that might be because she expected more of me. I was the eldest, her firstborn, the one for whom she had the highest ambitions. I knew she made a lot of fuss about how we looked, what we wore and how we behaved, but I also knew very early on that it wasn't for our sakes. It was always for hers. Unfortunately I was the clumsiest, the one who always tore and stained her clothes. It didn't help.

But accept evacuation in order to get rid of us? No, she didn't want that, any more than any other East End mothers wanted to be rid of their children. It was a most cruel canard of the day that should never have been allowed utterance.

That some evacuees in the post-war years stayed where they'd been sent, having become close to their rural foster-parents, and never went back to their own homes is true. For some the likelihood is that their parents were killed in the Blitz or in the services. For others it might be that the pressures of war and the pains of parting were more than they could cope with and they just gave up.

How many of those mothers, standing on the bridge at Stepney Green station that day in September 1939, watching their children go away to God knew where, not knowing whether there would be a London for them to come home to, or whether they themselves would survive the threatened bombing, lost their ability to cope and became ill?

Today there is much that can be done for people with depression of the sort many of those mothers must have suffered. Then there was no help. Evacuation shattered families and exposed children to all sorts of cruelty. Some of the pain was perhaps worse than being bombed in London.

Yes, it saved some of our lives, of course it did. And at the time I know the powers-that-be thought they were doing the best thing for the city children of Britain. But the trouble was that it was almost entirely working-class children who were sent off to total strangers as my sisters and I and our neighbours were.

Middle-class parents had their own and better ways of dealing with the risks of wartime living in London and other major cities. Most, if they were not of the select few who could afford to send their children to the safety of Canada or America, had friends, if not relatives, in safe areas. Those people, middle class like themselves, always preferred to have paying guests of their own sort as occupants of their spare rooms, rather than 'nasty smelly, nose-running, flea-ridden little horrors from the slums of London'* foisted on them by hard-pressed billeting officers.

So, when children like us arrived in country areas, we were seen as

---

* As I read in a novel published in the fifties. Evelyn Waugh was also *so* amusing about the horrid evacuees.

objects of patriotic duty first, which is a horribly uncomfortable sort of object to be – 'We're fighting this war for the likes of you and I'm buggered if I can see why we're bothering,' one farmer said to me, when he found out I was Jewish – or, perhaps even less comfortably, cheap labour.

When we arrived at our destinations, we were packed into the largest building they could find, like the church hall or a school hall. There, we were offered cups of cocoa by ladies in Red Cross uniforms or green outfits marked WVS, and were inspected by would-be hosts and hostesses.

Not all of them were willing would-bes: most had been told they had to take us in because they had the space, but those who were willing, even eager, to take a vaccie (the nickname arrived fast, and stuck long) were looking for very specific children. They walked up and down the lines into which we had been arranged, staring at us, conferring in whispers and being very picky indeed. They'd learned how to do that sort of thing at animal markets, of course, and found their skills transferred easily to London children.

I sound bitter, do I? You bet your sweet soul I do. Until you've experienced the humiliation of being inspected like a piece of highly dubious meat you can have no conception of the effect on you. Even after all these years I still burn with fury when I think of the way those hordes of frightened, tired, hungry children had to tolerate the bureaucracy of selection for a home on their arrival.

Big boys of thirteen and over were snapped up by farmers, some of whom were already losing their labourers to the armed services: a healthy teachable boy or two could be worth a fortune to them, because, first of all, they didn't have to pay them and, second, they were actually given by the Government 7s. 6d. a week – that's 37½p in modern money, if that matters – but then it was enough not only to feed a child but make a bit of a profit.

The next most popular were big girls of the same age group. Domestic servants were vanishing fast into the flesh-pots of the munitions factories, where they could earn far more than they ever had skivvying for the middle classes, or into the glamour (they thought) of the women's armed services. How many of them ended up skivvying for officers, of course, is not known, but it was probably a sizeable number.

Once they had all gone, it was the turn of the sort who wanted sweetly pretty little girls, who would be decorative and nicely grateful. The hardest to place were families – my sisters and I, my mother had said, were to Stick Together No Matter What and, even so far from her, we dared not disobey – and boys of intermediate age, who looked as though they might be a bit on the noisy side. Normal boys, in fact, but still too young to be put to work.

No doubt I will receive a flurry of letters from people telling me that evacuation was the best thing that ever happened to them, lifting them from the abusive homes to the care of generous country people who treated them well and whom they learned to love. And yes, of course that happened, but there is a great tendency for stereotypes to develop around such massive events as wars and the national evacuation of children. And the stereotype that was most carefully nurtured in the press of the time, and on many occasions since, was that the Great British Public Rallied Round in a time of war, and looked after each other and cared for each other, and settled cheerfully for the fairness of rationing and pulled their weight on all occasions and were all-round good eggs.

Well, let me tell you how it really was for some of us.

Seven

I have no memory of making the decision to run away from the country and go back to London. I can just remember it being there, a fully fledged plan, occupying every corner of my mind. Which was just as well because I had discovered, almost on the first day, that there was no library in the village.

This had come as a dreadful blow. What would I do if there were nothing to read? But I discovered then that I could do something else: I could tell myself stories. All I had to do was imagine I was in a particular situation, out on my own, say, walking in the horrid fields that were everywhere, then watch what happened. The 'action' would take off with no conscious control from me. I watched it the way you watch a film on a cinema screen.

Back in the early days of the war, daydreaming was my comfort and salvation, and I suspect the source of my decision to take some control over what was happening to me. In my daydreams I could do all sorts of clever and exciting things. Why shouldn't I try to do them for real?

So I set about the practical details. I would need food on the journey, so whenever I got the opportunity I would filch a little of whatever came to hand, such as a slice of bread and butter or, that special miracle of miracles, a biscuit. A miracle because they were usually kept in a tin on a very high shelf well out of reach, but sometimes they'd forget to put it back up there. I would hide my supplies in the old cigar box I had pinched from the man's study on the day we arrived.

I called him 'the man' because no one told me his name and I never saw him. I just knew he belonged to that very large part of the house where we weren't supposed to go. We had to stay up in the attics where the servants lived. That was where I hid my cigar box. There was a broken floorboard under my bed, and when I fiddled with it, it came up and left a space. Very useful.

I had been sent to the Manor House of the village with my sisters, because it was the only place big enough to take three.

'The master and mistress are away on a shooting holiday and won't be back till the end of the month,' a woman in a thin grey coat with a thin grey face told the billeting officer when we were shown to her, virtually the last of the batch to be selected for a home, 'so we can take them for that long. After that they'll have to go. Mistress wants to make the house a hospital for officers, she says, and she'll start as soon as they come back from Scotland.'

I wasn't prepared to wait till they found us a new home. I hated the house with all its big quiet rooms, which we dared not set foot in for fear of stinging slaps. I hated the grey woman, who was in charge of us at the house, and above all I hated the two maids who were there with her, because they jeered and sneered at us.

I doubt they were much more than teenagers, but at the time they seemed very grown up and very, very nasty. Especially after the first morning when, in spite of all my efforts to hide it, they found the wet patch on my bottom sheet. They put dandelions on my plate at dinnertime, because they said that was what Pissthebeds had to eat and wouldn't give me any other food at all. I seemed to be forever hungry in those days and Sheila, who was always the kindest of us, gave me some of hers.

Every day after school I walked down to the station to look at the trains and find out where they were going. There were no signs up on the platforms. All signposts and station names, even street names, had been taken down the moment the war started, in case of invasion. The Government seemed to think it would make fighting so hard for the German Army, because they would keep getting lost, that they'd get fed up and go home to their own country. From this distance it sounds both silly and rather touching, but those were more innocent days.

In the event I had to wait a little longer to make my breakaway. Instructions had arrived from Scotland, apparently, to get the vaccies out 'toot sweet', said the thin grey person with relish, and cheered on by my two tormentors, because the owners were coming home early to start looking after wounded officers. No one had seen any or even heard of any because, as far as I could tell from listening to the teachers at school and every other adult I came across, there wasn't much of a war going on at all. Still and all, that was why we had to go and I didn't mind a bit that they were lying because there weren't any wounded officers for them to look after.

'Not like last time,' the old people standing around outside the shop-cum-post-office would say to each other, looking at us with bright, malevolent eyes. 'That was a real war when people got hurt. This time it's just a lot of nancies mucking about.' And they would stare at us, hating the way we had invaded their village and wanting to be rid of us. But not as much as I wanted to be got rid of.

They separated us now, and that was perfect for my plan. I didn't want to get my sisters into trouble for what I did, and I knew everyone would think they'd known of my plan once I got away, even though I would have jumped out of a window sooner than tell them. It was my plan, and I had no room in it for two smaller people who wouldn't be able to keep up.

The new house I was sent to was worse than the Manor House had been. There was an old woman who never stopped shouting at everyone in an unintelligible roar that made my head hurt. There were three young women in the house, who I assumed were her daughters, but it was hard to tell since they ignored her all the time. They ignored me too, and I didn't mind that at all. I didn't like the way they looked, in thick dark green trousers streaked with earth, and raggedy jumpers, and the way they smelled of the cigarettes they smoked all the time, and of something more, thicker, nastier and unidentifiable. Above all I didn't like the food they ate and expected me to eat.

I would sit and look at what they put before me each evening – in my memory it was always exactly the same – and try not to heave. My mother's training stood me in good stead when I looked at the slab of greyish boiled suet pudding, speckled with scraps of glutinous half-cooked bacon fat and a few shreds of salty red bacon meat, with a pile of wet cabbage, boiled to a dirty green sludge, slopped down beside it.

I would push it around the plate with my knife and fork, hoping they wouldn't notice I wasn't eating it, but they did. The woman would roar at me, and the daughters would shout about wasting food in wartime, but it was no good. I couldn't eat it, so I'd be sent to bed without pudding. Not much of a punishment because that, too, was always the same: lumpy semolina – sometimes burnt – with watery plum jam on it.

I knew I had to go and I chose a morning when it was raining. I thought people wouldn't bother to look for me if anyone noticed I wasn't at school.

I went to the station and waited till the man who stood at the barrier when there was a train – he took the tickets from arrivals and made the people who were going to get on the train show him theirs – had run back into his warm little office. Then, moving carefully, I slid on to the platform. I walked close to the wall and slipped to the end, away from the ticket office, and stayed there, hidden round the edge of the building.

Was I scared? I can't remember. I just stood there and daydreamed, hugging my cigar box, till the next train came.

It slid slowly along the platform and I peered out. The ticket man was at the other end of the train where the engine was. This was a one-track station and the same little train went up and down all the time. When it went up the engine pulled it from the front and when it came back the engine pushed it from behind.

I heard the flurry of doors opening and didn't wait. I ran across the platform and along the train till I came to an empty compartment with an open door and climbed in. At once I lay down and rolled under the bench seat. I don't know how I knew to do that. It just happened. There was the seat, and there was the space beneath. *Ergo*, that was where I had to be.

I stayed where I was in case someone else got on, but after a while there was the familiar sound of steam getting up, then the whistle, and in a whoosh the train started to move, slowly at first and then faster, settling down to its familiar steady song, that lovely friendly diddly-dee, diddly-dum. It was like all those journeys I had been on with my mother on our way to find my father again. The only difference now was that I was doing it alone.

The little train stopped three times on its way to the last station, and each time I hid under the seat in case anyone got on. No one did, and then I could stand at the window staring out and feeling the rain on my face as the dank fields slid by and the smoke from the engine sent black sooty specks to stick to me and fill my nose with the delectable smell of a steam engine. I was happy for the first time in ages.

The big test was the last station. It was called the Junction. I knew that because I used to hear people talking about it when I hung around the village station while I was making my plan. Trains went from the Junction all over the place, but most importantly to London.

It was a bewildering place to be. So many platforms, so many trains, so many people. I got out, trying to look ordinary, but no one paid me any attention. Everyone was far too busy about their own affairs. There were no signs up where I was, no timetable to look at, nothing that might have helped an invading German as well as me. I would have to use my ears. I wandered from group to group of adults, trying to look as though I had left my own grown-ups up the platform. And I listened.

I was lucky. A woman in a tiny hat, which looked as though it ought to fall off because it was perched so far forward on her head, and wrapped in a fur that had feet at one end and a head at the other, gave a loud shriek of laughter. And at once I remembered two things. First, that the lady was wearing a fox and it was only rich people who wore them; my grandma had one – she had let me stroke it and put the front paws in the grinning toothy mouth, which was how it was fastened, and I had shivered with terrified excitement. Second, when I went out with Auntie Nancy she had made me speak quietly: she said it was common to make a lot of noise in public and disturb other people. But there were some people around, she told me, who talked in tight, tinkly voices and always shouted. That meant, Auntie Nancy had gone on, they were 'Society' persons.

Auntie Nancy clearly had small respect for Society persons, but I thought they were useful because you could hear what they said, instead of having to strain to hear the whispers of polite people like Auntie Nancy.

I moved closer to the shrieking lady and stood looking sort of vaguely at her, as though I was thinking. She chattered on to the man with her, who was wearing an overcoat and a black hat. I thought suddenly that he looked warm and realised how cold I was. My dress was only a thin one and the coat I had on top wasn't much thicker. They both had gloves, but I didn't and my hands were frozen. I put them into my pockets and listened hard.

I can feel the cold in my hands that day as I stood there waiting for the woman to say something useful about which trains went to London. I can still catch a hint of her perfume – she must have put it on with reckless generosity – and I can recall suddenly thinking of my mother. This was the sort of woman she used to talk to in the shops and tell them she was 'from Kensington, don't you know'. What would happen when I got home to her? What would she do to me? I nearly turned round and went back to the train I had come on.

But then the woman said, 'Darling, at last, here it is. I suppose it will be groaning with people, too ghastly. Look, sweetie, phone me, won't you? I'll be in London by – it ought to be before six but, these days . . . Just phone, yes? 'Bye, darling.'

She got on to the train and, walking very slowly so as not to be noticed, I followed her and got on too.

Eight

Trains. *Steam* trains. The smell of them, the sound of them, the look of them, the bustle that always surrounded them, all of it for me as a child was solid magic. With hindsight I find this extraordinary. If my experience of trains had been of going off in high excitement to the seaside for summer holidays the way other children did – I knew how wonderful that was because they boasted about their adventures when they came back to school afterwards – it would be understandable, but it was never like that for us.

A train journey in my life meant trouble of one kind or another. *Always.* We would be running away from something, or trying to get to something better (which we never did), and my parents, if they were both there, would be snapping at each other and bickering, which I hated. Or if it was just my mother we were with she would be grim and silent, doubly fierce in her anger if I did anything to annoy her. Which, of course, I managed to do all the time, however hard I tried not to.

I have tried to understand why they were so unpleasant to be with on such occasions. I have tried to imagine herding three small girls under eight on and off trains, trying to keep them amused, dealing with train sickness (Maxine) or a perpetual need to run to the lavatory (Sheila) or total forgetfulness of the need to run to the lavatory at least occasionally (me) and the results. I add to that the fear of whatever it was they were fleeing on these journeys and, I imagine, the considerable doubts and anxiety about how they were going to cope when they arrived wherever they were heading, and it is clear that the atmosphere around us was fully entitled to be thick with emotion.

And yet I loved trains. I still do. They make me tense and anxious, convinced that unless I'm there at least ten minutes earlier than the advertised time I'll miss mine, they make my muscles crawl with worry for hours before I am due to ride in one and I am always convinced there will be a crash. And yet they have for me the same magic they did in childhood, even though they are so much less beautiful now, with their dull smoke-free engines, and no hint of steam or the rich scent of the coal that used to fuel those glorious old machines.

When I think now of getting on that train at the Junction that rainy morning in November all that time ago, I am filled with the old heart-pounding, delighted excitement. What I was doing was wrong. If I were caught I'd get the hiding of a lifetime. If I wasn't caught and got back to my mother the chances were I'd get the hiding of a lifetime. Yet for that glorious moment I was getting on to a train and that was bliss enough.

My memories of the rest of that journey are mixed up with those of similar journeys I made after it, for I was to run away from being an evacuee four times in all.

I developed a technique, I suppose you could call it, for not being noticed as a runaway. I would attach myself to friendly-looking persons, usually a woman on her own but sometimes a couple, and say in a vague but unworried fashion that my mother and my sisters were further up the train and that I'd come down to this end to see if there were any seats. But of course there weren't. There never were. I would perch on the nearest piece of luggage and chatter to them in a cheerful sort of fashion until they were used to me being there. After a while I would say I was going back to the other end to see if my mother and sisters had found seats and set off to push my way through the unbelievably crowded corridors to the other end.

It is exceedingly difficult to explain to people who are too young to know about the way life was during the war what train travel was like. Even compared with the worst of overcrowded late-running commuter trains on our current benighted rail system, it was hell.

The windows were covered with criss-crossed anti-shatter beige paper strips, so looking out at the passing view for entertainment was not a real option.

Every compartment in every coach would have at least five, sometimes six people crammed into each side, which had originally been built to take four seated passengers. They were the lucky ones. The space between the two rows of seated passengers would be occupied by three or four others, often sitting on kitbags because soldiers were always the most numerous among the passengers, with sailors a close second. *They* sat on their duffel bags. After that, people pulled the windows up to help them shin up to lie down in the luggage racks. They were very content and comfortable up there!

The corridors that ran alongside the compartments were just as crammed and the crowd there seemed always to be heaving and rolling around, like an oily sea on a heavy day. The reason for this was that people needed to get to the lavatories at each end of each carriage as journeys that were meant to last no more than a couple of hours stretched to three, four and even longer. It was easier for me to get through, for I was small enough to crawl between people's legs or sometimes, if the soldiers and sailors were in a good humour, they'd pick me up and pass me along like a bundle of washing.

I learned early on these journeys to listen out for the cry, 'Tickets, please! If you please. Tickets! Tickets, per-lease,' of the ticket inspector. At this stage the railways still tried to use them on their trains; later they gave up in despair, for completing the job of inspecting a train full of tickets in those conditions had to be hell on earth. But they were certainly on the trains I used on my running-away trips and as soon as I heard the cry I would head for the lavatory. Even if there was someone in it, they were usually out by the time the inspector got to me; if they were tardy I'd bang on the door and plead urgency. It usually worked.

The trick then was to leave the lavatory unlocked, and press myself against the wall behind the door, alongside the pan. The inspector would push it open as he went by to make sure he missed no passengers, but didn't push it all the way to the wall so he didn't find me. I wish I had the build to do that now.

Hunger could be a problem. The cigar box had long since been lost. I found that when people took out their sandwiches, cakes or apples and started to eat I only had to watch them lift their hands to their mouths for a little while to have them offer me some. The first times I would say, 'No, thanks,' because I'd never been allowed by my mother to accept gifts from anyone, but soon I was grateful for what I could get.

And when the train arrived at the terminal, and people poured off it, I would attach myself to a couple who were talking eagerly, and walk out through the barrier just behind them as though I belonged to them. It still amazes me that I was never stopped.

And after that? Then the real fear began. The excitement of tricking my way back to London had been wonderful, but once I arrived I thought of my mother. I had to go home to her. There was nowhere else. I knew she would beat me. I knew, after the first time she did it, that she would promptly arrange to have me sent away again. But still I did it. Why? Because it was better than my evacuee life.

I seem to remember that my youngest sister, Maxine, also had a bad time, although she stayed put, but I know only what she told me, long after, because we were always separated after I started to run away. The authorities never sent me back to where I had been before, so I quartered the country, ending up in Wales, Wiltshire, Herefordshire, and Devonshire. When my own children were young and we went driving off on holidays, I would recognise an area and start to say 'Hey! I was –' and they'd finish it in chorus for me, '– evacuated near here!'

I remember one billet in Devonshire, in a small village close to Okehampton, on Dartmoor. They had a smallholding, and part of being their vaccie meant getting up at the crack of dawn or earlier to wash eggs in cold water, and bundle radishes, spring onions and carrots for market. All this before school and breakfast. It wasn't so bad in the summer, when there was a chance of pinching a carrot or two to gobble, earth and all – I never seemed to have enough to eat – but in the winter months when it was dark in the morning and bitterly cold all there was to do was wash eggs, because the vegetable season had finished. That was hellish.

Maxine told me long after that she had the same experience regarding egg-washing. They were always well covered in chickenshit – oh, the joys of free-ranging birds – and had to be washed in cold water. Warm water would cook 'em, they said.

Maxine described her hands as being like 'bunches of purple sausages', and I know exactly what she meant. I used to get dreadful chilblains, appallingly painful cold injuries on my hands and lips that would itch and hurt until I hardly knew what to do with myself.

And then there was the day I dropped three eggs and was sent to school with a black eye. Not that any of the staff noticed. It was probably easier that way.

Des, my husband, was an evacuee for a short time. The house he was sent to in King's Lynn was occupied by a couple and their teenage son, who took a strong objection to this small interloper invading his premises, and used to take pot-shots at him round the corner of the house with his shotgun. Oh, it was great to be a vaccie!

When I had run away for the fourth time and been taken back to Antcliff Street by the police (it was too far to walk from Paddington, which was where I had arrived this time, so I had had to ask for help) I think my mother gave up. If I was going to go on doing this I might as well stay in London with her and the baby.

Ah, the baby! He was born in January 1940, in the middle of an air raid, in the shelters under the Hackney hospital. I had only seen him a couple of times, but after this fourth runaway when I stayed in London I really got to know him. And fell head over ears in love.

He was so uncomplicated to love, that was the thing of it. If he was upset he cried, but if you rocked him and cuddled him he got over it and laughed and smiled great gummy smiles at you. He certainly didn't shriek at you and hit you or sulk at you half a day for some crime you'd committed unwittingly. And my mother would never tell me why she was refusing to speak to me. I was supposed to be able to work it out for myself, 'Since you're so clever!' So Lionel, the baby, was a great comfort.

We're all sitting round a table, eating. We're crushed up close to make room for the other people. I don't really know them: they are my mother's friends.

One is called Black Sophie because she has black hair and that makes her different from Sam's Sophie, who has yellow hair like my mother. I expect she makes it that colour with a saucer of smelly fizzy stuff and a toothbrush the way my mother does.

I like Black Sophie because she owns the shop on the corner of Antcliff Street. Every time I go in she gives me something nice: a screw of blue paper filled with broken biscuits, perhaps, or a salty, juicy pickled cucumber from the barrel by the door, or even, if she is feeling extra nice, a slice of rich Dutch cheese. No one asked how she got cheese to give away. A certain amount of this sort of black marketeering wasn't unusual.

The room we are in is Black Sophie's kitchen, which is at the back of her shop. It is a very bright, cheerful room with red curtains and a red rug and pictures on the wall. The table is covered with a nice thick red cloth that has bobbles all round the edge. On top of this cloth there is a square of thick, shiny American cloth that you can spill stuff on and it doesn't matter. This is one of the reasons I like being at Black Sophie's. No one shouts at you if you make a mess.

As well as the other women there are a couple of babies and, of course, the best baby in the world, Lionel. After a while I get bored. Lionel is asleep, and I can't play with him, so I slide off my chair and slip under the table. I like it here. I can see everyone's feet and legs and they amuse me: they have stockings on them that are wrinkly and they are mostly wearing slippers, though my mother has shoes on.

One of the slippers Sam's Sophie is wearing has a little hole in the toe. I take my pencil from my pocket and very slowly slide it into the hole. They are still talking, all at the same time, and not really listening to each other.

Sam's Sophie wriggles her toes and pulls her foot away, and I try not to giggle. After a while I put the pencil into the hole again, and again she jerks her foot irritably. But I get tired of the game and wonder what to do next.

I am just about to crawl out from beneath the table and go and play in the street when I hear one of the mothers of the babies say, 'But what do you do first? That's what I can't work out. What do you do first?' Her voice sounds so frightened it's as though she is going to cry, and that's a dreadful thing, so I freeze and stay where I am. To see a grown-up cry is awful. I once saw a mother at Rushmore Road Infants School cry when they told her her little boy had been taken ill and had been sent in an ambulance to the fever hospital. That had been so bad I never wanted to see it again.

'You've got a baby's gas mask, haven't you? Didn't they give you one when you got yours?' That was Black Sophie, a nice, sharp, juicy sort of voice, a bit like her cucumber pickles.

'Sure I got one. But what good is it if the gas raids come? What do I do? If I put my mask on first then by the time I put the baby in his, he'll be dead, and if I put him in first then I'll be too late to put my mask on, and who's going to keep the pump going in his mask if I'm dead? I lie all night, worrying and worrying . . .'

I can see it. There are the aeroplanes in the sky, hundreds and hundreds of them, all with their gas stoves in the back, popping and hissing with all the taps turned on and none of them lit, so the gas comes pushing out of the aeroplanes and down on to the people underneath. I can see the woman with the baby, and she is crying and putting him in the big baby's mask, that looks like a box with a glass lid on it, then taking him out and putting on her own gas mask, which is like mine with a long snout and a piece of mica across the front to see through, until it gets all misted up, of course. Then she takes hers off again and puts the baby in his and all the time she's crying, 'What do I do first? What do I do first?'

'And suppose, God forbid, I'm out of the house and I've not got the mask with me? It's a big thing, that baby mask. Even if I put it on the pram it's a big thing to shlep around. So suppose I just don't have the mask at all and the gas raids come . . .' The mother of the baby sounds as though she is going to cry at any moment so I sit still under the red tablecloth's bobbles.

'So don't go out if you don't think you can manage! I've been practising with Lionel and it's not so difficult. I manage fine, and so could you if you practised a bit!' My mother never has much patience with people who grizzle, and this other mother is certainly a grizzler.

Black Sophie, who is always nice and always wants people to be happy and comfortable around her, says as soothingly as she can in her pickly voice, 'So listen, I'll tell you what you do.'

She takes a big breath because she obviously has something important to tell them all. She always takes a big breath like that when she's going to pass on a bit of gossip. I listen hard when she does, because that is always the best grown-up talk to listen to.

'I was told this by the Feldman boy, the one what's a medical student over at the London. He works in the casualty department, he tells me, and they're having to learn emergency ways of dealing with things that might happen, right? What do you do if you're caught out in a gas raid, God forbid, and you've got no mask?'

She pauses dramatically, and I can imagine all the women sitting staring at her and, for once, not trying to interrupt.

'I'll tell you,' she says, just at that point when you could scream from waiting for her to tell you the answer. 'You take a big hanky. A man's hanky. And you fold it into a pad just big enough to cover your nose and mouth, right? And then –' another dramatic pause '– and then you pulls up your skirts and you pulls down your drawers and you pee on the hanky and you put it over your mouth and nose and, *shoin*, you got a gas mask! I swear to you, he says this is as good in an emergency as any lump of rubber!'

The women start to laugh and someone shouts, 'Sophie, you're as bad as you ever were, you *lobbus*, with your skirts in the air and your knickers down!' and then they're all laughing and chattering again.

Even the woman who was almost crying over what to do first for her baby is laughing.

I am not laughing. I am sitting under the bobbles, staring at them and thinking, They're liars. All grown-ups, they're liars, I hate them, I hate them. They are liars and nothing will ever be any good ever.

I begin to cry, softly at first, as the truth of it sinks into me. They said one day I would grow out of being a *pisher*, that all the horrible wetness would stop when I was old enough. I had believed them. I had been convinced that grown-up people didn't make all this hateful water inside that made me wet my bed and knickers. And now I knew it would go on for ever and ever.

My crying got louder and louder until suddenly Black Sophie's astonished face peered at me from under the bobbles, and then my mother was reaching under and pulling me out and I still couldn't stop crying.

'We've frightened her, talking that way,' Black Sophie said. 'It's all right, *boobalah*. Don't cry. There'll be no gas raids, I promise you, not a one. If that Hitler tries it I'll be there in Berlin in no time and I'll make *ashenblott* of him with my chopper, how's that, eh, choochie? No need to cry.'

They all fussed over me, trying to make me feel better, but there was no point in it. Nothing would ever be any good ever again.

Nine

I stopped going to sit under the table at Black Sophie's after that. I was afraid of what else I might hear. It was bad enough to know for sure that all grown-ups were liars and couldn't be trusted. I didn't need any further evidence and, indeed, if I'd overheard more, I'm not sure I would have been able to cope. The bedwetting got worse than ever, and I was hit a lot for it, but I just didn't care. In a way I thought it was their fault for telling me lies about growing out of it.

But life wasn't all bad. Life never is. The library relaxed its rules because of the war – 'New Rules for the Duration!', a phrase that became very familiar – and allowed me to borrow as many as three fiction books at a time. My mother let me go over to the library as often as I wanted. There was hardly any school: only one remained open in the whole area and we attended either in the mornings or the afternoons and rarely did any real work. It was mostly singing 'Jerusalem', which made the teacher cry, I seem to remember, and practising how to get into the shelters in a hurry if we had to. I had lots of time to read.

It was so hot, that September, I could sit on the sun-baked pavement outside our house if I discovered my knickers were wet, and they'd get dry in no time. In the evenings the women stayed outside in the dimness – no lights, of course, because of the blackout – until it was cool enough to go to bed. But then they started, searchlights picking out patterns of tiny dots in the sky made by aeroplanes coming over in waves, the humming getting louder and louder, then being drowned by the long whining wail of a distant siren, that looping, hooting sound that to this day makes me want to dive for the nearest safe place if I hear it.

At first they paid no attention, the women in the street (there must have been one or two men, but I can't remember more than a couple of very old ones), apart from squinting up into the deep blueness of the summer sky, and I thought the planes didn't matter. And then realised they were lying again, the grown-ups. *They were afraid.* They were pretending it didn't matter, were trying to pretend to themselves that muttering about the planes being a 'bleedin' nuisance, you no sooner get to sit down and catch your breath than the buggers come and drive you barmy' would make them go away.

But the noise got louder as other sirens nearer to us took up the wailing, and then they moved, dragging home the wooden chairs they'd brought out from their kitchens to sit on in the street, shouting for the children, hurrying each other along until the whole street was on the move. I would try to be one of the last to go, leaning in the shadows against the wall of the house, watching everyone and listening to the noise of the oncoming planes until my mother or one of her friends spotted me. Then they'd drag me by the arm, pulling painfully on my shoulder and making me go down into the shelter. Which I hated.

It smelled, our shelter, of cats, staleness and general nastiness, and wasn't at all smart like others in the street. Some people had done their shelters up with curtains and pictures on the walls, proper oil-lamps swinging on overhead hooks and rugs on the floor. Our shelter was just as it had been left by the men who had come from the council to make it: flattened earth floor, a couple of bunks and benches against the curving corrugated metal walls, a lidded bucket in the corner and a couple of candlesticks on a makeshift shelf.

My mother, Lionel and I shared it with the people who owned our house, and who lived downstairs.

They were an elderly couple who chattered ceaselessly at each other in low, grumbling tones, never seeming to listen to each other, just chuntering on and on. I know it nearly drove my mother demented because she got that look on her face. But clearly she couldn't say anything to them because it was their house and their shelter.

So, grimly, she would make me pee in the bucket – oh, the ignominy of it, with the old people there, not that they took any notice – then give me a blanket and make me lie on one of the bunks. Lionel in his basket, which was getting rather small for him because he was growing like a weed, was put beside me, and she would sit on the end of the bunk, her arms folded, chin resting on her chest, and pretend to go to sleep. I knew it was pretence. She was breathing all wrong to be asleep. But pretending helped, because when I tried it, I actually did fall asleep.

A few days after the raids had started, and we'd got used to spending the night in the shelter, we woke one morning after the all-clear had gone and emerged from our underground holes to find the whole street ablaze with gossip. The night before there had been a great many planes, but they had been heading further east for the docks. However, a couple of small bombs had landed over the road ('One of those stupid Germans what don't read the maps before they set out,' said the knowledgeable types) and there was now a pile of rubble over which you could see clear through to Commercial Road.

For the half-dozen children who lived in Antcliff Street it was wonderful. We didn't have to go to school the morning after a raid, which was cheering, and there was all the busy digging and cleaning up over the road to watch. No one had been hurt. The people there had been in their shelters and pulled out safely, so everyone could enjoy the drama with a clear conscience.

A couple of weeks or so later, the bomb-damaged area was so familiar to me that I couldn't remember what the street had looked like before. It was just part of my new mental as well as real landscape. And I liked watching the busyness of the big Commercial Road now that there were no houses in the way to block it out.

It was one of the hottest days ever. 'Ninety in the shade, I swear,' Black Sophie said, sweating heavily, her face the colour of a boiled beetroot. 'Tell your mother I'm sorry but the milk's all turned. I've got the whole lot dripping in the kitchen making cream cheese. I've got some tinned milk, tell her – not that she'll want it, not good enough for your little brother . . .' I went home to deliver the message.

Lionel was roaring in a frenzy of rage and hunger. She was trying to pacify him with boiled water, but he would have none of it. She swore under her breath when I delivered Black Sophie's message and shook her head at Lionel, who was now even redder in the face than Black Sophie.

'I'll go to the dairy,' I said. 'It's only just along Commercial Road.'

She looked at me and then at the clock. It was almost five. We were all getting used to the pattern of life in the East End now. No more sudden scares as lone planes came over, and the sirens got excited for nothing but real raids.

They usually started at around five, not waiting till dark any more. The sky was full of fat silver barrage balloons and it was the street's expert opinion that the planes came in daylight to make sure they could see them and keep out of their way.

Lionel screamed even more loudly and I sympathised with my mother. I knew how angry and bouncy he could get, throwing all of his considerable nine-month-old weight around.

'All right,' she said, 'and make sure you go straight there and get back in time.' She jerked her head at her purse on the table. 'Take a shilling and God help you if you lose the change. Run all the way – and don't go over the bomb damage.'

I was half-way down the stairs by the time she got to the bit about the bomb damage but shouted back, 'I won't, God's Honour,' and ran out of the front door, down the street, into Bromehead Street, then on to Commercial Road and helter-skelter along its wide pavement to Jones the Dairy on the far corner.

I was almost too breathless to speak when I got there but I had to wait anyway because Mrs Jones had a customer. She was patting into a neat cube a small piece of butter she had cut from a huge block. I loved watching the wet wooden butter paddles at work and I stood waiting happily, getting my breath back.

Mrs Jones and her customer had a brief gossip and I dared not interrupt to say I was in a hurry, but as soon as I could I asked in a gabble, as instructed by my mother, for 'A-pint-of-full-cream-sterilised-and-make-sure-it's-full-cream-please.'

Mrs Jones had just put the bottle of milk, with its special crown cork to keep it sterile, in my arms and tucked the change from the shilling, which was threepence ha'penny, into my hand when the noise began. The sirens from all around took up their wail together, creating a fearful racket and filling me with huge fear; not of the coming raid but of my mother's reaction to my tardiness.

'Now then,' cried Mrs Jones, heading for her shop door, ready to lock it, 'you'd better come down my shelter with me – it'll be safer. Come you now.'

But I dodged under her arm and out into Commercial Road. 'The baby's crying,' I shouted, in explanation for my rudeness, and ran as hard as I could, like everyone else in the street. Some of them tried to pick me up and take me with them, but I kicked hard and they soon decided saving me wasn't worth the trouble and let me go.

I came level with the bomb damage, over which I could see my own house in Antcliff Street, and hesitated. 'God's Honour' was the strongest promise a person could make, and the thought of breaking it terrified me. But then, as the sound of gunfire started somewhere away behind me, I stopped worrying about God and his wretched Honour and hesitated no longer. I was going to get home as fast as it was possible to get there, which meant taking the shortest way. I went belting over the rubble, slipping and sliding, trying not to hear the gunfire. That really did worry me.

Then the ground seemed to shake as the gunfire got louder and I slipped with a vengeance, slithering and sliding down into a hole. A fair bit of rubble landed on top of me and when the slipping and sliding stopped I was half lying, half sitting on what seemed to be a piece of wood, with quite a lot of other pieces of wood on top of me, my bottle of milk and my threepence ha'penny change.

And I suddenly realised my knickers were wet.

It was to be twenty-eight hours before they got me out again, or so I was told. It didn't seem all that long to me. I think I slept a lot and whenever I heard what sounded like people I shouted a lot, but it was a long time before anyone heard.

As Black Sophie told me, 'They'd cleared all that patch, you see, never thought to find anyone there, did they? They wasn't lookin' and they wasn't listenin'. Your *mazel*, *boobalah*, your *mazel*!'

I didn't feel lucky when at last the air-raid wardens, who had heard me calling, pulled me out of my hole.

I must have let go of the threepence ha'penny change at some time because it wasn't in my hand any more.

I dropped the bottle of milk as they pulled me up and it immediately shattered.

My knickers were sodden.

And I was expecting the hiding of a lifetime.

Ten

Being buried under seven feet of rubble was an important experience for me at the time, and I must have caused quite a commotion in Antcliff Street when I was borne back there.

Yet I have no glimmer of recollection of what happened next. If I close my eyes now I can almost smell the dustiness, the hint of broken sewers and escaped coal gas in that hole in the ground. I can feel the weight of the milk bottle pressing on my belly, and the shape and weight of the pennies and ha'pence held so tightly in my other hand. But the memory vanishes into nothing after the moment they pulled me out and I dropped the milk bottle, and realised I had not only lost my mother's money but that I had been a Problem Child again.

I then recall sitting all alone with Black Sophie – a rare treat since normally her back kitchen was where everybody spent their time – being fed all sorts of delicious odds and ends. I am eating Dutch cheese, all sticky and creamy in my mouth and glueing my teeth together lusciously as she tells me how lucky I was. I might never have been found. 'And then what?'

I agree with her about my good luck and let the cheese melt away, and as the taste of it goes so does the memory and I echo her question, 'And then what?'

I do know that eventually the house in Antcliff Street was bombed so we had no London home any more. Long after, in 1979, I wanted to set part of a big novel I was writing, about the Jewish diaspora, in Antcliff Street, so I went back to look at it for research. I knew the house had gone, of course, but I was not expecting to find that the whole street grid had gone too. The Bromeheads, Road and Street, as well as Antcliff Street, have been swallowed into what is now called the Sidney Street Estate. I felt bereft when I stood there and stared at that huge sixties housing development. I felt as though the town planners had eagerly finished what Hitler had started.

I also know, as a matter of family history, that my father had been in France with the British Expeditionary Force, and had been among the hundreds of thousands of servicemen who were evacuated from Dunkirk. The story goes that he was separated from his regiment (probably picking up bits and pieces of loot, which had always been one of his specialities) and reached the Dunkirk beaches virtually at the last moment, trailing a dozen or more Frenchmen behind him. They wanted to escape to England to join the British Army and fight for *la patrie*.

He was posted to an aerodrome, one of a circle of them in the Cotswolds surrounding the old Roman town of Cirencester, as part of the Air Force's military defence. He managed to find a flat for his wife and children and took us there. They brought Sheila and Maxine from their evacuation 'homes' and there we all cluttered up together again.

A flash of memory again. The 'flat' is an empty shop. There is a tiny back room with a gas stove but no sink, which is the kitchen and sitting room. There is a tiny upstairs room, their bedroom, and the three of us inhabit the huge empty shop part. It has a big window, with a sort of platform in front of it where goods had once been displayed, and we play on that, mostly doing putting-on-a-show because it is so obviously a stage, though it's really the others who play. I still read all the time. The rest of the space contains a double bed shared by my sisters and a single bed for me. The Problem has some beneficent spin-offs. I like having my own bed and I often didn't when I was an evacuee, which made the Problem ten times worse. There is a back door leading out to a yard where there is an earth-closet lavatory, shared by all the people living round it (some dozen or so families, I think), and a communal tap for water, which is fetched into the flat in buckets. I am the oldest so I do most of the bucket-carrying.

We are enrolled at a school where the headmaster is a vicious little man with a humpback called Mr-Henderson-Sir – that is how all the children are taught to address him – who prowls the playground at every break with a bendy bamboo cane under his arm.

My mother goes to see him when we are enrolled and tells him her 'I come from Kensington, don't you know' story, which completely beguiles him because, as we find out in time, the whole town is enmeshed in snobbery. I also think she flirted with him, fluttering eyelashes and the like. She was a pretty young woman – barely thirty – and often turned on her very real charm to get what she wanted. Certainly he never attempted to hit any of us, though he was generous with his beatings for everyone else and always grinned delightedly while he was doing it, which I thought was horrible to see. He particularly liked an audience when he beat someone but after the first time when I saw him grinning while his victim screamed I never went near again when he did it.

We lived in the 'flat' for a long time, and various things happened there. Once I developed huge swollen glands in my neck so that I looked like a pumpkin and was feverish to the point of delirium. I was admitted to the Evacuees' Hospital, a converted house in the middle of a shopping street set up out of charity collections: the local people did not want vaccies polluting their rather handsome Cottage Hospital.

Perhaps I exaggerate here and no one used the word 'pollute', but according to my mother that was the way of it. I remember conversations she had with my father, telling him how people in shops refused to serve her, ignoring her when she went in because as soon as she opened her mouth they realised she wasn't a local.

And I have to say I saw some evidence of that myself. She had taken me with her when she had gone into a rather fancy grocer's shop not far from the church in the big marketplace – very posh, I thought it – and had asked the price of something.

When they told her, with the sort of sneering face some shop assistants put on whenever anyone asks the price of their goods – it proves they're poor and not worth bothering with – she made it clear that she regarded them as war profiteers of the first order and told them they should be ashamed of themselves to treat a brave soldier's wife and child so. And we were escorted to the shop door and told, 'We don't serve your sort, so never come back or we call the police.'

I agree she was as much at fault as the shop assistant in that particular fracas, but there is no doubt that the local people regarded us as pretty scummy. Lots of parents told their children not to play with vaccie children for fear of catching things, and certainly my mother made no friends I can recall. In Antcliff Street she had been part of a busy gossiping network, but in rural upper-class Cirencester she was an outsider and never allowed to forget it.

But she got her own back in a way that was very typical of her. Name-changing was nothing new in our family. The Brandon episode was by no means unique and had been a method of getting out of trouble my father had often used. She now decided, and persuaded my father to agree with her, that it was time to get rid of all connections with the in-laws she so hated and find a new name that would be all ours.

The name she (they?) chose was a family name of the local swells, the earls of Bathurst. They owned a great chunk of the neighbourhood, including Cirencester Great Park, and I had seen residents of the town actually dip a little curtsy when they saw one of the family out shopping. So, because she wanted what they had, she took their name. It was a bit of magical thinking on her part, perhaps: taking the name meant that some of the money, fame and respect the earls had would rub off on her. It also fitted nicely into her 'refained' I'm-from-Kensington-don't-you-know persona, and made her feel, I am sure, that she was a cut above the mere masses.

My parents did the job in style. They did it by deed poll, with which no one could argue, publishing their intent first in the *London Gazette* so that objectors could complain if they chose. None did, so we became the Chetwynds. We were instructed by Mother to tell people if we were asked that it was one of *her* family names they had chosen to use instead of my father's so it really was ours anyway. A typical lie, and of course we did as we were bade and told it whenever we had to.

I have to say, I couldn't get rid of the name fast enough once I married because it felt even more phoney than Brandon had. I've been the happiest of feminists using my husband's name ever since. But it was as a Chetwynd that I was admitted to the Evacuees' Hospital and treated rather better than I might have been because I bore the name. Sickening.

Shortly after I recovered from whatever had caused my massive adenitis my mother got ill. I had an inkling of what it was all about, but only that.

Not long after we arrived in Cirencester, I woke in the middle of the night to hear my mother groaning. My father was on duty at the camp, so only the four of us were there, and I was terrified. But I got up and crept to the kitchen, which was where she was, and peeped through the crack of the door.

She was in her nightie, which was pulled right up to her middle, and was perched on the bucket we used as a pot when it was too cold or rainy to go out to the earth closet. The bucket seemed to be covered with blood. She had blood on her hands too, and I stared. Then, as she made a huge and obviously painful push that made her groan again, I fled back to bed in cold terror and hid under the blankets.

Next morning she was already up and about when I woke and I crept into the kitchen, expecting only horrors to greet me, but she smiled cheerfully. She was making toast and offered me some. I took it and said, 'Are you all right?'

'Never better,' she said. 'Why?'

I improvised fast, remembering the sort of things the women said to each other at Black Sophie's. 'Nothing, really,' I said, and bit into the toast so that I wouldn't have to look at her. 'I just thought you looked a bit pale.'

'Ah, well, that's very likely,' she said, and made a funny sort of grimace. 'As you'll find out. It's something that happens to women. I'll get over it. Go and get dressed.'

So when she got ill and told us she had to go to hospital to have an operation called a hysterectomy I guessed it was something to do with the bleeding in the middle of the night. Now, with a deal of experience of gynaecology behind me, it's clear to me that she had used the services of back-street abortionists when necessary – access to contraception for working-class women during the war not being what could be called easy – and had had to pay the price, though not literally, of course. She would have been a charity patient at the big hospital in Gloucester to which she was sent as 'an interesting case'.

I do remember she was very cheerful about having the operation. 'It'll save me a lot of trouble,' she said, and then, perhaps deciding it was time to teach me something she felt I should know, told me she'd give me something to read about her operation. There was a booklet in her bedroom.

It told me that 'The womb, which is removed in hysterectomy, is a small triangular organ towards the front of the female sex organs.'

Naturally I immediately investigated my own body to see what she was to have removed, and the only small triangular organ towards the front of my sex organs that I could find was a rather ticklish little knob that, at that stage of my life, I preferred to leave alone. I was into my middle teens before I got the nomenclature right and discovered that what I thought was my uterus was my clitoris.

Even simple anatomical knowledge was regarded as disgusting in my young years. It wasn't till I was old enough to go hunting out the right sort of books to teach myself that I got any sort of understanding and that made me angry. It also made me determined that one day I'd make sure girls like me would be able to find out properly about these things and not be made scared or ashamed of their ignorance as I was. The seeds of a future career were certainly sown by my mother's operation and the best bit of mothering I can ever remember getting from her: the booklet, although it misled me, at least gave me permission to be interested in such matters.

I can't remember who looked after us during her month in hospital (there were complications apparently) but I do recall I was the only one whom Lionel would allow to touch him. I would sort him out in the mornings, changing his nappy, feeding him, then leave him to the person looking after us and go to school. I rushed home in the dinner hour to feed and change him again, play with him and put him down for his nap. And after school I devoted myself to him completely. He became my favourite of all my family and still is, though today's sixty-plus-years-old Hollywood writer and film-maker is not quite as pretty as he was in his toddler days.

My mother came home, and life settled down again and went on its usual boring way. That is how life is for poor people, and much worse in wartime. It's just a steady grind, doing your best to get enough to eat and get to the end of each day. There was no money for anything, except once in a glorious while my mother scraped up enough to let us go to the swimming-pool in the summer. That was the greatest treat and the pool was a lovely thirties job of which the town was justifiably proud. I just wish I could have used it more, for I had a passion for swimming.

Instead I read my way through the whole of the children's library and was in despair until Miss Beasley, the librarian, a woman of great insight and tolerance, told me I could read grown-up books as long as she checked their suitability first.

She started me on J. B. Priestley's *The Good Companions*, and then I read everything else of his I could find. I fell in love with Arnold Bennett and Hugh Walpole, G. B. Stern and Jules Verne, H. G. Wells and Rudyard Kipling, Dornford Yates, Jeffrey Farnol, Jerome K. Jerome, and heaven alone knows who else. Clever Miss Beasley knew enough to add plenty of merely fun books to the more serious ones.

And then I read any number of playwrights, whom I borrowed as non-fiction, of course. Galsworthy, Coward, J. M. Barrie, Pirandello, Brecht (yes, indeed!) and a marvellous series of 'Plays of the Year', which introduced me to American writers like Saroyan, Tennessee

Williams, Thornton Wilder, Clifford Odets and umpteen others, with no TV or radio to distract me. My mother had a radio but she saved it for herself because it cost so much to get the accumulator recharged and she wanted 'to use it for good stuff, not stupid dance music.' But I had books so nothing else mattered.

Sometime in 1942 I came back to the old shop, which was still our home, at the end of the school day and was told, in an almost casual way, that I was to go away to school. I had won a scholarship, my mother said. It had all been arranged at my current school by the LCC, who still looked after London children as best it could even if they were vaccies – didn't I remember doing the exam?

I sort of did but it had seemed to me no more than one of the usual tests the school gave us. But there it was: I had sat an exam, the London County Council Junior County Scholarship, and passed exceedingly well, and all the glories of a *real* education lay ahead in a public school.

'As long as you work hard and try to remember to go to the lavatory when you have to,' my mother said, 'you'll be all right.'

I didn't know it but I was one of the lucky ones. At the start of the war, the LCC apparently arranged with all sorts of county education authorities to allow London children their chance at the scholarship, once they reached the statutory age, which they would certainly have tried if they still lived in London. When I started at the Cirencester school the arrangements had been put in place and, in due course, I sat the exam.

Others were not so fortunate. Des, two years older than I, had been sent to King's Lynn *after* the London children of eligible age already sent there had done the exam. His mother took him home after the shotgun incident but by then his school in London had already done the exam. He, like thousands of other London and other big city children of his age, never had the chance . Although in the future, after his National Service stint, he used his Air Force discharge gratuity to train at the Guildhall School of Music and Drama in London and get its diploma, he has never ceased to feel cheated by what happened to his education. We're both autodidacts now.

I was taken up to London, oh, joy of joys, to buy school uniform. I did ask why, if it was safe to go to London for shopping now the Blitz was over, it wasn't safe to live there any more. I ached for London in a physical way, my belly turning over with excitement as the train drew into Paddington, past great big black-and-white enamel advertisements reading 'Mazawattee, What a Tea!' and 'The Stephens, the Owl and the Waverley Pen, they come as a Boon and a Blessing to Men.' And then there was the smell of London, indescribably and perfectly of London and nowhere else.

My mother was short with me: 'We'd have to be mad to think it isn't going to start again. This war's not over yet by a long chalk. Now, come on. Don't dawdle. We've got a lot to do.'

It wasn't till we reached the glories of Oxford Street and my mother led me into the splendours of Daniel Neal's that a thought occurred to me, and Big Mouth lived again: I blurted it out without stopping to think.

'It must be very expensive here,' I said, remembering the humiliation we had suffered at the posh grocer's shop in Cirencester. This place had the same sort of atmosphere, and it alarmed me. 'Where are you getting the money from?'

For the first time in her life, my mother swore at me. 'Mind your own bloody business,' she hissed and sailed into the shop, taking it for granted that I would follow her.

I knew then. Grandma, I thought. My father had gone and begged it from Grandma.

And when we emerged a couple or more hours later with an amazing array of uniform for the City of London School for Girls, the establishment I had chosen from the list the LCC proffered, refusing to go to Christ's Hospital School for which I was eligible when they told me it was very much for Big Brains and I'd have to work hard every hour of the day, I owned more clothes and objects than I had ever had in all my life.

There was a hand-blocked beribboned black velour hat with elastic under the chin for winter, and a ditto straw Panama for summer.

There were dark red gymslips, and red-and-white striped crêpe blouses, and a handsome red-and-white silk tie, the colours of the City.

There were regulation dark red knickers, which my mother said scathingly looked like bloomers because they had a pocket in one leg, and stockings and suspender belts (oh, the hell of wearing those!), liberty bodices and a dark red swimming costume and white rubber bathing cap.

There were three pairs of shoes – *three*, when I had never had more than one at a time, ever. There were dark brown outdoor shoes with laces, lighter brown indoor shoes with one buttoned bar to hold them on and black sports plimsolls. Oh, and a bag to carry them in. It was overwhelming.

The best thing, though, was a handsome brown pigskin writing case and a pack of Venus pencils, which my mother told me my father insisted I have as a going-away present, though I suspected it was really Grandma. My father never had money for presents. The writing case had a design in one corner of three dots and a dash and of course everyone knew what that meant: it was V for Victory, the Morse code sign and therefore bang up to the minute in terms of style. I thought it very glamorous indeed, with its special pockets for paper, stamps and envelopes, and its loop for putting a pencil in safely. I thought it was absolutely the most glorious thing I had ever seen.

And I have to say it is one of the few souvenirs I have of my childhood. It is a poor, battered old thing now, but I wouldn't part with it for the world.

Until that moment, when my mother said it was a going-away present, I hadn't thought much about the fact that all this meant I was going away from Cirencester and all of them, but now, suddenly, my heart leaped in my chest so that I thought I'd be sick. Another train journey! Oh, life could offer no more!

Except that I would have liked to go and see Grandma and Auntie Nancy, away to the north of London in Stamford Hill, to show them all the things they'd paid for and say thank you.

But I had more sense than to say so.

Eleven

The City of London School for Girls (often pronounced 'gels') should have been in Carmelite Street in London but had, of course, been evacuated at the start of the war with its brother school, the City of London School for Boys. The boys went to Ashford in Kent and the girls to Keighley in Yorkshire. At the start of the September term of the year 1942 in which I was eleven I set out to join them there, all dressed up in my new uniform, looking like a character straight out of Angela Brazil's *The New Term at St Catherine's*.

There had been a nasty moment on the platform of Cirencester station at 6 a.m. where my mother had taken me and my rather battered old cardboard suitcase for the train to the Junction. It was a complicated journey to Bradford, where I was to pick up the local train for Keighley, with lots of changes, but I had it all written out on a piece of paper tucked into my new dark red woollen gloves. I'd be fine, I knew that, and was bursting to get away.

I stood there on the windy station in the new morning light, cringing as she engaged an arm-in-arm couple, the only other people on the platform, in conversation. She told them, in her most strained of tinkling cut-glass accents, that, 'Ai'm jest seeing m'dawter orf to college. The City of London College for Gels, don't you know. Boarding, of course.'

I couldn't bear it and took a chance. I'd be leaving her behind on the platform at any moment so she couldn't do me any harm.

'School,' I said loudly. 'It's not a college. Just a school.'

She made one of those tight little three-cornered smiles that always presaged trouble. 'Mother knows best, dear!' she said, with horrid brightness, and I saw the people she was showing off to exchange glances, trying not to laugh aloud. I wanted to hit them and to shout at her to stop making a fool of herself in front of such stupid, unimportant twerps, but all I managed was a choked 'Isn't that the train?'

It wasn't, and there ensued what seemed like an eternity of more of her dreadful chatter, with her accent getting more and more strangled and the other people staring at her and looking like stuffed owls as they struggled not to laugh.

If I had been feeling any sparks of regret about going away from the family to be on my own with strangers, that episode quenched them fast. I was so grateful when the train came that I almost wept. She saw it and thought the tears were for her, that I minded going away, but in truth I wept because I *didn't* mind and knew, somewhere deep inside, how sad that was.

I date my separation from family life to that morning in September. Oh, I would return to them in Cirencester, of course, at school holidays, and was to return to London with them after the war, but I finally lost any lingering emotional attachment to my mother, and through her to my father and siblings (with the exception only of the infant Lionel), as the train carried me away and I watched her on the platform, waving at me.

She would still be able to manipulate me, still be able to make me feel worthless, ugly and undesirable, still be able to make me fill up with guilt for some vast unnamed crime, but it wouldn't hurt as it had when I was small. Perhaps she had loved me, at some time, but all I knew was that I never felt she did – or that she even liked me much, come to that. That had been a source of misery as long as I could remember. But not any more, not once I went away to school.

I felt sometimes as though my brain was bulging with all the new things I had to learn. How to say 'Keethley' and not 'Keeley' for a start. How to cope with Yorkshire accents and Yorkshire prudery, too. I was removed from my first billet because the woman was too disgusted to put up with me: I was reading the newspaper after lunch on the first Saturday I was there and asked her what VD was, since there was a huge headline about it and I'd never heard of it.

'Diseases of filth that 'ave never bin talked of in this 'ouse before and niver will again once I've got thee out of it,' she snapped, and sent her mild, obedient husband immediately to fetch the billeting officer and get me bundled out forthwith.

'She's a right dirty-minded gurt nowt, that one,' she told the billeting officer, who arrived in a state of great anxiety because she had been told there was a crisis. 'Wi' 'er dirty talk! Send 'em back where they coom from, that's what I say, and let the nasty objects get themselves bombed and good riddance.'

The billeting officer asked me what had happened. 'I asked what VD is,' I said. 'I saw it in the paper,' and the woman cried, 'Eh, she's a right shameless 'ussy, sayin' it again!'

So the billeting officer took me away and delivered me to the nicest people I was ever evacuated to. The Exley family were lovely, warm, affectionate and, above all, courteous people, who made me feel welcome and wanted. Almost all the adults I had ever met treated me as a half-wit because that was how children always were treated. They could be shouted at, ignored, beaten and commanded to do things with never a please or a thank-you, though heaven help us if *we* forgot to use those magic words. But the Exleys treated me like a person, asking my opinion on things, reading the paper with me and discussing the war news, asking me with real interest about the books I read and the work I did at school.

They took me to the theatre with them every Saturday night, which was a revelation to me. They had had the same three seats, front row dress circle centre, ever since their son, their only child, had been old enough to accompany them. Because he was now in North Africa, one of Montgomery's Desert Rats at El Alamein, I was able to sit in his seat and see *Love from a Stranger* and *Poison Pen* and *Dangerous Corner* and *Hobson's Choice* and *The Maid of the Mountains* and *Chu Chin Chow*, and so much that was wonderful. I owe a lifelong delight in the theatre to the excellent Exley family.

I spent a couple of years with them, never wanting to go back to Cirencester in the holidays but having to, and doing well at school because I knew they would be eager to hear what work I had done that day and what my marks were. I wanted more than anything to please them.

I learned Latin, French, science (that was a first! And I loved it) and English literature as well as English language, both of which I enjoyed greatly, for Miss Beasley, back in Cirencester library, had guided my reading well and I was top of the form in those subjects, and history, geography and mathematics – all separate subjects taught *properly*. It was a different universe from the primary school in Cirencester, where all we did was Religion, Reading, Writing and 'Rithmetic, with sewing for the girls and woodwork for the boys.

That school, like so many country and small-town schools for working-class people, existed to produce servants for the houses and farms of the upper classes and little more. But the City of London actually was a *school*. It was amazing in my eyes. So were the new ideas with which I was bombarded.

One teacher, the remarkable Miss Peach, was my form mistress as well as the teacher of English literature, and I liked her a great deal, even though she was somewhat ugly, bearing a vigorous tuft of luxuriant grey whiskers on her chin, which she never seemed to notice though we all did, wretches that we were.

She gave me John Stuart Mill, Thomas Paine and Thomas Hobbes to read, and Mary Wollstonecraft and sundry other 'disgraceful texts', according to another teacher who disapproved of her radical ideas and methods of teaching. (I once eavesdropped shamelessly on a row between them: my Miss Peach won, of course.) They were even more of a revelation than Saturday nights at the theatre with the Exleys.

I also learned to develop my own ideas and express them vigorously, and it says much for the quality of Miss Peach as a teacher that she listened to the views I developed and didn't punish me for them, as many other teachers would have done. She might have disagreed with them – I never knew because she didn't tell me either way, although she always put up a good argument – but accepted that my views were honestly held and carefully thought about.

The thing was, I used to try very hard to be a religious believer. I wanted very much to believe there was a kindly God who cared about me, personally. I wanted to believe there was a Tooth Fairy, that Father Christmas really was a down-the-chimney mystery, that there were fairies at the bottom of the garden and that adults told the truth. But I never managed it.

I must have been a tiresome child with whom to deal, because I argued so much. I was told by both Uncle Max and Auntie Nancy that I had perfected the extremely infuriating use of the word 'why' almost before I learned to say 'shan't!' and I have a vivid memory of being stingingly smacked at infant school (not, of course, by the wonderful Miss Delight) because, when a teacher told me that Jesus would cry if I was naughty, I asked her how he would know if I was naughty. And when she told me it was because he watched all of us all the time, I remarked that he must be very rude if he watched people in the lavatory and, anyway, I'd see him watching if he did, and kick him for it. That was what we'd been told to do if any of the little boys in our playground came spying on us in the lavatories. I thought she'd understand that. But she didn't.

I rather think the belief business almost bit the dust for me after that experience. I was labelled a troublemaker from then on: the walloping made me so angry that I told her there wasn't any Jesus anyway and she'd made it all up, just like they'd made it up about Father Christmas. It was put to death for ever after the business of going across the bomb damage, even though I had said I wouldn't and had used my mother's sternest promise to obey, 'God's Honour'. If this supposedly kindly God they all went on about really cared for me, he wouldn't have thrown me into the hole full of debris just because I'd broken my promise in an effort to get back home in time to reach the shelter. I came to the conclusion that whoever else this

God was interested in it certainly wasn't me, so I wasn't interested in him.

I don't for a moment think I was all that unusual. I think the majority of children are natural sceptics. Watch them watching conjurors and you'll see the brightest of them trying to look under the silk scarves and boxes and other tricksy bits to see how it's done. It takes a very deft magician indeed to fool children; that's why the successful ones are those who make jokes and allow the children to laugh. They forgive the pretence of magic in exchange for the fun.

The trouble is that these children go on to be bullied into irrational belief. It used to amaze me, when I reached City of London school where they taught us physics and chemistry, that the selfsame teachers who taught us about the rules of scientific evidence, of the way experiments had to be repeatable to be true, of the way mathematics provided incontrovertible evidence of so many of the laws of nature, could stand in daily prayers with hands folded and eyes closed, praying to a supernatural, unproven being. Weird or what?

Even weirder was the way some of them were enraged and punitive if a pupil – all right, if *I* said that Darwin (Miss Beasley had given him to me, too) had proved that Genesis was a myth at best, nonsense at worst. Miss Peach saw my point; the biology teacher didn't.

The thing I found most difficult, I have to say, was feeling such an outsider. All the other people in my form were believers, swallowing grown-up duplicity in large lumps, reading newspaper horoscopes eagerly, playing with home-made Ouija boards and suchlike, and it was lonely thinking differently. I used to pretend to believe in the same things they did, until a Walt Whitman poem, encountered in Miss Peach's English class, brought me up short again.

In 'Song of Myself' he says, 'I think I could turn and live with animals. They are so placid and self contained. They do not bow down and worship one of their own kind,' and I had a sudden absurd vision of a rabbit making a deep bow to another rabbit and saying, 'Hail, Your Royal Rabbitness . . .'

The sheer stupidity of it all got to me. It not only confirmed my disbelief in supernatural gods (what was Jesus but a man, after all?

They kept telling us that at the same time as telling us to worship him, daft objects!), it also made me a republican. But that's another story. Anyway, after that poem came into my life, I stopped trying to be the White Queen, who could, Lewis Carroll said, believe six impossible things before breakfast, and settled for being the form outsider on the matter of religion. It might be lonely, but it wasn't too bad. After all, Walt Whitman sort of agreed with me . . .

As time went on, I discovered at last that there were other real live people, not just dead poets and philosophers, who thought like me, and that I wasn't weird after all. From then on, the struggle to be a believer disappeared into the other horrors of childhood memories. I was a real live grown-up at last and refusal to share others' illusions/delusions no longer marked me out as peculiar at best, despicable at worst.

Though I have to admit, of course, that I came by my own rationalism not because I was deliberately taught it but because I found it for myself in the books I was given, which I chose to read. As long as there are teachers like Miss Peach, children with enquiring minds will find their own ways through the labyrinth of truth, falsehood and fairy tales.

If life had gone on like that, and I could have stayed with the Exleys at a school I loved, with a teacher I trusted and respected, I suspect my life would have turned out very differently. But everything went dreadfully wrong.

I don't know why it happened, but I had to change school. I liked the City and I thought they liked me, so I was shattered when I was taken away and sent to Welwyn Garden City in Hertfordshire to attend a school of equal quality, also a public school, the Skinners' Company School, but given no explanation for the change.

Here I was sent to live in a hostel with other children rather than in another family home, which was something to be grateful for; no one could be as good as the Exleys had been. My sister Sheila was there and attended the school, too, for which I was far from grateful.

I have to admit I was sick with anger, and jealousy of her because she was sweet and biddable, and everyone at the school adored her. The more they liked her, the less they liked me, so I hated everything: the school, the hostel, the whimsy-mimsy town, which was a

garden city and looked like something from a revoltingly sentimental greetings card, as far as I was concerned. I even hated the street
names, I remember – Applecroft and Cherrycroft and the like. I
despised the tweeness of it all. More to the point I missed my old
friends, I missed Keighley's Yorkshire grittiness, I missed my City
teachers. Above all, I missed the Exleys.

I stopped being interested in working. I shirked lessons, ignored
prep, never did any homework at all. I played truant, ignored what
was said to me and was generally a pain in the neck to all around me.

Some of the trouble was my age – I was pubertal and fizzing with
hormones – and part was, I think, that I suffered my first depressive
episode. I think this because every hormonal change I've ever experienced has been accompanied by clinical depression. I mean the real
psychiatric illness, not just a change of mood. Each pregnancy and
birth plunged me into an attack, mild at first but worse with each of
my three babies. The menopause, and later the loss of my residual
oestrogen when I developed breast cancer, had the same effect. If all
those hurled me into black depression it's reasonable to suppose that
puberty did too. Looking back at the way I behaved – sulky, aggres-
sive, refusing to eat, unable to sleep – it sounds logical to me now.

But in the forties no one would ever have considered it possible
for children to get depression. Actually, no one thought adults got it,
apart from psychiatrists in the know, because the condition was
never discussed in public. What would be the point, since there was
no effective therapy for it?

I was just labelled Problem Child again, and harassed, punished
and nagged, not only by my mother, in letters, but also by teachers
and hostel staff, who took their cue, naturally enough, from the
things my mother told them about me. I became ever more difficult
and hell to have around.

I look back on those years, which took me almost through to the
end of the war, and wonder how I managed to live with myself, I was
such a misery.

Though I still had libraries, of course. There was always reading.
Glory be.

Twelve

And then it was over. The war, which had dominated every thought, every daily experience, every aspect of our living, was over at last.

We had talked of the possibility, sometimes, spoken of being bored all the way through to our middles with the hunger and the tedium, and tried to reassure ourselves it was 'just for the duration' as a way of tolerating the misery. For a long time we had used the mantra 'When the war's over, we'll . . .' in the same way that children's stories start with 'Once upon a time' and end 'And they lived happily ever after', without anyone believing it would happen.

War was all we could remember, all we knew, all we could think about, really. To be told that it was all finished, that the Germans had been defeated, Hitler had died in a Berlin bunker, the soldiers were coming home, the blackout was over and done with and there were to be no more blitzes or V1s or V2s – how could we possibly be expected to take all that in?

It is 8 May 1945. We wander around the streets of Cirencester – for we are back there and have left Welwyn Garden City and the Skinners' Company School, though don't ask me why for I've long since forgotten. I have Lionel in a pushchair, because even though he's four years old he likes to ride when he can, and I like to push him. My sisters have gone off somewhere to look for some signs of excitement in this dismal town where, even on VE Day, no one seems particularly concerned about what is going on: they're as totally wrapped up in the minutiae of their own rural lives as they always have been, and do not apparently see any reason to celebrate on this cool May morning.

The only people sharing the market square and the surrounding streets with us are GIs from the nearby US Army camp and a few local children like ourselves. Now I suppose that their grown-ups were at home, relishing the suddenness of a weekday holiday, and sleeping later to make the most of it.

Those of us who are out and about this early – it is barely half past nine – do our best to be jolly and celebratory, especially the GIs who are breaking out great bundles of bunting from the backs of their jeeps and draping it wherever they can. Some of the local citizenry will disapprove, no doubt, but for the moment the red, white and blue flaps valiantly in the breeze and I try to lift my own spirits to match it.

And fail. I know what the problem is. My father was at the cottage last night, on a short leave from the blissfully silent aerodrome. The cottage is where we now live. It is on the other side of the town from the shop 'flat' and, I have to say, is considerably smaller in real terms, though it is a proper cottage for living in and not just an empty lock-up shop. It is stone-built, sits low in a tiny valley called Quern's Hill (no doubt, in ancient times, they quarried millstones from the area; hence the name) and provides two upper rooms just big enough to hold a double bed each, in one a cot and in the other a small camp bed, unlit except for small deep-set windows. At night we burn candles.

There are two lower rooms, about the same size, which are gas-lit – I learned to be very effective with handling delicate incandescent gas mantles. The front one is the main living room, which has an open coal range for both heating and cooking; the one at the back is the kitchen, which has a tiny gas cooker in it and a deep yellow stone sink, but no water supply. There is neither bathroom nor lavatory; just an earth closet (a double-seater, which is a novelty) fifteen yards from the back door. For household water there is a pump in the centre of the yard used by all the residents of the Hill (about thirty families, I think; we were at number twenty-one and that was by no means the last in the row).

These arrangements are so similar to those at the lock-up shop that I accept that this is normal living in Cirencester for poor people, and a sergeant's family definitely counts as poor.

He had sat there last night talking to my mother about plans, now that the war is over. He'll be demobbed. We'll go back to London, as soon as he can find a place for us all. It'll have to be the same sort of size as number twenty-one Quern's Hill, but at least it will be in London and will have mains water. Maybe even a proper lavatory. He'll get a job soon and we'll all live happily ever after.

I sat and listened to the plans and knew I couldn't bear it. Ever since I had escaped to the City of London School for Girls and the bliss of life in the Exley household I had known that I couldn't bear *ever* to live with my family again. I'd been dragged back to them in Cirencester from Welwyn Garden City against my will, though, as I say, I can't for the life of me remember why. And now it seems I have nothing to look forward to but having to live with them all for ever and ever. I can think of no worse fate.

I sit in the market square with Lionel in his pushchair, watching the GIs trying so hard to celebrate, and I feel the tears in my chest trying to push up and out. But I can't cry. That might make Lionel cry.

So I don't. But I sit there and start to make plans of my own. I've run away before, I tell myself, I can do it again. Only this time I won't run towards them, the family in London, but away, far away, somewhere on my own. I'd even give up my passion for living in London to escape being with them. I'm also prepared to give up seeing Lionel, but I know he'll grow up and away from me on his own because that's what children do. I'll lose him anyway.

And, as always, daydreaming provides comfort. I see myself walking away from my family with a suitcase in my hand and not looking back. I see myself hunting for a job, for I will never again go to a school I don't like to be nagged at, sneered at and constantly criticised. In my dream I am looking for a job where I'll be useful and important and people will be happy to see me and never, never tell me I'm lazy or stupid, the way they did at the Skinners' Company School when I was too frozen with misery to do any work.

And, oddly, in my daydream I suddenly see myself in a hospital, wearing a nurse's uniform.

I am startled by the road my daydream has taken and pull myself out of it, staring down at Lionel in his pushchair where he is happily bumbling over a picture book I bought him for a penny in a jumble sale, and try to think about it properly, not just as a daydream. Me, a nurse? Where on earth had that idea come from?

Where it had come from I still don't know – but I do know that from that moment it never went away.

The place Peter found for us to live in was a small house in the depths of South London, as far as it was possible to get from the East End of my infant memories. So far that I didn't really feel I was back in the London where I had so yearned to be for such a very long time. Yes, there were big red double-decker buses and hordes of black taxis, with a sort of flag near the driver that he pulled down to show he was hired or left up to invite new fares. There were vans and whistling boys on bicycles and people, people, people. Yet it didn't smell like my London and, oddly, I was as homesick for London while living in that little house in Norbury, just beyond Streatham, as I had ever been in Cirencester.

They tried to make me go back to school, choosing Selhurst Grammar this time, in Croydon. Sheila and Maxine went off there amiably enough, but I dug in my heels and flatly refused. And discovered, to my great interest, that I wasn't as helpless as I used to be. Before, if I'd said a flat 'No' to something they wanted me to do then the reaction would have been a good hiding for being so cheeky. But I'd passed puberty now, had had my growth spurt and at five feet eight and a half inches I was taller than my mother and almost the same height as my father. They were somewhat nonplussed by that.

But I wasn't. I was delighted. It meant I could do what I wanted to do when I wanted to do it, and what I chose to do was get a job at Woolworth's, selling rubbishy earrings and necklaces at threepence and sixpence a go. They paid me twenty-two shillings and sixpence a week for working five nine-hour days, and a four-hour day on Wednesdays, which was early-closing day. This gave me an hourly rate of just fivepence.

If I could have kept it all I would have felt rich, but my mother demanded I pay for my board and lodging at home at the rate of fifteen shillings a week. Out of the remaining seven shillings and sixpence I was to save up to buy my own clothes – when she could spare me the coupons, that was, for clothes were still heavily rationed – and cover all other expenses. I have a vivid memory of her refusing to walk along the street with me one day because I looked so scruffy and didn't even carry a handbag. 'Every girl has a handbag!' she said scornfully and crossed the road to walk on the other side.

'How do I get a handbag, for God's sake?' I called after her. 'I've got no money!'

'Then earn it,' she shouted back. 'You want to run your own life? Then go ahead and see how far you get. And you don't have to swear, either.'

I thought that parting shot most infuriating because she said 'for God's sake' all the time and she claimed to believe in religion. I didn't, so how could my saying 'for God's sake' count as swearing for me? But I didn't argue with her. Instead I got on with The Plan.

It wasn't very complicated. First I did indeed save every penny I could, never going to so much as the pictures, which cost sixpence for the cheapest seats. I went to the library on every possible occasion (in those halcyon days the libraries remained open till eight-thirty every evening except Sunday) and found my pleasure in books as ever, but also spent a lot of time in the journals and newspaper section.

I must have looked a bit out of place among all the old men who spent long hours there. Then I assumed they liked reading newspapers. I now think they were there because, even in the coldest weather, the library was warm, comfortable and deeply peaceful. Just the place to spend the day if you were on your uppers and had nowhere to go and nothing to do when you got there.

I found the *Nursing Mirror* and the *Nursing Times*, and devoured not just the articles, most of which were on very esoteric subjects (one title that I still remember with affection was 'The Role of Gruel Enemata Following Extirpation of Piles', which at that time impressed me as much with my own ignorance as admiration of its high seriousness) but also the advertisements.

Page after page, they offered me open doors to freedom all over the country. It was bewildering at first. For a start, I had to learn the language in which they were couched. What on earth were emoluments, for example? That wasn't too difficult. I just had to nip into the reference library in the next room and use the dictionary. It meant, I discovered to my delight, not just the salary a person might get from an employer but also payment in goods and services rather than in cash, and included such things as board and lodging, laundry, and even, in some cases, provision of uniform. Was this why nursing seemed so attractive? That I could earn the roof over my head and my own keep was of huge importance.

I soon learned to identify the posh training schools where student nurses – or, rather, Lady Probationers as they were called in some old-fashioned establishments – were expected to pay tuition fees and provide their own uniforms, and lesser establishments where they were looking for Nurse Cadets or Nursing Assistants and were willing to pay them for their labours.

It took me several months to get the whole Plan in place. I wrote to lots of the advertisers, using the post office as an address and telling them that I had to do that 'because we were bombed out and the family is still trying to settle on a permanent home. Meanwhile we are in lodgings but might move before you can answer me, so I thought the post office would be best.'

Where did I learn to be so mendacious, so slippery in my dealings with people? I can only plead that I had two excellent mentors in this field. Both my parents could lie like Ananias and wriggle their way out of almost anything they chose to, just with weasel words.

They did it as much for fun, I always suspected, as from necessity. My father's motto, he once said, was 'Why not give 'em a good story, when the truth's usually so boring and always puts you in a bad light? You'll always get a better deal for yourself if you've made it interesting for them.'

I comforted myself with the thought that I wasn't doing all this for fun. I *had* to be devious. If I had received letters at home I would never have got them. I am certain they would have been intercepted by my mother and thrown away. She would have done it not just to stop me doing what I wanted or simply as a method of controlling a rebel but because it would give her malicious pleasure to watch me waiting for something that she knew would never arrive. She'd done that sort of thing to me before and I wasn't risking it again.

If I wanted to get away from it all I had to be as twisty and mendacious as my parents were. The only thing that worried me was the way it was, to be honest, fun to be so secretive. It felt wicked, somehow, and then I remembered Mrs Exley and felt worse. She had told me that it was always better as well as simpler to tell the truth, and added that when people were open and honest with each other they enjoyed life more. In her house that had undoubtedly been so. It never was in mine. I had to behave as I was doing, I told Mrs Exley inside my head. They forced it on me.

It all took time. Not all the matrons I wrote to answered me. Some did and sent information about their hospitals that frightened me: huge mental hospitals that held hundreds of patients, miles out in the country – no, I didn't like the thought of that at all. Nor did I want to go too far away from London. I had lived in rural and small-town Britain long enough. I might not feel as though I lived in London at present but I still wanted to be nearby.

Then something else turned up to interest me and take some of the urgency out of my search for a hospital job. An election was called, and I read about it in the papers at the library, gobbling up all of them from *The Times* to the *Telegraph*, the *Daily Sketch* and the *Daily Mail*, at first in a casual sort of way and then with more and more interest.

It was amazingly exciting, I thought. Here was the chance, some politicians said, to build a better future for ourselves, better schools and hospitals and better care of everyone, and an end to the terror that illness caused poor people because they couldn't afford to be looked after by doctors.

It was this that caught my eye and, I have to say, my spirit. I remembered the time my mother cut my head with the saucepan lid and how my father had had to take me to the chemist for help because people like us didn't go to doctors. They cost too much.

I remembered that I had seen a doctor for the first time in my life when I started at Rushmore Road Infants School at around four because I had picked up scabies and impetigo, as well as headlice. I remembered my sister Sheila sitting in her cot, looking utterly miserable, her nose running a deep and disgusting green, then seeing her choking and how they boiled a kettle to make the room steamy for her so that she could breathe better. No doctor then, either.

And I also saw again my mother sitting on that bucket in the lock-up shop and knew then that she should have been looked after by a doctor. If she had been maybe she wouldn't have had to go away for a month to have the operation that had made her so bad-tempered and miserable for so long after she came back.

I took time off from The Plan and one Wednesday afternoon, when Woolworth's closed for the half-day, I went to the place described on the poster in the library as Labour Party Headquarters for the constituency. It was a rather grubby shop near Thornton Heath pond, just a short tram-ride away and well worth a three-ha'penny ticket, I thought.

I asked them if I could help with the election. The place was humming with people. One of them, looking harassed and a bit vague, handed me a pile of leaflets and told me to deliver them to the streets on the list he also gave me.

And I did, marching up and down those interminable streets, shoving bits of paper into letterboxes and then making the long walk back to the Party shop. I asked for some more leaflets to deliver, tired as I was, but this time the person I spoke to looked up sharply and said, 'I've never seen you before. Are you a member of the Party?'

'No,' I said.

'How old are you?'

'Fourteen,' I said.

She laughed, 'On your way, ducks. Come back when you're old enough,' and shoved me out. I was mortified – but that was the start of a real interest in politics that was to burn even more strongly as the years went by. It was also a lesson that I stored away for future use.

Then, three days after the election, won by the party I had wanted to win (maybe my few leaflets had helped?), I got a letter at the post office that was to change my life.

The Matron of Epsom Cottage Hospital had responded to my application for a post with an invitation to attend for an interview.

I was on my way, at last.

Thirteen

I felt I had come home. The moment I set foot inside the big double front doors everything about Epsom Cottage Hospital felt right for me.

It was a mild morning, with a very English autumnal nip in the air, and there was a fire burning in an open grate in the large entrance hall. The hall itself was panelled in a pale wood, which had clearly enjoyed years of hard polishing, and the plain wooden floor gleamed to match. There was a bowl of chrysanthemums, deep bronze and yellow and red, on a low table, and a couple of armchairs with bright rugs before each of them. The place looked warm and welcoming, and smelled utterly delicious.

I have always been susceptible to interesting smells and they don't always have to be what most people regard as sweet to be attractive to me. For example, the smell of horse manure is anything but unpleasant in my estimation and the smell of a weary sweaty man I love is totally irresistible.

My ideal-smell environment is a mixed one, and Epsom Cottage Hospital provided that. Lots of beeswax polish, of course, and a thread of chrysanthemums, but also a remote hint of ether and carbolic, scrubbing soap, toast, coffee and roast meat and that odd scent

I was to learn so well eventually, but which was still new to me that morning; a damp, weary, faintly chemical yet yeasty stink that makes a healthy person uneasy with the desire to escape from it as swiftly as possible. But I found I rather liked it.

It is the smell of disease, of much disease in the same place. Individual illnesses have their own odours and that can be very useful to a trained clinician who can, in time, let his nose make his diagnoses for him. Or could; few modern doctors have this ability, as far as I can find out, and don't really need it, but the doctors and, of course, the experienced nurses I worked with in the forties, when I first entered this extraordinary world of sickness, bodily deformity and death that made my life so interesting, absorbing and completely enjoyable, all had the ability to use their noses as one of the tools of their trade.

I stood there, wondering what to do. I was precisely on time for my 3 p.m. appointment – indeed, had hung around outside for ten minutes for fear of being early, and now feared being late. I'd read somewhere that being punctual to the second was the mark of a thoughtful, well ordered person, and I was determined to be that if I possibly could. I coughed politely but quite loudly to announce my presence.

The effect was comical. A door on one side of the hall popped open and out came a very short, very round butterball of a woman, with a great deal of frizzy hair pinned tightly to the top of her head, and large horn-rimmed glasses that looked too big for her small face. 'Well, dear me, Nurse Chetwynd, I do hope you do not bring infection with you to the hospital, for it is the duty of all good nurses to maintain their own health at all times in order to protect the vulnerable patients for whom they care.'

I desperately wanted to giggle. She had a high, tinny little voice, her glasses kept slipping down her nose and had to be pushed back, and she had called me 'Nurse'! It was all hilarious and I could feel the laughter pushing hard behind my nose. But I managed to say, 'Oh, no, Matron, it was just to sort of say I was here, the cough, not an infection, no infection at all.'

Few of my memories are as vivid as this one. I can hear her voice, hear my own, hear every word we spoke as though it had happened just a few moments ago, yet it is close on sixty years. Why should I remember it so vividly? I've tried often to work out the answer but I can't.

I expected some sort of interview, but she took me on a tour of the hospital at once, whisking me along more highly polished corridors and into the wards.

There were precisely three. A Men's Ward, a Women's Ward and a Children's Ward. These were their names, Matron said. 'We don't go in for fancy labels here,' she went on sniffily. 'Roses Ward or Lilac Ward – makes a hospital sound like a florist's shop. I can't be doing with it,' and she looked at me severely as though I were about to contradict her, which I could not have done under any circumstances. I was still trying not to giggle, for a start.

She let me look through the little window of the closed door of the operating theatre at which I was suitably awed, which encouraged her to make an approving little sound, and also the Casualty Department where there were no patients but a nurse was sitting cutting up swabs. She showed me the X-ray department, the small pharmacy, the kitchens – large, unfeasibly clean and glittering with well-polished chrome – and, almost as an afterthought, the nurses' accommodation.

This was a huddle of rooms at the back of the main buildings, including some single bedrooms for lofty people like sisters and Matron herself, dormitories for four to eight people for the rest of us, a large sitting room with a highly polished pianola and fairly full bookshelves, and a dining room that smelled of old cocoa and long-forgotten dinners.

I loved it all. Every bit of it. I thought the whole place was designed just for me, and I walked back through the main hospital to the front door behind Matron with my fingers crossed behind my back, for fear she wouldn't take me when she got round to the interview.

I need not have worried. This clearly was not a woman who wasted time on formality. As we walked down the long main corridor she looked up at me over her shoulder and said, 'And how old did you say you are?'

I hadn't said at all, but I thought of all she had shown me, thought of how much I wanted it, thought of my father and his lifetime of lying, thought of what it would be like to be forced to live with my family any longer, and said firmly, 'Seventeen.'

The fact that I had to be almost six inches taller than she was and was built very much more like a seventeen-year-old than a mere fourteen might have had something to do with it – a size thirty-eight bust must surely have an ageing effect on the very young? – but the fact is she just nodded and swept on.

When we reached the front door again she said severely, 'You must never again use this entrance. Always come to the garden door at the side. *That* is for staff. *This* is for members of the Governing Board and the Doctors.' I could hear the capital letters without any difficulty.

'Yes, Matron,' I managed, bursting with questions. Was I to be interviewed? Would I get a chance to ask questions of my own?

Clearly I would not. 'Send me your measurements for your uniform in the next post,' she said, as she opened the front door. 'And get yourself good black shoes and stockings. You will be paid on the first Monday of the month after the month you take up your post. You will receive twenty pounds per annum and must find your own shoes and stockings. You will be responsible for payments for any breakages you cause. Good afternoon, Nurse Chetwynd. I shall expect you on October the first. Do not forget to bring your ration book.'

And the door closed behind me.

I spent the next two weeks trying to work out what to tell my parents. The house in Norbury felt more claustrophobic by the day, and I thought yearningly of the dormitory, the sitting room and dining room that awaited me in Epsom. Compared with this, it was like the palace at Versailles.

I bought black shoes and stockings without coupons by being truthful: I told the people in the market in Croydon where I went that I had to have the things because I was going to be a nurse, and discovered for the first time the huge goodwill there was towards the profession.

'There y'are, ducks. These'll see you through. Not your glamorous nylons, I'll grant yer, but nice warm lisle as'll see you through a treat. Good luck, gel.' And as he wrapped up the stockings, three pairs of them although I'd only paid for two, he whistled the then popular song 'Nursie, come over here and hold my hand, Nursie, there's something I don't understand, round my heart there's such a funny pain . . .' I was to get to know it well in the coming months.

I hid my purchases in my locker at Woolworth's and bought an elderly suitcase for a shilling at a jumble sale in the local church hall. Two days before I was to leave, I packed everything up, put it in the left-luggage office at the railway station and went home to deal with the matter of my ration book. My mother was surely not going to part with that without a battle. I was sick with terror as I went into the house that evening after work, but I knew it had to be done.

All my life my mother has puzzled me. Until then she had always been capricious, unreliable, someone whose moods came and went like thunderstorms, and certainly someone whose reactions could not easily be foreseen. That day she ran absolutely true to form. She listened to my bald announcement that I had arranged to start nursing and would be leaving in a couple of days, and please could I have my ration book as I would be living in the hospital?

She looked across the supper table at my father with her eyebrows up, then back at me and said calmly, 'Well, it could have been worse, I suppose.'

I blinked. 'Worse? How do you mean worse?'

She shrugged. 'You might have been going after a job as a parlourmaid. In domestic *service*. Or on the halls or something of *that* sort. Anything's possible with you, isn't it?' And she stared at me, with the single raised eyebrow that throughout my infancy and childhood had controlled me with fear, and I knew she was hinting at something very nasty indeed. And couldn't for the life of me work out what it was. It would be years before I was to understand the depth of her implied insult.*

----

*And once I grasped what she had meant, I was amused as well as angered. I was well on the way to fifteen then and had never spoken to a boy of my own age, let alone any men. To imply, as she did that evening, that I would consider setting up as some sort of courtesan was utter rubbish. But the sort of rubbish a person remembers. It certainly hurt to realise what she had meant.

But she gave me my ration book and I tucked it away safely, not before noticing, however, that all my clothing coupons were gone and I'd not had a new stitch since the war ended. But that was par for the course with her.

My father was nicer about it. 'Good luck, Berrela' he said. 'It'll be hard work but you'll be good at it, I bet. And remember my motto. *Nihil illegitime carborundum . . .*'

'Never let the bastards grind you down,' I said with him. I know he meant kindly, forgetting he could be one of the bastards.

I went to Epsom by bus, clutching my suitcase, terrified and excited in equal measure. I remembered to use the garden entrance, but it was dark by the time I got there and there was no one around, and I had to go wandering to find where I should be. Fortunately the person I found was a Nurse Jenson – that's the name I seem to remember anyway – and she took me into her care.

I could have had a much harder start-up. Many of the other nurses were tough little cookies who ran a tight, self-important clique; one of its pleasures was picking on the new bugs. But Jenson had been through all that and wasn't about to let it happen to me. (I hope she had a good life thereafter. She left Epsom to go into full training a couple of months later. I never saw her again, and she had been so kind to me.) She showed me my bed, helped me put the necessary studs and buttons into my uniform, gave me safety-pins to do up my apron (I hadn't expected the need for those!) and finally, very importantly, showed me how to fold my cap.

We were provided with an oblong of heavily starched lawn, which had to be twisted and bent and pinned and feathered out into a concoction of starchy folds and frills, which sat on the top of our heads and looked, I have to say, very beguiling.

It took me a month to learn how to make a cap, and I can still do it. There was a skill to wearing them because they hung well down to shoulder level at the back, so sitting in an armchair and throwing your head back did a lot of damage. To this day if I sit in a high-backed chair and I'm very tired I may still make the necessary flipping gesture to get my cap out of harm's way.

I fell into bed on that first night, and slept like a hibernating bear.
I was on the brink of a great career, I was certain, and I was going to
have the most wonderful time being useful and clever and making
people feel better.

Well, yes, up to a point.

Sister on the Women's Ward, a tall dark woman with a great deal
of experience, took one look at me and, I think, got my measure.
'Nurse, you must never jump into anything, however well-
intentioned you are, without asking me or Staff Nurse first, do you
understand? I am sure you are keen and willing, but you can do a lot
of harm if you don't know what you're doing. Do you understand?
Never be afraid to ask.'

'Yes, Sister,' I said, and waited for orders. They came fast.

'Nurse, scrub these mackintoshes, please, use lots of disinfectant –
the patient is incontinent of stools – and wait! For God's sake, put on
a big rubber apron, and use gloves.'

'Do that mack again, Nurse, it's still got shit on it.'

'Nurse, why haven't you done the sputum mugs yet? What? Didn't
anyone tell you? Well, do them now. Collect them from the lockers
by the beds. Empty them and wash them out – it's a horrible job but
it has to be done – then scrub them and put an inch of Dettol solution in the bottom of each one and hand them out again.'

'Nurse, it's bedpan rounds – come with me and I'll show you how.
Lots of paper in your pocket? Good, you'll need that – and when we
get to bed seventeen make sure you show not a hint of anything on
your face, you understand? She has a form of coeliac disease and her
stools, I have to say, smell very offensive indeed, and you've got
quite an expressive face, haven't you? Well, you must keep it in control or patients' feelings are hurt and that must never happen, you
understand? They are always to be treated the way you'd like someone to treat you, and never forget it.'

'Nurse, why haven't you been to lunch? Not hungry? Rubbish! If
you're going to lose your appetite to a few shitty bedmacks and a
clutch of sputum mugs you're not going to last a week. Wash your
hands properly, change your apron and go to lunch at once.'

'Nurse! Go and change bed eleven. Poor woman has just been violently sick all over it. Scrape some of the vomited material into this specimen pot, then wash the linen through before it goes to the laundry. They fuss if we send it down without rinsing it first. Off you go!'

It was amazing. By the end of that first day I was awash with the most pungent of disinfectants, and my hair reeked of it. My hands were red raw despite the gloves – they tended to leak – and I was sure the smell of human body waste had entered every pore of my body and lodged itself in my throat and nose for ever. I would smell of it till the day I died.

But when I went to Sister to ask if I might go off duty for the evening, which was the proper thing to do (everyone was very keen to make sure I learned all the necessary protocol fast), she looked up from the patient's chart in which she was writing and at my tousled hair, my sodden apron and wrinkled black stockings – lisle never stayed up properly. Then she smiled with great charm. 'Heavens, look at you. You take me right back – now, listen, child. Go and strip off, take a bath, wash your hair and change all your clothes – and don't worry. The laundry understands when you new probationers put in so much for the first few days, so don't fret over that. And you'll be surprised how good you'll feel and how much better the world smells.'

She was absolutely right. I never enjoyed a bath or shampoo more. I never tasted hot cocoa as ambrosial as that supplied to the dining room for our night drinks. And I slept even better than I had the night before.

Fourteen

Within a couple of weeks I was completely absorbed into this extraordinary new world of pain and disease, sickness, body fluids and money.

That the last on the list was of the most enormous significance in our day-to-day activities was undoubted. Not a penny was wasted that could possibly be saved. All leftovers from the ward dinner, for example, after Sister had gone through the ritual of serving it, were removed at once to the kitchens so that they could be recycled. There was a great reliance on shepherd's and cottage pies for staff suppers, not surprisingly since the basic light diet for patients each day was mince and mashed potatoes.

Any food left on patients' plates – and there was severe quizzing by Sister if they didn't eat: had they been committing that major sin and nibbling rubbish brought from home between meals? – went into carefully marked swill buckets, which we had to use with great care because they were bought by local farmers to feed their pigs and hens. Vegetable waste into one, meat and fish into another, and again Sister was excoriating in her comments if you made a mistake or failed to scrape plates with sufficient vigour: as she said, over and over again, 'This buys medicines, Nurse!'

Our own dining room also had its row of selected swill buckets, though I have to say we wasted little. We were always far too hungry to leave our plates anything but almost licked clean, and it was pretty good food as food went in those austere days. Still, the daily collection of swill by van each day brought useful income to the hospital.

Probably more than the much-hated collection tins. We were expected to choose fairly among ourselves the one who would have to wander round the town centre each Saturday afternoon in full uniform, surmounted by the classic red-lined short cape, rattling the tin in an attempt to lure donations. As the newest and youngest, I was cast as Muggins and it was a rare Saturday afternoon when I was off duty that I didn't spend trudging round the shops with the hated tin.

Not that I did badly as a beggar. One old lady, scrabbling in her purse for three-ha'pence, said sweetly, 'Oh, you poor thing! You look so sad – I do hope this will help all your poor patients get better.' Quite what she thought we could buy for them for three-ha'pence I never knew, of course, but she meant well. Every time she saw me I got the three-ha'pence.

It was a great relief when Matron decided to stop the practice of tin rattling, because one of the governors had seen me 'looking very forlorn', she had reported to Matron, 'standing in the rain with the tin. The staff will all go down with pneumonia and that will cost far more than we get so we'll have to find a better way.'

'Your trouble, Nurse,' said Matron, 'is that you have a speaking countenance.'

There were other economies, some of them familiar war-time techniques, such as turning worn sheets sides-to-middle and making those too worn even for that into draw-sheets, the shorter cross-sheet that patients sat on, which was supposed to protect the under-sheet and thus reduce the need for laundering. We even had to patch the worn parts of the rubber under-sheets, those dreaded macks I spent so much time scrubbing, a practice that sometimes made sore patches on patients' bottoms. So that had to be rethought, too.

There was much talk around the hospital of the newspaper reports of the plan being made by the new Government to make medical care free, but it drew only lukewarm support.

'It'll mean that every hospital is like the metropolitan ones, you know, the sort the county councils run. Horrible places. You can't beat the good old voluntary system, can you? Imagine Bart's or Guy's or one of them being government-run! It'd ruin them. Anyway, the doctors won't like it and if they don't like it, it won't ever happen.'

This was Sister on our ward, holding forth one Sunday afternoon during visiting time when the ward staff occupied themselves folding swabs, rolling bandages, patching rubber gloves and packing drums with dressings to be sterilised. I knew I should behave and be quiet but I had to join in: 'But won't it be better when people don't have to be scared of being ill because they can't afford a doctor?' I ventured.

'Such nonsense!' Sister said roundly. 'People could afford to pay a doctor if they didn't waste their money on football pools and going to the pictures and cigarettes! All this socialism!' I shut up.

I had already been told that Sister was a 'local girl', a dentist's daughter who had trained in London as a Lady Probationer – her family had paid for her to train – and had come back home to work in the cottage hospital where she had now been for many years. And I had seen enough of the surrounding district, with its rows of pretty suburban houses in tree-lined streets, to know that she couldn't have the remotest idea of what life was like in places like the East End of London.

But life at Epsom wasn't all penny pinching and mack-scrubbing for me, although it took a chunk out of most days. Sister, for all her reactionary views on the Government's plans, was a good, deeply caring professional and went to a lot of trouble to teach me, as I was the only junior probationer she had at that time.

I knew for certain that I had found my world, that I wanted to be a nurse for the rest of my life and never, ever wanted to live in an ordinary home again, not ever. I told Sister as much, one evening when she had shown me how to apply an ankle spica, a tidily patterned bandage that would hold a sprain most snugly and for which I had an aptitude that surprised even me.

She looked startled. 'You never want to live at home again?' she repeated, and the amazement on her face made me careful. She would never understand, I knew.

'I mean, this is where I feel so comfortable,' I said, 'being with patients and doing the work – it's the best thing in the world.'

She relaxed. 'I'm glad to hear it,' she said. 'It means you have a vocation. You're meant to be a nurse, you see. You're not just using hospital life as a hiding-place. Some people do, you know. They take up nursing after broken love affairs and so forth, but then it never works. If you don't love the work and the patients for their own sake, it just doesn't work. You could never be a good nurse without a vocation.'

This was a widely held belief at the time and, to an extent, still survives. The idea was that women – male nurses were rarely spoken of outside the psychiatric hospitals, where they were considered necessary for their muscle-power over male patients – went into nursing almost as a religion. Nurses were not supposed to care about themselves at all, and a nurse who showed too much (any!) interest in what she earned, her working conditions or career prospects was regarded as very odd indeed and quite unsuited to the profession. You were there simply to do as you were bade, either by senior nurses or Matron who in turn did as they or she were bade by doctors and governors.

Even though I had learned by now that this was the received wisdom in the hospital I was convinced it was wrong. My main reason for wanting to work in a hospital was to get away from my family and home. Here I could earn my keep, do useful things and be able to hold up my head as a worthwhile person to have around, something that had never before been possible. Furthermore, the life offered the possibility of academic training in due course, if that was what I wanted.

Matron herself, I had discovered, had been a Sister Tutor, a Nurse Teacher, and held the highest qualification a nurse could have, the Diploma in Nursing. She was only at Epsom to take her last working years easily after a tough war, nursing soldiers overseas. Maybe I would be a Sister Tutor some day, but definitely without a vocation. I hated the idea of doing something that had an overtone of religiosity about it. So I said no more to Sister about my ulterior motives and asked her instead to explain to me about Angela.

Angela was a spindly sixteen-year-old, older than I was although I didn't of course tell anyone that, who had been coming in and out of the hospital since childhood. She had been readmitted that afternoon, and hadn't stopped crying until Sister had given her a dose of chloral to get her to sleep.

Sister looked suddenly sad as she stared at me. Then she sighed. 'Well, you might as well know. She has kidney disease. Had it since she was a two-year-old. Picked up an infection as so many children do, but hers became chronic and then – well, we do what we can with a poor prognosis. Her mother says she won't stick to her diet. She mustn't have protein, you see, or salt – I'll give you a textbook so that you can read up the disease.'

I read the book in bed that night for as long as I could keep my eyes open, and tried to pick out the meanings of words I hadn't come across before, like 'prognosis', and made a note to ask Sister to lend me a medical dictionary until I could save up enough to buy one of my own. And fell asleep to dream of Angela shouting at me for being younger than she was.

I don't think it was the next day, though it might have been. Probably a few days later. Anyway, I came on duty at 7.30 a.m. as usual to find Angela perched high in her bed and grinning hugely. She looked flushed and happy and waved at me to come and talk to her. She liked me because I wasn't as old as everyone else on the ward, she said.

I shook my head. There were rules about what happened in the mornings and I dared not step out of them, so she pouted. I got on with my set tasks, the first of which was to clear the sluice – the place where bedpans, dirty sheets, macks and all wet, undesirable objects had their being and where I spent much of my time.

After that I was to help in the ward cleaning. More senior nurses had the agreeable job of giving the patients their breakfast while I scrubbed and polished lockers and helped the senior probationer make the beds down one side of the ward. Inevitably she made the decision about which side we were to do, and of course it wasn't Angela's. I made a little grimace, meant to express regret, at Angela but she pouted even more.

I got glimpses of Angela as the morning wore on, but I couldn't get near her. The staff nurse who was on duty – Sister wasn't due on until 10 a.m. that morning – was a bit of a madam: she enjoyed being in charge because she could tell people off loudly in the middle of the ward where everyone could hear and see her victim's discomfiture. I wasn't going to risk that, even for Angela.

We were sent to change our aprons and have a break at nine-thirty, by which time I was as hollow as if I'd not eaten a vast porridgy breakfast a couple or so hours ago. I hurried off without making any more effort to talk to Angela. It could wait till I came back and Sister would be there by then: she never complained at me if I talked to patients. She quite liked her nurses to do that, so that they got to know them properly.

I came back, stuffed with bread and jam and hot tea, in a clean apron with my stockings well pulled up. I'd even had time to brush my hair, repin my cap in place and put a dab of powder on a very shiny nose.

There were screens round Angela's bed and I assumed a doctor had come to see her, although usually they did their rounds later in the morning, after their morning surgery and home visits. All our doctors, except one, were local GPs and worked amazingly long hours, almost as long as we nurses did. The exception was a very newly qualified young doctor who looked after Casualty and held the fort for senior doctors, sending for them in any emergency.

I wondered then if it was perhaps the young doctor who was seeing Angela. I wasn't as scared of him as I was of all the others and, anyway, maybe Sister would be there too. She wouldn't mind me coming in as long as there was nothing else I was supposed to be doing. I looked round at the rest of the staff, just two other nurses this morning, and they were with patients, so I walked across and stepped inside the screens.

I had never seen death before. I knew about it, had heard hair-raising tales of the damage done to bomb victims in the East End when I had sat listening to my elders, under Black Sophie's table, but this was something quite different. This was real. This was Angela. And she looked – well, not like Angela now. Her face had always been smooth, but now it seemed stretched to a paper thinness over the bones of her cheeks and jaw. Her eyes were open, and the pallid blue of them was clearly a dead colour, even in the dimness here behind the screens.

The doctor had been using his stethoscope as I came in and now he straightened his back. 'Massive myocardial infarction,' he said, with some satisfaction as the words rolled portentously off his tongue.

Sister looked at me and said, 'Big heart-attack. Coronary thrombosis. Sad, though we expected something like it, of course.'

I knew she was talking to me and realised I had lost control of my facial expression. I made a lot of effort these days to remember Matron's acid comment about my 'speaking countenance'. I smoothed my face and said nothing, standing there as I had been taught, with my hands crossed on my clean apron, glad that I looked tidy for this important moment. Angela, I thought, I wish I'd been able to talk to you this morning.

'She was very happy,' Sister said, apparently speaking to the young doctor. She bent and, with one hand, neatly closed Angela's eyes, then pulled up the counterpane to cover her face. 'She had her first period. Started during the night and she was cock-a-hoop, Night Nurse said. Poor child had been so upset it hadn't happened to her yet. Thought she'd never be able to get married and have children, you see. No one ever had the heart to tell her that even if she lived long enough babies were out of the question for her, with those kidneys.' Ten years later, I read for the first time of the use of renal dialysis, a system that could have saved Angela.

'I'll do the certificate,' the doctor said. 'I'll get it checked by the boss this afternoon after the round.'

Sister, who had been about to speak, closed her mouth, smiled at him approvingly and said, 'I'll call her mother, poor soul. She won't be surprised. Only heartbroken.' Then she made a grimace and walked out through the screens, followed by the doctor and, lastly, me.

'Stay there,' Sister said. 'We must do Last Offices. You can do it and I'll help you,' and she went away down the ward. After a moment or two I returned to the other side of the screens and waited for her.

I stood and looked at the draped form that had once been Angela, so anxious to talk to me this busy morning (about her period? Probably) and tried to work out what I felt.

Was I upset? Well, not really. Sad for the dead girl and her family, of course, but not for me. I had hardly known her, and to be deeply sad would make me like one of those gooey cards I had seen in shops, with sentimental verses about remembrances and heaven. I just couldn't be like that, and I wondered if I was supposed to try.

Was I frightened of seeing a dead body? Well, no to that too. I had gone through a patch of being terrified of death, when the raids had started, and on one particular afternoon, when I was at school in Keighley and broke a thermometer during a chemistry experiment. I had collected the running globules of mercury on my desktop and played with it – until I discovered that I had a tiny cut on one finger. Waves of terror flowed over me: I was immediately convinced that I was about to die of mercury poisoning. I never want to live through an afternoon like that again, for there was no one I could talk to about my fear.

As the days wore on and I survived, the terror died and I realised, young as I was, that the fear of something, the expectation of it, is much worse than the reality. I truly was no longer frightened of dying, and standing there next to dead Angela caused me no distress at all. Except for a sort of guilt that I was so serene about it. Surely I should be upset? Was I too phlegmatic to the point of being heartless? A horrible thought, that.

In the event, I need not have worried. Several weeks later, we had another death on the ward, again a young person, a girl of seventeen. She died because, Sister explained unwillingly, 'She had been a bad girl and rather than face the consequences of what she'd done had gone to a dreadful quack who had done an illegal operation on her, which had led to the terrible sepsis that she died of.' She had gone on to give me and the other nurses a long lecture about the importance of chastity and the dreadful effects of illicit sex, making it clear she regarded what had happened to the girl as her just deserts.

For my part I was furious. How could a girl so young be blamed for dying like that? To listen to Sister and the others, you'd have thought she'd committed suicide rather than just made love to someone. I couldn't bear it, but to my shame I said nothing, chicken that I was. Long after, when people started to question the laws on abortion and the inevitability of back-street abortionists killing women, I was right at the front of the protestors asking for changes. Legal abortion had to be better than what I had seen happen to that girl all that time ago.

Just as renal dialysis arrived too late for Angela, so did more liberal attitudes to women, and their need to control their own fertility safely, come too late for the other girl – whose name, to my shame, I have long since forgotten.

Sister came back with a trolley, carefully laid with all we would need, and under her instruction I carried out Last Offices. This consisted, first, of being quiet and reverent, Sister said. Then I had to wash the body completely, remove all surgical dressings and replace them with clean ones. In Angela's case there was just the puncture wound in her arm where blood had been withdrawn the day before.

Then every body orifice had to be plugged with heavy brown tow, 'because leaking is inevitable and would cause distress to the family and has to be avoided at all costs', and that included nostrils, ears and mouth, as well as the other more obvious ones.

Finally, we dressed her in a shroud, made of disposable cotton, brushed her hair and put a ribbon in it. We tied up her jaw with a bandage so that when rigor mortis set in she would be left with a closed mouth and look good to her grieving family.

There were disconcerting moments. Sister helped me turn the body over to wash the back, and it produced a long, deep sigh as the movement emptied the lungs. 'Sometimes,' Sister said, 'it sounds like a groan as it passes over the larynx and vocal cords. I'm glad that didn't happen this first time for you.'

I was, too. We set·Angela in her shroud on the trolley the hall porter brought, then covered her with a purple pall and wheeled her out of the ward, while the other patients studiously avoided looking at us, and took her to the mortuary. And that was that.

Or was it? Perhaps I was more affected by Angela's death, over fifty years ago, than I realised at the time. It was my first death and it has stayed with me vividly.

Fifteen

The weeks pleat softly into each other as people live and die in Epsom Cottage Hospital and I, as the most junior of junior probationers, do my small part in helping them do it comfortably. I am still queen of the sluice, a dedicated scrubber of mackintosh sheets and rinser-out of foul linen and bedpans, which amuses me a little: now that at last my Problem seems to have cured itself, I am dealing all day with the effects of others' Problems. But slowly I widen my nursing horizons.

Under Sister's sharp guidance I learn to give blanket baths without making the patient embarrassed, or leaving her with itchy damp patches and goose-pimples from being exposed to the cold ward air for too long because of my slowness.

I learn how to position and move patients, and how to care for their skins so that they don't get bedsores. It is a matter of huge pride to Sister that there has not been a bedsore on her ward since 1937, and that one had been due to self-inflicted injury – the patient couldn't be prevented from scratching at her bottom until she had torn her skin to ribbons.

I learn how to clean a semi-conscious person's teeth without choking her or otherwise causing any damage.

I learn to clean the bed and skin of a desperately unhappy doubly incontinent lady, who is so painfully aware of her situation she wants to cut her throat, she says, yet leave her smiling as well as clean and comfortable.

I learn how to spoon-feed helpless elderly ladies with the minimum of messy dribble and the maximum of nutritious intake, just before going off duty to eat my own lunch – and still enjoy it.

I learn to listen, to observe, to tell Sister or Staff Nurse what I have noticed about patients that might be important, without being a know-it-all pestering type.

I learn, above all, how to fit in with the other nurses as part of the team and generally become a comfortable part of the ward staff, enjoying the company of the others and quite relishing my status as the baby of the ward – even the occasional teasing that goes with it.

What I was experiencing, of course, was classic apprenticeship. As a system for training nurses it had a great deal to commend it, certainly from the point of view of this apprentice.

I learned the right way to do hands-on tasks under the direct supervision of persons who were themselves fully qualified and knew exactly what had to be done, and also knew the theoretical – philosophical, if you like – reasons for it being done in a particular way.

These were told me as I carried out the tasks, and at the same time Sister, or whoever was deputising for her, encouraged those patients who were able to communicate to tell me why it felt better to have something done one way rather than another. That was the most educational thing of all. Even more so than the nursing books Sister lent me and made sure I read by quizzing me on them.

Years later when I went into training properly and became a true student nurse, rather than a mere cadet, the same system was in use, though with more formal lectures, lists of required reading and formal examinations added to the clinical – that is, bedside – work.

But it was in the wards, clinics and operating theatres, rather than in the lecture rooms, that my skills slowly and steadily developed until I was able to perform the most complex technical tasks without ever forgetting the underlying imperative of watching over and catering to my patients' comfort. I learned then to accept responsibility and, in due course, to teach as I had been taught.

It went on for three years with an added year of 'internship' (something my training school demanded, though others did not), after which I was deemed to have earned my Hospital Badge as well as State Registration. Thereafter I was free to take on as many post-registration courses as I wished, specialising where I chose.

And all through those training years I felt that I was not only learning how to be a useful member of my future profession: I was useful while I was learning and was a valued member of the team. This gave me an intense loyalty to, first, the ward on which I worked; second, to the hospital; and, third, to the whole system of medical care in Great Britain at that time. I *belonged*. It was a heady experience.

All this has been swept away now. Modern nurses in the UK are produced via a university-degree system called Project 2000. They are not let anywhere near the wards for a long time after they start their nursing education. The very thing that gave me most pride, pleasure and incentive to learn is withheld from modern students. In many areas nurses are taking on tasks once regarded as the responsibility of junior doctors. This is encouraged by the masters of the NHS and the medical profession because it releases valuable medical time.

But I find myself wondering who is going to do the real nursing while the nurses are doctoring – that is, the feeding, washing and comfort-caring of frail and ill patients. Untrained cadets of the sort I was, I suspect, without the sort of supervision I got, because who has the time to supervise even their own practice, these busy days?

As a patient, herself once a Sister Tutor who had taught young nurses, told me recently, when she was in hospital with terminal cancer, 'These nurses are dears, but they aren't the nurses I need. Any one of them could, no doubt, write me a superb essay on the Gateway Theory of Pain Transmission but not one of them knows how to relieve my pain and make me comfortable.'

And whatever happened to that emotional attachment to 'your' hospital that made you care deeply about the look of the place? It used to be always a nursing responsibility to see that the place was warm, clean, and a pleasure to be in, if possible. Matron spent a lot of time running her finger along high shelves looking for missed dust, and although this may seem a degrading job for a highly trained professional, the fact is we had much less cross-infection and resulting antibiotic-resistant strains of bacteria because, as everyone agreed about asepsis: 'It all starts with ordinary dirt control.'

Christmas comes and goes in a flurry of ward decorations that, according to long tradition, I am told, go up the day before Christmas Eve and come down the day after Boxing Day. This practice has the effect of making the tawdry tinsel and general tra-la-la seem really beautiful instead of cheap and tacky, which was how I had always regarded such decorations in the past.

On Christmas Eve all the nurses put on clean aprons, turn their capes red side out and go round the three dimly lit wards bearing candles and lanterns and singing old Christmas carols with as few flats and sharps as we can manage. It must sound all right because all the patients weep a little when they hear us, including some of the men. ('Maybe,' says one of our more sardonic staff nurses, 'they're musicians.')

On Christmas Day three senior doctors arrive at twelve noon sharp to carve a turkey in each ward. Actually the 'turkeys' are extra large capons from a local farm, since only black-marketeers can get their hands on the bigger birds, and the hospital couldn't possibly afford them. They put on chefs' caps, tuck sprigs of mistletoe into them, then carve mightily, ending up with a mock ward round during which they contrive not only to kiss each and every child and female patient but all the sisters and nurses too, amid much giggling and cries of 'Ooh, sir!' It is all great fun and I love every moment.

Excitement comes in the first week of January, usually a dead, dreary season, when a very special case comes in that involves the entire hospital in excited surmise. I still remember, almost with awe, what appeared at the time to be little less than a miracle.

A young man in his thirties is admitted late on a Sunday afternoon.

He has a raging fever – 'Almost 105°, I'm afraid,' Sister says, looking deeply ominous – due to a staphylococcal infection picked up in his job as a dustman. He is put into a side ward on his own so that he can have all the care he needs without disturbing any other patients. (This was long before the development of intensive-care units of course: it was to be almost twenty years before the NHS created them.)

A team of available staff is collected from all over the hospital, including some of those off duty, to give him twenty-four-hour cool sponging. There is no other way (at that time) to bring down a high fever, except for aspirins, and he is not sufficiently conscious to swallow those – anyway the dose needed would be risky to his stomach lining. Sponging is the answer, together with a couple of electric fans set behind bowls of ice to blow cool air on to his exposed damp skin.

I am one of the team of spongers and we all take it in turns to prepare fresh bowls of water as the cool water we use for him heats up, and to replenish the ice. His temperature goes no higher but also shows no inclination to come down. And his semi-consciousness is accompanied now by the restlessness and distress of delirium.

It looks very much as though the next step will be to check his religious affiliation to see if the Last Rites would be appropriate.

'Where's his doctor?' I ask, as I change places with someone who has been working over the young man for thirty minutes without a break. 'Shouldn't he be here?'

'Gone to Aldershot,' she says pithily, and leaves me to take over the sponging in a highly puzzled state. Aldershot? With a dying patient in the ward? It seems very odd.

Not because death in the hospital is rare. Far from it. But it is comparatively rare for acutely ill young patients. I would have expected this patient to be transferred at great speed to one of the major London hospitals. Except, of course, I think then, he's so ill the chances are he'd arrive there dead already.

Half an hour later his doctor arrives. He drops his coat on to the floor, bellows for Sister, who comes running together with almost all of the rest of the staff, and we gather round, wide-eyed, to hear him explain that he has brought from the Army Hospital at Aldershot a treatment for our patient that is not meant to be available yet to civilians but that he scrounged from a colleague from the old days.

We watch and listen as he prepares his treatment and lectures us about it, clearly pleased as punch to be doing so and revelling in his role as a medical knight-errant. 'Penicillin,' he announces, and launches into the tale of Alexander Fleming and the culture dish left near an open window into which the spores of what would prove to be the most magical of infection-fighters drift. It's a well-known tale and still exciting, even if later knowledge shows that the miraculous drug wasn't produced by Fleming on his own but that Howard Florey and Ernst Chain made it possible to produce in large quantities and therefore available as a usable therapy.

Until now it has been available only to soldiers in Britain and never civilians, but because *our* doctor was an Army doctor, lo and behold, we have a miracle at Epsom. Our pride is massive.

We watch the drip set up and the first dose of penicillin run into it, then drift off duty, very tired but feeling good and hopeful, leaving our patient to the night staff.

And, yes, we had our miracle. Next morning when we come on duty there he is sitting up in bed, still with his penicillin drip but also drinking a cup of weak tea.

Things go back to normal and the young man is discharged home after a fortnight to everyone's delight. Then it is the end of the month, almost, and my birthday.

And in a moment of idiocy, as I stand there in the sluice cleaning out the bedpans and vomit basins with Vim, which has to be done at least once a week, I tell this to Sister who has come to check on the quality of my work. What a supervisor that Sister was, to be sure. I don't think I ever met another quite so conscientious! And she says kindly, 'Happy birthday, Nurse! How old are you?'

And I tell her.

Idiot that I am, I say, 'Fifteen, Sister,' then almost choke with the horror of what I have done. I just wasn't thinking. I want to cry, 'Ask me again and let me lie to you! Ask me again!'

'What did you say?' Sister says, staring. I can feel her eyes on me, even as I stare down at my work trying to look absorbed in it. Not easy when it's just battered bedpans.

I look very closely at the one I am scrubbing and mutter, 'Um. Sixteen, Sister.' It is hard to make an f sound like an s, I have to say.

'Well, have a nice birthday,' she says at last, and rustles off – to tell Matron, I am certain, that while it is one thing to have a Baby of the Ward it is quite another to have an Infant of the Ward.

Nothing is said about it, and I begin to think I have got away with it. February bursts upon us, and the first snowdrops appear in the hospital gardens with crocuses belting along behind so fast it's as though they're racing and then there are daffodils all bawling their great heads off everywhere and I feel wonderful. I have never lived in so beautiful a place among so many flowers. I have the perfect job that promises me a golden future. I live in the perfect home in which I am blissfully content. I am at last free to be my own person and never again need I worry about *them*. The family.

Even as the thoughts form in my head I try to banish them. I am filled with the sort of primitive superstition that tells you that taking conscious pleasure like this is hubris and those bloody gods'll get you—

They get me. Matron sends for me one morning, and I slide miserably into her office, fear filling me to the brim. She doesn't look angry; indeed, she looks almost as miserable as I feel. 'My dear, there is some sort of situation at home and you are needed there,' she says.

'Situation.' Not a question. I just repeat the word.

'Your sister phoned me. Says to send you home at once.' She is brisk now.

'Not my parents?' I feel a bit better. Maybe this is all nonsense. I don't have to do what Sheila wants: she's not *them*—

'They are away. On holiday,' Matron says and I feel the chill of her disapproval. 'How old are your sisters, Nurse? I understand there are three of them at home.'

'Two sisters, one brother,' I say, miserably.

'And how old are they? Truthfully, please, Nurse.'

I turn the colour of a sunset, sick with shame, and mutter, 'Well,

Sheila is – um – thirteen and Maxine is eleven and Lionel is just turned five.'

Her face is, as they say in lots of my favourite books, a study. She is clearly horrified to think of children of this age being alone in a house but kindly does not say so to me. She just nods and picks up an envelope from her desk. 'Here is your pay up to date, Nurse. You had better pack quickly and go home to sort out what is going on. You are yourself much too young to be in charge of such a family, but there, times and ideas have changed since my day, I suppose.'

'I'm sorry,' I say, not in tears of rage yet, but feeling them inside me, not too far down.

'Not your fault,' Matron says. 'If you ever need a reference I will give you an excellent one. You have earned it. Good luck, my dear. It has been a pleasure to have you with us.'

And that is the end of my first try to escape into nursing.

Sixteen

I was quite grateful for the anger. It did at least stop me feeling sorry for myself.

When I knocked at the door at number forty-four Northborough Road, Norbury, my suitcase beside me, I was as ice-cool as I could manage to be. I knew that whatever had happened it was hardly likely to be Sheila's fault. If they had gone off on holiday, as she had told Matron, then I would just have to wait for them to return before I could express my feelings.

Of one thing I was sure: I would never again cringe in front of either of them, never again let them get away with whatsoever they wanted to do without protesting. Not only was I now bigger than they were, so that there could be no more thrashings – and I remembered what a good feeling *that* had been the first time I realised it – I had now managed to escape, albeit for a short time.

I had proven to myself that I was able to take care of myself and I knew I always would be. I wasn't a dependant any more. And most importantly, they would know that too, so I could say whatever I wanted to say. And I looked forward with great ardour to doing just that, while refusing to think about the other weapons they had, which I found harder to deal with than the beatings.

I knocked again, and listened harder this time. I thought I had heard a sound when I first knocked, but then it had stopped. Now I rapped harder. The same scuffling sound happened and once more stopped.

'Open the door,' I bawled, losing my temper suddenly. 'Open this bloody door!'

I think that was the first time I ever used a swear word in my siblings' hearing – and I was sure Sheila was on the other side of the door: that tentative sound was precisely the sort she would make – and I found it a remarkably liberating thing to do. In the forties Nice Gels didn't swear, and I just had! Amazing. And I bashed on the door again, paying no attention to a passer-by, who was clearly fascinated by evidence of some sort of show about to begin and waited by the gate to watch.

I stopped paying no attention, turned on the passer-by, took the three steps down the minute front path to the gate, leaned into her face and said, very loudly, 'Bugger off!' She blinked and buggered off, very fast. This swearing thing was marvellous! I felt like Napoleon, like Julius Caesar – like Alexander the Great.

I returned to the door, which had opened, and there was Sheila peering at me from the dim hallway.

'Oh, I was so afraid! I thought it was Them again,' she said.

'Who?' I pulled my case inside and left it in the hallway deliberately, although of course it was in the way there. It was my way of announcing I would not be staying any longer than I had to. I marched through to the kitchen. No one there at all. 'Where are they?' I asked, meaning Maxine and Lionel.

'In Lugano,' she said.

I gawped. 'Where?'

'Lugano,' she said, and added helpfully, 'It's a lake, in Italy. Or Switzerland. Or both. I'm not sure.'

'I meant the kids.'

'Oh. I thought you meant Mummy and Daddy. The others are at school.'

My chest tightened. It had been years since I had been able to address either of my parents by the childish labels. When I spoke to either of them I addressed them as 'you' and no more. To hear Sheila speak so now underlined just how much I had changed and grown up in the past months.

'Why were you so afraid to open the door? Who did you think I was?' I demanded then, trying to get my head together.

'Oh.' She made a face. 'The bailiffs.'

I sat down now. The joys of swearing had been evanescent in the extreme. I felt awful and very much not like Napoleon. 'Let's have all of it,' I said, and she nodded, but went first into the scullery to make me some tea, which was a very Sheila-ish thing to do. I looked round at everything. It was all tidy and the place shone clean. I could even smell some furniture polish, which was rare in this house. My mother hated housework, always had. Obviously Sheila had been doing it. 'The place looks very clean and tidy. Did you do all of it on your own, or did the others help?'

'Well, Lionel's only little' she said.

'And Maxine?'

Sheila just shrugged. I could see it clearly. Maxine wouldn't have argued with Sheila or made any sort of fuss. That wasn't her style, though I have to say I had seen so little of her over the years that I hardly knew what her style might be now. But I could see her just shaking her head sweetly when asked to do something she didn't want to do, then disappearing.

I put that to Sheila and she shrugged again.

'Tell me about the bailiffs,' I said. 'All of it.'

She told me, and she looked very scared as she did so.

He had started a shop in West Croydon, calling himself *Peter Chetwynd, Bespoke Tailor*. I knew that: he had got me to do some work for him, notably travelling around London after I left Woolworth's in the evenings to pick up packages from the outworkers he used to make waistcoats and trousers. He did the basted first fittings of the jackets the customers ordered but the rest of the work was given out to CMT houses – cut, make and trim – a common East End tailoring process.

He'd done well, partly because of the hunger for decent suits in men coming out of the services with a few bob to spend on themselves, and partly because he had access, as of course he would, to black-market cloth.

I'd known all this and pretended to myself that I didn't. I hated the notion of black-marketeering. All those books I had read, all that Paine and John Stuart Mill and Hobbes and others that had taught me to be interested in politics had also filled me with the notion that fair shares for all was what it was all about. Why should there be big people at the top to get more than the little people at the bottom? It was very juvenile political thinking but I was, after all, still just fifteen. Why shouldn't I be a juvenile thinker?

When I found out – actually, he boasted about it – that he was buying fabrics in the black-market, fear of him kept me from saying anything so I just tried to keep my distance, though it wasn't easy. I couldn't refuse the journeys to fetch and carry his parcels, first because of the inevitable row if I had tried, and second, because I was so glad to get out of the house.

Anyway, I had escaped to Epsom and left him and his black-market-based business and knew no more about it. Sheila filled in the rest as best she could.

It was a classic tale in the Peter repertoire. He wasn't content to build a business slowly and surely: even one based on ill-gotten materials still needs time, care and constant reinvestment of any profits. What he did was spend all he could, with my mother's eager co-operation, the moment any cash came into his hands, and the devil take tomorrow's bills.

They bought new clothes – he had a heavy Crombie overcoat that must have cost a bomb and she had a fur. Black-market again, of course – where else would they get enough clothing coupons? I think they even got a few things for Lionel and the girls. But not much.

Back to Peter's dabbling in the market. The holiday had been the *coup de grâce*. With creditors already phoning at frequent intervals to pester him, and a couple of episodes involving two large professional debt-collectors on the doorstep making a fuss that brought the neighbours out, Peter and Betty had opted to go away on a very swish holiday indeed, a week in Lugano with their new clothes and new suitcases (essential, Betty had insisted), leaving Sheila to hold the fort.

'They said never to answer the door, and only to go out when I had to. They said a week off school wouldn't hurt me but the others should go and they'd be back in no time. And if anyone makes a nuisance of themselves I was to tell them I was only twelve.'

Lie upon lie was built into this story. And consequently, she had had an awful week, clearly. It wasn't just the business of trying to make enough suppers for everyone – the other two had school dinners. They'd left her, for a week's meals for three, some potatoes, a few onions, a tin of dried egg and a few odds and ends like that, as well as a few bob 'in case'. The bailiffs had come on the second day and the brawny debt-collectors had come again the day after. She told them all the same: she couldn't do anything, she was only twelve and go away, please. Amazingly they did, but she was still scared they'd come back, and there were still the phone calls and that was why she had called me. 'I didn't know what else to do.'

I felt wicked, because all I could think of, once I'd got all the details, was that the worst had been over when she'd called. There were just two days left before they were due back. If she had held on a little longer I'd still be a happy member of the nursing staff at Epsom.

And then I remembered my idiocy in telling Sister the truth about my age and stopped feeling bad or even guilty about resenting Sheila's phone call. It was no one's fault, no one was to be blamed – except, of course, our parents, and that was something we were all thoroughly used to. I'd find another hospital job as fast as I could and go to it the moment they came back. 'I'm not even going to unpack,' I said aloud and stood up. 'I'm just going down to the newspaper shop. I'll be back soon. Before the kids get in from school.'

I bought the *Nursing Mirror* and began to look down the advertisement columns as soon as I got back to the house. Maxine came in from school, seemed unsurprised to see me and vanished upstairs to do her homework. Lionel trotted in a half-hour later, having stopped, 'as usual', Sheila said, on his way home to play with his friends.

It was lovely to see him again, though he had grown greatly and seemed far less interested in me than in his latest exploits, which involved the swapping of some of his possessions at school. I realised then that he actually had toys, and relaxed about him. Clearly, as the only boy he was favoured in a way his sisters never had been. I need not worry about his welfare. Well, not unduly.

The bailiffs came again the next day, and this time I assured them that the man they wanted would be here in just another day, and to hang around for him – which they did. I was very charming and co-operative – I look back at myself behaving so with amazement, because I was as scared of them as Sheila had been. I rather think that kept other creditors away from the door.

Anyway, after that there was peace and I could concentrate on job-hunting. And I found what I wanted remarkably soon. A long way from my London admittedly – Epsom had felt Londonish because it had red double-decker buses – but that at least meant that I would be far away from them too. Weighing one against the other, I reckoned it was worth it. Anyway, this was a seaside town, which was a major plus. I loved swimming and there it would be free of charge, a potent attraction.

I used the phone – daringly: my mother screamed blue murder if anyone was extravagant with it – to apply to be a junior probationer at the Deal and Walmer War Memorial Victoria Cottage Hospital in Kent, and all I can say is that they must have been desperate for staff. Matron interviewed me there and then on the phone, and asked me what I had done before. I took a deep breath and talked about Epsom and how I had had, unhappily, to leave because of a domestic emergency. I knew that when she called Epsom for a reference my old Matron might feel she had to spill the truth about my age, but it was a risk I had to take. Anyway, I thought then, maybe now I can get away with the truth.

She sailed over what I was saying, obviously as happy as Larry. 'You've had some experience? That's excellent, excellent. I won't hide from you that we're very short-staffed just at present. Very – um – and when could you be available? Soon? Dear me, how splendid. When could you manage to come, do you think?'

I blinked at the phone. Was it to be so easy?

'Well,' I said, and gambled. They had assured Sheila that they would be back on Saturday. I would have to risk them failing, then having to call this Matron again about having a problem with getting to her as soon as I had hoped, but if she wanted people so much that she took them on just a phone call it shouldn't prevent her taking me. Should it? If I'd believed it would do any good, I would have prayed. Instead I just hoped and wished as fervently as I could. 'Saturday night,' I said firmly. 'I'll have to check the times of the trains from here in London.'

'You can get a Green Line bus from Victoria', she said, and her voice seemed to buzz with eagerness. I hoped she would always be so nice and unfrightening. My old Matron had been nice but very scary. 'We'll expect you then – and I'll collect all your details when you arrive. Goodbye, Nurse Chetwynd.'

There it was again. And she had never even seen me!

That was Friday afternoon. And on Saturday, as they had said, they returned, at about eleven in the morning, having just caught, as she said in a throwaway sophisticated-experienced-traveller's sort of voice, 'the first ferry from Calais, a glorious morning, as flat as a millpond, delightful'.

This is where it gets very difficult to tell my story coherently, because something odd has happened to my memory.

I know that during those days while I waited for them to return to Norbury and set me free to live my own life again, I daydreamed with an intensity that had startled even me. I had dreamed of the conversation I would have with them. Well, perhaps it would be not so much a conversation, more a vitriolic verbal attack. I would *harangue* them.

I would tell them what dreadful, wicked people they were to leave three children as young as my sisters and little brother on their own. To have left them with debt-collectors prowling round the house like so many wolves. To do again for a whole week what they had done on that dreadful night in Besses O' The Barn when they had gone out to a cinema, leaving us alone with me in charge when I was just seven. I'd almost forgotten that night, when policemen had come to the house, alerted by neighbours, but it was worth remembering now. I would go on and on about their wicked selfishness, their all-round awfulness, and they would just have to stand there and listen to me, because they were so obviously in the wrong.

That had been the daydream, but what actually happened? To this day I don't know what I said to them. I did complain that I had had to leave my job, but added that fortunately I had managed to find another hospital. She looked at me with those brown polished-marble eyes of hers, raised her eyebrows and said, 'Fine. Better be off, then, hadn't you?'

Peter laughed, and said, 'Stick around, Berrela. I've got plans, ideas. It's a great time to be doing things now the war's over—'

'Let her go if she wants to go,' my mother interrupted. 'She doesn't care about us. All that time in that stinking little hospital and she never even phones us. She doesn't care about us, selfish cow. Let her go.'

Seventeen

Life at Deal Hospital promised to be very satisfactory. I had arrived too late to be able to see much of the outside of the place in the dark winter night, but the room I had been taken to, which already had my name on the door, quite took away my breath.

Well-sized, fully carpeted in dark red, with a suite of furniture in pale polished wood, curtains and cushions in bright reds and oranges to contrast with pale papered walls, it had stepped straight out of the pages of a magazine. There had been a time in Cirencester when we had got from somewhere a pile of old American magazines called *House Beautiful*, or whatever, on which I had based many a happy daydream about a better life than the one I knew. And here it was: a daydream made concrete.

The parlourmaid, complete with goffered cap and frilly pinny, had brought me from the front door to my room, which was at the end of a long corridor. She dropped my case at my feet and turned to go. 'Bathroom and lav are over the other side of the corridor, there's a buttery half-way along where you can make yourself some cocoa, if you like, breakfast is at seven thirty and they'll expect you to be on time, the dining room is in the main hospital building across the courtyard, goodnight,' she said, and went.

Her surly resentment at having to look after someone so clearly at the bottom of the pecking order didn't perturb me in the least. I just stood there and looked around, entranced. Pictures on the walls, of flowers in vases and animals grazing in green fields. A bookshelf. A bookshelf! I could display those second-hand ones I had already bought and look out for more now. I opened drawers and cupboards in escalating delight. I had never in all my life had such accommodation all to myself. Even at the Exleys' house, where I had occupied the attractive bedroom of their son who had been away fighting at El Alamein, I had had to keep my clothes in a chest, because the wardrobes and drawers had been filled with his possessions.

I unpacked my few odds and ends, slept like a baby and woke only when peremptory rapping on my door and a muffled 'Good morning, Nurse!' insisted I should. It was still dark and, not owning a clock or watch of my own (such luxuries!), I had to guess that that had been the night nurse who had the job of rousing all the day staff – we had used the same system at Epsom.

I washed and dressed as fast as I could and, not having any uniform yet, put on a skirt and jumper, which was pretty much all I had in the way of mufti. (Because of the origins of modern nursing in Florence Nightingale's experience of Army nursing in the Crimea, there was an inherited use of a great deal of service jargon. Nurses reported on and off duty and went on leave, not on holiday. There were Staff Nurses, just as there were staff officers, and when you were not in uniform, you were in mufti. And, oh, yes: we all addressed each other by our surnames or nicknames derived from them, and never, *ever*, by first names.)

Walking into the dining room – not hard to find: I followed the smell of tea and porridge – I was as self-conscious as it was possible to be. I hovered at the door, watching a couple of dozen sleepy, newly scrubbed nurses drooping over teacups and porridge spoons, and waited to be noticed.

A dark-haired, pleasant-looking person in what appeared to me to be a Staff Nurse's uniform caught my eye and beckoned. I went over to her, feeling like a hippopotamus on the move, as one does in such circumstances.

'You must be – um—' She looked down at a piece of paper in her hand. 'Nurse Chetwynd?' And she pronounced it as in winding a ball of wool.

'No. Wind, please, Nurse,' I said. 'I mean, it's Chet*wynd*.'

Someone else on her table giggled and said, 'You'll find plenty of that here, ducky, the way the kitchen feeds us all on beans, never mind the patients on their gruel.' The giggling spread around the table and beyond, until several people were staring at me.

'No need to be coarse, Vale, especially at the table,' the Staff Nurse said, and the giggler subsided but only a little. Now everyone stared at me and I wanted to die.

'Sit down, Nurse,' said the Staff Nurse. 'Porridge?' She lifted her head and waved at the maid, who was standing at the serving table.

I had hated porridge since my earliest vaccie days, when it had so often been lumpy and burnt. At breakfast at Epsom I had put away a great deal of bread and marmalade, unless I was lucky enough to get near enough to the open fire and the use of a toasting fork. But now I dared not complain of what I was offered and was grateful that the porridge was well made. And even more grateful when the giggler, Vale, pushed a pot of jam towards me and indicated I should put a spoonful into the porridge. I did, and it made it quite delectable. I perked up a bit.

Five minutes later, a sister came in and everyone stood up in a flurry of starched aprons. She shook her head crossly and sat down in the chair my Staff Nurse, as I now thought of her, pulled forward. 'Good morning, Night Sister,' everyone chorused, and sat down again.

Night Sister grunted a reply, took a cup of tea from the maid, drank it thirstily, then settled down to read out the notices. She looked very tired, I thought.

Several nurses were to change wards and departments, and there was a hiss of whispers that made Night Sister look up with a frown, which immediately silenced said whisperers. She returned to her papers.

'Is there a Nurse – um – Chetwynd here?' I was so grateful she had pronounced it right that I almost sang my response.

'Here, Sister.'

'You'll be going to the Men's Ward,' she said. 'But go to the sewing room first and get some uniform sorted out. That is all, nurses. Go to your wards quietly.'

'Yes, Sister,' they chorused again, and a cheeky one called from the back of the room, 'Sleep well, Sister!' which made the tired woman scowl even more.

I was lucky. My Staff Nurse took it upon herself to show me where to go, and now that I could see the hospital more clearly I liked it even more.

It was built in the clean art-deco style of the late 1920s because, as the Staff Nurse told me, 'It took a little while to raise all the money for the war memorial so it wasn't built immediately after the Great War. I think that's why it looks so modern.'

The site was fairly large and dominated by the long, low E-shape-minus-the-central-stroke main building. There were wards in the long wings: men's on one side, women's on the other, and a children's ward tucked away behind. There was an operating-theatre section, very modern, with the big sterilisers called autoclaves that were used not only for boiling theatre instruments but for the sterilisation of every item used surgically anywhere in the hospital, and a small casualty-cum-outpatient department. There were about a half-dozen single rooms for high-class patients willing to pay a bit more for their care and, of course, the nurses' home in which I had taken such delight on arrival.

When I got to the sewing room to be equipped with uniform, the woman in charge looked at me, shook her head and made the sort of noise through her teeth that plumbers make when they look at a leak, or motor mechanics produce when faced with a car in trouble: disparaging, doubtful, uncertain of any sort of success in putting matters right. 'My,' she said, 'you're a big girl.'

I felt the muscles at the side of my face knot into lumps as I clenched my teeth in an effort to stop myself saying something I would regret. I ought to be used to this by now. I really ought to be used to it. Because all my life people have been saying it to me. At three and three-quarters, starting at Rushmore Road Infants School, the teacher looked at me doubtfully and said, 'My, you're a big girl,' and in every succeeding class I entered the teacher said the same thing: 'My, you're a . . .'

It happened everywhere. In shops, in the street, in the library. Sometimes it was said approvingly, 'My, you're a nice tall girl – could you get that book down from the top shelf for me?', but mostly it was said with amusement, or a note of accusation, as though I'd grown tall on purpose as a deliberate act of rebellion.

I have never been able to understand why well-brought-up people who consider themselves to have good manners and who would die rather than make any comment to a stranger about his or her complexion, squint, sticking-out ears or purple birthmark will think it perfectly reasonable to say to a young woman they have never seen before, 'My, you're a big girl,' or to make hugely unfunny jokes along the lines of 'Is it cold up there?' and 'I'll bet you have snow on your head six months of the year.' Where do they get the right to take unto themselves the responsibility for pointing out to me and women like me *something we know perfectly well*?

Because it is, of course, true. As a child I was always a head or more taller than the other children in the class. At twelve I needed size seven and a half in shoes – actually, I needed size eights but they were never available so I squeezed painfully into seven and a halves and have paid the price in ghastly, twisted feet ever since.

When I started at Deal Hospital, at the age of fifteen, I was well past puberty: I had first menstruated at eleven, much to my amazement, since I had been given no warning or explanation of this imminent and inevitable event – bless the libraries again for providing books to help children in such a state! and now I was almost five foot ten inches tall. I measured 38–28–40, which looked in proportion to my height, the size of my feet and hands, and the length of my arms and legs. I was a normal young woman in a world where the only young women who were allowed to feel normal were the small ones – and this is as true now as it was fifty years ago.

Be five foot five – all right, six – or under, be a 32–22–34-sized person, and you're in. No one will point out your faults to you in the street. They might whistle after you, but they won't jeer at you because 'My, you're a big girl.'

For my first weeks at Deal Hospital I had to wear the same uniform, which had to be let out to accommodate me, until two new sets arrived a month later from the factory. Every night I had to wash out the heavy striped serge dress and struggle to dry it (I often went on duty all damp in my personal places, very uncomfortable) and wash, starch and iron the apron. It took me over an hour every night and I fell into bed when I'd finished. I hardly got to know anyone or go anywhere till that damned uniform arrived and I was at last freed from one of the effects of being a 'big girl'.

I spent almost two years working at Deal and, by and large, they were happy times. I was paid better now; a princely thirty pounds per annum as well as emoluments, of course, which put in my pocket two pounds ten shillings a month – at least I wasn't liable for tax! – and that meant I could do jolly things with friends from the hospital who were off duty at the same time.

It was a first for me, that sort of socialising. In all the years hitherto I had never had the chance to make friends for long. I was shoved from school to school, from home to home: how could relationships be built in such unpromising circumstances? But now there was time, and there were people who shared my interests and activities. I was deeply content.

In morning off-duty time it was fun to go to the teashop in town and get a table near the open fire, which burned from October till May, to dispose of lots of tea and toasted teacakes. We were always hungry, though the hospital food, to the best of my recollection, wasn't at all bad. But there was a widespread saying then: 'You can always spot an off-duty nurse: flat feet and a bag of buns.'

In the afternoons in the winter there were shops to wander round, though never much to buy. We had too little cash and there was always the problem of coupons.

In summer, of course, there was the beach, a stony expanse licked by usually very cold water, but I loved it and spent all the time I could there. I had a battered old blanket I'd liberated from the hospital somewhere, and a precious cushion I had also found lying around unloved: with them, a book and a modicum of sun, life was perfect.

Some of the other girls tried to persuade me to go with them to dances to meet Marines, who were part of Deal life in every way. They were barracked at Deal Castle, and there is no doubt that the town hummed with testosterone from all this male talent, which encouraged girls to visit from all over this part of Kent. Our nurses, being on site, as it were, could have a whale of a time, if they were so inclined (and several were, enthusiastically).

I wouldn't. First of all, there was the height issue. If I went to a dance I dared not sit down in case someone asked me to dance and, when I stood up, turned out to be three inches shorter than me. If I stood all the time I got tired and my feet hurt, and no one asked me to dance anyway because they could see how tall I was: most of the boys were stocky five-foot-eighters or less.

Anyway, I disliked popular music of the sort that was played at dances as well as on the ward radios. I put up with it when I had to, but I daren't tell anyone that I had developed a taste somewhere along the line (Miss Peach, perhaps?) for classical music. I would sneak off to concerts sometimes on my own. If I had admitted that, I'd have been written off as a complete freak.

My final reason for avoiding Marine-encrusted parties and dances, however, was even more inadmissible. After what I had seen of male–female relationships in my childhood the very last thing I wanted was ever to get involved in one. And dances and parties would have been very much a step in that dangerous direction, in my opinion.

They were tranquil months at the hospital and I fitted in happily. It wasn't quite as . . . well, cosy, I suppose is the word, as it had been at Epsom. Here at Deal we had the same Cottage-Hospital system, including the rattling of collection tins at regular intervals to keep the funds up, with local GPs providing medical care and surgery, a

resident medical and surgical officer for Casualty, and general supervision. But we had much tougher cases than we had had at Epsom.

There was a lot of trauma work: one of our GPs was exceedingly
good at dealing with major accidents, after a hectic war in which he
had honed his skills, and we picked up quite a lot of cases of injury,
some very complex, from the nearby coal mines at Betteshanger,
from the seamen in the town (the Channel could be vicious) as well
as the Marines. I became, like all of us, adept at bandaging, plaster-
ing and dressing difficult wounds.

After a while I was sent to work in the operating theatres and I
loved that. I enjoyed the anatomy I got the chance to see – a body
with a sizeable incision in it gives you a good close look at the interior – and the drama of it all, though Sister Theatres (all sisters bore
the names of their departments and wards when on duty) I have to
say, was a horror.

Very flirty and, I think, a bit desperate for a reliable man to call
her own, she was petite, pretty and, gossip said, had had a lovely time
in the war but was now over thirty (shock, horror!) and wanted to
settle down. And there seemed to be no one of the right age or
income available in Deal. Visiting surgeons got the whole wide-eyed
glamour treatment of fluttering eyes above a snowy mask, and her
eyes were indeed a gorgeous blue, but sadly it never seemed to work.

Christmas came and brought one deeply warming experience for
me. All incoming post for staff was piled on a particular window-sill
in the long corridor outside the private patients' rooms. I never
stopped to look, although everyone else buzzed round it like hornets
on holiday, because I knew no one would send me Christmas cards,
and my family was certainly not sending me letters. One of the
others, a good friend called Ann Wilson of whom I was very fond
(she was several years my senior and appointed herself my guardian,
which was very agreeable), noticed I never looked and asked me
why.

'Oh, no one would ever send me a Christmas card,' I said. 'I've
never had one in all my life!' Which was true. 'It's not precisely a
family thing with us.'

Two days later it started. Someone called to me out of the scrum that there was letter for me. I looked and went scarlet with amazement. There it was – plus two more.

The next day there were half a dozen and the day after that I stopped counting. Everyone in the hospital, including patients and people I had never met, had sent me a card and I bedecked my room with them – refusing to take them down until almost Easter.

There was one other episode that I shall always remember about Deal. I had been sent to work on the private rooms, which most of us hated, me included. The people here differed from ward patients only in that they had to pay for their care. Ward patients did, too, if they could afford it or belonged to something like the HSA (Hospital Savings Association) but not so much as the private patients. If necessary, ward patients were treated free. That was one of the things we rattled tins for.

There was a lot of tea-making for visitors, a special private-patient privilege, and many of our patients loved nothing better than to send us running round after them like servants.

But there were very ill people too, and one of them was a nice lady we all liked a lot. She and her husband lived not far up the coast. She had cancer and suffered dreadful pain. Sometimes you could hear her cries of anguish all over the hospital as she howled, unable to stop herself, and I know how hard she tried. I would tell her to shout as loud as she wanted if it eased her and, oddly, that used to help her stop, but that wasn't why I said it: I really thought shouting might help.

I was very unhappy about Mrs X and spent as much time as I could with her, because she liked to have her forehead bathed with eau-de-cologne and liked me to do it. Sister didn't mind – I think she was glad that I was willing to be with so difficult a patient because none of the others wanted to. I don't think Sister wanted to be with her either.

This, remember, was 1947. There were none of the therapies we have now for cancer, no chemotherapy, and only basics in the way of radiotherapy, which is infinitely more sophisticated now. As for pain control, that was always a problem because essentially all we had were opiates like morphine and sometimes diamorphine (heroin). Now, with nerve blocks and a range of alternative drugs and therapies for pain, the picture is very different, cancer care having been largely redrawn by the Hospice movement.

And doctors and nurses operated under a widespread professional anxiety about the risk of making patients into addicts by overuse of pain control. Sister explained this to me when I asked why they couldn't give Mrs X more. She had to wait the full four hours every time, and within two hours of every injection she was in agony.

I thought it was crazy and cruel, too. These patients were going to die anyway: they wouldn't have time to become addicts. But there were rules about how much morphine, or whatever, could be used and when, and that was that. The result was that many terminally ill patients went through hell.

I was off duty one afternoon, and when I came back Sister asked me if I'd like to give an injection. Would I! I was avid for everything I could learn, and had been practising injections assiduously on apples, as we were taught to do. And here was Sister giving me the chance to do a real one.

'It's for Mrs X,' she said. 'Her next injection is due, and I've got it all ready for you. I'll come and supervise.'

Mrs X was already showing the restlessness, making little mewing noises, that usually preceded her howling, and I didn't really think what that might mean. I just eagerly did as Sister told me, swabbing the pitifully thin skin of Mrs X's forearm as Sister held her hand firmly, then gently introducing the needle on the syringe just under the skin, for it was a hypodermic injection, not an intra-muscular, and slowly, slowly, pushing home the piston.

Mrs X settled peacefully after that, and when I went off duty that evening about three hours later she was asleep when I put my head round her door to say goodnight.

Next morning when we came on duty we were told she had died, and although I was sorry I was also relieved for her. She'd had a bad time of it.

At break-time one of the other probationers on the private-patient rooms came and sat with me over our morning tea. What she told me I couldn't check, but I believed her when I remembered how Mrs X had only just started whimpering when I was taken by Sister to give the injection, and the way she had still been sleeping three hours later when usually her injections lasted barely two hours.

Nurse Carroll had been listening at Sister's office door. 'I do it all the time,' she said bluntly. 'It's the only way you get to know what's going on. No one tells us, do they?'

I couldn't disagree with that. She went on to tell me in direct terms that Mr X had been so distressed by his wife's condition that he had sat in Sister's office and begged her to put Mrs X out of her misery. He couldn't bear to see the state she was in. It was cruel to leave her like that.

Sister had called the doctor who, fortunately, was on the ward, and he came and joined in the talk. Carroll, ostensibly polishing wooden meal trays with Friar's Balsam to get rid of heat marks, had stayed outside and listened hard.

The doctor had agreed, written up a double dose of morphine, then left. Mr X thanked Sister, in tears, and went to see his wife again. Then he left the hospital too.

I came back from my afternoon off duty and, Carroll said, was given the injection to do. 'I daresay they – well, certainly Sister couldn't bring herself to do it, so she gave it to you. Maybe she thought if you didn't know it wouldn't matter. But I think you're entitled to know.'

So did I. I thought a lot about it, almost confronted Sister Private Rooms, a rather sweet but dithery woman, but I knew it would cause an uproar, and to what purpose? I'd already thought it was wrong to keep Mrs X like that when she was suffering so. If they'd asked me I'd have given the injection gladly. I just wished I'd been asked.

And why, I wondered, hadn't the doctor done it? Why had he pushed it on to the nursing staff when, ultimately, it was he who had decided what should be given in the injection?

I can offer no answer to that, of course, only conjecture.

That is all there is to tell, really. Except that years later, on an *Any Questions?* programme for the BBC euthanasia came up and I told that story to illustrate the need for properly written laws about it. Letters in the *Nursing Times* that week attacked me viciously.

No decent trained nurse would dream of doing such a thing as I had reported. Therefore, no decent trained nurse did. *Ergo*, Claire Rayner is a liar.

I am not, but I fear there are many professional nurses and doctors who would prefer to think I am than that such a thing could happen. There are still a lot of blinkered people in the nursing profession who deny that morphine is used to give the double effect – that is, primarily to relieve pain but if it causes death, well, so be it – but I know it happens.

Eighteen

My years at Deal and Walmer War Memorial Victoria Cottage Hospital gave me, I think, what I most desperately needed at that point in my life: a breathing space. I felt at fifteen that I had spent my life on a perpetual helter-skelter, soaring up only to come swooping down into misery again before the next upturn. I remember hearing Churchill's famous speech in which he spoke of 'the sunlit uplands' to which our wartime efforts would bring us and thinking, somewhat wistfully, of how lovely that sounded. And knowing perfectly well that the chance of finding so much as a hint of sunlit anything anywhere near my family, even in peacetime, was slender in the extreme.

But now the sun did come out and smile down on me. I got a brief letter from my mother, the first one she had ever sent to me at Deal, announcing that they were all going to Canada to live and would send for me when they got there and could get me a ticket.

Canada! A million miles away! Well, three thousand, anyway. It was a wonderful thought that there would be so huge a distance between us, and for the first time in my life, I think, I relaxed, stopped fearing what might happen next, what misery might be about to be inflicted on me. I felt safe and, much more importantly, free. For some reason, I ignored the sentence about being sent for. Probably I didn't believe it. I certainly didn't *want* to believe it.

It was not just freedom from the awareness of them being too near, too able to make trouble for me, that I felt, but also freedom from the brooding sense of something-nasty-about-to-happen that usually filled me. When I first saw *Hamlet* in a school performance at the City of London School and Hamlet said, 'Thou wouldst not think how ill all's here about my heart,' I had wanted to jump up and shout, 'I know, I know, I've got the same horrible feeling!'

Now, it melted away. I became more able to make friends with people, as the self-absorption – which must have looked to others like offhandedness at worst, shyness at best – caused by my constant fearfulness melted away. That, shored up by the memory of the generosity everyone had shown me with the Christmas cards, made me a much friendlier person.

Instead of spending my free time curled up on a sitting-room sofa (winter) or on the beach (summer) with a book, I joined in hospital events. I helped build our float for the big event of the summer, the town's fête and parade, which brought in a major chunk of our running costs each year.

I joined some of the other nurses in making Christian Dior-style New Look outfits of the sort the papers were making headlines about to wear at the hospital ball – the one dance I was prepared to go to – and thought they were the last word in glamour. Someone with an enterprising boyfriend in the Marines had managed to get hold of a great deal of 'parachute silk', as we called the amazing nylon fabric that was such a revelation to post-war young people, and we pooled our clothing coupons to buy watered moiré taffeta. With the nylon we made great swirly skirts, using umpteen layers to get the proper bell shape demanded by the great Paris couturier (the *Daily Mirror* was our guide), and with the taffeta tight-waisted peplum-style jackets to wear over them. All of us used different-coloured fabrics, and thought ourselves *le dernier cri* of fashion.

I even started to listen to some of the records the other girls played and, though I didn't particularly enjoy the music, I enjoyed the togetherness that came from listening in a crowd.

I was even willing to misbehave for the sake of my new friends. In the autumn the local churches sent us all the fruit offerings they got at harvest festival, which was wonderful, not only for the patients but also for us. Great baskets of top-grade Kentish apples and pears made a welcome addition to a rather dull, if wholesome diet. But we never got as many of the apples and pears as we would have liked. Some of us suspected the sisters of hogging them and grumbled greatly – until someone suggested we should help ourselves to a few. 'They keep them in the mortuary,' she said, 'where it's nice and cool. I know where the key is.'

So far so good. But who was to do the dirty deed? To my own amazement I volunteered. And on a cold and much too bright half-moon night, with various interested persons skulking in the shadows of the buildings to watch me, I strolled in the most offhand manner I could muster across the big quad that lay between the nurses' home and the main hospital to the mortuary building.

I wasn't stopped, and no one whistled the alarm we'd planned, so I unlocked the door and crept in. Now, indeed, everything was ill about my heart. I was sick with fright, but it was a different sort of fear. Almost an agreeable one. It was an adventurous fear, not at all like the way thoughts of my family made me feel.

Dark isn't the word for the inside of a mortuary at night. There wasn't so much as a chink in the tightly covered windows and even after my eyes had become accustomed to the darkness, I could see nothing. I had a small torch, although I'd been warned to keep the beam low, and I managed to get the courage to switch it on.

There were three ordinary high-wheeled ward trolleys, with suggestive, covered, body-sized shapes on them, and in the far corner the baskets with the apples and pears. I could smell them above another, rather less agreeable, smell of formaldehyde and Dettol, and something nameless I preferred not to think about.

I had to do what I was there for, so I wove my way past the trolleys, and when I got to the baskets I realised one major flaw in our plan:

Myself when young. This well bundled up photograph was taken in my grandmother's home (the chair is deeply etched into my memory)

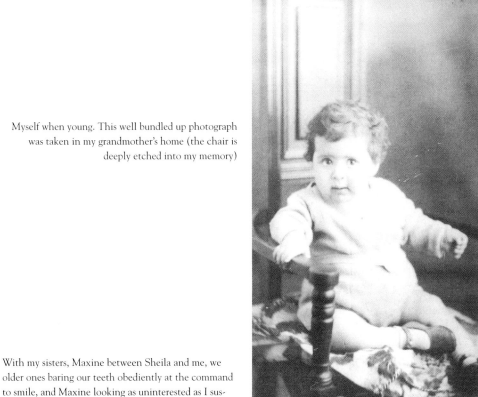

With my sisters, Maxine between Sheila and me, we older ones baring our teeth obediently at the command to smile, and Maxine looking as uninterested as I suspect Sheila and I felt

My paternal grandparents' engagement picture. She was sixteen, he twenty or so. I first saw this photograph when I was around twelve and was very startled by the likeness between Grandma and me. I still am

My parents at the end of the war, when she was about thirty-three and he thirty-five. I have doubts about the authenticity of the medal ribbons. I never heard any mention of his being awarded one, let alone several, and modesty was not his strong suit

Squinting into the sun on an outing to Epping Forest

My brother Lionel in Toronto at age eight. I treasured this for years after returning to London, though by the time we met again he had virtually forgotten me

Class Two at Rushmore Road Infants School around 1936 when I was five. I am hard to spot in so large a class – over forty – so check the back row where I stand looking sulky holding a large toy rabbit

The cast of the first Christmas Concert I produced at the Royal Northern Hospital in 1952. No men, because even though they had taken part they were excluded from the photo by Matron

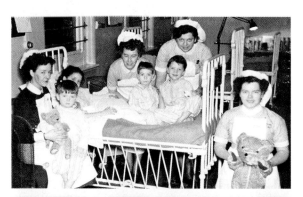

Sister and staff of Ward Eight, the children's ward at RNH, around 1953. I can still remember the children in the photograph – the little boy on Sister Friel's lap was called Teddy

Prize-giving at the end of my first year of training. I value this photograph mostly because it is so accurate a picture of RNH's Matron, Miss Darvill, whom I feared and admired in equal measure. The man giving me my prize is probably some Lord or other. Matron liked titles on prize-giving day

A brand new SRN bursting with pride in 1954. Matron was horrified by my choice of books for my Medical and Surgical prizes which dealt not with surgical operating theatres, but real dramatic ones, and with Impressionist art. But she let me have my choice, which was quite a climbdown for someone as powerful in her world as she was

The picture of Des I kept on my bedside table in the Nurses' Home at the Royal Free Hospital after we were engaged. Highly theatrical of course – it came from his job-hunting CV, vital to every young actor. The other nurses were mostly impressed and thought he looked exceedingly romantic. They were of course quite right

I felt a complete fool in all the satin and tulle I was assured the occasion demanded, but was blissfully happy all the same. Des had a migraine as a result of all the strain of the day and looked almost green in consequence

My cousin Susan is the bridesmaid on my right, and Jenny, on the left, is Des' cousin. She is now Jenny Diski and a fine writer

In our beloved flat where we spent the first three years of marriage and I began to learn to be a writer, using Des' ancient typewriter. It was one of his presents for his thirteenth birthday, so even in 1957 it was over fifteen years old. Des still uses it . . . Note the feature of every trendy fifties home, a lamp made out of a Chianti bottle and adorned with a handmade shade

A memento of a rare day out in the sixties *without* the children, when we went to Brighton and ate fish and chips, and window-shopped and sat on the beach before hiding ourselves in a photo-booth to make a permanent record of our summer tans no one had thought of providing something in which to carry the fruit.

I used my initiative. I pulled up the corners of my starched apron and filled the bag so formed to the brim. It was exceedingly heavy and I probably looked like a pregnant elephant, I thought.

Another problem. I couldn't use the torch now as my hands were full holding my overloaded apron. So, slowly, trying desperately to visualise the way, I crept towards the door. I hoped.

When the first trolley moved under the impact as I hit it, and almost sent me flying, I managed to keep my feet and my bundled apron.

When the second did the same but, worse still, allowed me to push it over so that its burden hit the floor with a thump, I fell hard on my rear and inevitably let go of the apron corners. The noise as fruit rolled all over the place was so loud that I thought someone would come in and find me. I sat there, frozen. But it all settled down and no one came so, using all the courage I had, I began to crawl towards the dark space where I hoped the door might be and somehow, eventually, found it. I fell out of the mortuary almost headlong, I was in such a rush to get away.

We never heard a word of what happened when the mortuary was opened next morning and the sprawl of fruit, trolley and, heaven help us, body was found. I suspect it suited the hospital to hush it up, for fear of the uproar there would be if local people realised how poorly protected their dead relatives were, which was a stance we agreed with heartily.

It was an episode that melded us into an even tighter group of mates, which I liked a great deal, though I have to say I was left with a nasty guilty conscience for some time, remembering how my favourite sister at Epsom had taught me to be respectful and sensitive at all times when dealing with the dead. But she was fun, too, so I suspect she would have forgiven me. I hadn't dropped the body on the floor deliberately. Just greedily.

I hardly noticed time passing. Another classic hospital Christmas, and then I reached my sixteenth birthday and felt very adult and contented. I was all set for the next year, I thought, after which, as soon as I was old enough to train properly for the profession, I would go up to London and, in due course, become a proper State Registered Nurse, and after that a State Registered Midwife. And after that, who knew? I had lovely career daydreams to keep me happy while I waited for my age to catch up with my ambitions.

It couldn't last, of course. Matron called me to her office one afternoon, much to my surprise because I knew I was in pretty good odour among the senior staff at present and hadn't done anything I shouldn't, not lately anyway. So I wasn't worried and knocked on her door cheerfully.

She looked at me and said, without any preamble, 'Nurse, you never told me you don't get on with your parents.'

I went crimson. I felt the heat fill not just my face but all of me and it made me giddy. She said sharply, 'Sit down, do.'

I did. And waited.

'I've had a letter,' she said then, 'from your mother. It enclosed one for you. Here you are. You'd better read it.'

It took a while because I couldn't concentrate properly but it made sense in the end. I looked at the letter and the piece of paper that had come with it and said, 'She wants me to go to Canada. This is a ticket for the ship.'

She nodded. 'Yes, I know. And of course you will go.'

She said it very firmly and I was puzzled. I'd always found her a friendly sort of person, someone you could talk to, not a bit the heavy sort of matron she could have been. And here she was, being very heavy. 'But I want to stay here,' I said. 'I'm very happy. I want to stay here and then go to London to train properly.'

'I know, but there it is. You can't. You have to do what she says and go to Canada.'

'Why?' I was getting myself together now. 'If I don't want to go, she can't make me. I'll send her ticket back.' I looked at it then and marvelled. Thirty-five pounds! I couldn't imagine her spending that much on me, ever. Even when I had to have all the uniform for school it had been Grandma who had paid for it. Grandma, I thought, and put the thought away.

'Oh, yes, she can make you,' Matron said, and sighed sharply. 'I told you she had written to me too.'

'Yes! Why? I mean, it's my business, isn't it?' I didn't want to be rude, but she understood.

'I wish it were, Nurse, really I do. I'd keep you here like a shot, if I could have my way. You're a very good nurse, and once you're trained you'll have a superb career. You were born for the profession. The patients love you and the sisters say you do a good job. I'd keep you like a shot. Good staff are very hard to find.'

'Well, then—'

'But it wouldn't be legal.'

I gawped. 'Not – how not?'

'She says she'll sue the hospital for enticing a minor away from her legal guardians. Her parents.'

'She can't do that,' I said. 'I don't believe it, it'd take ages and, anyway, I'd say to them I wanted to be here and that I didn't want to be with them because I hate them and—'

'I'm sorry, Nurse, I really can't discuss it.' She looked upset and flushed, but was very definite. 'I do sympathise with you, truly. My mum wasn't exactly – well, I do sympathise, but a threat like this, I can't take any chances. By rights I suppose I ought to have got their permission to take you in the first place, but I've never had to do it for any of the other cadets, and there it was, you'd had experience so I assumed – well, you'll have to go. You'll have to use that ticket. I'll write and tell her you'll be coming.'

Nineteen

I wonder now what would have happened if I'd called my mother's bluff and frankly refused to leave England.

I lay in bed night after night, trying to compose the letter I would write to tell her in effect to go jump in the lake. I also, I think, discovered that I had perhaps inherited aspects of my parents' morality: I considered the possibility of cashing in the ticket for the MV *Ascania* and pocketing the thirty-five pounds – more than a year's salary to me, after all – then changing my name (nothing new there!) and going to work in another hospital until I was old enough to start training properly and— But I couldn't sustain that daydream.

She kept appearing in the middle of it, vengeful, raging, attacking me with fists and objects like saucepan lids. I don't think I ever felt more trapped than I did at that time.

I felt ill too, in a way. The sense of foreboding that had been part of me all through my childhood came back with a vengeance. I called it my Hamlet feeling and sometimes talked back to it, telling it to shut up, to go away and leave me in peace or to make the bad things it was warning me were about to happen hurry up and happen, because the waiting was driving me potty. And then I'd think I *was* potty.

It was the physical symptoms that bothered me most. First, a gut problem that Sister Theatres liked to call 'intestinal hurry' when she noticed how often I was diving for the loo. She insisted I send a specimen to be tested for infection-causing organisms. (She was right, of course: I couldn't work in theatres if I was a carrier of salmonella or something of the sort.) Fortunately it came back clear, so she sniffed and said I was a worry-guts and to stop being so silly.

Then I developed some sort of lesion, which I later discovered was a verruca, on the sole of my right foot that made walking hellishly painful. I told no one, fearing I would be told again that I was a worrier, or 'neurotic', the greatest insult that could be hurled at any patient, let alone nurse. I would die of shame, I thought, if I was ever called that. So I simply walked through the pain, and pretended it wasn't there, but it didn't do much to help my general sense of unwellness.

I slept poorly, waking in the small hours to toss and turn, thinking of ways not to go to Canada, then was desperately sleepy during the day. Was it clinical depression of the sort I had first suffered when I started my periods and recurred most months in the days before a period? Not that I knew that the way I felt then had a fancy label. I just knew that I hated the world as much as the world hated me, and the only way to cope was to lock myself up inside. In other words, I used to sulk for hours and refuse to talk to anyone, eat or drink, and sometimes sat up in the living room all night because I couldn't bear to lie sleepless in bed. It wasn't as bad as that now, at the hospital, but if I was ever going to have a row with someone, or get into trouble, it was always in that few days before a period. But who knew about PMS then?

I don't think I was suffering from depression at this time, just before the dreaded departure for Canada. True depression, in my experience, occurs without obvious triggers and does not vanish when the trigger does. In other words, had I found a way not to go to Canada I am certain I would have felt marvellous. The sense of illness I had – that is, a feeling of things not being right in my world – was a reasonable reaction to a set of horrid circumstances that I could not control.

I make this point now because the issue of depressive illness recurred often over the coming years. But then, in spring 1948, I was just another adolescent whose life was being screwed up by her elders.

I was to sail on 6 May, and if there was any compensation for my plight it was the idea of a nine-day sea voyage. The ship was to leave from Liverpool and, after picking up more passengers at Cork in southern Ireland, would cross the Atlantic to enter the St Lawrence river and cruise up it to Montréal, passing Québec on the way. At this time of year, they told me at Cunard when I made enquiries, the pack ice was gone and the river was navigable. In winter, ships had to use Halifax, Nova Scotia, as their port of arrival, which meant very long train journeys for passengers going further west.

For the first time I had a moment of agreeable anticipation and spent a lot of time with the battered atlas in the nurses' sitting room, seeing how I was going to cross half the globe – well, almost half – and feeling rather sophisticated about it.

When the time came to leave I put on a great show for my friends. I would miss them, of course, but I was off on a great adventure, and smiled, laughed, hugged them all and shed not a tear. I was howling inside.

When the train from Deal at last took me into Victoria I dragged myself and my luggage – just one cardboard case – to a taxi, feeling very extravagant but shored up by the generous gift of a guinea (a pound and a shilling for those who never knew them) from the Nurses' Benevolent Fund, given to me by Matron as a parting gift, and my savings from my salary. I had fully four pounds in my purse. That was a lot of cash to me. To a lot of other people at that time, actually.

Why I imagined they would be there I just don't know. I hadn't seen them for years, though I know my parents had, late in the war, when my grandfather had died of cancer in his early fifties, but they might have moved – anything could have happened. I hadn't written or phoned but I gave the driver Grandma's and Auntie Nancy's address (they lived in adjoining flats in a small block in Manor

House near Finsbury Park gates) and travelled the whole way with my fingers crossed.

I knocked first on Auntie Nancy's door. She was the nicest person, after all. I had been told vaguely by my father at some time that she had married, though not until her mid-thirties, considered very old in those days, and that she had a small boy. I now discovered she had a daughter too. I told Auntie Nancy of all I had been doing and she looked impressed, which was nice of her. I thought she might regard nursing as – to use a phrase my mother had once thrown at me when she wanted to be particularly unkind – little more than skivvying with shit-removal thrown in. But she murmured about it being a respected profession and she hoped I meant to train properly and get the full qualifications.

'Of course.' I glowed at her, so grateful for her reaction I could have hugged her, though of course I didn't, and was about to tell her how miserable I was about having to go to Canada, then do what I should have done weeks ago, I now realised, which was ask her to help me stay in London, but she had to feed Susan, who was suddenly screaming blue murder.

The household settled to baby worship for the next hour, with Susan's four-year-old brother Maurice making a pest of himself the whole time, eaten up with jealousy as he obviously was. I understood entirely the way he felt.

By the time the baby was fed, with Maurice having his lunch immediately after, the moment for talking to Nancy about my needs was well past. I talked a lot, however, while all the feeding was going on, some of it coded anger directed at my parents. I had never complained to Auntie Nancy directly about them and I couldn't now. They were grown-ups, after all, and I most certainly was not. But I made it clear that I thought families were horrible, that I wanted no part of them, that I was going to be a totally free individual and never marry and have children. She listened and nodded and said nothing.

And, heaven help me, it never occurred to me, idiot that I was, that such sentiments spread before a woman who had just given birth to her second baby and who was living a totally domestic, family-centred life might have been interpreted by her as personal criticism.

At the end of lunch I said I had to be on my way to Euston to catch the boat train to Liverpool, and she nodded and said she was sorry I'd missed Grandma, and do write and let everyone know how I was getting on. She wished me every success with my career, then slipped a piece of paper into my pocket and waved me goodbye as I made my way down to the pavement below to get on the Underground to the mainline station.

I can still see her waving down to me from her living-room window. When I put my hand in my pocket later I found that she had more than doubled my reserves: she had given me a great big crisp white five-pound note.

The journey was indeed a dramatic experience for a very inexperienced sixteen-year-old. I was put in a cabin to share with five others, including a couple of small babies, just over the screw. The noise and vibration once the engines started was unbelievable, but I could and did sleep through anything. And I had had worse accommodation than this in my time.

And suddenly I felt good. It was as though all the bad feelings, the sleeplessness, the inner qualms, had vanished. I was on the ship, the journey was a *fait accompli*, so I might as well relax and enjoy it.

And I did. The food amazed me. I had been living in austerity, under severe rationing, ever since childhood. I couldn't remember what it felt like to have enough things to eat, or to have nice things to eat. From the start of the war until I left home to be a nurse, I never tasted butter. My mother used to say that margarine was best for children because it had added vitamins – which, in fairness, it did – but that the taste of it made her sick so we had the margarine and she ate only butter. But on this ship we had butter at every meal, never margarine, and what was more we had it on WHITE BREAD.

How can anyone who did not live through the same years that I did have any conception of what those two words meant? I have not the least doubt that the wartime bread we ate, which was wholemeal and used all of the grain possible, was exceedingly healthy but, ye gods, it was dull and tough and hard, and made very inferior toast. The stuff they gave us on the ship stood to what I had been eating as brioche stands to *pain paysan* in France. It was like eating the softest and most delicious cake after living on a diet of hard ship's biscuit.

And that wasn't all. Proper eggs from *shells*, as many as you wanted, bacon ditto, sausages and ham and steak (there was a miracle!) ditto, ditto, ditto and all sorts of goodies (cream! ice-cream! chocolate galore!) that convinced me and my fellow passengers we had died and were in Paradise, and that Canada was going to be all ambrosia and manna after such a start.

People danced a lot – there were lots of young men off to make their fortunes in the new country – even me, and we spied on the people in first class who dressed up in white ties and tails and long dresses every night for dinner. It was easier to get around on first-class decks without being caught if you went up after dark. There was a certain amount of cuddling and kissing under the tarpaulins over the lifeboats, which became the game of the journey for the young people in steerage – more, I think, for the joy of dodging stewards and officers as you crept up to the boat deck and clambered in unseen than for the cuddling. And if someone was already in the boat you chose and a ruckus followed, so much greater the fun.

For my part I have to confess I didn't like the kissing and cuddling much. For all that I had so deep a suspicion of male–female relationships I did feel that I would need to have some sort of attachment to a man to enjoy all that physical groping. Perhaps my hormones were not riding as high as they might or maybe I was a late developer.

There were one or two other single girls aboard who seemed to have a new chap to take to a lifeboat every night – sometimes two – and I watched them with a sort of scientific surprise. I could not understand what the pleasure was. I didn't disapprove of them: I just thought them odd. I imagine they had an even ruder label for me.

By the time we started up the St Lawrence, I felt I had been at sea all my life. There was a pleasant peacefulness about having all day to yourself with nothing special to do, except turn up for meals and read or whatever you wanted to do. But after seven days of it I was beginning to be a little edgy. I watched the views from the rails of the ship as the Canadian houses and countryside passed us as we moved further and further west, and they fascinated me. I had read *Anne of Green Gables*, of course, and though I knew her part of Canada was Prince Edward Island, and far behind me, it helped me to try to make some sort of connection between the books I had known and loved so well and this frankly terrifying new country.

It was almost as though I could feel its immensity stretching on each side of me, thousands of miles in every direction. At home in England I had always been able to 'feel' where I was in the country. I knew how far it was to the sea or to London or wherever, and that made home feel right, manageable and, well, right.

But once I left the ship, I was lost. I looked back at her rather rusty, grubby bulk looming over the Customs sheds and yearned to get back on board where it was safe and familiar. I didn't mind her shabbiness: the crew and stewards I had talked to called her 'the old Ashcan' and that had endeared her to me. Much more fun than the spanking newness of a perfection one couldn't touch or relax in.

I couldn't get any sense of where I was, that was the trouble. My legs wouldn't obey me. On board they called it getting 'sea-legs': after a couple of days at sea you learned to walk with a roll to accommodate the ship's roll, and the *Ascania* was a mighty roller. No stabilisers on liners then! Once back on land, you had to unlearn your sea-walk. It was not easy and made me feel like a baby, a toddler out with no one to hold my hand and keep me safe. A horrid feeling for an independent-minded person.

And landing at Montréal was terrifying. So much noise, so many people, so much pushing and shoving, and everywhere voices I could not comprehend. On the ship most people had been English and felt homely. Here in Montréal, on the docks and on the railway station where I eventually fetched up, they were mostly French with an accent quite unlike the one I had learned at school, and the people using it made no effort to speak to us anyway.

Happily for me, a nice couple from the ship were also going to Toronto. They took me to the right train and even saw to it I had a bunk to sleep in. I suspect now that they might have paid for it for me – I suppose I might have been a figure of pity, a young girl alone on so long a voyage! I was certainly far and away the youngest of the unattached passengers.

I arrived in Toronto after two days and, I think, as many nights on the train. I can't remember now. I was tired, very disoriented, and all the horrible feelings had come back.

Oh, Hamlet, I thought as the train slid into the station to where I knew they'd be waiting to meet me. Oh, Hamlet, it's worse than ever. All the bad feelings that had seemed to melt away when I stepped on to the ship had come back with a huge rush. I couldn't have been more miserable.

Twenty

They met me at the station, all five of them, and it was over-whelming. Both parents gave me huge hugs and great slobbery kisses, and I felt sick. It felt like a performance, a show they were putting on for any watching strangers – and there were plenty around in the crowded station.

Why were they doing this? They didn't care about me, I decided, not the real me. I was a sort of symbol of their success in making me do what they wanted, a 'here-we-all-are-together-again-in-spite-of-you'. I could understand that they would have a sense of failure about me. I hadn't conformed to what they wanted of me, and all this show of affection was a way of pretending to themselves that they could make their family life work out the way they wanted it to. But it was much too late, and I knew that. They had to learn to see it too.

They'd brought something called a corsage, and went on and on about it. I said I'd never heard of them and my mother said, in her high I-live-in-Kensington voice, 'Oh, how quaint you are, child! They're all the rage!' and insisted I must put it on at once.

I looked at the transparent box they had put into my hands. Maxine, ever-impatient, pulled it open and showed me a garish purple orchid dripping with ferns and glittery silver wrappings. 'You have to wear it on your left shoulder,' she said, pinning it on to the shabby old winter coat I had been wearing for three winters, and which showed it. 'It's the height of fashion.'

I looked at the mirror window to which they dragged me and I felt even sicker.

They took me back to the three or four rooms they were renting at the top of a house in a shabby inner patch of Toronto, and showed me the tiny space I would have to sleep in 'just till we find the right house and move'. It was clear I was supposed to be grateful to have a space to myself. I thought of my room in Deal, and the tears only just stayed in my throat.

They wanted me to go to school, like Sheila and Maxine, and I laughed in their faces. With the sort of life I'd been living I thought it highly unlikely I could cope with that, but they nagged me to try and I gave in out of sheer exhaustion.

I sat in a schoolroom with a bunch of people of my own age – sixteen – but at least five years younger in mind and outlook, and fled. I wanted to go back to nursing, I told them, and I would. Thank heaven they knew when to stop pushing, at least at that point. And let me alone to sort myself out in the great alien city to which they had dragged me so unwillingly.

The main feeling I experienced startled me. I hadn't thought about the possibility of it happening to me. I was, after all, not some little homebody who had only just ventured out of the cosiness of a secure life, I told myself. I'd knocked about a bit, suffered a bit, been toughened by life. I wouldn't be bowled over by anything as puerile as homesickness.

But I was. I was desperately, gut-wrenchingly homesick. Homesick for familiar voices, familiar sights, even, amazingly, familiar food and drink. The alienation of those first weeks stunned me. When it didn't make me furious.

Take the plethora of food and drink everywhere, from loaded grocery-store shelves to candy stores outrageously full of every sort of chocolate and sweet confectionery imaginable, absurdly large num-bers of restaurants and eating houses, and street-food vendors of all kinds, and all with immense menus. Access to all of it was governed only by the contents of your purse.

I thought of the people at the hospital in Deal. About the women in their ward and how they would respond to the possibility of buying half a dozen eggs, just for their own breakfast. Of the children in their picture-decked ward and the way their faces would look if they were given just a single box of Laura Secord chocolates, a Canadian product, quite stunningly delicious and rich. I imagined the men in their ward faced with shops full of cigarettes and all their favourite tobacco mixtures, and no refusal to let them buy because they weren't regular customers. I thought of my colleagues, and how much fun they would have rampaging through a dress shop with never a thought of coupons in their heads.

And I wept bitterly, soaking my pillow in a way I never had before in all my life, no matter how hard I'd been hit or how miserable I was.

Homesickness, I discover to my relief, can be assuaged temporarily if I go to the pictures – 'the show', in Canadian parlance – whenever I can, and spend the whole day there so that I see the film three or even four times at a sitting. But the films I choose are very specific. They must be English and the best English there is.

Henry V, Olivier's perfect piece of propaganda for a nation weary of war and hunger, I manage to see thirty-five times till I know every glorious word of the script, every nuance of every performance, every note of William Walton's music. To this day I can reel off great swathes of the text (if my family are around when I'm triggered into it by some passing reference, they groan and forbid it). It gave me great comfort at the time.

And so did the next Olivier film that came to Canada. I managed to be at its première in a fancy Toronto cinema, and every time I went, which was often, I saw every showing in a day's continuous performance. *Hamlet* and I therefore clocked up almost thirty meetings in the happy darkness of the dusty cigarette-smoke-filled, popcorn-flavoured Toronto 'shows'.

And then there was delicious, gentle, witty and perfectly pain-soothing *Passport to Pimlico*, which gave me not just English voices and English characteristics, so different from those around me, but also my very own brave and beautiful bomb-battered London. I adored that film and still do. I lost count of my viewings but I think it must have beat fifty.

Obsessive? Of course! I was obsessed with misery and loneliness, and those cinema hours took that obsession away just for a few hours. I am still grateful for all they did for me.

I am arguing with my parents. Again they nag about wanting me to go back to school, and then on to university or medical school. Once, that might have appealed, perhaps, and I think, just for a moment, when they first make the suggestion, that things have changed and they are thinking about what would be best for me and what I might want to do.

But then she says, 'At least then I'll be able to talk about you and what you do if you go back to school! I could never tell people what you were doing at those hospitals. I was too ashamed of you. You can do better than that because you're clever.'

And I remember her on Cirencester station boasting I was going away to 'college' because she thought it a cut above a school, and here she is doing it again, trying to use me to aggrandise herself. I can't bear it so I'm arguing and they're shouting at me and I feel sick.

Grace Hospital is a Salvation Army maternity hospital where the staff nurses are called Captain and the Sisters are called Major and Matron is a Brigadier and I quite like working there. They seem to like me, and trust me with basic nursing tasks of all sorts, even temperature-taking, though not, of course, with any of the obstetrics. But I help the mothers feed their babies and show them how to bath them and put on nappies, now that Major Sister has shown me the right way, and I am generally content enough, though I have to return to the family house at the end of the day. I would like to live in at Grace, but they say they must have my parents' consent. I wouldn't even ask.

One day in August we have a strange experience amid the smells of Dettol, baby powder and flowers. There is a parade going on outside with men in suits and bowler hats banging drums and blowing wind instruments that are unfamiliar to me, and wearing great orange-coloured sashes.

Right outside the hospital's front door someone throws a stone: a young man is hit on the cheek and bleeds copiously. His anxious fellow marchers pay no attention to the word 'Maternity' on the sign outside, only to 'Hospital', and bring their bleeding friend in.

Major Sister says this is not an emergency room but she will do the preliminary care, then send for an ambulance to transfer him to a proper hospital. She sets about it, as I stand by with bowls and swabs and so forth, and she mops up his face as he lies on an occasional table in the middle of the entrance hall. She is trying, with some difficulty, to reduce the blood loss by pressure when a group of patients in frilly nighties, dressing-gowns and fluffy bunny-rabbit slippers, clearly alerted by the hubbub and the news travelling round the hospital at the speed of light – in the normal hospital manner – appear at the top of the stairs.

They start to shout at Major Sister and the young man, clearly enraged, and I am amazed. I nearly drop the bowl of bloody swabs I am holding when one of the patients runs down the stairs, nearly pushes Major Sister over, spits lavishly into the face of the man on the table and goes straight into a violent attack of screaming hysterics.

After the hubbub dies down I am told the patient behaved like that because she is a Catholic and they all hate the Orangemen. Furthermore her own dad had been killed in Ireland at the height of the Troubles during a scuffle at an Orange parade.

It takes a lot of explanation before I even begin to comprehend what it is all about, and why people in Canada should still be fighting battles that had started three thousand miles away and hundreds of years ago. This is the first time in my life I have heard of the Irish Troubles in a real way and not just as silly cartoons in the magazines *Film Fun* and *Radio Fun*, which I used to read when I could get hold of copies. I had thought the IRA and the Troubles were cartoon inventions. I never knew they were real. I do now, of course.

I am working as a not very good or very fast machinist in a dress factory on Spadina Avenue, which is in the heart of the rag trade in Toronto. It is horrible, boring, backbreaking, and I count the minutes away and comfort myself with a daily bar of raisin chocolate, which I make last for the whole day by sucking each tiny piece for as long as I can. I should be putting on weight, but in fact I am getting thinner. My clothes don't fit and I have to take them in. I seem to do nothing but sewing, and I hate it so much I could kill someone.

But I have no choice, it seems. My mother has announced she needs more money from me because my father has gone off again, I don't know where to and care even less. I do as I am told and leave the hospital but the old urges are stirring. Runaway time again, surely?

New York. That is what it says all over the place at the bus station where I got off the bus, all stiff and still half asleep. I can see myself there, looking at posters, buying a newspaper, reading it in a coffee shop, and counting my money under the cover the paper provides. I had the wit, when I arrived in Toronto, to keep the fact that I had some money well hidden, like the money itself. If my parents had known I had managed to amass seven pounds, even after spending some of it on the journey over, they would have had it out of my hands in seconds. I have been wearing it – three notes, two single pounds and one fiver – sewn into a piece of white rag picked up at the Spadina Avenue factory and tucked into my bra.

I changed it in Toronto into Canadian dollars, so that I could buy the bus ticket. I remember nearly choking when they asked about a passport, but I told them I was English and was waiting for my Canadian one, and they believed me and let me on to the bus. No one seemed to care much at the border when we got to Buffalo about passports, so I suppose they have taken the Canadian authorities' word for it that their cargo of passengers is legal.

Looking back now from a post-11 September 2001 world, I am
enchanted by this. Imagine wandering around in North America
now without a passport or other suitable documents, looking for a job
and somewhere to stay!

So here I am, with just under thirty Canadian dollars, which is
worth rather less in US dollars, but should still see me through until
I get a job and somewhere to stay.

And this time, I swear to myself, I am never going back to them.
I will not, I will not, I will not.

I am tired of working in this disgusting place that calls itself a restaurant. It stinks of rancid oil and dead old cheese, and meat that is
perilously close to rotten, yet the people who come here never seem
to notice. They eat the boiled salt beef and cabbage, the hot chicken
sandwiches – a real North American concoction, this, white bread
slices, lots of sliced chicken between them, mashed potatoes and
green peas on the side, and gravy poured over the lot, especially the
bread, which takes on an oddly gummy texture.

I have become expert at waitressing. I can take six orders, however
peculiar – 'Hold the mayo, lots of mustard, no white bits in the cabbage' – and remember them all. I can stack the plates along my arm
so that I have to make fewer visits to fetch them from the kitchen. I
can dodge the short-order cook's bottom pinches (I had a regular
crop of bruises at the start, not now), I can sweep up a tip left for
me – or anyone else, for there is no shame in these matters and the
other waitresses robbed me naked at the start – in a trice.

And I am so bored I could scream. No time for going to see movies
now. I have to work extra hours because they let me have the small
room over the restaurant as part of my wages. It is very small, very
stuffy, for it is still hot although it is September, and I cannot believe
I am in New York. I could be anywhere. There are no skyscrapers to
be seen, no fun at all. Just hot chicken sandwiches over and over
again . . .

(Many years later, when I am a successful writer, journalist, TV
performer and all the rest of it – and, yes, quite rich – I am invited by

my publisher to make a national tour of the USA to publicise my novel, *The Running Years*, starting in New York. It is all very glamorous and exciting, and I love every moment. Now I have skyscrapers galore and limousines and the best seats at the hottest Broadway shows, and it's bliss. And then one lunchtime, sitting in the Waldorf Astoria on Park Avenue with my husband, eating perfect Caesar salad and heaven knows what else, I am suddenly transported in my mind back to that god-awful restaurant and its horrible food, and I weep painfully. What else could I have done?)

A girl comes in who is a regular, a youngish one, though clearly older than me. She seems to like talking to me – because I have an English accent, she says. It is a quiet night, we don't have many customers in so I have time to talk, which is nice. She smiles at me a little sadly and sits down, and I notice that tonight she is carrying a complete Shakespeare. At once, without thinking, I go into 'O! for a muse of fire, that would ascend the brightest heaven of invention, a kingdom for a stage, princes to act and monarchs to behold the swelling scene.'

She is delighted, and we talk about the film and about *Hamlet* and also about the Elisabeth Bergner and Olivier screen version of *As You Like It*, which I saw in Toronto once, and it is all very friendly.

Eventually I remember I have a job to do and say, 'What can I get you?' She looks embarrassed and says, well, actually she is broke, the most she can manage is a cup of coffee and one of yesterday's doughnuts, which are a couple of cents cheaper than the usual price. Actually the doughnuts are five days old and, I suspect, horrible. I feel sorry for her and say, 'All right.'

I order the ham omelette and fries, because at least they don't cook the eggs if they are bad, and you can't say the same about the meat dishes. When I take it to her she starts to cry and I tell her not to worry. All the waitresses do this sometimes for their friends and the boss is out and no one will pay any attention, so enjoy your supper.

And then we really start talking and I begin to believe that there is fun to be had after all.

*

I had never heard of Wilmington. I'm not sure I really believed Vermont was a real place, although I loved the song about the pennies in the stream. But Barbara, my new friend, assures me that it is not all that far – you go to upstate New York and sort of turn left and you get there – and it is much nicer than the awful Third Avenue places we had both been living in. And, of course, she's right.

There are nine people in the group, four girls and five men – and if I'd had any sense I'd have realised at that point that this was a crazy enterprise. They are going to do Shakespeare for the ordinary people, Barbara says, no fancy costumes, no fussing over scenery, just let the wonderful words speak for themselves.

I know my Shakespeare. I love the plays, and have ever since schooldays. And I know that there is no play that can be cast properly with so few men and so many women unless the women play men's parts, which is never quite as satisfactory with Shakespeare as the other way about.

The first thing they do is have a whip round for money. They are sitting in this damp barn sort of place beside a farm, and they say, 'This is where we work and play and live the rest of the summer.' Again I am puzzled. I have learned, in my short time in America, that after the first Monday in September, which is called Labour Day (sorry, Labor Day), the summer is officially over. Everyone goes back to work, and holiday places by the sea and in the country are empty.

It is now the second week in September but no one seems to worry about it, so I don't. But I lie and say I have no money left from the bus fare that brought us here. Barbara assures me they'll be thrilled to have me, once they hear my accent, even though I've only done a little amateur acting, at Deal Hospital when we did a show to raise some money for the hospital. Oh, yes, and at school, where Miss Peach had said I was good.

I blush to remember all this. The way they tried so hard to make it all work, and stretched their money to give me equal shares in everything when I had an undeclared over thirty dollars in my bra – I'd saved a little to add to what I had at the restaurant. It was shameful.

But I worked as hard as I could, although it was difficult. I had started to feel ill again. The loo and I knew each other far too well. I was getting thinner all the time, although I ate like a horse at every opportunity (the people at the farm were generous, though they obviously thought we were mad) and I sweated and shook with every effort I made.

Indeed, I sweated and shook most of the time. I checked my pulse once with the stage manager's stopwatch when I was feeling particularly tremulous and was amazed to discover it was pounding along at 182 beats a minute, which was very fast considering that the norm, as I had learned at Epsom and Deal, was around 72.

I put it down to trying too hard to pull my weight as they fixed up the barn with rows of home-made benches and fashioned a stage of sorts. I tried to relax but that didn't help. I couldn't sleep at night, though once again in the daytime I was dreadfully dopey.

They cast me as Gertrude in *Hamlet*, and although I was thrilled I was terrified too. I was seventeen and looked well enough made (for all I was getting thinner, I wasn't that thin!), but could I convince an audience that I was a sexy, mature woman and the mother of our Hamlet – a heavily built chap of around twenty-six – as well as a queen?

I was full of doubt and trepidation but I learned the lines, most of which I already knew, having seen Olivier's film often enough, and we headed for a first night as best we could. I hardly noticed what the others were doing. I really was feeling more and more ill.

So ill I began to think I ought to go back to Toronto. Because if I had something really bad wrong with me, to be alone in a country where I didn't even have a passport might be very tricky indeed.

Twenty-one

I am sitting in the consulting room of Dr Liebel in Toronto, and falling more and more heavily in love with him at every word he speaks. His name had been given to me by the doctor in Wilmington in Vermont to whom the nice people on the farm had taken me. One afternoon I did a spectacular faint while standing on a bench and holding up a curtain for ten minutes while one of the others fixed it: the prolonged arms-over-head posture had been all that was needed to fell me. Landing on the hard floor was what had made it a spectacle. It had scattered what little wits I had left, what with feeling so lousy anyway, and I have no doubt I thoroughly alarmed the nice people.

They were extremely kind, I thought, as they drove me into the town to a doctor. On the way we stopped at a diner and had coffee and pie, because Mrs Niceperson thought I might be hungry (brilliant woman – when was I not?) and while we sat there they gave me a piece of paper to sign to the effect that it wasn't any fault of theirs that I had fallen. I signed it gladly, if shakily, because of course it wasn't.

Later, I heard from Barbara that they had gone back after the trip to town to tell them all to pack up and leave because they had no insurance for what was going on in the barn. As they said, while it was one thing to pick up a few bucks from letting a bunch of lunatics fool around on their property it was another if it made them liable for damages.

Not that it mattered by then because the leader of the group, our Hamlet, had also been so frightened by my fall that he had decided it might be wiser to slope off before I came back and sued him. The idea had never entered my English head, of course, but apparently it was the first thing every American around me had thought of. Which left all of them scrabbling around to find their bus fares back to New York.

So, a sorry end to what I had thought might be fun. It had undoubtedly been better than the restaurant and it also gave me the chance to show off a little in later years about the time I worked in summer stock in Vermont. As long as I didn't go into details I felt I wasn't lying because I *had* been there. But, oh dear, what a fiasco!

I don't remember much about the journey from Wilmington to Toronto. I know it was expensive because my dollars had dwindled to little more than ten by the time I got back to the house in Mount Dennis, a suburb not too far from the airport at Malton where the family was living. My mother found the money in my pocket, because it had stopped being convenient to keep it in my bra, and that was the last I saw of it.

I do, however, remember being haunted by what had been said in the doctor's office in Wilmington. He had with him when he examined me a nurse in a very fancy all-white uniform, including white stockings, which I considered very odd since in England every nurse wears black ones. When he said I had a disease of the thyroid gland called Graves' disease she had giggled and said brightly, 'Hastening to the grave with Graves' disease.' He had frowned at her and said hurriedly to me, 'Well, that is what they *used* to teach, but nowadays, of course, it is *much* easier to treat.'

I did not believe him, of course. He had been in too much of a hurry to reassure me and had told me nothing about the disease, except that it involved an overactive thyroid and that his old friend in Toronto was a specialist in it. I was convinced I was going to die and did a lot of thinking about that during the journey back to Toronto.

Generally speaking, people of seventeen regard themselves as immortal. However, the Blitz years and my Epsom and Deal experiences had taught me that even immortals can die. Could I be about to die from this Graves' disease? I knew nothing about it, apart from the fact that it made me feel dreadful, and I was not in a position to look it up in a medical book. I no longer had the sort of access to a medical library that I had had in Epsom and Deal.

And another great wave of homesickness almost overwhelmed me, as I had a sudden vision of the nurses' library at Deal Hospital with its rather battered books and out of date copies of *Nursing Times* and *Nursing Mirror*, where I had spent a great deal of contented time. It almost made me wail aloud.

All I could do was remind myself of the Greek philosopher, whose name I couldn't remember, who had said that before we are born there is oblivion and we don't care about that, and after we die there is oblivion again so why worry about it? Or something like that. I knew I had the quotation wrong and spent the rest of the journey trying to get it right. That, at least, gave me something to take my mind off my imminent death.

Dr Liebel is doing a lot to take my mind off my death, which is why I am developing a passion for him. He has explained all about the overactive thyroid and the way it has been making my heart beat at double time or more and my body burn up all available energy at double time too. He explains the result of the Basic Metabolic Rate test he did on me, and how it proves that this disease is why I have been so breathless and sweaty and agitated and hungry and irritable and sleepy all day and insomniac at night and tearful and all the rest of it. 'And why you have such dreadful dreams when you do sleep,' he adds.

This is the point at which I know I am for ever in love. How does this wonderful person know what hellish dreams I have been having for so long? I gaze at him with soulful eyes and hope he notices.

He doesn't. He just says he wants to put me on some pills which, if they suit me, will slow down the thyroid, after which all will be well.

'And if they don't?' I ask.

'Then we must think again. Perhaps surgery.'

I catch my breath. 'Would you do that?'

'No. I'm an endocrinologist. I would have to hand you over to a surgeon.'

I decide I don't want surgery and say so, and he nods. 'Naturally not. But it may be necessary.'

'How soon will I know?'

'What you need now,' he says, failing for the first time to answer a direct question, a fact I note carefully because it alarms me, 'is a chance to rest. Can they look after you at home?'

That makes me laugh. 'No,' I say, and try to imagine my mother actually taking care of me, try to see myself lying in bed or on a sofa and her fetching tasty little somethings to tempt me. My imagination fails totally. There are some things that could never happen.

He looks at me thoughtfully and then says, 'Why do you run away so much?'

'Oh. They told you that? My parents?'

He shakes his head. 'I haven't spoken to them. I sent a message after you booked your first appointment, asking them to come here with you, since you are a minor, but I was told that you must look after yourself. Is that – um – does that surprise you?'

I don't answer but he seems to know anyway, and I say then, 'If they didn't tell you I run away sometimes, how do you know?'

'You told me.'

'Me? I never said—' and then I stop. 'Have I been talking a lot?' I ask, and he laughs for the first time. A new wave of adoration for the small dimple that appears in the corner of his mouth nearly ruins me, and makes me yearn to throw myself at his feet.

He nods.

'Well, all right, I suppose I have chattered a lot,' I admit, and think about Matron at Epsom warning me about my 'speaking countenance'.

'Has it helped?'

'Oh, yes,' I say, and smile at him as nicely as I can. I have never, I swear, behaved like this in all my life but, then, I have never before met anyone so devastatingly wonderful in every way.

'So, why do you run away?'

He's persistent, I'll give him that. 'It's the only way I can cope when it gets bad. I don't do it till I have to.'

'I see.' He is quiet for a while, just looking at me, and then a sudden thought hits me.

'You said you had to ask them to come because I'm a minor and they said no, but you're still seeing me.'

'Yes,' he says, then smiles again. 'Don't worry about it. It doesn't matter.'

I now know exactly what my parents are up to. They are refusing to admit any responsibility for me because that might cost them money. I have no idea what Dr Liebel's fees might be, but I know I can't pay them. Just as I couldn't pay the doctor in Wilmington, and his nurse had said, in that horrible bright way of hers, 'Well, not to worry. He can put a claim in on the City for treating a vagrant, seeing you have no fixed address.'

I hadn't minded that in Wilmington. There I *had* been a vagrant, after all, and anyway what could I do about it? I dared not tell them I had a few dollars or I'd never have got back to Toronto, which at that point seemed to be the best thing for me to do. I had to let the City pay, whatever that meant.

But now I am not so sure. I'm in Toronto, where there are people who are supposed to be interested in me, who claim to want me to be with them, who had forced me to come to this lousy country when I didn't want to. And they are refusing to see the doctor who wants to take care of me and my hurrying-to-the-grave-with-Graves'-disease because if they do they will be liable to pay his fees. Liable for Liebel's fees, I think, and want to laugh, but once more I am weeping, howling, sobbing disgustingly, with my nose running. Dr Liebel sighs and gives me some paper tissues from his desk.

After I manage to sniffle down to a less revolting state of misery he says kindly, 'I want you to just wait outside for a little while. I'll sort something out for you.'

Obediently I go to his waiting room, and there his nurse, who is much nicer than the Wilmington one, although she too wears all white, gives me a cup of tea and a couple of biscuits. I look at them and am surprised to see they are lovely thin sugary Nice biscuits, which I haven't seen since I left England, and didn't see often there on account of rationing and shortages. 'English!' I say delightedly, and the nurse smiles.

'Dr Liebel trained at Guy's Hospital in London,' she says. 'He likes a lot of English things.'

Once more I am amazed at the all-round perfection of this man, and as I sit and wait for him I doze off as I usually do when I am sitting anywhere tolerably quiet during the day (I'd even done it over a meal, once or twice) and dream nicely for once, all about him. Very agreeable.

He wakes me, and I see from the clock that I have been dozing for half an hour and am embarrassed, but he says not to be, I need all the rest I can get. He sits down beside me, there in the waiting room, and seems to think for a while, staring at me. Then he says, 'I have made an arrangement for you that might surprise you, but if I tell you it will be the best thing for you and that you will be very well looked after, will you take my word for it?'

He looks so serious and – well, worried, is the word that comes to my mind, that I am alarmed. And say so. 'Are you trying to scare me?'

He smiles but it is still a worried smile. 'No, not at all. But the hospital I want you to go to – let me explain. I think you need to rest for a long time. A couple of months or more. I can't get you into one of the beds in my ward at Toronto General because there is this problem of the bills. Even in one of the open wards, which apart from anything else aren't very restful, there are some bills and if you can't pay them I can't keep you there as long as you need to rest. However, if you go to a different sort of hospital, which in some ways is as relevant for your condition as my own hospital—'

'I don't understand what you're saying,' I complain, and he sighs.

'I have a bed for you at a hospital where they are not too concerned about failure to pay bills. In fact, they're quite used to it. They do a lot of university-based research and education so that funds them. But some people might be put off by the name of the hospital. And its specialty.'

He took a deep breath then and said, 'It's the Toronto Psychiatric Hospital. I know your illness is physical but a lot of your symptoms – the anxiety and the bad dreams and the agitation . . . ' He stops, looking at my face, and I dare say he is surprised at what he sees there. A psychiatric hospital? What an interesting idea, I think. When I was at Epsom, which at that time was surrounded by several large psychiatric hospitals, I was taken one afternoon with some of the other cadet nurses on a visit to one to 'widen your nursing horizons', Matron said.

And I had thought the hospital splendid. I had little experience of what it might be like to be inside such a place but I had liked what I saw. I was much taken with the wide lawns around the separate patient pavilions, and the openness of the wards and the entertainment facilities there were for patients. Those we had seen had been quiet but far from unhappy. Maybe it wouldn't be so bad, I think.

And I think, too, of the films I have seen about people having psychiatric treatment. I had seen *The Snake Pit* a few months earlier but I didn't think this Toronto hospital would be like that rather scary institution. I thought – hoped? – it would be far more like the lovely place in the country where Ingrid Bergman had looked after the gorgeous Gregory Peck so successfully in *Spellbound*.

(I looked back with embarrassment on this piece of thinking when I first wrote it down. Allowing your decisions to be seriously affected by what you see on a cinema screen has to be the pits, so naff, so immature; and then I reminded myself that I was only seventeen at the time and blushed at being so patronising an old woman. Odd to think of patronising one's younger self, but that is what I think that reaction meant. I report it now as an apology to that younger self.)

And then I think of something else: for me a hospital, any hospital, feels like home. During my two cadet jobs the hospitals where I worked were more than my workplace: they were homes in every sense of the word, havens from a harsh world. A hospital would always be preferable to a house, I told myself, there in Dr Leibel's waiting room. There is a potent mixture of satisfaction in them. First of all they are safe, whether you're a patient or a nurse (it is an index of my naïvety at the time that I forgot patients could be anything but safe because of their illness) and second – I could only repeat my mantra. They feel like home.

And there was at that time another extremely good reason for going to a hospital – any hospital, whatever its name or speciality.

I would not have to live with my family.

Poor Dr Liebel, I think, as I see the surprise on his face when I say cheerfully, 'I think that's a great idea! Can I go there now, and not have to go back to Mount Dennis? Because that would be the best thing of all.'

Twenty-two

I stayed there for fifteen months. During that time my parents once sent me a box of old books and my sister Sheila once came to see me. Obviously there was great anxiety in Mount Dennis about the sort of bills for which I might make them liable. So they stayed remote and I liked it – dammit, I loved it – that way. My only anxiety once I was admitted was that one day they would tell me I was well again and I would have to return to the bosom of my family.

That I was physically ill on admission was undoubted, which re-assured me I'd have to stay there for a while. Virtually every medical student in the place, and as a university establishment it was crawl-ing with them, came to examine me, quiz me and try to make a diagnosis for their consultant, who would stand magisterially beside them as they fumbled about.

If they were nice and I liked them I would whisper it to them. If they were off-hand and came the I-Am-A-Doctor bit at me, as some raw medical students try to, I left them to flounder.

I have the haziest memories of the early months. I was given better food than I had had for a long time, for I truly had become very thin, something I simply can't imagine now. I was made to rest a great deal – they gave me a lot of barbiturate drugs to ensure sleep but that only made my dreams more lurid than ever and, indeed, gave me noisy nightmares – and I was made to talk to a doctor at regular intervals. What about, I can't remember, but I do know I liked the doctor because he listened to me seriously, and made me feel, while he was with me, that I was the only person in the world who mattered. He even managed to expunge from my mind the memory of the divine Dr Liebel, whom, I'm afraid, I never saw again.

But there was a risk in all this responding to niceness. I wanted to please the people who were trying to please me. If a night nurse was gentle and soothing when I woke up screaming from a nightmare and tried to get me to describe what I had seen in my dreams, I would make up things that I thought she wanted to hear, following her guidance. So, yes, I would say, gulping back the tears, I dreamed of snakes and men with big sticks and being on top of tall towers – whatever she suggested.

My nightmares actually took the form of my being very small and surrounded by the huge faces of very large strange people who first tried to eat me up, then left me all alone in the middle of black nowhere. I had been having them from time to time ever since I could remember, and I knew that they had come back to me in the hospital because of the barbiturates.

Once before, when I had been ill in Epsom with a chest infection, Matron had given me a dose of barbiturate to 'give you a quiet night's sleep, dear', but all it had done was summon up my noisy nightmares. And she had warned me that I must never take them again because they clearly disagreed with me.

But I did not tell them that at Toronto Psychiatric Hospital: first of all, because I liked feeling important enough to have the senior nurses come to find me at regular intervals to give me my medication and, second, because I liked the feeling it gave me before it hurled me into sleep. Woozy, giggly, relaxed, a bit like having a drink but without the sick feeling alcohol always gave me. I always threw up if I had alcohol, never if I had barbiturates. I had discovered something rather fun, I thought, and well worth a few nightmares.

Wanting to please led me further and further away from telling the staff, and particularly the doctors, anything truthful about myself. I thought it would bore them dreadfully if I admitted that my only problem, apart from an overactive thyroid gland, was that I had had a miserable time as a child, and had come, over the years, to hate and fear my family – except, perhaps Lionel – so much that I couldn't bear to be in the same room with any of them, especially my mother because she was so very manipulative and such a – well, such a liar.

That is what I should have said, but I never did.

I now think it possible that had I been truthful I might have been rehabilitated sooner. They would have seen, as Dr Liebel had, that my prime need was for treatment for the thyroid disease, and that although there was a psychological overlay to the physical illness, as there always is with any illness, I was not in fact psychiatrically ill. I wasn't depressed, I wasn't manic, I did not have schizophrenia. The nearest thing they could come to for a diagnosis (and, of course, I peered into my notes and charts whenever I could) was 'Acute Chronic Anxiety State'.

I knew that meant I was anxious most of the time, with episodes of the anxiety getting much worse from time to time. An overactive thyroid of course fed it. Essentially the psychological problem was that I was just very unhappy in a situation over which I had no control, and looking for ways to deal with that unhappiness. What I needed was treatment for the damned thyroid, which would banish the anxiety, and almost certainly that meant surgery, since I had responded badly to the only available anti-thyroid drug at that time. That I chose bad ways for getting over my unhappiness was unfortunate to say the least.

And very bad ways they were. I began to imitate other patients – mainly, I have to confess, because I was jealous of any attention anybody else had. I had landed amid a group of people who were nice to me and liked me and wanted to care for me, and then some other damned patient made a fuss and dragged them away from me.

I reacted like an infant faced with a new sibling. All ill people do this to an extent. They regress to a form of childhood behaviour, and become helpless, clinging, weepy, demanding. That's where all the jokes about men dying of colds in the nose come from. I regressed in spades. I began to copy the behaviour of my rivals, most of whom had really worrying psychiatric illnesses, throwing things, having tantrums, going into prolonged sulks, refusing to speak to anyone at all and, the one that really worried them, refusing to eat.

As a result of that, and my stubborn refusal to be tempted by even the nicest of dishes, they told me, regretfully, that they would have to tube-feed me. I didn't believe them. That was what the police did to suffragettes: I'd read all about the Pankhursts and their friends long ago. It wasn't the sort of thing that would be done by these nurses and doctors I knew and trusted.

Another twenty-four hours without food or drink and I had given them no option. I was tied down with heavy straps on a trolley, had my head held back by ungentle hands and an ice-cold tube as thick as a hosepipe shoved up my nose and, with me gagging horribly, past my throat and into my stomach. The sense of fullness that followed was disgusting but at least they had given me a hefty dose of barbiturate at the same time as the high-calorie, high-vitamin mixture and, almost immediately after the tube was pulled out of my stomach – and I could feel every inch of the huge thing – and from my stinging, running, horribly hurting throat and nose, I slept.

It got worse. I developed, obviously, a reputation as a troublemaker and 'acter-up', a common phrase used for any behaviour unadmired by the staff. My original nice nurses and doctors moved on to new jobs and a different crowd came. They were much less interested in me and I became even more miserable.

The refusal-to-eat episode happened again, and again, even though I knew what the outcome would be. Was I trying to punish myself? I don't know. I only know that I was unhappy and fearful of being sent home, and 'acting-up' both ensured I wasn't fit to be discharged and took my mind off my misery.

Once when I threw up immediately after being force-fed – and it had been an accident, by no means self-induced, as they accused me – they were furious and swept me off to the dreaded tubs.

These were used, they said, to soothe agitated people. A row of four very large iron bathtubs standing on higher than average legs, all with extra water inlets round their sides and extra outlets along the bottom, stood in a dismal row in a dimly lit room that had all the ambience of a cheap Turkish bath but none of the charm. The room smelled of chlorine, Johnson's baby oil and excreta. There were fans blowing damp hot air in all directions so the smells were thrown at you and there was, particularly horrible to my mind, a constant trickle of tinkly, reedy, violin-mawkish Muzak played at just below the level at which it could be properly heard and just above the level where the sound of it could drive you really mad.

People who were manic and screaming, or swooping about singing at the tops of their voices and refusing to keep away from the windows – which though barred were still dangerous to the vulnerable – and who couldn't be controlled in any other way, were brought here. So were the deeply depressed who needed to be on suicide watch, which was easier to do in the tubs than anywhere else apparently – I learned a lot from eavesdropping on every possible conversation among the staff – and so were those like me who needed to be taught a lesson.

They stripped me off completely – modesty meant nothing here and no one tried to respect it – and, wearing great plastic-coated gloves, the nurses, two at a time, and maybe a third if I was being extra awkward, smothered me in baby oil. It might have been a little heavier duty than that but that was what it smelled like to me. Cloying, sweetish, nasty. And degrading.

Then – and from my point of view, this could be fun – they had to get me into a bath in which the warm water was already running and which was filled almost to the brim. It was too tempting. I was slippery with oil, and though they were now in towelling gloves to improve their grip and were covered in plastic aprons and so forth, I managed to wriggle and make a great splashing performance of slipping out of their hands into a tub and – straight under the water.

This terrified them. They needed to use the tubs to control difficult patients but if someone managed to get her head under the water for even a second the nursing staff went into overdrive. I had heard that they had once lost a patient who was so determined to die that she had put her head into a basin of water and deliberately inhaled enough to kill herself.

I don't believe this was true. It doesn't sound possible, knowing what I have since learned of the way the human respiratory system works, but there it was. The tale was in the fabric of the hospital and everyone, especially the staff on duty in the tubs, seemed to believe it.

After the fighting and silly games, I had to let them do the rest of their job, which was to tie a great heavy tarpaulin over the tub with me in it, with a soft-lined collar that went round my neck and a small padded section behind on which to rest my head. There was a small flap of canvas that acted as a sort of waist-high hammock in the water and arms and legs were tied down with buckled straps inside the bath so that there could be no kicking or splashing or attempts to get out.

And that was it. There you lay, in a bath of regularly changing water, kept at a constant temperature, peeing into the water, even defecating if you had to, until they deemed you compliant enough to be let out.

I look back on this therapy, for so it was labelled, and I wonder. Properly used it could have been beneficial, I think. I know that whenever I had been miserable in Cirencester the best cure had been to escape to the swimming-pool so that I could lie weightless in always forgiving, always friendly water. Once I was in a place where I had access to a proper bathtub, like Epsom and Deal, my idea of heaven had been to stretch out in silken, scented water and snooze, read, listen to music and just relax until I was as wrinkled as a passion fruit. Yet here, in what was supposed to be a hospital for treating unhappy ill people, water was seen as a punishment. Why did they not see its full potential? Talking to unhappy or disturbed patients in that sort of damp, hot, womb-like environment could surely have been the best sort of psychotherapy. But it never was used that way. It was just a threat.

I was luckier than some patients. I was never given insulin-coma treatment. For this, patients, usually those diagnosed with schizophrenia, were injected with massive doses of insulin, then allowed to slip into coma. They were kept there as long as the doctors and nurses dared – it's a life-threatening state, after all – then brought out of it with high-sugar drips. They sometimes had reactions in the small hours and were always being given special meals, much as I still was, which caused some jealousy, but I don't think any patient would have chosen the treatment. And, to this day, I wonder what the long-term effects of it were on those patients. There is a price that many sections of the body – eyes, blood vessels, heart – have to pay every time diabetics slip into coma. That is why their treatment ensures they never or rarely do. Yet these people were deliberately put into prolonged insulin comas three times a week for three weeks on the trot. I shudder to remember it.

Equally distressing to me were those women who drifted regularly through the ward with shaven heads and rough scars on their scalps from brain surgery for their psychiatric illness. It was fashionable at the time to carry out these essentially brutal attacks, lobotomies, on brain tissue, separating pathways that were suspected on the most slender evidence of being involved in the sick behaviour of the patients, usually those diagnosed with schizophrenia.

I can see one of them still: Alison, middle class, with rich, adoring but desperate parents, who only wanted her to be normal. She had been an extraordinary presence on the ward, lively, poetic, singing absurdly rhymed songs she wrote herself, unpredictable, of course, and in need of constant watching but wonderfully funny and clearly enjoying her life, even though to onlookers she was patently quite mad. They sent her for a lobotomy and she came back grey, shuffling, scarred, and didn't know any of us, her old bedmates. They took her away to the State Hospital to stay there for ever after with all the others for whom the operation had been a dreadful experiment and total failure.

And then there was another 'therapy' they used for the recalcitrant and noisy. Cold Wet Packs, CWP, it was called. Patients were stripped, oiled and then wrapped in sheets wrung out in ice water, and pulled dreadfully tight. But it worked. You would lie there totally helpless, unable to do more than wrinkle your nose, looking exactly like a modern Egyptian mummy. As the pack warmed up with the heat of your body, then dried on you, you would get very, very sleepy, then go out like a light for up to twelve hours and wake up very peaceable indeed. I have been told there are spas in Germany where they use a modified version as an expensive beauty treatment.

And, yes, on one occasion I pushed the nurse on duty so far with my cheekiness that I ended up there too. Not surprisingly, some restless, sleepless patients would ask for a CWP to help them settle for their night. But that sort of self-assessment was never welcome and they never did get one on request. Some, however, asked for – indeed, begged for – electroconvulsive therapy, ECT. And they would be listened to.

This has had a bad press over the years and it could be nasty in the old days, when I was in Toronto. It was given without anaesthetic, the whole head was involved and the resultant terror of the treatment, plus loss of memory caused by it, made many patients very unhappy about it.

Today, when general anaesthesia is always used, and only half the head is involved in the electric shock with much less risk of memory loss, it is used for the very ill or those for whom no other therapy works. And work it does. I've seen its value both by observing fellow patients long ago and by nursing people with depression, long after my own brush with patient status. Some of them used to do so well, climbing out of their pits of appalling black despair, that they knew when they next needed it and asked for it. And that happens today with patients who have depression and do not respond to modern treatments, just as it did in Toronto back in the late forties.

I try to look back on those days, and those doctors and nurses, with fairness. They had so little in their armoury to help people whose lives were made a misery by psychiatric illness. Only barbiturates, which were terrifyingly addictive and limited in their clinical range. No anti-schizophrenia drugs. No anti-depressants, no tranquillisers, major or minor. Although in some patient circles today there is much sneering at drug-based therapies for the psychiatrically ill the truth is that they have revolutionised life for the better for millions, and emptied the long-stay hospitals. Despite that, I think we could do with just a few today for those who are so battered by their illness and time that they need what has been lost from the care of the mentally ill: the concept of asylum.

Toronto Psychiatric Hospital provided that for me for fifteen long months. I did not step out of doors for the whole of that time, getting my fresh air, such as it was, from open windows. I had known nothing of what had been happening in the world outside since I was seventeen and now I was eighteen, well on my way to nineteen. I suppose I had missed what should have been my fun years, meeting fellas, getting around, building a career, but there it was. Yes, I had been locked up, but I had felt safe.

And then one day a new doctor came to look after me, and after a lot of examinations and tests he said, 'You shouldn't be here, should you? You're thyrotoxic. It's the cause of all your symptoms. You need surgery. Then you can start living again.'

I know I lost every bit of colour, and then my face flooded with it. 'I can't – I mean, who would pay? My family won't, you know, you must have seen that in my notes and even if they would, I mean, how much would it be? They – and anyway—'

'Hey, hey, come down out of the trees! Of course you can't get it done here! I know what it's like. They can be right bastards about the children of immigrants like you. They only want the healthy ones, and if any of them get sick and expensive they say, "Send 'em back to the UK. Now they've got this National Health Service back home in the Old Country let 'em get their operations and medicines there. Why should we pay? We got enough sick folk of our own, why should we pay for these people?" That's what they say over there in Ottawa. "Make whichever shipping line brought 'em here take 'em back and let us get on with the nice healthy immigrants who work and pay taxes. We don't want these sick ones."'

I wasn't sure what I was hearing. 'Go home?' I said. 'Have an operation at home in *London*?' I was so agitated that 'London' came out as a squeak.

'There is a way,' he said. ' You may not like it, but there is a way. It's up to you. Now, listen . . .'

Twenty-three

It had been decided that I would obtain no further benefit from extending my already long stay under the roof of the Toronto Psychiatric Hospital. My main problem, they said, was an overactive thyroid gland, possibly caused and certainly complicated by personal stresses of various domestic kinds over which they, as psychiatrists, had no control. The time had come, therefore, to clear the bed I occupied and give it to a more interesting – ahem – worthy case. TPH was, after all, a university hospital.

Dr McKenzie was considered by his colleagues the best person to deal with me and my thyroid, so he told me. In fact, he told me all about everything, because he thought patients had the right to know about their condition and treatment and should not be treated like half-wits incapable of comprehending medical information. 'Everyone can understand if it's explained properly,' he said.

A doctor out of his time, indeed. His was a medical stance – indeed, philosophy – that is widely accepted today, after many painful years of trying to teach and encourage it, in order to break down and remove the medical arrogance of centuries. And there he was, in 1950, a fully fledged whole-person, patient-centred, communicating doctor *circa* 2002!

The plan he had made for me was a simple one. I would have to be transferred to the State Hospital in Oshawa – I stiffened and he said, 'I told you you wouldn't like this bit. But listen.' I listened – so that the health authorities in Ottawa could be made to see that I was not expected to get any better.

'As long as you stay here, there is a belief that you might turn out to be well, after all. We get all sorts of people here who are severely mentally ill when they arrive but who do get better.'

I knew that. I had seen and become friendly with a couple of new mothers in my ward, who had descended into severe post-birth psychosis, but who had eventually got well enough to go home to their families.

'As soon as we transfer you, your case will become live. That is, Ottawa will make a deal with Cunard – they brought you? Yes – with Cunard to take you back.'

'Who pays for my ticket?'

'Cunard does.' I opened my eyes wide and he laughed. 'I told you. It's the deal they make with the immigration authorities here. If they bring in anyone who has to be deported, they have to carry the can for it.'

It was the first time I'd heard the word. Deported. I rolled it round in my mind. Deported. It sounded horrible. I didn't say so but I think my face did, because he put out a hand and patted mine. 'You can handle it,' he said matter-of-factly, and I thought, He's right. I can. To go home I can handle anything.

'Now, who is there in the UK who'll take you on?' He looked at me very directly. 'This is crucial. If you have relatives or friends willing to take responsibility for you, then fine. If not, you'll be taken straight to a psychiatric hospital when you get to the UK. And I have to tell you that it can be bloody hell getting yourself uncertified once it's been done. If you're deported, you'll be certified here. I told you it's no fun but there it is. If you want to go home and you can't pay your own way, and I know you can't, then this is your only hope. Undignified and so forth, I can't deny, but it could be the way to a decent future for you. There sure as hell isn't one here for you. You mightn't even survive long. They're not going to pay for costly surgery for you here.'

I understood and thought hard, but I knew I had no choice. I hadn't been in touch with them since I left London, but there had been so many years when I hadn't been in touch. The point was, there was no one else.

'Grandma,' I said, 'and my auntie Nancy. They'll look after me. And once I'm home and I've had the operation I can start my nursing training and then I won't be any trouble to them and—'

'One thing at a time,' he said. 'Walk first. Full names and addresses, please.'

And so it was. He was a rock, that man. He knew exactly how to tell me what was to happen to me in a way that made it possible for me to accept it. The whole process took, it seemed to me, for ever. I was transferred to the State Hospital in Oshawa, which was exactly like the one I had visited in Epsom, all modern brick pavilions and glorious grounds, with typical Canadian additions such as a full-size bowling alley and a baseball diamond.

I hated it there and I had to stay for several months, even spending my birthday there. That made me really miserable. I found the other patients impossible to get on with, for many of them were, indeed, severely ill. Although they put me into a low-security pavilion it was an oppressive atmosphere, much more so than TPH had been. Here the staff seemed to relish their roles as controllers and watchers, and would rattle the great bunches of keys they wore at their waists with noisy pleasure, like prison warders rather than nurses.

Many, if not most, of the staff were grim-faced and hateful indeed. I learned early to keep my mouth shut and to stay in line. I had only to hold on a few weeks longer, only a few weeks, and the deportation order would come through and I would go home. And even when the weeks pleated into months I used the same mantra to keep me going. Only a few weeks more.

Dr McKenzie came to see me late in the summer, with what seemed to me to be hateful advice. I should, he said, make the effort to go and live in my family home, just until the order was made. It would show goodwill, he said, and, more importantly it would be a just-in-case.

'Just in case of what?'

'Just in case your grandmother refuses to take you. Have you heard from her yet?'

I felt cold with fear. I hadn't considered the possibility that she would refuse. How could I? But she was old now, wasn't she? I tried to think how old, but I couldn't. She had always been very secretive about her age. But she had to be over sixty, surely. In 1950 that was more than old. It was elderly. Maybe she'd be too frail to agree to take me.

'Auntie Nancy will manage it, though,' I said, thinking aloud, 'even if Grandma can't.'

'Well,' he said, 'to be on the safe side go home to your family for a while. I'll talk to them, see they understand. Then if your family fails to turn up trumps for you, and there's no one else in England to take responsibility for you, you'll be able to argue you were coping all right before you left here and therefore won't need to go to hospital in England.'

It was good advice but taking it was hell.

In the event they behaved amazingly well, I thought. My mother was all smiles and fussing over the arrangements she had made to give me a bedroom of my own. There was a slice of space split off the main living room that became mine. She'd even put a radio in there for me, with long-wave on it so I could listen to the BBC when I wanted to. I heard every episode of *Take It From Here*, which I think kept me sane.

My sisters were friendly too, as far as I recall, but I have to say some of it is now lost in memory's black holes again. I can't recall if my father was actually there when I came back to Mount Dennis from Oshawa that late summer, though I know he turned up for a while, then vanished again.

They were always like that, those two. Either parted and miserable (well, *she* was, I never saw what he was like when they were apart, but he always came back, which is an indicator) or fighting and shrieking at each other – and I have a sudden visual image, bright as the morning sunshine pouring through the windows of the kitchen in Mount Dennis. She is screaming furiously, throwing plates at him, and I am cowering by the door and weeping in real terror, and that makes them stop.

But only for a few seconds and then she is off again, and her words are horribly clear. This row is all about their sex life and I really, *really* do not want to know. I put my hands over my ears, shut my eyes tight, push the back door open and run out, falling over the step as I go because my eyes are closed. And that is all I recall, I am glad to say.

I get a letter from the authorities to say that I will receive further letters in due course regarding my departure from Canada. I am to confirm with them the addresses of my UK contacts. I phone Dr McKenzie in a panic. Is something going wrong? He reassures me that this is normal bureaucracy and advises patience. All will be well.

I discover later that he immediately phoned Ottawa and raised hell over my case and they promised to get a move on. It is now late September and they will have me out of the country before the end of the year, they tell him. Wisely he does not tell me this, in case they let us down again. But he phones often and reassures me. Lovely man.

Suddenly the family loads me with presents. Even Lionel, who has avoided me since I returned, I think – or is it just that he is a normal ten-year-old schoolboy with better things to do than hang around elderly sisters? Anyway, on the present-giving day he is there.

It is an odd day in other ways. I have had a job for a few weeks, selling modern art prints in Eaton's, College Street, the posh department store that shares Toronto with its nearest rival Simpson's.

I am very successful at the job because, I think, of my rather BBC-ish English accent picked up in my City of London schooldays and somehow retained. It makes me sound classy to Canadian ears, or so the manager of the department says. (Me? Classy? If they only knew!) However, it is true that if I tell a customer a painting is a good one, they believe me, and they buy. I am popular with the manager.

That afternoon a young man comes into the department and buys a present for his mother. I can still see it, one of Picasso's Blue Period paintings of a boy, a lovely piece, and I say, only half joking, 'I shall miss it, it's a favourite of mine.'

He looks at me for the first time, then says, 'Haven't I seen you at the Sir Ernest Macmillan concerts?'

These concerts are held all through the summer under the bleachers at the sports stadium, a very canny Toronto-ish use of space. Great classical music for just a few cents, if you don't mind sitting way up at the back; and for music it doesn't really matter where you sit.

'Yes' I say. 'You could have seen me. I go a lot.'

'Great! I can't manage tomorrow's concert,' he says. 'Do take my ticket so it isn't wasted,' and he goes away and leaves me with a ticket for the very front row where you can actually see the sweat on the performers' faces.

I am tickled to bits about this because I have so little money. All I earn has to go into the family kitty, and I get back just enough for car fares, work lunches and occasional tickets for a film show. Now this!

And then they give me presents. They take me into my room, all of them, and, yes, my father is there, all beams and big laughs and jokes, and they show me the presents spread out on my bed.

Three matching suitcases, hard-sided and certainly not cardboard, all pretty and smart in beige and maroon.

Clothes. Two suits, one in white barathea and very handsome, and another in grey worsted. And dresses, underwear, several pairs of nylon stockings and a full-length bright blue cloth coat that my mother used to wear but which fits me because it has been lengthened.

I am struck dumb by all this and my immediate thought is: Who did they rob to get it?

I can't help it. These are the parents who never have any money, even though they both work now. These are the parents who once, not all that long ago, went on a trip to Niagara Falls in a car they hired and when they came back without it, but with their pockets full of extra cash, pretended to us they had forgotten to bring it back. And then assured us it didn't matter because the company'll soon find it.

This is the father who regularly pinches his children's savings from their jobs if he can get his hands on the cash. This is the father who, to the best of my admittedly poor memory, has never given me a present in his life. Yet there is all this . . .

My mother gives me the reason for it all, eventually, and I feel . . . not better, precisely, but less uncomfortable because at least I understand why they did it, even if it doesn't explain where they got the stuff from.

'They won't be able to sneer at me when you get there now, will they? I wasn't going to have you turning up on their doorstep looking like a waif and stray,' she says.

'Thanks,' I say. What else could I say? The motive for my farewell gifts is exactly what I would expect of my mother. A present to her daughter, not for her daughter's delight but to adorn her own reputation with her hated in-laws.

Ah, well, I think, trying to be philosophical, *plus ça change, plus c'est la même chose*. I consider for a moment being hugely noble and honourable, since I have these deep doubts about the source of their largesse. I would like to push it all aside and cry, 'Take it all away! I will manage as I am, with my old cardboard suitcase!' But I am not strong enough for such a gesture. Dammit, I need those clothes. And the cases are very pretty. But to this day I fret over where the presents came from.

Later that evening I had a sudden thought. I said, 'How can you be sure I will be going to Grandma, anyway?'

My father answers before she has a chance to. 'Nancy wrote. Last week. Or was it the week before?'

I light up. 'She did? What did she say?'

'She'll meet you at Liverpool with Max. Right, Betty?'

I look at my mother and she is clearly annoyed with my father. More than annoyed. She is furious. But 'Now you've ruined the surprise,' is all she says, and my father looks at her properly for the first time since the conversation began and realises what he's done.

'Oh, well,' he says uncomfortably, 'it wouldn't have been as good a surprise as your presents, would it, Berrela?'

I say nothing. I daren't, for fear of the words that might come out of my mouth.

She had known how anxious I was about the forthcoming journey, about what could have happened to me if my London relatives had refused to accept me, because Dr McKenzie had spelled it out to her very clearly when he had sent me to Oshawa. She knew that what I feared could happen to me without Grandma and Nancy's help, yet she hadn't told me of Nancy's wonderful reassuring letter and given me the peace of mind I so badly needed to get me through the wait for my departure. I don't think I ever hated her more than I did that night.

I finally leave Canada in the second week of January 1951, with a passage booked on the MV *Aquitania*. I am picked up at the house in Mount Dennis by a social worker who is to take me to the train.

She is obviously shocked to find that I am alone in the house with no one to say goodbye. I explain I am alone because everyone in the family is at school or work.

I do not explain that my father has gone off again after yet another fight. Nor that my mother had been the last to say goodbye to me. She had stood on the doorstep pulling a hat and earmuffs on against the bitter Canadian winter and had said only, 'Be lucky and be careful.' No hug, nothing.

She had gone walking down the road to the corner, carefully avoiding the half-melted slush in the gutters as though it was the most important thing in the world.

And I had watched her all the way, until she turned the corner and vanished. She never looked back.

I never saw her again.

Twenty-four

During the long and desperately tedious train journey to Halifax, whence the *Aquitania* had to sail because of the ice on the St Lawrence, and under the watchful eye of my social worker chaperone, I did a lot of daydreaming about how life would be from now on.

The first almost twenty years of my life – I was just seven days away from my twentieth birthday – had not been much fun, to put a gloss on it. There had been some things that gave me pleasure, books in particular, but taking it all round being me had been a miserable business.

However, this was not necessarily a bad thing, I told myself, staring out at the blank Québecois landscape sliding past. Obviously no one can have a life that is blissful all the time. There have to be bad times as well as good, and when the bad times come you need to have a bit of stamina to deal with them. And when better to develop that stamina than in the bad times? Misery makes you stoical in my experience, I told the passing view, and that can be useful when you need it. Better than making a huge fuss, anyway.

I remembered something Grandma had taught me to say, long ago, when I got excited about a new toy she had given me that I then dropped and shattered and became broken-hearted. 'The best four words in the world, Dolly, are "This Too Will Pass." You have to say it when nice things happen and when nasty things happen too. They help you to remember that nothing lasts for ever.'

I remembered being cross when she first said it to me, thinking it was silly, but I was only six or so at the time. Now I know she was right. It also came to mean that, on balance, the best time to be miserable and have bad things happen to you was when you were young, because first of all you're strong then, and second, anything that happens after that has got to seem lovely.

So now, once I was freed from my censorious companion (who was there, I decided in one of my fancier flights, to make sure I didn't steal anything on my way out of Canada – 'Hide the spoons, Québec, here she comes', which was not unreasonable, perhaps, with parents like mine) I thought I would have a peaceful journey home. Auntie Nancy and Uncle Max would be there to meet me, and then I would go to Grandma's flat, and then – but I could see no further. It didn't matter. I was going *home*.

In fact, the whole journey was blighted with watchful companions. At Halifax, after spending the greater part of a day and night locked up in their version of Ellis Island (and I mean locked up: there were iron bars on the doors and windows), I boarded the *Aquitania* and at once found myself held by two uniformed hospital Sisters who spoke to me in English accents, which was some comfort in an odd situation.

I was so startled I said and did nothing but let them take me where they wanted to, which was a special pair of heavily locked cabins off a fairly high deck aft where, I was told, I was to spend the whole journey. My food would be brought to me, and that was that.

I remembered the sea stories I had read and said, in amazement, 'Am I in the brig, then?' A crewman, who was also walking alongside me and whom I had not yet noticed, laughed and said, 'No, love. The brig's a sight rougher than what this is. You got your own bathroom 'ere, you 'ave! But I suppose you ain't far wrong, at that.'

Indeed I wasn't. The two hospital sisters had come out from Southampton General Hospital to escort me home, because that was what Cunard did to any of its customers who had the misfortune to be rejected by the Government of Canada on medical grounds. Whatever their problem, they were clearly considered unfit to move about the decks and saloons of a Cunard liner at sea.

They did worse, those officials in Ottawa. During the journey to Liverpool I was able to see my passport, which I wasn't allowed to hold, of course. One of the sisters, who was a kind woman and didn't approve of the way the officials had behaved, showed it to me.

My passport was stamped, in large letters on the Canadian page, DEPORTED: INSANE. APPEAL DISMISSED.

I was mortified. 'I didn't appeal!' I told Sister. 'I was aching to get away and come home to London, and I wasn't insane, I've got an overactive thyroid, that's all. Do I seem insane to you?'

'Whatever insane is, love, no. You're just someone needing some looking after. Which you'll get at home now and no worry about the costs. That's really why they don't want to keep you there in Toronto, isn't it? I've seen your notes. But it's all right now. We've got the NHS and no one ever has to worry about doctor's or hospital bills ever again.'

And she chattered to me for a long time about the new system and I was grateful, because I wanted to know how my future working life would be in the NHS, and also because it took my mind off the humiliation I felt about my situation.

I would never be able to travel anywhere, ever again, because of that disfigured, blighted passport. How could I? How could they have lied so? And how could they treat ill people so? Whatever my diagnosis was, physical or psychiatric illness, whatever my condition, they were wicked to treat me like a robber or some other dangerous criminal who had to be put behind iron bars in ports and locked in special quarters on ships.

As I said, I had nowhere to go but up, and up I went. Max and Nancy, Peter's brother and sister, the two best relations anyone ever had and amazingly good to me, were waiting for me in Liverpool, and came aboard to take over from the sisters full responsibility for me. I was never so happy to see anyone in my life. Nancy, small and plump with black curls and very bright eyes, and so good-natured that she was smiling and showing real pleasure at seeing me, rather than looking tired and strained and anxious at what she might be taking on with me; and Max, who was a much better-looking version of his older brother, my father, exuding good sense and reliability, also smiling and happy to see me. I wept, I think, out of sheer gratitude and bliss. I had escaped, I was home; everything from now on would be roses and happiness and fun.

Well, sort of. There was first the matter of my thyroid to be dealt with. Grandma, scorning the shiny new NHS, took me to the private consulting rooms of a great thyroid specialist and I was most upset. Why pay when she need not?

'I choose to,' she said, rather grandly, but once he had seen me, said I needed hospital admission at once and probably surgery when I was fit enough for it, she changed her mind.

The surgeon was very brisk about it: 'My dear lady, your grand-daughter would not be happy alone in a private room. At her young age, she needs company! So why spend the money when you need not? Save it for a convalescent holiday. I will admit her to Fitzgerald Ward at St George's at Hyde Park Corner on the NHS, and I assure you she will do very well.'

I did. The hospital was a comfortable, beautifully run place, with excellent nursing care. How could it be otherwise when every Sister was so devoted to her ward and her patients that she not only aban-doned her own identity to take on the name of her ward as was common practice – so I was under the care of Sister Fitzgerald – but also lived in a flat that ran off it? That made her available for all emergencies and for constant supervision. It was comforting thing for her patients to see her coming round late at night, shaded torch in hand, to check on us all just before going to bed herself. Lady of the Lamp *circa* 1951.

I used to lie there listening to the traffic at Hyde Park Corner and feel so grateful for the newborn NHS that made it possible for me to be there without anxiety. And now, whenever I drive past the Lanesborough Hotel into which St George's Hospital was transmogrified or go into its sumptuous interior for a party or to lunch, I remember Sister Fitzgerald and her shaded torch and I'm grateful all over again.

The operation was done some eight days after I was admitted, after several tests and enforced bed rest. I had no idea it was to be done on the day it was, because the system was to 'snatch' the thyroid, since it was considered safer that way. That is, the operation was done without giving the patient more than an hour or so warning at most. Sometimes they were sedated without their knowledge.

With one of the main features of the disease being over-anxiety and a rapid pulse, a patient who knew too far in advance that she was to have the operation was likely to fret about it. Excessive pre-operative anxiety could lead to excessive bleeding during surgery and a host of other complications. So 'snatching' (or 'stealing', a term others used) the thyroid from comparatively relaxed patients gave them a better chance. People could die of the effects of runaway tachycardia – fast heartbeat – so it was a legitimate action.

I guessed, unfortunately, and spoiled their snatch. I hadn't had any injections since admission, and one that made me woozy was a dead giveaway. But I only had a little while to think about the operation because the sedative took over fast and they got me to theatre quickly.

I woke to discover that I had not only lost enough of my thyroid to bring my pulse down to a reasonably normal rate and get rid of the trembling, the sweating, the 'intestinal hurry' and the Hamlet sensation in my chest and belly, but also my voice. I remember the doctors and nurses peering down my throat with torches and mirrors as I struggled to come out of the anaesthetic and trying to make me 'Sing out!' but all I could produce was a croak like a cross between Tallulah Bankhead and a bullfrog. And nothing they or I did could improve it.

I had always had a fairly ordinary female type of voice, of medium pitch, a little on the high side. But during the operation a nerve was severed that should not have been; it was the recurrent laryngeal, and severing it caused one of my vocal cords to become paralysed. Now, instead of having two of them lying side by side in my larynx – voice box – widening and narrowing on demand to give various cadences, all I had was one utterly still vocal cord, and what are known as the 'false cords' nearby. They, too, can help with speech, if necessary.

I eventually trained myself to use my remaining vocal cord and also my false cords to give me back speech in a voice that no longer croaked, but was a good deal deeper and likely to become husky under pressure like fatigue or illness. Today patients with this problem will be referred to speech therapists, of course. In 1951, I don't think there were any in the NHS.

After the operation I only ever saw the senior registrar. I never again saw the surgeon, and one of the junior, rather chatterbox doctors told me it was because he was so upset about having destroyed my voice. I am actually grateful to him for his moment of surgical ineptitude: the result has been a most useful voice, because when I started broadcasting some six or seven years later, I found myself in possession of a very distinctive timbre that made my voice memorable and me with it.

The only problem was that after every broadcast – usually on *Woman's Hour* in the early days – I used to get kind, anxious letters from nice doctors and nurses advising me to see an ENT consultant about my hoarseness. They would fear I had a cancer of the larynx, though they rarely said that. I would assure them that I was fully aware of my laryngeal paralysis and they really need not worry. But I appreciated the thought all the same.

I also found that my voice acted like a man magnet. I plumped up a good deal after the operation, as is often the case with thyroid overactivity once cured, and though I wasn't massive I was, well, certainly a bit on the magnificent side. I used to describe myself as 'a Rubens inadvertently clothed'. I would tell chaps who tried to chat me up on the phone that if their taste ran to Dresden-shepherdess types they should go search elsewhere. But there were some men I met who quite liked the combination of magnificence and huskiness, so I wasn't left entirely alone.

One other outcome of that operation: my daughter, born almost ten years after I had that operation, with two perfectly normal and active vocal cords, by the age of sixteen or so sounded so exactly like me in pitch, tone and timbre of voice that people always thought she was me on the phone. It came in handy, she said, for booking 'hot' theatre tickets and over-popular restaurants . . .

I left hospital and went home to Grandma, feeling like a different person. It was wonderful not to feel ill and tired and anxious, and instead to have sudden surges of real energy that made me want to go swimming or running. Grandma at once suggested a holiday to recuperate in Vichy in France. I told her I suffered from seasickness and, anyway, Bournemouth would be much nicer – I knew she had old cronies there in the various hotels and loved playing cards with them – so that held off the passport problem at least for the present.

Sooner or later, I knew, I would have to deal with that damned lying document. It made me feel sick and guilty, almost like blackmail bait, having it tucked away deep in my chest of drawers. Nancy had given it back to me without examining it, being a sensible, honourable lady and seeing it as my property.

After the holiday in Bournemouth, which was like spending a couple of weeks inside a Terence Rattigan play with a bit of Noël Coward thrown in, I wanted to start nurse training. I had bought the nursing journals, looked carefully at all the ads for students, knew exactly where I wanted to go and why.

No, said Grandma. Rest first. The staff at St George's had told her I was to wait until at least July and lead a simple, quiet life in the interim. But this was just February in Festival of Britain year when there was so much going on and so much excitement, after the austerity years, that no one could possibly live a quiet life in London. Certainly not at the age of twenty!

I got a job as a filing clerk in a government office. Dull but easy, short hours and excellent pay, which Grandma insisted I kept in its entirety. I felt very rich. She and Nancy still had the dress shops in Letchworth and Hitchin, with Max having some input too, although I think he was most busy with his own clothing factory by then.

Anyway, between them they decided I needed more clothes, and Max made me a lovely suit and also a grey skirt with a matching long coat, which was all the rage. Grandma and Nancy chipped in with dresses from the shops and underwear and also, to my great joy, took me to a cousin of my grandmother's who was a Bond Street dressmaker for a made-to-measure, full-length, full-skirted evening dress, strapless in true Hollywood style, with a long stole, all in sky blue tulle, to wear at the very smart wedding of the daughter of a family friend. I never felt so glamorous in all my life, although I don't think I looked anything other than what I was: a rather unsophisticated barely-out-of-her-teens *ingénue*.

But I was happy whatever I did or did not look like, and I spent evening after evening at the theatre, seeing every play on Shaftesbury Avenue and everywhere else. I remember *The Little Hut* and *Seagulls over Sorrento* and the *Lyric Revue* and Ivor Novello's *Gay's the Word* and *Waters of the Moon*, with marvellous Edith Evans and, joy of joys, *Caesar and Cleopatra* and *Antony and Cleopatra* at the St James Theatre with the Oliviers and Robert Helpmann, and Alec Guinness as Hamlet at the New Theatre and everything that happened at the Old Vic, where I drooled from the gods at the likes of Alec Clunes – years later I took part in *Have I Got News For You*, the TV show, with his son Martin – and generally wallowed in Shakespeare.

And then, of course, there was all the fun of the South Bank where the new Festival Hall preened itself beside the Dome of Discovery and the Skylon, which Noël Coward dismissed as 'that permanent erection on the South Bank'. I wandered in the Festival Gardens at Battersea Park, and through the tree walk that Ronald Searle had devised, and laughed at the Guinness clock every time I saw it. I went to the zoo and St Paul's, to the Tower of London and Madame Tussaud's, to Hampstead Heath and Portobello Road, Regent's Park and Petticoat Lane, riding my lovely red buses everywhere and sitting right up at the front of the top deck.

In other words, I behaved like a tourist in my own city and I was blissfully, utterly happy. It was a feeling I had never known and I wallowed in it, and could re-create at will, just by trying something new.

Grandma, to her eternal credit, accepted this late-adolescent incursion into her tranquil life, with normally just her resident companion, and didn't seem to mind how often I was out, as long as I told her when I'd be back.

Max and his very young – only six years my senior – beautiful wife Muriel and their small son Jeffrey were always willing to welcome me when I wanted to visit them.

Nancy listened to me chatter about all my comings and goings, and her husband, the silent Louis, just smiled and said nothing. As usual.

They all seemed to look on indulgently as I picked up the threads of a hitherto wasted life and plaited them into a thick, warm fabric that I can wrap around me to this day, just by remembering the perfect summer of 1951, the summer when I discovered that families can be all right and not always a sick, miserable threat hanging over your head and filling you with anxiety.

Then July came, and I was allowed to start out on the ambition that had kept me going these past five years or more. The weather was foul, raining every day. And I loved it.

Twenty-five

The Royal Northern Hospital in London sits almost at the foot of the hill that leads northwards up to the Archway, Highgate and Hampstead, yet manages to seem to be looking down a little loftily on Holloway and Islington, for which borough it stood as a war memorial to the events of 1914 to 1918, away to the south. It is a red-brick, very Edwardian sort of building, and in its heyday was considered an architectural gem, with a famous block of round wards unique in British hospital design at the time.

Nowadays the building has been absorbed into a modern housing project. All the functions of the old hospital have been taken over by the Whittington at the top of the hill. This makes old Northern-trained doctors and nurses, like me, feel slightly uncomfortable. In our snobbish young days we despised the Whittington, referring to it as 'that pile of yellow bricks on Highgate Hill' and dismissing it as much lower class than we were: in pre-NHS days it had been merely a municipal hospital built and supported by local government. The good old *Royal* Northern, like its great friends and colleagues Bart's, St Thomas's, Guy's and so forth, had been a voluntary hospital maintained entirely by charitable gifts, legacies and public subscription. That, we believed, made us vastly superior.

I had chosen RNH as the place where I would spend the next five years at least of my life not, I hope, on snobbish grounds, but precisely because it was not a teaching hospital. This meant it had no undergraduate medical school, although it offered opportunities for postgraduate medical study. I had done my homework carefully, checking the nurse-training systems of all the big London hospitals, and realised quickly that where there were medical students nurses got the dirty end of the stick every time. They were rarely more than mere handmaidens to the scions of Aesculapius and had little opportunity to get their own hands-on experience of tricky medical techniques.

Also, the Northern had been the hospital to which Epsom Cottage Hospital had been linked and to which it sent its cadets to train, so there was a sense of continuity. Finally, Grandma and Nancy lived a mere three-ha'penny bus ride away at Manor House. I could have walked between the two places at a pinch.

It helped, too, that Matron wanted me. I was honest with her. Well, up to a point. I told her I had started as an Epsom cadet under age, due to my excessive enthusiasm. I told her about my long stay at Deal. No problems there. Then I said I had been a cadet in Canada, too, during the past three years, and if she got the impression I had spent all the time I was in Toronto at Grace as a cadet rather than at the psychiatric hospital as a patient I couldn't really be blamed for her misapprehension, I told myself.

Actually, if I had been put to it I would have had to give her the lie direct. One of the Cunard sisters had told me candidly that I should give up all hope of a nursing career because no matron, however needful of nurses, would take on someone with a psychiatric history. Bugger that, I had thought furiously. I will train, no matter what anyone says, I will.

Matron, all unwitting of my mendacity, I thought gleefully, agreed that I should train with her at the RNH. She looked down at me thoughtfully, a rare experience for me. For once I was not the tallest female in the room. I looked back, keeping my face as smooth and uncommunicative as I possibly could, knowing perfectly well that my relationship with this woman was to be one of the most significant in my life in the coming years, and very much wanting it to be a good one. After a moment she managed a wintry smile. 'I hope you will work as hard at your education and at developing your clinical skills as you have worked at trying to impress me this morning, Nurse,' she said. 'Now, go to Sister in the office outside and she will make all the necessary arrangements with you. And I look forward to tranquil, mutually satisfactory years together. Good morning!'

Well, I thought, as I went to see the Assmat, as I was to learn to call the assistant Matron behind her back, at least I know where I am with that one. Eyes everywhere, sharp as a tack, knows a hawk from a handsaw. I liked that better than a rather remote and uninvolved Matron as the one at Deal had been.

That was the start of what was to be the most consistently happy time of my life up to that point. The past few weeks, enjoying London and my new freedom, had been huge fun but had felt temporary, a sort of amusing limbo before real living was to begin.

There had been short bursts of tolerable living, even in the old Hackney days. Once I had learned to read, life had been much easier to cope with, and the beatings, shoutings and nasty things my mother used to say to me when she was in one of her bad moods – about how ugly I was and how no one would ever want to marry me because I was so stupid, lazy and clumsy as well as ugly, and what good was a girl no one wanted to marry? – hurt less when I knew I could escape eventually into a book.

The war years had given me one period of real contentment with the Exley family, the only experience I had ever had of living in a normal, happy household where people were nice to each other and didn't keep telling each other what was wrong about them.

But now it was all to be very, very different. From now on my nearest and dearest were to be the other nurses, my life was to be run by the lofty sisters, Matron's office and Sister Tutor's department. Thinking for myself would be regarded as highly suspect, and something I kept to myself when I did it – which, of course, was often. No system yet devised can change a basic personality entirely!

This new life would also be lived in layers, the subtle and never-changing layers of a strict military-type hierarchy. It was an essential part of hospital life then and mattered hugely to all of us.

And don't think we disliked it.

We wanted it to be that way, because we found that it was comfortable to be part of so powerful a pattern. To know who you were, where you belonged and to whom you could safely turn in times of trouble was deeply reassuring and, in a curious way, imbued us with a sense of power. Others would rely on you, you would rely on others, together we could cope with anything. A lovely feeling to have when your work is literally a matter of life and death, and your hands can bring either rescue or disaster.

Certainly to young us it seemed a great deal better than living a shapeless sort of life dependent entirely on our own conception of what you should do in a particular situation. That is the life most adults have to lead and as a new student, even though I was twenty, I was well aware that I was by no means an adult. It was to be the hierarchical life that would show me how to become one, the sort of adult who can think a problem through, come to a decision about its remedy, then apply it. That takes a lot of self-confidence and it was the way I was to live in those early years of the fifties that gave it to me.

That hierarchy has now vanished. Modern doctors and nurses are on first-name terms, there is little or no deference shown to senior members of staff and there is a great deal of self-reliance demanded of all nurses and doctors when they are working alone. This is tempered by the fact that many today work in sizeable teams in which all problems are shared and decisions are group decisions.

Is this better or worse than the way we were supported and, to an extent, controlled by the hierarchy? Honestly, I don't know, although I do get the impression, when speaking to modern young nurses, that they are rather less content with their professional lives and its rewards than we were.

Be that as it may, I was launched into my place in the hierarchy that wet July morning in 1951. I was to be, for the coming years, totally reliant on the nurses with whom I trained for friendship, support and encouragement, and notably on those in my own training set of around fifteen young women.

We went into the Preliminary Training School for three months before being allowed into the wards, and a new set followed us as soon as we moved out. Thus, four sets a year came in and each set maintained their sense of separation from all the others in the School throughout their training. Our role models, a term we never used, of course, although we knew what they were, were our seniors, the girls who had come into training before us. In a very short time we became role models for our juniors.

And all through training years the demarcation lines were adhered to strictly. Juniors never addressed seniors directly unless they had been sent to do so by someone even more senior, such as Staff Nurse or Sister. Juniors got to their feet when seniors came into the room, even in off-duty times. Juniors held open doors for their seniors to sweep through. We all addressed each other by our surnames at all times – or diminutives of them or nicknames among our friends. The hierarchy was built on this sort of detail and it was always taken incredibly seriously.

The three months of lectures, displays and essay-writing, as well as weekly tests of our knowledge, were, to be honest, a little tedious for me. I had already spent long hours in the wards and ached to get back to them. Also, I was a little disappointed by the level of material we were given in lectures. I thought some of it rather juvenile, and wondered, for a panicky moment, whether I was going to enjoy training as much as I had hoped. The need for enough satisfying academic work was very much a part of my overall feeling about the profession and I had hoped it would be more mind-stretching than some of the stuff we got.

There were lectures from various outside specialists on such subjects as the history of medicine and nursing, all of which I discovered I had already absorbed over many years of reading about my favourite subject. Less enthralling were the lectures on invalid cookery, still in the syllabus although Sister Tutor admitted that we would be unlikely in the extreme ever to require the skill, 'Unless you go into private nursing, of course,' she added, with a perceptible sneer. Of all the hospital's nursing staff, Sister Bishop had seized the ethos of the National Health Service most eagerly and had no time or use for anyone who wasted her skills working outside it for mere money.

Even less enthralling were dry-as-dust harangues from a retired engineer on the design of towns, their water and sewage systems. It should have been interesting, but he managed to make it deadly and I hated him for it. I opined to my new friends that Mr Parker should be put head first into one of his own sewers for being so dreadfully dull.

The only amusing part of that lecture, I remember, was a visit to a working sewage farm on a rather warm afternoon, when the most useful thing we learned was that tomato seeds travel through the human gut unaltered by enzymes, and for that reason a rich growth of lusty tomato plants is usually a feature of the premises. Enjoy your tomato soup!

But there were other subjects that were better: anatomy and physiology with which I fell into immediate love (I can drool with delight over a well-dissected muscle group), Materia Medica, which was to open the mysteries of the pharmacopoeia to us, and, of course, practical classes in which we made up post-operative beds, used stethoscopes on each other and checked our blood pressures, blanket-bathed each other, passed tubes down each other's throats, and learned the hands-on skills of the job.

Then there were the other nurses to enjoy. There were serious people and solemn ones, gigglers and grumblers, flighty ones itching to get their hot little hands on the doctors they hoped to meet, and a little group of fresh-from-the-country Irish girls, who were bowled over with amazement at the excitements of London. One of them, Mary Burnell, became my closest friend, and a great deal of fun we had, swanning around town while I showed her the sights of London, and visited the Festival, which was still running, and trying local cinemas and shops, and always, always being broke.

We had our allowances, of course. We were not paid much as student nurses, but it was more than I got in my Epsom and Deal days. I think in my first year it was about a hundred pounds per annum, but by the time we had paid our National Insurance and income tax, we had about six pounds a month in our pockets. I didn't think that was so bad, seeing we had our board and lodging, uniforms and laundry all provided.

But of course we all complained about being poor, and a lively internal banking system was soon in operation with canny savers acting as our support, lending to those of us who were bad managers between pay days and collecting at Matron's office door as our envelopes were dished out. It is interesting that we were an honourable lot. No one ever welched on a loan that I heard of, and no one ever tried to extort extra cash from a borrower.

I do remember the warm glow I felt at the reaction I got one pay day when we collected for afternoon tea in the nurses' dining room and I told my set the tale of the time when I was working at Grace Hospital in Toronto. The weather was quite hot and I ran out of cash and desperately needed new underwear. I had to choose, I told them, between a bra and pants. I couldn't afford both. 'Well,' I said, 'I was a big girl and I thought a bra was definitely the thing I needed most, and everything was fine until one day I was half pulled over a bed by an agitated mum who had gone noisily mad after her baby was born, and made me display more Chetwynd than the staff or the patients felt they required. But the Captain forgave me and lent me some voluminous and altogether awful elastic-top-and-bottom empire-type knickers in pink satin to tide me over till pay day when I could buy my own.'

All my set sympathised greatly, and fell to discussing what choices they would make in the same situation, an enthralling over-the-teacups subject. I wondered briefly what they would have said if I'd then told them I'd had to make do with the Salvation Army passion killers for three months because it took that long to save up some money to buy my own, on account of my mother taking every penny she could get out of me. But I didn't, of course. Together with the others, I just collected my weekly rations of butter and sugar and thought how lucky I had turned out to be as we made our way back to the classroom.

About twice a month I visited Nancy and Grandma, who fed me like a fighting cock, gave me goodies like freshly baked cakes and biscuits to take back, and sometimes added a little cash to the package, which I took with pink-faced embarrassment but intense gratitude.

It was on one of those visits home that Nancy did something very special for me. I tried long afterwards to tell her, before she died, but she just smiled sweetly as only she could and didn't really understand. To her it was the most natural and ordinary thing in the world. But it changed me and my attitudes in a way that was to lead, eventually, to an amazing (to me) second career.

It was the end of my first month in PTS. Sister Bishop had a mini-exam for us, she said. She wanted to measure our level of comprehension and to see what had actually gone into our heads of the things she had taught us during that hectic and heavily lecture-loaded four weeks.

Some of the set worried about the test and sweated over it, doing revision, but I behaved as I had in school where I never did any work if I could possibly avoid it. I just shrugged away Sister Bishop's test and planned to get round to some revision, but somehow never did.

I did the exam with no preparation at all and, to my amused amazement, came top of the list with rather remarkable grades. I felt pleased in a general sort of way but of course I knew it was a fluke. I'd done it entirely by accident so I was certainly not going to show off among my set, and be labelled a nasty swot.

But all the same I did want to tell someone, so just as we sat down to one of Nancy's nicest Friday-evening chicken dinners I said casually, 'It's the daftest thing, Auntie Nancy. We had an exam this month and I came top with a crazy ninety per cent! And I never did a stroke of work. I suppose it was a mixture of luck and the stuff I'd already learned at Epsom and Deal.'

It was amazing. She stood there and stared at me, then clapped her hands together and cried, 'Did you all hear that? Berry's top of her class! With ninety per cent! Did you hear?'

There was a lot of chatter. Grandma was there, as usual, and, of course, Uncle Louis and my other aunt and uncle, Bessie and Sidney, up visiting London from Letchworth in Hertfordshire where they lived and Uncle Sidney had his grocer's shop.

'Attagirl,' Louis said, which was special as he wasn't a great talker. Uncle Sidney grinned and winked at me and mouthed, 'Congratulations.' Grandma beamed and said, 'So I should think, already,' but she was pleased, I could tell.

And then Nancy reappeared, coming back from the kitchen to which she had hurried, bearing a bottle of champagne.

I sat there like a lump of soppiness. No one, but *no one*, had ever done such a thing for me ever. To drink a toast to me in champagne for accidentally coming top in an exam? It was ludicrous, it was absurd, it was crazy, it was lovely, and as they all sat there and lifted their glasses to me, I grinned like a great oaf and knew that from now on no power on this earth would stop me from being the swottiest of swots in the world.

It was the least I could do for Nancy, I told myself, looking at her standing there, beaming at me with her kitchen-flushed face and her black curls in a hubbub of excitement, her glass raised to me. The very least.

It was a moment that I will never, could never, forget.

Twenty-six

We are having a Study day on infections. A huge subject and the cause of much illness, though not as much as there used to be, thanks to penicillin and all its followers, streptomycin and chloromycetin and the rest. There are about thirty of us attending – a large group – because Sister Bishop has brought in top-ranking outside specialists and not just our own consultants to deal with this very important matter.

This morning we heard *inter alia* about post-operative infection from the great Rodney Maingot, Senior Surgeon of the Royal Free Hospital in Gray's Inn Road and a world expert on gall-bladders, who regaled us with disgusting pictures of perfectly revolting abscesses, which actually put some of the girls off their lunch – a considerable achievement because, as everyone knows, nurses are never hungry, they're always *starving*.

Now we have reassembled for a lecture that is mysteriously labelled 'The Other Infections' and I am suddenly alert. Sitting there at the back among my own friends, but with a small bevy of nuns fluttering away alongside on my right – RNH has always trained nursing nuns, ready to be sent out to Africa to meddle with people's beliefs while treating their bodily ills – I realise that this is going to be a tricky session. I have seen the lecturer arrive: he is our own VD specialist, who normally inhabits a set of Nissen huts in the grounds known simply as the 'Special Clinic' because even among professionals discussion of such a matter as sexually transmitted disease is frowned upon.

I can guess what has happened. Matron, deeply religious as she is, is away on a Retreat. And Sister Bishop, a strong-minded and sensible woman with a robust approach to matters that make some lesser types feel squeamish, has no problems about teaching her girls what they have to know – even if some of those girls are nuns – and has made the most of her opportunity. Matron would never have allowed this doctor to talk to her nuns, for whom she has, naturally, a special concern. But Sister Bishop is hard to stop on matters she thinks important. She will, I have no doubt, have warned Dr T to be aware of the nuns' sensibilities. But all the same this should be interesting.

It is. Dr T leaps on to the rostrum and marches to the front of it, sets his hands on his hips, leans forward and fixes his gaze on the most senior nun, a skinny young woman with a rather frightened expression, called Sister Winifred.

'No use to stand upon the seat!' he cries at her, his brows up and his eyes fixed firmly on hers. 'The spirochaete jumps forty feet! But I can assure you, ladies, that although the organism that causes syphilis is unlikely to be picked up in a lavatory, it is extremely likely to attack you during the more amusing direct method of transmission. So beware!'

A moment's stunned silence, then some of us, and I am definitely one of them, fall about laughing, while the nuns, after a very short period of frozen stillness, agitate themselves into a susurration of skirts and rosaries and after a frantic whispered colloquy follow Sister Winifred out in a rush.

I wonder why Sister Bishop didn't know Dr T was a rabid antireligionist. Has she never heard him hold forth over a ward patient he's been called to see and who had dared to murmur the word 'God' in his hearing? I have, and have enjoyed it greatly. And I enjoy the rest of his lecture too. He knows his stuff. However, I decide I have no wish to work in his field. Too many body fluids altogether for my taste.

Night duty on the children's ward. I'm senior nurse tonight with just one junior and a nursing cadet to help me with seven toddlers, five school-agers, three of them post-operative, and six babies. Getting them to sleep has been hellish, what with all those babies' bottles to give, and the toddlers' bedtime rituals to remember, and the medicines and dressings to do. But by midnight we've managed it. I send the other two to their belated midnight meal and settle to writing my report.

I hardly hear him at first. Then he gets more urgent and it's very clear.

'Nurse-Mummy,' he says. He is three and a half and has been with us for some weeks with a resistant osteomyelitis, a bone infection, in his right leg. His mother never visits, the day staff say, because it upsets him too much. Lots of the parents feel that way, encouraged by Day Sister, who likes to keep the children to herself and prefers parents at arm's length. So the parents stay away on Sunday afternoons, the only visiting time in the week, or come and peer through the windows, staying out of sight to prevent tears. It can't be good for them, I think, they'd be better off crying, as long as their own mums are there to cuddle them better, but I am just a second-year who has no right to an opinion. Maybe later, when I'm more senior . . .

'Nurse-Mummy,' he says again, and I go over to his cot. He drags his plaster-splinted leg up with both hands and somehow stands up and hurls himself at me. I only just manage to catch him because he's a fast mover.

He holds on tightly, pushes his face into my neck, lifting his chin to clear my stiffly starched collar and rests his heavy plastered leg on my hip. 'Nurse-Mummy,' he says again, and immediately falls asleep. I stand there for half an hour till the others come back and together we can get him back into his bed without waking him.

*

Christmas yet again, and as well as the usual carol-singing to make the patients cry and tree- and ward-decorating, I get a bee in my bonnet and persuade the rest of my set to help me put on a Yuletide concert for staff and patients.

The project becomes ever more ambitious as other people join in and to hell with the rules about who talks to whom. I find myself using every spare moment being Madam Producer.

I borrow evening suits and top hats from the local undertaker so that four of us can do 'The Stately Homes of England'. I devise a twenties line-up to the tune of 'The Black Bottom', and working on the basis that if you don't ask you don't get, take myself in full uniform, so that I look more worthy of assistance, up to the West End to the Windmill Theatre where they do super nude shows, so I'm told, and even better costumed ones, and march backstage, since I have more cheek than good sense, to ask for the free loan of seven flapper costumes. Bless them, they oblige, and I bear my treasure back to the hospital to show the girls.

And they are thrilled because the costumes are divine, all beads and scraps of tulle and fringe skirts falling from the waist to a couple of inches above the knee.

And that is all. No knickers. No bras. They are meant to be worn without such items (shades of my poverty days at the Grace Hospital). We have to make them out of the nearest matching fabric we can find, or Matron will have several fits and we'll all be for the high jump.

We manage it and the girls look splendid indeed, even if their singing and dancing is a touch on the wobbly side, but with those skirts, who cares? And the sight of our best friends in such getups is all we need to make the act a huge success.

There is also the 'Hippopotamus Song' for which I have to persuade the Theatre Zoo mask shop in New Row in the heart of the theatre district to make me hippo masks and also to scrounge umpteen sacks from the post office to sew into hippo skins. These work out rather well – and I still enjoy the memory of Sister from the private St David's theatres, a tall, gangling lady who never smiled, singing 'Mud, mud, glorious mud' at the top of her voice. Marvellous!

The junior doctors want to do a shadow operation, a stand-by of all hospital shows, with axes and choppers, hammers, strings of sausages and water-filled balloons to wobble like bellies behind a brightly lit sheet. This is agreed by one and all to be a *tour de force*.

The X-ray staff come up with a sketch involving knights in full armour – I daren't ask where they borrowed that from – and they write a song that goes to the tune of 'The Vicar of Bray' and starts 'In days of old when knights were bold and X-rays weren't invented, they diagnosed their broken bones by where their armour dented . . .', which we all think is wildly witty and gets them a standing ovation.

At the end of the last performance, by which time I am frazzled beyond repair and everyone is drooping about wondering why the hell they let themselves be talked into this project, the cast have arranged for me to be given a pot plant in thanks. It's a large heather, and I am so amazed when Matron, in the front row, gets to her feet and beckons me to come and get it that I take an almighty pratfall and land on my belly at her feet. This gets the biggest roar of the evening and the whole cast assure me that it was worth all the trouble just to see me in such a battered state.

Next day I start again the trek all over London, limping a little, to give back the costumes, and wonder why I get these wacky ideas. Next year, I promise my weary bones, I'll stay in my room all through the Christmas run-up and read.

I did three Christmas shows altogether.

It started like just another cold snap when the weather had been muggy. Anyway, it was not expected to be any worse than the usual winter fogs that had afflicted London for decades. But I knew the moment I came out of the Nurses' Home into the courtyard that something was very wrong. It was so dark. Normally when I came on night duty in those early spring days – I always did my night-duty spells between January and March or April – there remained a hint of light in the sky, the remnants of the smells of earth and early flowers from the gardens beyond the Nurses' Home, but tonight was different.

Tonight there was just the smell of soot, thick and tickly in my nose, chewy and crisp between my teeth and tasting disgustingly of sulphur, cinders and petrol. That, I discovered, came from the flares that had been set up all over the place to supplement the meagre outside lighting the Northern usually relied upon. I pulled my cape over my face and, with my head down, ran for the Casualty entrance.

The ward I was on that night was one of the long rather than round ones, and from the ward door I could not see to the end of it. The first three beds on each side were visible but after that they dissolved into the general yellowish grey that surrounded us. Sister emerged from the gloom and made me jump, for she looked larger than she usually did, until she got up close. 'Not good,' she said. 'I'll give you the report when I have a chance. We have seven oxygen tents going and we're running low on cylinders. I'm going down to Supplies to raise hell. Check everyone and remind 'em that if they smoke they'll blow us all to hell and back again.'

The night went downhill from then on. Ward three was a female medical ward and normally not too hectic. We would have diabetics in to have their insulin and diet stabilised and those needing complex endocrine investigation and chronic heart patients to be freed of some of their oedema, if we could, and at least to give them a little rest, and a few slightly dotty old dears, who just needed a little TLC.*

But tonight even the not-too-ill were gasping and blue about the lips. All the heart patients, and two asthma sufferers, were in oxygen tents that Sister had clustered together at one side of the ward for convenience. The effect, however, was to make the whole area look horribly alarming to the other patients, who stared at it in a semi-mesmerised fashion as though it were from outer space. The row of slightly moving opalescent plastic tents threw long, oddly shaped shadows and gleams through the gloom. Each one whispered and hissed and sometimes seemed to shudder as the patient inside tried to cough or move.

I shed my cape, collected my junior nurse and set her off doing a

---

*Tender Loving Care: a common and useful prescription.

Horlicks and cocoa round for the patients who were not too ill to want it. It would help them all, I said. Make sure it's good and hot and sweet, and pinch some of Sister's biscuits to go with it. They need a bit of coddling. She went very happily because she was only a second-set first-year, had been on the wards less than six months, and was clearly terrified at the sight of all the oxygen-tent gear and the intravenous drips that went with it.

It often startled me to realise how much I learned on night duty. This was my second session, for I was a third-set second-year, which meant I had had approaching two years' bedside experience as well as four two-week study blocks and umpteen study days. Not enough, though, to prevent me being nervous as I pulled back a flap gently and slid inside one of the tents against the bed of the patient.

Who was dead. In the few minutes between Sister going off to seek further oxygen supplies and my coming to the bedside – six or seven minutes at most – the poor creature, who had been admitted with chronic heart failure two days ago, had given up the struggle to breathe the thick, soupy stuff that passed for air in London that night; even when oxygen was mixed with it it was barely breathable.

I lost three more patients that night, all needing to be laid out and their paperwork sorted while the rest of the ward tossed and turned fearfully and kept asking for hot drinks, or water would do, anything to reassure themselves that they were still alive and would stay so.

We comforted them all we could – I distinctly remember promising one old lady that I would not let her die in her sleep, but would watch her and if I saw any risk of it would wake her at once; she slept like a baby after that – but it was difficult when, within a moment or two of starting to listen to them, we had to rush off to admit another patient brought up from Casualty: 'On O_2, continue O_2 via tent, urgent.'

I marvel now at how we coped with so little equipment apart from the tents and our own experience. There was no system for measuring oxygen saturation of the blood. They use a simple finger-tip clip now that gives an instant reading, but we had to guess how much oxygen our patients had in them from the sounds of their breathing, the colour of their lips, their inner eyelids and fingernails, and whatever past experience we might have had in respiratory medicine. There were no monitors with beeps to alert us to failing hearts. There was only a bedside vigil for the ones we feared for most.

By off-duty time in the morning we had seven tents going – Day Sister had come up trumps with extra oxygen cylinders – with patients we doubted would last the day, but we didn't feel as bad as the children's ward staff did. They told us, when we all trailed in for our unwanted morning meal, that they had lost seven babies who simply couldn't cope with the effort needed to breathe the foul air.

There were similar horror tales from all over the hospital, newborns dying as well as old men, schoolchildren dying of asthma attacks so quickly they never left Casualty, a dreadful, dreadful time. Eventually we learned that during the three or so days that the fog lasted, four thousand people died. And we, the staff, had never been so dirty. I remember that I sneezed and sprayed my apron front with black specks, and all my white underwear was a dark greyish yellow.

It was at around this time that I heard once more from my father. It was my twenty-first birthday and I received a telegram from Acapulco in Mexico. I stared at it and tried to recall what the place looked like – I'd seen it in films – but couldn't. 'Happy Birthday,' he said. 'Key of the Door. Great.' I threw it away, but three days later I had a visit from two serious-looking men who told me they were from Interpol and asked me about him. Did I know *exactly* where he was? No, I did not, I said firmly, nor did I wish to. They went away and I wondered for days what he'd done this time, then never thought of him again.

Exam time on the horizon. I spend every spare half-hour I can steal in the School of Nursing, my cap on the floor, my apron hanging over the back of my chair and my collar gaping open because it's so hot this summer, and swotting, swotting, swotting. Over textbooks, over books of anatomical and physiological diagrams, over my own notes, my friends' notes and every crib I can find, stuffing my head with the names of every bone and its protuberances, every nerve (well, every major nerve) and its pathways, every important blood vessel and the tissues it serves. Sister Bishop comes in and scolds me for virtually stripping off but fetches an electric fan. I dress properly to please her and carry on.

Books go with me everywhere, meals, the loo, everywhere. But only the Bish knows how hard I am working. I would die before I let friends and colleagues in my set know that I was just a nasty swot. They seem willing to forgive me cheerfully enough for always coming top when they believe it's a sort of accident or a side-effect of having a good memory. Which I do. It is eidetic, that is, photographic, to an extent.

But I can't just trust my memory. I have to work hard, have felt it incumbent upon me to do so, that I have no right *not* to ever since the night that Nancy gave me champagne. I have made sure to get to the top of every list, every exam, every possible thing that would show Nancy how much her support matters. I hope she knows, and that she also knows how appreciative I am.

Not that she has as much energy right now as she should have. I worry a bit about that. She has told me little because she doesn't talk much about her ailments, but I know there are problems.

Grandma never stops talking about her ailments. She enjoys ill-health and, indeed, is the most active and remarkable of hypochondriacs. We all know it and indulge her, showing all the interest in her symptoms she could possibly want. Max also indulges her by plotting routes in the car that never, *ever* go near a cemetery. She is obsessively afraid of death and has a great raft of absurd superstitions to protect her from it. Above all, death must never be mentioned in her presence and the sight of a gravestone – well, it doesn't bear thinking about.

But Nancy is very different. I believe she really isn't well, although she won't talk about it, and I wouldn't dream of nagging her – yet I have to say the family are beginning to defer to me somewhat on matters of health. Now I am in my final year they see me as, if not the fount of all wisdom, certainly someone who is a bit damp from it and could pass it on.

I do my modest best, scared to say much in case it's the wrong thing, which might be accepted by my dear relatives as your real *echt* wisdom, and I couldn't bear to take responsibility for that. I also can't nag Nancy to talk to me about herself in case she tells me something I know is awful and my speaking countenance creates problems. It's all very complicated.

So I just do my exams and settle down to wait for the results. When they come in I should be, I pray I will be, please let me be, a State Registered Nurse. I managed to pass my intermediary exams with great grades two years ago. Now let me pass these.

I fall asleep each night making the same pointless prayers because, of course, in the absence of a god in my universe they aren't aimed at anyone but Providence and blind good fortune in general.

Only another six weeks and then we'll know. Can I last that long?

And if I have passed, then what?

Twenty-seven

Matron posted me to the private-wing theatres to spend the limbo of waiting for finals results and I suppose I should have been flattered. Everyone knew it was a tough posting, Sister-in-Charge being an eagle-eyed obsessive about every detail of her department and its workings, which of course was highly commendable and perfectly proper in such a vulnerable unit, but didn't make for a jolly working atmosphere full of cheerful chit-chat and gay badinage.

It would have been more fun on ward six, the male surgical ward, especially if there were a few Arsenal footballers in, as we often had in the summer, dealing with their minor sprains and niggles to get them fit for the next season. We were the team's own special hospital and, as far as many of the players were concerned, RNH nurses were their own special harem. In those more innocent and careful days that rarely meant more than dates to the local flicks and a goodnight cuddle by the Nurses' Home gates where every passer-by could take a lively interest in your activities.

Not that I ever dated a footballer, finding talk about sport the perfect soporific, but it would have been fun to be on ward six to be asked, and to find agreeable witty ways of saying, 'Not on this earth or Fuller's, mate, and never you think otherwise,' or something equally sweet and girlish.

So I reported on duty to Sister Mack. She could stand at the operating table in theatre for up to eight hours yet never seemed to need to escape to the loo. We had long ago decided that she wore mackintosh knickers to make this feat possible and had dubbed her accordingly. I settled into a world where high drama was relieved by the most appalling boredom while we scrubbed and cleaned everything from top to bottom ready to do an hour's operating, then got ready to start from scratch and do it all over again.

At first I missed the contact with patients, those living, breathing reasons for everything we did and thought at RNH. In the theatres patients arrived at best in a woozy haze from their pre-operative medication, at worst already flat out because of the severity of their trauma or their basic condition.

Not that the theatre staff could have had chats with them, even if they'd been awake and eager to converse. They came to theatre accompanied by very junior ward nurses whom we, the snooty theatre nurses, dismissed as mere 'hand-holders'. They were there, we told them cruelly, only to make sure frightened patients didn't attempt to leap off their trolleys, and supervised the patients while we made sure the theatre was all set for their reception.

It was a busy department, with two working theatres and matching anaesthetic rooms, and I had a huge amount to learn, from the contents of the beetle cupboard – a vast, compendious storage unit – to the names of literally hundreds of different instruments. And not just their names: their uses, their alternatives and even their histories. Many had been invented by surgeons in the past, and modern ones loved to show off their expertise in their origins and current uses – and heaven help nurses who couldn't keep up with them.

Thus, Spencer-Wells forceps, invented by the great surgeon of that name, were the first self-retaining artery forceps. Before their invention the surgeon or his assistant had to tie off bleeding points immediately to prevent excessive blood loss, and that hampered surgery enormously. It's a lot smoother with a bristling collection of Spencer-Wellses fringing an incision while the surgeon busies himself deep inside.

I remember with great affection one particular surgeon's invention, which sounded so much more exciting than it turned out to be. The 'Lockhart-Mummery Bung' is used in rectal surgery and was just a curl of rubber tubing with a catgut tie attached, but it sounded exceedingly impressive, I thought. I imagined Mr Lockhart-Mummery as being very tall and *soigné*. When I met him years later he was precisely that. Which was nice.

Within a couple of weeks I was well settled. I started out as a runner – that is, during cases I did not scrub up but was the one person in the theatre able to move about freely, to fetch, carry and be the dogsbody. A very privileged dogsbody, mind you: no other unscrubbed-up person, apart from the anaesthetist, was allowed into theatre and if Matron herself had peered in through the glass window in the door, I would have had to send her away.

I also had the job of counting swabs so that none was left inadvertently inside the patient to rot and fester. I remember one dreadful case, not mine, glory be, where a big swab was left inside a poor chap, who almost died as a result. Then I had to double-check the instrument count with the scrub nurse for the same reason.

Sister Mack and I got on rather well, despite her nit-picking, which I rather respected, and her miserable expression, which I did not. In truth, I felt rather sorry for her. She loved her job and was brilliant at it, yet was never entirely happy. I suspected that, like many of her generation and, indeed, most of the RNH senior nursing staff, she had been reared to regard herself as a failure if she didn't have a man to put a wedding ring on her finger.

She was taller than I was – over six feet, I think – and very thin, with a stoop to compensate for her height, which simply made her look gawky and not at all prepossessing, sadly. She never dated, to the best of the hospital's knowledge (if she had we would have known!), in spite of drooping hopefully around all the eligible doctors who came to the theatres. She had an amazing gift for ferreting out their private histories and left the married and engaged men strictly undrooped-over, for she was an honourable woman in such matters.

I remember her with sad anger: today she would have taken much more pride in her success in her job and would have valued herself much more highly than she did. She'd probably also look handsome to today's eyes: she was so quirky she'd have been a wow in fashionable modern clubs. And she was a great teacher and taught me how to be a scrub nurse. I loved it. First, there was so much expertise to develop, and I took huge delight in that. And then there was the drama of it all.

I liked the way I looked in scrubs – the thin, loose, pale blue tunics we wore in theatres over white ankle socks and special soft shoes – and I knew that having my head covered in a white cap and just my eyes showing over a mask did wonders for my appearance. We all looked better like that, unfortunately, so it gave none of us any leverage. Poor Sister Mack had been gazing soulfully over her mask at assorted chaps for years to no avail.

But I certainly felt special in the job. Sometimes I would look down on my smooth brown-gloved hands under the clear, specially focused white light, as I handed instruments, threaded needles, snipped catgut ends and sometimes sewed up the skin after the operation was otherwise completed – a treat some nice surgeons liked to give us and themselves: they got to their tea sooner – and glowed with pleasure at the sight.

The drawback to being in theatres was unreliable off-duty times. If a case was running late you stayed to the end, no matter how long that might be.* Also, you had to be 'on call' several nights a week to take any emergency cases, and there were plenty of those from severe road-traffic accident trauma to Caesarean sections. I suspected one of our less scrupulous obstetricians of deliberately leaving his private-

---

* I was shocked to discover that modern scrub nurses actually hand over to a different one in midcase when a shift ends. We would never have let anyone else finish what we had started. Much too proud!

case emergency Caesars until the middle of the night so that he could charge the patients more. We got not another penny, of course.

And then there were the surgeons, an unpredictable lot of men, some of whom were downright horrid. (I remember very few, if any, women in senior surgical posts; it's a bit better now but not nearly as fairly balanced as it should be.)

Mr William Bashall Gabriel, a rectal surgeon inevitably known as the Arse Angel, roared and moaned at you interminably if you dared move an inch at his side except for what was absolutely necessary. He was a particular bugbear. Another was his anaesthetist, a waggish fellow who thought it the acme of exquisite wit to discharge syringes full of cold water at my feet and ankles during Gabe's cases. He knew I daren't protest and the lousy coward said nothing to support me at the end of the case when Gabe, seeing the great puddle at my feet, said, 'Well, really, Nurse, you only had to ask.'

I became a sort of anti-heroine for the other nurses on St David's theatres at that time, all of whom, excluding Sister and me, of course, happened to be Catholics. One of the busier gynaecologists using the theatres for his private patients had a large and very lucrative prac-tice in Harley Street and good friends among psychiatrists. As a result he brought to theatre a steady stream of women he insisted should always be referred to as ladies needing 'aspiration of retained products of conception'.

This term is normally used after a miscarriage or birth has left bits of tissue or afterbirth behind, but the gynaecologist didn't wait till that stage. He brought his patients before the foetus was born. In other words, he was an abortionist. What he did was perfectly legal, even though abortion in general was not. It was not until 1967 that a limited system of abortion was permitted (excluding 'social' abor-tion) under an Act of Parliament pushed through by David Steele, for which many women are grateful every day.

Our surgeon acted under a piece of case law of the 1930s, known colloquially as 'The Case of the Horse with a Green Tail', in which a young gynaecologist, Alex Bourne, brought a fourteen-year-old girl, raped by two soldiers who had promised to show her a horse with a green tail, to his hospital, St Mary's in Paddington, to abort the pregnancy that had resulted. He was a brave man: his actions might have jailed him for years and destroyed his career and life. He notified the Director of Public Prosecutions of what he was doing and called the police to his operating theatre to see him do it.

The case came to court before Mr Justice McNaghton, famous for the McNaghton Rules. Bourne was acquitted and the case made it legal for the first time in the UK to abort a pregnancy in a woman who, in the opinion of more than one doctor, was at risk of loss of life and/or damage to their physical or mental health.

So, a woman who could afford to find a nice Harley Street chap to get one of his psychiatrist chaps to agree that her mental health would suffer if she were forced to go to term would be brought to a nice, clean, safe theatre like ours to have a safe, clean abortion carried out. Poorer and even more desperate women had to make do with back-street abortionists, for 'legal' interventions cost a great deal.

Of one thing I was convinced even then, from what I had learned on the RNH gynae wards: there is no power on this earth that can force an unwilling woman to go to term with an unwanted infant. She'll kill herself first. Many have.

But the Catholic staff refused to have anything to do with these cases, not even rinsing off an instrument or picking up the surgeon's discarded gown from the floor. That left Sister Mack and me to take them all, and we did. It got the nurses off the hook – refusing to work could have led to dismissal by the governors in those hierarchical days without employment tribunals to turn to, however much Matron approved of their stance – and since the work was done in the private theatres Matron was able to shut her eyes to it, however much she hated it.

For my part I saw no reason why any woman should be forced to have a baby she didn't want: I never forgot the girl who had died of her back-street abortion in Epsom and I never would. If these were the choices to be made, let them choose the Northern any time they can, I thought. If they can afford it.

I wished I could have liked the surgeon who was helping at least some women to have some control over their own fertility and their own bodies, but I couldn't. He was so patently in the business because it was money-coining, which sickened me as much as it distressed my Catholic friends.

There was another sort of operation the Catholic nurses jibbed at: sterilisation. It is possible that our egregious Harley-Streeter, who did operations other than abortions, tied the tubes of some of his abdominal cases when he was ostensibly doing a laparotomy, say – surgical short hand for 'let's-go-in-and-have-a-bit-of-a-look-around-and-see-if-we-can-see-what's-going-on'. No one fussed over those because if they didn't know and only guessed, being involved didn't count as a sin on their part.

But male sterilisation was another animal altogether and, to a woman, they downed tools when any were booked with us. The surgeon who performed them for us was called Hamilton Bailey. He was enormously famous but had lost much of his drive and capacity to work when his only child, a boy of sixteen, was killed in a bizarre railway accident. His fame rested on his co-authorship of a standard surgical textbook called *Royal Northern Operative Technique*, which had, over the earlier part of the century, become the Bible of every medical student in the country. His co-author was McNeill Love and he, too, was a regular operator in our theatres. Both were on the shaky side now, being what was described tactfully as in late middle age.

The amazing thing about both men was that although their ageing hands trembled visibly as they approached the operating table, the moment they started work their hands were like rocks, and they never put a finger wrong.

Watching McNeill Love in particular was a deep pleasure. His hands performed a sort of ballet, with little flourishes of the wrist that must once have been studied and affected but were now part of him. Sometimes his movements were so swift and deft that they seemed blurred, while at others he seemed to be performing in slow motion. He knew the effect of all this perfectly well and was inordinately proud of it. I would have been too, had I had his ability.

Ham spoke hardly at all while he did his vasectomies, signalling his wishes with a pair of fairly fierce eyebrows. He grunted when he left theatres instead of offering the more customary 'Thank you and good afternoon,' but knowing his personal misery we forgave that. But we could be a harsh and unforgiving lot to doctors who we thought misbehaved. Coffee would appear cold and there would be only stewed tea, no biscuits, and damp scrub suits until they learned to treat us with the respect to which we, in our own high-flown opinions, thought we were entitled.

We could do it because we knew how much they depended on us. On the wards we would never be so uppity: it wouldn't be good for patients. But in theatres it was different for we knew the value of our own expertise. Looking back it was probably good for the surgeons, especially the new young ones. It helped them to learn. As McNeill Love would say to every new houseman he broke in, and he always did it over the operating table, 'Young man, do you know the three stages of a surgeon's career? Skin forceps, please, Sister.' I was always called Sister when I scrubbed for him. It was one of his courtesies.

'Er – no, sir.'

'Scalpel, Sister. The first stage, my boy, is to get on. Swab, Sister. And the second stage is – ah, Allis's forceps here, I think, just so – yes, the second stage. To get honour, young man! Catgut tie, please, Sister, and you, young man, hold that retractor there for all you're worth. And the third stage is, of course?'

He would wait for the houseman to respond, but he never did, and McNeill Love would tut-tut and say, 'Oh, Sister, when will they learn! To get honest, of course! On, Onner, Onnest – and don't you ever forget it!'

I doubt they ever did. I know to this day, over fifty years later, that if I am speaking at a conference of medical people and I tell them that I scrubbed for both Bailey and Love it rocks them back on their heels for it makes me sound very old indeed. Which I suppose I am now.

They were happy weeks, and I even stopped worrying about the results of the finals and what I would do after them. Until one evening when I was in my bedroom on the far side of the main Nurses' Home and someone bashed on my door.

I jumped and reached for my uniform, then stopped and shook my head irritably. 'I'm not on call tonight,' I yelled back. 'Sister Mack is. Her room's over on—'

'You got a phone message, Nurse Chetwynd.' The little junior outside sounded scared, but delivered her message carefully. 'I was to tell you it's about your grandmother and you must call home at once.'

Twenty-eight

Grandma was probably around sixty-five when she had her fatal coronary thrombosis. We could only guess because she had been a very successful secret-keeper. Part of her fear-of-death superstition had included never saying how old you were in case the devils heard and snatched you away for boasting of your longevity.

She had been the adored only girl and youngest child amongst five brothers of a successful middle-class family in that great segment of Poland and Russia known as the Pale of Settlement. There is no doubt that her parents tried to protect her from contact with her poorer neighbours so that she wouldn't pick up either nasty infections or the wrong ideas.

They failed with the latter, and all her life my otherwise intelligent, often witty and always-full-of-vitality Grandma was plagued by these absurd beliefs that she took horribly seriously. So I hoped she didn't know what happened to her when it happened. She had been complaining for a few weeks of indigestion – that is, vague pains in her chest – but because she complained ceaselessly of assorted symptoms everyone soothed her and made comforting, reassuring noises, including her own doctor. And – I still feel bad about it – me. I knew that chest pain should always be taken seriously, but Grandma had had what she called chest pain for ever. So, while I feel bad I feel no guilt.

She had gone to bed, according to her companion Mrs J, at half past seven saying she didn't feel well, so early that Mrs J thought Grandma might need a nice cup of tea before she went to bed herself three hours later. She went into my grandma's room, found her breathing noisily and impossible to wake up, and had run shrieking next door to Auntie Nancy.

Nancy was ill herself, as I had suspected. I knew she had been to see a specialist at the Westminster Hospital, who told her husband – he had refused to talk to Nancy alone about it, which she, easy-going soul that she was, accepted without a murmur, apparently failing to see it as a hint of serious problems – that she had 'a breast lesion', which he would try to disperse with hormonal therapy. They were not told about the treatment, or that it had side-effects. She was put, I think, on massive doses of testosterone, the male sex hormone, to suppress her own oestrogen, which was almost certainly causing the breast cancer. The result was that she thickened in face and body, became rather hairy about the chin and her voice deepened, which alarmed everyone. I worked out that she had an inoperable cancer of the breast, but I couldn't talk to her about it, couldn't offer to help, because I wasn't supposed to know that she was ill and, anyway, in our family, like most families in those days, *we didn't talk about such things*.

The word 'cancer' was never mentioned. Old ladies playing cards with Grandma would speak in a whisper of 'The Big C ', and when I argued with them and said it was unhealthy to be so fearful they got so agitated that I learned to shut up.

It was the same with the other major disease they all feared: tuberculosis. It was nothing like as bad as it had been in the thirties and early forties. We had special drugs now that cured it, and I had spent three months attached to a companion specialist hospital of RNH to educate me about it and its treatment. I knew it didn't always kill people, but I couldn't speak to my family or their friends about it. They wouldn't listen, only whispered about 'a touch of chest trouble'.

It was not their own stupidity or superstitious attitudes that made them so fearful of information. It was the general medical approach to giving patients information that made them react with silence and sick terror. It was normal practice throughout my own hospital, and I am certain every other in the NHS, to tell patients as little as possible.

The reasoning was kindly. There were so many diseases for which there was little that could be done, apart from offering drugs to relieve pain, that telling patients they had, or might have, such a disease would only create fear to no purpose. That was what the wisdom of the period dictated. If we had had reliable, effective treatments then, of course, we would talk to them about it. Orthopaedic specialists had no trouble in telling their patients which bones had broken, sometimes in eye-popping detail, but when it came to many other conditions silence was the golden rule.

And if the doctors were silent the heavens would open on any nurse who dared to give a patient information that had not been sanctioned by the doctor. Only Sister could speak to them if they insisted on asking, and even she had to be circumspect to protect them from fear and worry, and herself from medical fury.

The result, of course, was often more fear, more worry, more tension. I still wonder to what extent watching what was happening to her younger daughter and applying her own not inconsiderable intelligence had enabled Grandma to work out what the cause and outcome might be. And what effect that had had on her heart condition.

The other big difference between now and when Grandma died was that not the smallest effort was made to save her. Her own GP called as soon as he heard, shook his head sadly at her bedside, said he was sorry and went away, 'To leave the family in peace,' he said. She was still breathing when he saw her, but never for a moment did he consider hospital admission. Why bother? They could do nothing.

If a woman of sixty-five today with a history of diabetes type two told her GP she had vague chest pains and called it indigestion, even if she were the most accomplished cryer of 'Wolf', the likelihood is that she would have an immediate blood test for cardiac enzymes to see whether there was any heart tissue damage and an equally swift ECG.* The result would almost certainly be treatment either with one of the new clot-buster drugs that literally dissolve the blood clot causing the circulation blockage to the heart, or perhaps insertion of a balloon to the blocked coronary arteries to clear them, or the offer of an operation called a CABG.**

If that had been possible for Grandma, the chances are high that she would have had at least another ten good years, maybe more, and would have known most of her sixteen great-grandchildren. She certainly would have given her family much pleasure as well as enjoyed plenty of good living herself.

She would also, of course, have been part of what is now frowned over by worried prognosticators of doom: the so-called demographic time bomb. That is, a steadily ageing population requiring more and more costly care while themselves being unproductive. There are more centenarians now than there have ever been, and it is the new and amazing therapies the NHS can offer to the majority of sick people that have created them. People are also better fed, housed, warmed and cared for than they have ever been, and mostly happier too, which all leads to long life.

Not that I was either aware of this, or looking forward to the time when, some fifty years or so later, I would be sitting on a Royal Commission to consider the funding of the care of older people in the UK. But looking back to that day from where I am now, it intrigues me to realise that even then I was being put in a position to learn about such things as demographics and medical progress and what they mean in the lives of ordinary citizens.

Not, of course, that I was thinking any such thing at the time. All that went through my head during the short bus ride to Grandma's flat was 'She's too young to die yet. There's lots I have to tell her still.' And I cannot deny that as I wrote that sentence

---

* Electrocardiogram, to measure errors of heartbeat and rhythm.
** Coronary Artery Bypass Graft, to restore full circulation to the heart. Popularly called a Cabbage.

on an April afternoon in 2002, I found myself repeating exactly the same thought. There is so much I would still like to talk to her about.

Masses of people at the funeral, masses of people at Grandma's flat in the succeeding week, all arriving bearing cakes and chocolates for the family. As Max says, with some bitterness, 'You lose your mother and you're swamped in sweeties.' He writes letters to distant relatives including my parents about Grandma's death. The only one not to respond, of course, is my father.

I return to the hospital afterwards to be greeted kindly by so many people, with all the Irish girls using the same lovely phrase: 'I'm so sorry for your trouble.' That makes me feel surprisingly better.

The theatres are hectically busy and I bury myself in work for weeks, visiting Nancy whenever I can and wondering how and when I can talk to her about what is going on. She looks less and less good but never fails to put on a great show of delight when I arrive and chatters cheerfully, usually contentedly, about the children and about her memories of her mother, though she weeps occasionally. Well, of course she does. Me too. We both snivel and then we laugh and I make a cuppa and it's all very cosy.

But I wish she looked better.

The results come out. I am in my room that morning, as I have a day off, and there is a knock on my door. It is Sister Bishop and I stare at her and cry, 'Oh, Sister, please, have I passed?'

'Passed, you silly girl? Of course you have. You've got the Gold Medal, too.'

I gape. That means I topped ninety per cent in every exam, including the practical. I find that hard to swallow. 'Are you sure Sister?' is all I can manage, and she laughs like a drain.

'Thirty years a tutor and now she asks me if I can read a list of exam results! Charming! Congratulations, my dear. I must go and see that everyone else gets their results,' and she plods away down my staircase like a rather wobbly owl.

I rush after her. 'Sister, do you remember when I was on first-year night duty on Casualty?'

She is puzzled, trying to look back over three years in the lives of all the two hundred or more girls she has trained. And then she smiles. 'Of course I remember, ruined my breakfast.'

'I'm so glad you do, though I'm sorry about the breakfast. I just wanted to say thank you. You were right, of course.'

'I usually am,' she said serenely, and went on her way, and I sat on the stairs and looked out at the June gardens through the rather grimy window, and remembered.

First-year night duty on Casualty was like working on a battlefield. Well, the weekends were. Monday to Wednesday or so was mostly RTAs, road traffic accidents that the ambulance men had scraped off the Tarmac like so much raspberry jam – no compulsory helmets or leather urban armour in those days. There were cuts and bruises among the kids mucking about on the swings in the park and a few 'I-only-slipped-on-the-stairs' excuses from half-drunken housewives, terrified of being identified as alcohol abusers: in those days, women who drank were considered the lowest of the low.

There even used to be time sometimes for a little flirting with the local police, who regularly 'popped in for a cuppa', bringing their own mugs because we never had enough to go round. Many are the pints of tea I've drunk from jam jars and splendid tea it always was.

But weekends were different. It started on Thursdays because one local firm paid its labourers then. It rose sharply on Friday, and by Saturday night would hit a crescendo that sent it shrieking away off the charts. We ran around like demented bees, slipping in blood, vomit and worse that no one had time to mop away, keeping the drunks from bashing each other to death, and us too while they were at it, coping with the almost dead and often very dead after-pub bashers and bashed.

Weekends brought the women and children too. Women with faces beaten to a pulp, too terrified even to moan. Children wide-eyed and white-faced, because they had seen far more than they should and had the bruises to prove it. And sometimes dead babies and toddlers killed by their parents, by accident, by bad luck, by who knew what?

I looked at the women and their clinging, fearful children, and remembered hearing screams on Friday and Saturday nights outside our Homerton flat when I was small and asking my mother what it was and what was happening. I can still see the way she looked at me and then away, with her mouth primmed up and tight. 'None of our business. We don't mix in. Take no notice.'

But now I had to take notice and I did the best I could, as we all did. We washed and cleaned the injuries so that they could be stitched. We checked for other damage, belting up and down to X-ray with wet plates for the doctors to study and decide on. We admitted weary women to the wards when we could. Some refused: 'Gotta get the old man's breakfast – I'll be a bloody sight worse than this if you keep me 'ere. And, anyway, the baby's at 'ome.' We tried to unfreeze frozen children and admit them every chance we had, for they would be better off in ward eight, poor scraps, than with their own parents at home.

And then, in the small hours, the prostitutes, equally beaten up but more cheerful about it than ordinary married women. Some needed us to rescue wads of money they had hidden about their persons to keep it out of their pimps' hands, only to find that they couldn't hook it out again.

As one woman said gleefully, peering down between her wide-spread knees at the doctor brandishing in his forceps the little *gutta-percha* packet he had got out of the depths of her vagina and which contained three white fivers, 'Not bad for a night's work, eh? And I've done better than that this week already!'

I remember comparing that with my six quid a month and sighing. Something was badly wrong somewhere.

It was one particularly awful Friday night that did it to me. As soon as the day staff signed on I stormed out of Casualty so fast that I almost ran – not bad after more than nine hours of unremitting busyness. I didn't even go to night-staff breakfast but instead made a straight line for the School of Nursing. It was a lovely crisp sunny winter morning and I should have felt good. I was about to start on a couple of nights off, which was always pleasant, but I didn't feel at all good.

I found Sister having her breakfast and interrupted her shamelessly. 'Sister, I'm giving up,' I gabbled. 'I've had enough. It's all a waste of time. I feel like the little Dutch boy with his finger in the dike trying to hold back disaster. I had two children BID* tonight, a drunk who was only eighteen who had choked on his own vomit and died in the street, and then there were two women who – I can't take it, I'm giving up. It's an impossible, pointless job because it will all be the same again tonight. I can't bear it—'

And the Bish sat there, didn't even bother to get up, and fixed me with as icy a glare as I had ever seen on her amiable round face.

'Nurse Chetwynd! Who the blazes do you think you are? God? You are here, like the rest of us, to do the best we can, as much as we can, and leave the remainder to others. The arrogance of you to think you can do all there is to do and no one else need bother! Now, go to bed, have a good day's sleep, enjoy your nights off, and I never want to hear another word of such nonsense.' She returned to her coffee and waved me away.

I stood there, swaying on my feet with fatigue, and I thought, Well, she's usually right and I'm too tired to argue. And I said, 'Yes, Sister. Good morning, Sister,' and went.

By the time I had had a bath, crawled into my pyjamas and crept into my room the maid from the Nursing School had arrived in my room with a tray of hot buttered toast and tea.

I do hope there are senior nurses like the Bish still around.

---

* Brought In Dead.

Twenty-nine

Achieving a lifelong ambition can be a depressing experience. After years of being focused on becoming a State Registered Nurse I found myself rather nonplussed when I got there. My grandmother's death added to my sense of dislocation and, for lack of something better to do, I agreed to study midwifery. Not because I had a burning desire to care for mothers and babies but because it was the obvious next step, as far as the RNH was concerned, for its graduates to seek a post-graduate qualification. To this end the hospital had organised a combined course with Guy's Hospital, by London Bridge, and our own maternity ward.

So I went to Guy's and, apart from a few moments of agreeable melancholy when I remembered Dr Leibel in Toronto who had studied there, I found it rather dispiriting after RNH.

It was a very large hospital, antique, snobbish about its own significance as a very old establishment, and alive with young men – and very few women – from the medical and dental schools. They sashayed around the big quad with an irritating air of superiority that greatly impressed the rest of my set and made their eyes light up with anticipation of fun.

It gave me, however, small pleasure for I took great delight in my emotional freedom and was double-damned if any bloke was ever going to take it away from me. Crushes on remote, unobtainable doctors were one thing, the real thing something quite other, of which I wanted no part. With an example like my parents, who were undoubtedly besotted with each other in a most destructive way for themselves and their children, how could I feel otherwise?

Midwifery in the fifties was a two-tier training: half was done in the hospital, half 'on the district' caring for mothers having babies in their own homes, because it was NHS policy to provide hospital beds for only 60 per cent of births. Childbirth, ruled the gurus of the day, was not a medical problem but a normal physiological experience. If provision was made for all first-baby deliveries, in case of problems, and for all those suspected of having problems – such as those who had had past difficulties or who had already given birth to four or more babies – that would be ample.

The result was that middle-class women became very manipulative about getting hospital beds. The powers-that-be might say it was safe at home, but they didn't believe it. Women's magazines were full of articles telling expectant mothers how to persuade their doctors and midwives that they really needed to be in hospital. And the Government, always very sensitive to the demands about care of mothers and babies, which made such luscious tabloid headlines, obliged.

Now there is the so-called too-posh-to-push movement, in the US mainly but also arriving here. Mothers who can afford to pay for all their care in the private sector are pressuring their consultants to perform Caesarean sections on the grounds that it is less effort for the mum.

I have to say, as both a mother and a midwife, that I reckon what matters most is a healthy baby born of a healthy mother after a pregnancy and birth that leaves them both in the best possible nick. It seems to me that trying to make labour into some sort of all-laughing, all-singing, top-of-the-range experience for the mother rather loses sight of the reality of the business.

Not that all the practice at Guy's, in my time there, was an example I would wish to hold up to modern midwives or mothers. Not all the experiences I had were those I might have chosen, but I learned a lot even if it was mostly in a negative sense. As in: 'I'll never do *that* when I'm in charge!'

Babies and mothers were kept strictly apart, babies in nursery, mothers in ward. The babies were doled out at feeding times, then taken back with expedition. Every woman admitted to the ward who was not wearing a wedding ring was loaned one – with insistence that it was put on – from a collection of Woolworths' best, kept in the desk drawer of the admission suite. The reason for this treatment of unmarried women was an altruistic one, of course. It was – wait for it – to avoid upsetting other mothers in the ward. I can remember only two brave women who refused a ring and sailed into the labour ward then the lying-in ward after delivery with naked left hands. I also remember the amazed rage of the senior midwives, who could not comprehend such behaviour.

If babies were stillborn they were whisked away to prevent their mothers seeing them, even if they asked. In cases where the baby was severely malformed it perhaps made some sense, but I recall having to sew into her shroud – Sister liked things done with needles and thread – a beautiful stillborn baby. It might have helped her mother to see her, and I said as much to the senior midwife.

She stared at me as though I had just suggested we should start feeding the babies on steak and chips and suet puddings. 'What a very morbid suggestion,' she said icily, and sent me to take the little parcel to the mortuary.

Despite the existence in the ward of single rooms for those mothers who needed them (mostly saved for infectious cases), all mothers of stillborn babies were put in the general lying-in ward. They sat there in utter misery all through each feeding time as babies were fetched and carried past them, and slurped and gurgled and cried on all sides. On one occasion I stopped to sit beside one such mother, hold her hand and talk, and the same senior Sister called me away and told me 'not to be so sentimental. She has to get used to the fact sooner or later and the sooner the better.'

All the babies wore special binders over the stump of the cord, since it was Sister's proud boast that none of her babies ever developed umbilical hernias.

Every morning half a dozen of us would sit in the nursery, bath babies, then dust them with talc – never used now, I'm told, as it's dangerous – and roll a wide crêpe bandage round the belly, making it fairly firm, to hold a dressing in place, the whole sewn neatly at the back. A row of us with babies bawling on their bellies on our laps while we sewed them must have been an extraordinary sight.

Mothers who moaned, or cried out in pain or otherwise produced more than a low whimper in the toughest stages of labour) were regarded by Sister and her senior colleagues as spineless creatures who didn't deserve the gift of the pain that brought their baby. Sister was one of the religious sort, just like my Matron at RNH. The more that they cried or shouted, the less swiftly would Sister agree to pain relief. 'If they have it now what will they do later when it gets stronger?' she would say, if we tried to persuade her. 'The woman's just a spoiled brat. Tell her to pull herself together at once.' However, doctors' wives who cried or shouted were regarded by Sister as 'deeply sensitive' and fussed over accordingly. An interesting woman, was this Sister.

Her most despised *bêtes noires*, however, were not the shriekers but the swearers. 'Wait till I get my hands on him – I'll tie a fucking knot in it!'

'Next time he comes crawling round me I'll have his bollocks round his neck. I'll kill the bastard, I told him to be careful – I'll—'

'The next time that shit tries to put anything in my—'

Sister had a real gift for being well out of the way when the patients got that expressive.

When a severely malformed baby, such as an anencephalic,* was delivered, Sister, the senior midwives and sometimes the consultant in charge of the case would rush it away from the labour ward, then

---

* Born with no brain, apart from the brainstem that maintains breathing and heartbeat.

confer but never with us, the pupil midwives, who would be most involved thereafter.

The baby was not taken to the mother: she was told it was too ill for her to see. It would be left in a corner of the nursery out of sight of casual visitors, and fed only on warm water. The notes carried some sort of hieroglyphic to this effect, although I never managed to work out what it meant. The baby was to be cuddled a great deal, and never to have the bottle propped up in the cot as we sometimes did under pressure. It died within a few days usually.

Do I feel guilt at contributing to the care of these babies and thereby to their deaths? No, I don't. They had no capacity for more than the vegetative functions of breathing and swallowing. There was no person there, no consciousness, nor would there ever be. The burden on the parents of those that lived, albeit only for a few years at most, could be catastrophic for families. I just wish, as I had wished in Deal, that we had been consulted and our co-operation not taken totally for granted.

A girl of sixteen, very pretty and very frightened, screamed mightily. Sister said, 'Do be quiet, girl. You should have thought of this nine months ago when you had your fun.'

Another girl in her teens, admitted in the routine way via the admission room where we bathed, pubic-shaved and gave enemas to all incoming patients, went white when asked to get into the bath and said she couldn't possibly. She hadn't bathed ever since she found out it wasn't safe and only washed herself very carefully. Sister said loudly, 'That is a very dirty way to be – you can't wash properly unless you get into a bath. So in you get, my girl, and stop being so silly. Of course it's safe. You won't slip. Nurse here will hold on to you.'

She did so, with a little urging from Sister's hand in her back, weeping helplessly, and wept throughout her labour. Afterwards, when she was delivered of a fine healthy boy, I asked her what had upset her so. She said she'd been to these special classes 'about how the baby grows before he's born and they had said the baby got his oxygen by breathing through the cord between his belly button and mine. So I daren't bathe in case I drowned him.' Oh, the things that are done in the name of teaching!

I would not want to generalise, but I have to say that medical students, who may be charming, courteous and kindly young men when they are on their own or with just one companion, turn into monsters in groups. One such group had taken to prowling our ward at night, looking for something to eat and drink. Constant hunger is as great a burden to them as it is to nurses and all other students, no doubt. But these were still austere times, with sweets and biscuits still rationed. There was little available.

But because we were on the maternity ward, half a dozen of them picked on me one night while I was putting together the hot drinks for the newly delivered mums. 'You must have dozens of bottles of milk here. Cream, too, I wouldn't be surprised. New mothers always get the treats. Come on, give us a drink and a biccy. Go on, don't be mean.' On and on they went.

Too tired to argue, I told them to come back in half an hour and made a half-dozen mugs of very rich Horlicks for them, using the National Dried Milk of which we had a fair supply and plenty of saccharine. I doubted I would have to do the job again. Tonight would be the one and only time, if my experience was to be the same as that of the senior pupil before me who had been equally pestered and who had found the ideal answer.

I made it thick and sweet and they adored it. ' Lovely,' they said. 'Knew you'd come up with the goods! Another cup going?'

'Sorry,' I said sweetly. 'I barely had enough breast milk from the bank to manage that lot. Try tomorrow night – the mums'll have expressed some more by then.'

I never saw their greenish faces again. They fled from my ward kitchen and I laughed at their departing backs.

And then thought again and this time was livid. Why should they be so sickened at being told they'd drunk breast milk? Not that they had: I wouldn't have wasted it on them. Why should they find the idea so offensive? And I took offence myself at their horrid maleness.

When I had done my required number of deliveries in the labour
wards – and I'm not sure who sweated most, the mother or me, for
either way labour is well named – it was time to get a taste of 'the district'. I looked forward to that. The ward was overhung always by
Sister's prickly personality, and I thought life with just one senior
midwife and two other pupils to make up a small team would be
much more interesting.

It was. But first there was the matter of transport.

At least I'd had some experience in riding bikes from the days in
Cirencester when I borrowed them from friends and went tooling off
for hours and many miles. I looked at the bicycles we were being
offered with great dubiety, however. Heavy iron-framed sit-up-and-
beg machines, they were painted in broad yellow and black stripes all
over, like metallic wasps, and deeply engraved on the handlebars
(no way could this be wire-wooled off) was 'STOLEN FROM GUY'S'.

As we were not yet qualified midwives our uniforms did not include
their regulation caps and coats so we had to go out in our ward uniforms of striped cotton dresses topped by starched aprons, our little red
and black capes and our caps pinned precariously to our heads. At least
we were no longer wearing butterfly-type caps. We had progressed as
qualified State Registered Nurses to frilled Sister Doras, much more
senior-looking and, of course, less likely to blow off. In theory.

That first morning I mounted the bike with some trepidation but
found it was true: once learned, bike-riding is a lifelong skill. I went
careering over the cobbles of Snowhill, the street just outside where
we would sometimes advise husbands of mothers who were taking
their time getting their labour started to take them riding in the
family car with the tyres let down a little. 'A few ups and downs,'
we'd say, 'and she'll soon break her waters.'

I had no doubt now that our advice was superb. I bounced like a
demented Tigger and thought I'd ruined my underpinnings for ever.

The Old Kent Road greeted us, Sister in charge of the District more
sedate in front of us, with hoots of laughter. And no wonder. My friends
were not good cyclists and wobbled all over the place and I kept getting
my wheels locked into the tramlines. At one point I feared I'd have to

ride all the way to the depot to get the bike out, but a nice copper managed to do it for me. (The depot trip happened another day.)

But we got there, way out by the docks where the new flats were being built on bomb-sites and also to the little streets that had survived the pasting of the Blitz. It felt oddly like home, even though it had been so long since I had lived in Antcliff Street: it was the same sort of terrain.

We trailed behind Sister from house to house and flat to flat, talking to the new mothers, then weighing the babies on Sister's portable meathook-type scales, checking the bigger children if Mum asked us to and being generally useful. I was fascinated by the rooms we saw. Some were furnished much as our Hackney flat had been, with basic wooden furniture and not much style, but others were very fancy, with draped silk and satin curtains and bright plastic flowers on low tables, all very reminiscent of the Festival of Britain.

These dockers were prosperous, Sister told us, on the way between addresses. Because of the need for post-war exports they were working long hours, which made life for them better in one sense but worse in another. The women were left alone more, and with new babies, Sister said, that could lead to depression.

That was the first and only time the subject was mentioned to any of us during our training. It would be some years still before midwives accepted the commonness of post-birth depression or the need to be active in helping mothers deal with it. You have to ask them to tell you about it, insist they do and refuse to take no for an answer. Mothers who are depressed are very good at denying it, which I was to find out for myself eventually.

I had to do one night on the district just before we transferred to the Hackney hospital for the next phase of our training. The maternity ward at RNH had had to be closed down because of a severe case of staph aureus infection in the very fabric of the walls.*

---

* This dangerous bacterium has been a hospital threat for at least fifty years, though nowadays it is worse than it was, being resistant to almost every antibiotic there is.

It took a long time to sort out so I never worked there at all in the end. No bike this time. I had been assigned to the Flying Squad ambulance. There were, I think, three attached to Guy's but they co-operated with other hospitals in the area and other District Midwives' offices and could be called to almost any part of East London. Most nights on which the pupils were in the ambulance it was quiet. On my night it was not. And I shall never forget it.

It was the fifth floor of a block of flats almost on the edge of the river down at the Isle of Dogs and the lift, to no one's surprise, was broken. We hauled ourselves up the stairs, all carrying heavy equipment, for we had been told it was a case of post-partum haemorrhage. At the time the message came in, it was not too urgent, but the lead doctor on the Flying Squad ambulance said something about post-partums always being tricky and made us hurry. We arrived at the top of the stairs panting like dogs.

The husband was at the door watching for us and almost dragged us in. There were four small children in a front room with an older woman. 'They're scared to go to bed,' she told anyone who caught her eye. 'I told 'em it was late but they was scared so they're better off here with their old granny, eh, girls?' The children sat and stared at all the comings and goings and said nothing. They looked, I thought, under six. If our patient was their mother, and she probably was, she was having a fifth baby. Didn't that make her a grand multip?* Shouldn't she have been in hospital?

The district midwife, whom we didn't know, was in the bedroom. One look at her when we got in there told everyone all they needed to know. The bed was a welter of blood and the midwife was kneeling in the middle of it, the legs of the patient on each side of her. As far as I could work out she had one fist jammed into the vagina and the other holding an ice bag to the patient's belly. She said, over her shoulder, 'It was very slow, no real problem, knew you were coming, pulse reasonable for a PPH and then suddenly she shot this.'

---

* A mother who has had several deliveries, and is therefore at greater risk of complications during birth.

The team moved with amazing smoothness. I was just a pupil appendage there to dogsbody so I stood as close to the wall as I could, with the gear at my feet, ready to hand over what was needed. The doctor joined the midwife on the bed and I could see nothing. Then someone called for oxygen and I was able to deal with that, getting the cylinder round the bed fast. The woman's eyes were half closed and she was the colour of scrubbing soap. I'd only ever seen someone so exsanguinated once before and that had been a man who had suddenly burst an aneurysm in the middle of the night and become, for a few brief moments, a blood fountain. Although this was different I was afraid for the same outcome.

But they worked well, and after a while it seemed she might be all right. They had drips going fast to replace her lost fluids and heaven knows what else going in as injections of one sort or another. They put more ice on her belly, and then the doctor got the midwife to climb off the bed, which she did stiffly and awkwardly. I put out a hand to help her. Behind her the patient on the bed seemed to jerk, and the doctor, who had turned back to look at her, said, 'Bloody hell, she's fitting.'

The jerking went on for what seemed like an age. The team gathered round again and I could see nothing, and then, slowly, they all pulled back. The doctor looked at his watch and said, 'One fifty? You agree? What's the date? Right,' and he wrote carefully in the notes.

There was a silence as we all stood about awkwardly. Then the midwife reached across and pulled up a sheet to cover the patient, who was lying sprawled and exposed.

'The autopsy will tell,' the doctor said. 'I imagine it was her heart at the end. Is the baby all right?'

The midwife blinked and then said, 'Oh yes, he's in the crib in the children's room. He was fine, a bonny boy. He—' She stopped. 'It was why she went in for a fifth,' she said. 'Her husband wanted a boy.'

'I'll check him,' the doctor said 'and we could take him back to the hospital for care, under the circumstances. If the family want that, of course. Shall I talk to the father or will you?'

'I will,' the midwife said, and she looked almost as yellow as her patient and was clearly on the edge of tears. 'She's my patient, I'll talk to them.'

On the way back to the hospital, as I sat looking at the baby sleeping contentedly in the crib, the doctor said suddenly, 'Well, pupil midwife, what have you learned with us tonight?'

'That all babies should be born in hospital where it's safe.' I said it without stopping to think, and when I did, I wouldn't have taken back a word of it.

'Yes,' he said, after a moment. 'I know what you mean. You could be right.' No one else said a word all the way back to Guy's.

Thirty

I couldn't cope with midwifery training after that. Part two, with its emphasis on delivery in the patients' own homes, struck me as taking part in something that was downright wrong. The risks were too great, and I was certain I would never tolerate such care for myself if I were ever to have a baby. That was an unlikely scenario but I needed a yardstick for the sort of care I was prepared to give patients. And if it was care I would refuse for myself then I was damned if I'd ever provide it.

So I did the exams just to have the qualification, for what little it was worth to me, and headed back to RNH as fast as I could. Matron took me back to Private Theatres, with the nearest thing to open arms I had ever seen from her because I returned in the middle of a staffing crisis. They happened at least once a month, mind you, which goes to show that nothing changes in the NHS except scale. We had monthly staffing crises; today they have daily or even hourly ones.

But I was still restless. I loved my job, always had, but there seemed to be no point in anything without a specific aim in life of the sort that getting my qualification had been.

I went out with friends from the hospital, swimming, maybe, or wandering over nearby Hampstead Heath or sitting around in the new frothy-coffee bars that were just arriving in London, or using the free tickets the West End theatres used to send us, then eating in Lyons' Salad Bowl or Carvery restaurants where we could stuff ourselves cheerfully for under half a crown.

To make friends outside the hospital, which Nancy had long ago told me I should do, I had got involved with a youth club in West Hampstead that she knew of, and people there were good fun with their drama group and sports activities and a mock-Parliament, which I enjoyed. But that was all. Just a bit of socialising, really. Not an *aim* in life.

I visited Nancy often, watching her look less and less well and still refusing to talk about whatever it was and pretending it was nothing. I was informed quietly by Homey, who was more family now than housekeeper, because she thought I should know, that Nancy had been told she had to have some sort of operation – Homey had no idea what – and they were even now making plans about the care of the children 'as though I couldn't manage perfectly well!' she said, and of course she did. She was the classic treasure.

Belonging to the club gave me something to talk about to Nancy because for the first time since the night of the champagne I didn't want to include her in hospital gossip. Not when I now knew that she'd soon be seeing all she could possibly want of hospitals.

Then something happened to give me my goal. One afternoon when the operations were done for the day and the junior staff were cleaning up, I was sitting in Sister's office preparing the operation lists for the coming week. One of our senior consultants came in and I was surprised to see him. He was our radiologist and a fine therapist of great reputation but he rarely came to our theatres. I looked at the lists. He had nothing coming up that I could see. 'Sir?' I stood up in the proper manner, folding my hands on my apron.

'Staff Nurse Chetwynd?'

'Yes, sir.'

'The clever one.'

I went puce, I think. Certainly very flushed. 'Sir?'

'I've been asking around. Sister Bishop and Matron both say so. Would you like to train as a radiographer?'

'Sir?' I was amazed. Train as a radiographer? Doing X-rays? I'd be bored out of my skull just being a photographer.

'There's much more to it than merely taking films, you know.'

I reddened even more at his mind-reading skill. 'Sir,' I said, highly embarrassed.

'We're developing a major department downstairs for radiotherapy for all the cancers we can possibly treat. I have new ideas, new plans – we could really make a major difference to the treatment of cancer, you know. But I need the right staff. Doubly trained staff would be perfect to lead the unit. Someone who is both nurse and radiographer, don't you see? It will take you just three years and you'll be fascinated, I'm sure you will. And you'll be unusual – a doubly trained nurse and radiographer, a remarkably useful person and perfect for me. It needs intelligence but they all say you have that.'

I stood and stared at him for several moments, then opened my mouth to answer. He shook his head. 'Just think about it. No hurry. Think about it. Great future for you, if you do it, and Matron said – yes – well, she seemed to approve, as did Sister Bishop. But I think I already told you that, didn't I? Yes,' and he smiled and trailed away.

'Sir,' I managed to say to his retreating back, and that was all.

Of course I thought about it. I thought a great deal, and two days later when McNeill Love came into the theatre I got him in a corner. If I could be considered as suitable for a second qualification in radiography, then I could do it in something I'd find more interesting.

'Please, sir, is it true you're the Dean of the Royal Free Hospital as well as being one of our consultants?'

'Something of the sort.' He grinned, then, 'Want to invite some of our medical students to a dance here?'

This was a sly dig, and it amazed me that he knew enough of the hospital's gossip to make it. A year or so earlier I had organised a dance for all the nurses of every year and invited doctors from various sister hospitals, including Highlands Hospital where we had done some of our training. The acceptances came with flattering rapidity and there was much agreeable anticipation around the place.

Then, two days before the dance, Matron called me to her office. 'Nurse, this dance you are organising. You have invited Highlands doctors, I hear?'

'Yes, Matron.' I was puzzled. I'd done dances before, and music evenings and all sorts. This was nothing new. Why the fuss?

'I have discovered that five of their doctors are black men, Nurse. We can't have black men at the Royal Northern! You will have to withdraw the invitations. I can't have black men here.'

It was the first time – indeed the only time – I ever dared to argue with her, but I did. I pointed out that the senior consultants at Highlands would be mortified if I insulted their staff now by dis-inviting them, that our nurses would be devastated if I cancelled the dance, but since the latter was my only choice under the circumstances—

The dance went ahead and was very successful. Matron took the evening off, and left the hospital premises, which was very rare for her.

I'd love to see her in practice now. Of course she was racist all the way through to her middle – and so was almost everyone else in those pre-Windrush days. It's taken a few decades to make racism of my old Matron's up-front sort unacceptable.

'This isn't about dances, sir,' I said now. 'It's just that I've decided I'd like to do medicine. If you could get me a place at the Royal Free—'

He stared at me, pursed his lips, shook his head and generally fussed at me. 'You're mad, woman. Don't you know that one good nurse is worth two doctors any day?'

'Possibly, sir, but all the same, I'd like to try. Will you help me?'

He thought for a while. 'Matron'll kill me,' he said.

I smiled happily at that. 'No, sir. She won't be able to refuse me.'

'How's that?'

'She let one of the other consultants offer me a different training so she's got the idea in her head already.' I explained the offer I'd had.

'Good girl,' he said at length. 'Nasty place to hang about, a radiology unit. All those invisible rays! Did for Marie Curie, you know. Yes. All right. If you've got first MB—'

'Sir?'

'Botany, zoology, chemistry and physics at senior matriculation level.'

'Not yet. But I'll get it,' I said. 'Just watch me.'

I was right. After the business of Dr Anthony Green's invitation to me, Matron couldn't refuse my request for transfer to Outpatients so that I could be on duty all day and go to evening classes.

When she'd agreed and the details had been worked out I headed for her door but she stopped me. 'I wish I were like you, Nurse,' she said.

This was a facer, and I said what anyone else would have said under the circumstances. Nothing.

'You can talk, you see. And write. Your ward reports are so well done they leave me – well, I wish I were you. Those BMA essay competitions you won. I remember those.'

So did I. A considerable time ago the Bish had sent for two of us, Mildred Simpson, a droll, bespectacled girl from the set junior to mine who looked as though the proverbial butter would remain for ever unmelted in her mouth but who was a witty, often wicked and delightful person to know, and me. She informed us – she didn't request or suggest but *informed* us – that we were to enter the British Medical Association's essay competition for nurses. 'There are prizes,' she had added evilly. 'Twenty pounds for the winner, ten for the runner-up.'

So we did as we were told, and that year Milly won first prize and her twenty quid and I was highly commended and contented with my tenner. The second year when we were Bishoped into entering again I got the twenty pounds and Milly the ten. We had both found this symmetry highly satisfactory.

And now Matron was looking at me and saying she envied me.

Had she ever said it to Milly, who was away now being a midwife? I'd never know. It was bad enough that she was saying it to me.

'And you can talk your way into and out of anything, can't you? Well, good luck with this new plan, and do remember that nursing will always be there for you if you need it. It isn't second best to medicine. It's itself, a practice and a vocation all of its own, and it will never let you down. One good nurse is worth two doctors, they say, and I believe it. But all the same, Nurse, good luck with your ambitions. And take care of your health. A full day in Outpatients, then every evening studying means you will need to eat and sleep well. No socialising.'

'Yes, Matron,' I said. 'No, Matron. Thank you, Matron,' and fled.

I signed on at the Northern Polytechnic, a short walk away on Holloway Road, and settled to work. It was blinding hard work, frankly, almost too hard to enjoy properly. It was a case of keeping doggedly on week after week.

Each day I was in OPD by 8 a.m. to set up my day's clinics, and until six it was a blur of busyness as we dealt with an average of seventy patients per clinic per day. Then, after the panic of clearing up, I almost ran down to the poly for classes, which started at six thirty, and stayed there till nine. Then a walk back to the RNH, where Matron had arranged for supper to be kept for me every night in the main dining room. I didn't eat it very often: I was too tired. A phone call home to Nancy, then a long hot bath and bed with a book. Not that I got through more than a page or two before I conked out completely.

All this hard work had another virtue: it took my mind off Nancy, who was admitted to hospital to have her ovaries removed as part of the preventive treatment for her breast cancer.

The ovarian removal did not help. The cancer, it seemed, was growing. So the surgeon performed an adrenalectomy, removing both her adrenal glands so that thereafter she had to swallow a battery of steroid drugs just to stay alive.

That didn't work either, and the surgeon was planning to perform a removal of the pituitary gland, a major brain operation, to see if that would control the hormone production which was supporting the cancer, when he realised Nancy had secondary deposits in her lungs and bones. She could not survive long now. No point in performing more heroic surgery on such a fragile patient.

I phoned home regularly and visited most weekends, and worked and worked the rest of the time. And it paid off. At the end of the term I had passed botany and zoology with over 90 per cent because of the work I'd already done in human biology in my nursing course, and managed to get a decent pass in chemistry. I ploughed physics, however, unsurprisingly as I had always hated maths and the two marched hand in hand. I'd have to do a resit. But I was almost in medical school.

And then came the call I had been dreading. I was to go to Nancy's new house urgently. Amazingly, in the middle of all this illness, Louis and Nancy had decided to move to a big new house in Edgware, the one Nancy had always wanted. She got there just in time to die in her own bed a few days later, still not yet fifty years old.

Again, masses of people at the funeral, masses of people at the house, masses of chocolates and sweets. Lots of silly people, it seemed to me in my raw state, saying singularly silly things, like 'It was a blessed release' and 'She's in a better place now' and 'In the end it was peaceful.'

I know it's hard sometimes to find the right thing to say to bereaved people, but you don't always have to say anything much. Just a warm hug and 'I'm sorry' can do wonders. I remembered the lovely Irish phrase, 'I'm so sorry for your trouble,' and thought, They've got it right. I wish these people could.

Except for one, who lifted me out of the worst of it. She had been a great friend of my grandmother and she turned to me, her face streaming, and said, 'Oh, thank God your grandma didn't live to see this day. It would have killed her!' I laughed till I cried, which was what I needed most.

It was less than a year since Grandma's death and now I went through a particularly disagreeable sort of *déjà vu*. The sense of loss I felt was exactly like the dreadful homesickness of the Canadian years

from which Nancy, with Grandma and Max, had rescued me. I
wanted to tell Nancy that because she would have been interested.
But, of course, I couldn't and there was no one else I could think of
who would really understand.

That was what I needed most, right then. Someone of my *own* to
talk to.

Thirty-one

I have never subscribed to what I call the Jigsaw Puzzle Theory of human mating a.k.a. the Mr Right Theory, even though it is extremely popular in romantic circles. This suggests that for each and every one of us there is, somewhere in the world, a person who perfectly fits our assorted protuberances and hollows, both physical and emotional. The only problem is to find him or her. Once found it's a case of Happy Ever After.

Poppycock.

When I became an agony aunt one of the things I learned very early is that those who subscribe to this notion are the ones who seem to come a romantic cropper faster than anyone else. 'What happened to my soul-mate to make him treat me that way?' they cried, in letter after letter, and I never had the heart to reply, 'You woke up, love, and discovered you'd been dreaming.'

What matters is *readiness*. There comes a time in the lives of most men and women when their various circumstances – age, work, finances, domestic lifestyle, hormones, just for starters – coalesce into a powerful need for a partner. The next person of the right sex (and all this is just as true for homosexual people as heterosexuals, of course) who turns up and who has one or two other useful triggers, such as a physical likeness to a person the would-be soul-mate has loved before (have you ever noticed how many women choose carbon copies of their dads and how many men want a girl just like the girl who married dear old Dad?) *and who is also ready* will seem devastatingly attractive.

Any less charming aspects of their personalities that inevitably show themselves as time moves on will become acceptable by the besotted one as part of the love object and even become adorable in time.

But if an individual isn't ready then someone who is a cross between the Angel Gabriel and Robert Redford (or Cleopatra and Julia Roberts – take your pick) could grovel at his or her feet and they wouldn't even notice.

Of course, there are other factors that complicate the simplicity of the readiness theory, but it's one I've seen operate so successfully so often that I can't help but adhere to it. But it took me a while and some experience to work it out. I was certainly not thinking about it on a cold February evening when for once I had no classes at the poly and decided to go and see Oliver.

He was one of the people who spent time at the youth club in Hampstead I had joined so long ago, where he directed the drama group in its efforts. We had been friends for ages, tooled around on various trips and generally enjoyed each other's company. He was also homosexual and brave about it, in those cruel days before John Wolfenden's resounding report. He made no attempt to hide his tendencies and I admired him for that. He made me laugh, and people who can make me laugh are my friends immediately.

He had been saying to me, for months, 'Darling, you really must come along and see my little amateurs some time – they're very ducky and not at all bad,' but I'd had no time. Till now. So, that evening I threw on a coat over my uniform because I was too tired to change, and possibly brushed my hair when I took off my cap, and that was about it. No makeup, not even lipstick. I rarely bothered in those days anyway, but that evening I think I looked particularly scruffy. And I didn't give a damn.

I walked into the big hall that doubled as the club's theatre, a respectable space that could hold over two hundred in the audience, with a sizeable stage and good backstage accommodation, and the sophistication of a separate light box at the back of the hall. A rehearsal was in full flow, and I watched and soon recognised Noël Coward's *Tonight at Eight Thirty*. They were steaming away at it with great vigour and I was most taken with their performances.

As I watched I wanted so much to be part of what was going on. The cast clearly liked each other greatly and there was much laughter and bawling from Oliver out front when things went wrong on stage, and great giggling when they made errors which led to more laughter. It was *fun*. And I was so very short of fun.

And then the act came to an end and they broke for coffee. Oliver saw me standing quietly by the door and roared in the deep, strong voice which was one of his most attractive assets, only not for me that evening. 'Darling! Here at last from the arduous business of saving lives – how *divine* to see you.' He gave me a huge hug and kiss on both cheeks (very theatrical in those days, commonplace now). Then he looked down the hall towards the back and called, 'Desmond! Come here! I want you to meet the most wonderful woman in London.'

No, my heart did not turn over. Nor did my loins leap or whatever it is they're supposed to do, according to the romantic love-at-first-sight brigade. But I did look at this tall dark chap in the red sweater with a somewhat supercilious expression on his face, which said, 'Oh, yeah?' to Oliver's description of me, and thought, Ooh, yes, please!

I asked him once, long after, what he thought that first time he saw me, and at first he said he couldn't remember, which was altogether too masculine a response for my taste, but under a certain amount of pressure he managed eventually to dredge up a recollection of thinking a vague, Hmm. Interesting.

That was the start of it. I suddenly became utterly fascinated by *Tonight at Eight Thirty* and turned up at every rehearsal I could, including the all-night dress rehearsal, even if it meant hurrying there after my physics classes.

I 'helped' with lighting, which involved being in the light box at the back of the hall with Desmond, where the propinquity was delightful. We did real work, of course, making sure that all the light cues were followed and the effects came in on time, but there was so much accidental brushing of hands and shoulders that the little box seemed to me to hum with an erotic charge.

For three whole weeks I took up fencing, which was played at the club and at which Des was an expert. He had to teach me, of course, which involved much wrapping of his arms around me to get the right stance. It nearly ruined my inside thigh muscles, though: it's an amazingly tough sport for all its apparent elegance. I was so glad when he finally got the message and I was able to quit the world of foil, épée and sabre.

I also went to a lot of trouble to be first in the queue at the hospital for all the available free theatre tickets. He rose to them like a plump trout to a juicy fly, of course. Free theatre to an actor! It was like *aqua vitae* to a midwife, I quoted at him, and he laughed. But he didn't deny it. He must have been content to be with me as well as at the theatre, though; there was much hand-holding and sometimes he would oh-so-casually drape his arm across the back of my seat. It was all your real fifties-style slow escalation of contact that built a head of sexual steam that was terrific. We may not have leaped into bed immediately but we certainly had fun on the way there. Lots of romance and none the worse for it.

So, after years of conviction that I would never marry and inflict on another person the misery I had seen in my childhood, and particularly the misery of children caught in the crossfire of a marriage, I went and married.

I was dressed up in tulle and satin to make Des's family and Max and Bessie happy and felt a complete ass. I had two bridesmaids, my own cousin Susan, Nancy's daughter, and Des's cousin Jenny (who grew up to be the remarkable writer Jenny Diski), and it was altogether too traditional for words. I kept remembering my original plan, which was just to shack up with Des, but he had insisted that I should make an honest man of him, so what could I do?

I would have preferred a quiet trip to a register office but Des wanted the works – and so did his family – so there I was all tarted up in a synagogue and not liking it at all, but it didn't really matter. It was just the two of us I cared about (all that religion!).

I hadn't told my parents I was marrying – they would have taken that as an invitation and they were the last people I wanted with me that day.

As I say, I'd hit a period of readiness for a mate. That is not to say I wanted to marry. I most certainly did not, but I wanted very much indeed to get into bed with Des as soon as possible and as often as possible.

It was interesting to me to feel this way (to put it mildly) because although I'd met and gone out with a few men it had been a very few. I was incredibly choosy for someone so far from a glamour-pants. Even if I was broke when a night out at a film, with supper thrown in, was on offer – considered by the other nurses as worth the dreariest of company – I still stayed in.

The interesting thing about what happened when I met Des was that although he was certain he had no right even to consider a relationship, seeing he was an impecunious actor of small prospects (I said we were very much fifties people: well, he was even more than I was), he didn't jump at my offer of – well, in essence – a love affair with no strings.

Many men would have. If I'd been a man I would have! But he, too, had come from a miserable background and what he wanted above all was stability: someone he could trust never to let him down, a world with a solid base that would not shift under his feet. It was clear to him, he said, that if we just became lovers that would be all we ever were and that it wouldn't be for long. We'd drift apart and that would be that. But if we were to be as he wanted us to be, a solid-for-always pair of lovers, there was only one way that he knew of to make it happen. And that was marriage.

It wasn't as easy as that, mind you. He got an appalling attack of the coldest of feet and broke it off For Ever. I was desolate, but no power on this earth would have got me to run after him – badly as I wanted to. Pride isn't in it with me.

But I didn't have to. Three days later he phoned me. He'd been as desolate as me and, oddly, on the Saturday morning of For Ever we both happened to hear a radio playing Ella Fitzgerald singing, 'It Was Just One of Those Things'. My friend in the next room was startled when I stamped in to her and shouted, 'Turn that bloody thing off!' And Des's mother was equally shocked when he did the same thing so hard that he almost broke her radio.

That was the last time we were parted, ever, except for occasional stays in hospital for the next forty-six years and counting.

Does it sound odd today that I responded as I did? Maybe. But the fact is that I accepted his view. As he said, if I wanted him – and oh, boy, did I! – I had to make an honest man of him.

We're still lovers, and we have been married since 23 June 1957. That is one hell of a lot of years. We have never had an affair, either of us. What's more, we were both virgins when we met each other so neither of us has ever had another sexual partner.

Why have we been so sexually faithful? I always have, and still do, enjoy admiring a neat round male bottom or a chap in a really tight pair of jeans swaggering towards me down the street. But the fact is I never wanted to have sex with anyone else, and often found the mere idea repellent. For me sexual pleasure has always been closely tied to the man I married.

Sometimes we sit and read or whatever and don't utter a word for ages, but that isn't boredom. That's just being comfortable together. The closer you are and the more you know each other, the more there is to know and the more interesting it is to be with each other. That's why when we're apart for a day – I may be working in another town or he may be spending a day at the galleries instead of painting at home – we phone each other two or three times. There's too much to tell each other to wait till the evening.

Does all this sound soppy and sentimental? Or unbelievable? When we took part in a BBC series called *The Other Half*, in the eighties, about couples who work together as well as live together, people said we were 'absurdly close' and 'over-involved'. Yet we are not unique. We live our version of the state called marriage. It's somewhat old-fashioned, perhaps, but we know lots of couples just like us (some of whom are gay). Other people run their marriages differently, and I would never dream of saying to them that our way is best.

In terms of financial prospects and meeting the costs of making a home for ourselves we had as little as each other. I was a nurse earning under five hundred pounds a year; he was an actor more out of work than in it and having to visit the labour exchange more often than he liked. He did earn a little extra from time to time working on the shows at the club, bringing a professional touch to the lighting (as he had been doing the night we met) and later the direction. Neither of us had any savings. I can remember us sitting over a cup of tea in Temple Gardens on a summer afternoon and working out that we needed a thousand pounds to put a basic home together. It was such a ridiculous sum that we laughed. We'd manage somehow.

And we did. We found a beautiful flat in Muswell Hill in North London, which cost a massive £1995 for a ninety-year lease. The LCC granted us a hundred per cent mortgage because we were both City people by birth and residence, reared and educated in London, and everyone who came to our wedding was encouraged by the families to give us money to buy furniture.

The most vivid memory of my wedding was sitting in the train going to Bournemouth for our honeymoon with the lid of Des's case open, so that we could hide behind it and count the loot. We'd got enough for a living room and half a bedroom.

Because of the erratic nature of an actor's career and earning capacity Des lived with his parents, which he hated because he did not get on with his father, an inveterate gambler who lost the family two homes and two businesses and never saw what was wrong in his behaviour. My people – Max and everyone – were affectionate and nice to be with but I was very much an independent operator and kept myself on my own income. Which was minute.

I could expect nothing at all from my parents. In fact, when Max was sorting out Grandma's estate (and, of course, she had died intestate, much too scared of death to make a will, so it took poor Max ages) he wrote to my father suggesting that, as he had had no contact with his mother for decades and I needed money to train as a doctor, it would be nice to let his share of Grandma's small estate come to me.

Max got a lawyer's letter by return post demanding every penny, pronto.

I wanted Des to continue as an actor. I discovered I had seen him on the stage of the Old Vic, when he was in *Henry the Eighth* in Coronation year, although I couldn't pretend I'd noticed him.

He wanted me to go on with my medical-training plans. I talked to McNeill Love, who made it patently clear that there was no way this side of Armageddon that the medical school would tolerate a married woman medical student. I had to choose: did I want Des or the title Dr?

The only thing that surprises me now is that I didn't even think of protesting about the injustice of it. But it was the norm then, and hard to buck.

Then Des chose to leave theatre. I was heartbroken. I'd built up this great scenario involving blissful love in an attic until he achieved a howling success when he took the world by storm. He was more rational, knowing that at any given time some eighty or so per cent of his profession was unemployed and that he, as a young character actor, might have to wait years to grow into his ideal age. He said, 'I've done some good work. The RSC at Stratford, the Old Vic, Donald Wolfit's company, some Greek tragedy, regular slots with Tony Hancock, but not often enough or enough of it. I keep getting hungry.'

He was amazingly staunch. The decision once taken, against my most earnest pleading, he got a job at Simpson's in Piccadilly selling ties and shirts, which he hated, and even when he got a call from a major BBC producer offering him a good part, he stuck to his guns. 'I've left theatre,' he said. And that was that. Later he went into advertising at which he was very good, though he found it boring after a while, but still he stuck to his decision. He had, he said, responsibilities. He was now a husband and he couldn't do just what he wanted.

He went on doing what he believed he ought to do rather than what he might have wanted to do for almost the first fifteen years of our marriage, after which everything changed and his work with it. But whatever personal ambitions he had in those years he kept to himself.

I was very proud of him then and I still am.

We had agreed to choose our marital home near to where I could get the best sister's job, for we needed the better pay a sister got and I was well qualified to apply for a senior post. I hunted about for a remarkably short time and was offered a cracker of a job in the theatres at King's College but Des blenched and said in horror, '*South* London?'

I had to agree. That would be like emigrating.[*] So, we found our flat in Muswell Hill after I got a job at the Whittington Hospital. It was a job I could enjoy and still get home in time in the evenings to do the housewife bit. Also, of course, it gave me free weekends, a rare treat in nursing circles. The pay was about £675 per annum, which I thought splendid.

We both thought we started off our marriage on a really auspicious note. I was blissfully happy.

---

[*] There are North Londoners who think there should be customs sheds and immigration officials on the bridges . . .

Thirty-two

There were times in those first few years of marriage when I felt like a character in a woman's magazine story. Des was all I could have wanted in a companion. Being his lover was easy: it felt right from the start. We laughed a lot, we learned a lot, we were surprised and gratified a lot by our own responses.

But the companionship element was startling to me. I had been fearful, as a fairly set-in-her-ways twenty-six-year-old who had run her own life for many years, about how I would rub along with a twenty-eight-year-old just as set in his ways who was, in addition, a somewhat traditional person compared with radical me.

But it was fine. He wasn't that traditional for a start. He was very willing to learn new things. Neither of us could cook, really. I'd lived in hospitals for too long so never had the chance to learn the skill. He was better than I was because of his years of living in digs when on the road, and sometimes catering for himself, so between us we learned.

The same applied to cleaning, sewing, ironing and generally being householders. It never occurred to either of us that these should be female-only tasks, and years later, when the newspapers and magazines were full of paeans of praise for the New Man who mucked in at home and in due course took on his share of babycare, I was exceedingly amused. I had a *circa* 1957 model.

We also had some spectacular rows. My scruffiness, his nit-picking, my disorderliness, his obsessive neatness. My rushing at decisions, his mature deliberations that went on till they fell off the tree because of overripeness. My short temper that made me fly up in the air like a Harrier jump jet, and his tendency to go all strong and silent when he was upset. My extravagance, his parsimony.

And here I must admit, dammitall, that in this department he was right and I was utterly wrong. When we picked up a bit of extra money from a cheque paying an extra fee for the sale of a *Tony Hancock Show* to the United Arab Emirates or wherever, or I earned a little on the side, my instinct was to blue it on fun. 'We'll go up to town, catch a show!' I'd cry. 'We'll have a slap-up Soho dinner!'

'We'll go to a local flick, and have a fish and chip supper,' he'd say. 'That way we get a bit of fun and save a bit too.'

We settled to an agreeable lifestyle, seeing friends from the drama group where we still did shows and Des still earned the odd cheque for providing lighting or directorial skills, giving coffee parties in our tiny shiny new flat and feeling no end proprietorial when we did it.

And I started to write.

It was all rather casual and accidental, really. I had been bitten slightly by the writing-for-money bug back in those days when the Bish made Milly Simpson and me enter that BMA essay competition and we had both won money. That cheque had concentrated my mind wonderfully, I must say, but it had still never occurred to me that I was in any sense a writer. But it was fun to have a go, so I started, in a small way.

I tried articles for tiny magazines catering to young mums. I wrote bits for the *Nursing Times* and the *Nursing Mirror*. I kept the pieces I did as short and crisp as I could, wrote them out in my best handwriting and sent them off to the editors complete with stamped addressed envelope for return.

One editor sent my piece back with a terse note. 'Get it typed.

Then I'll read it.' So I asked Des if I could use his typewriter, which he had had since he was thirteen. He, careful chap that he was and knowing my clumsiness with equipment, offered to type it for me.

He not only typed it: he commented on my grammar, something on which I had always quite prided myself, and punctuation. Des has some remarkable views on commas and semicolons, and we have had some spectacular rows about them. We once tried to collaborate on a piece of writing and gave up after the first paragraph and the worst day of our entire marriage. We can, we decided, sleep together, burp together, fart together, but by all that's intelligent never let anyone persuade us ever again to write together.

The articles began to sell. I was entranced. I got more ambitious and was sending off articles three, four or more times a week.

It was strange. In our very early months of marriage we had both taken on little part-time jobs – moonlighting, in fact – to earn the extra money we needed to buy a fridge and a vacuum-cleaner. Des did a drama-teaching job and I got a gig teaching sex education to twelve- and thirteen-year-olds at a local youth club, and we got our kitchen extras.

Now we were in the heady situation of not needing to buy more gear. We had all we wanted as well as all we needed, and we could save real money, have a busy bank account like rich people. For the first time in my life I had more than I needed. I felt rich, rich, rich, in a way I never have since, although I've earned a great deal over the years. And so much I owe to Des and his careful management and his 'nit-picking' and 'parsimony', about which I teased him.

I can see us now. We are standing in the minute hallway of our gorgeous flat, which I had come to love dearly and that Des had painted in half a dozen colours so that it looked like a Delaunay painting, only to my eye much better, and he was holding in his hand an envelope he had just picked up from the floor.

'It's going to be you who'll make us rich,' he said. 'You're going to build a great career out of writing,' and he looked down at the envelope. It was from the Central Council for Health Education and we both knew that it contained a cheque for eight guineas – government bodies paid better in those days! – for a leaflet I had fashioned for them out of an article I had originally written for a magazine about helping children with the going-to-hospital experience.

I shook my head in protest, but he wouldn't let me argue. 'Of course you are. Don't be so silly. You've earned more this week by writing than you get for a week's work from the hospital. Of course you're going to have a career.'

I stood there and, I have to say, I didn't stop to think. I just asked the question: 'Will it make you miserable if I go on? I want everything to be the same as it is now. I'll give it up gladly if there's any risk of you being unhappy about it.'

I have no doubt that modern feminists will squirm at this. They will despise me for not being strong enough to throw my head back proudly, throw myself into writing and throw my marriage to the dogs.

Well, I wasn't that concerned about feminism then. I wanted exactly what I had, which was a fair and equal partnership with a man I loved and admired and respected, and who felt the same for me.

Des said briskly, 'Are you mad? Don't be so daft. You've got a skill, you use it, girl, and I'll help all I can. It'll be fun. Now, come to bed and stop talking such nonsense.'

Thirty-three

Being miserable gives a person lots to write about. Being happy gives remarkably little.

We worked, we looked after our little flat – it was cleaned and polished, buffed and loved to bits – we played the fool. Childish, silly stuff of the sort both of us had, I suppose, been deprived of when we were children. His situation as the only child of warring parents had been miserable and had made him sometimes painfully tense and sometimes quite severely depressed. And, to tell the truth, being their daughter-in-law wasn't easy either.

But we were dutiful. We visited them regularly, just as we visited my aunt Bessie and her husband Sid, and also visited Max and Muriel and their two children, and various elderly cousins of my grandmother, collectively known as 'the girls' although the youngest was well past fifty. The prime effect all this duty had on me was that I swore then that when/if I had children of my own I would never, *ever* make visiting rules the way some of my elders did.

Every Sunday, for example, my in-laws took it for granted that we would either go to them for lunch and stay for supper, or provide lunch and supper for them at our flat. We would sit there grimly through those impossible afternoons of small-talk until I thought I would explode.

Des loathed the ritual as much as or even more than I did and eventually could bear it no longer. He told his parents that in future we would visit and be visited much less often and when we did, it would be for lunch or afternoon tea only. No more marathons. There were scenes and sulks but he stuck to his guns, glory be, and that helped maintain the fragile relationship we had with them.

Once again I found myself thinking, Well, I won't be like them! It was a form of learning that I was using more and more at work as well as at home.

My department was the outpatients' unit for the Whittington Hospital, which at that time was the largest in London (and the shabbiest). Since we dealt primarily in ear, nose and throat conditions and paediatrics most of our patients were children and their families.

The senior paediatrician, a remarkable children's doctor called Simon 'Sam' Yudkin, believed and taught me to understand that no child is ever ill alone. Whatever happens to the child happens to the entire family. And sometimes the child's illness is actually that of the family, not of the child who has the symptoms.

Thus, warring unhappy parents would bring us a child with severe asthma always made worse when his parents argued. Who, then, was the patient? The child-and-the-family, obviously, and not the child by himself.

I also discovered the problems of the 'scapegoat child', in which a family torn by a number of divisive strands seems to appoint one child as the one who is 'always ill, always having problems, the one without whom the whole family would be fine'. That struck quite a chord with me.

It was fun working with Sam. In 1959 the Platt Report on Children in Hospital was published, which recommended among many other things that children should be given much more freedom in hospital. They should be allowed to be with their parents all the time (sleeping accommodation with or near the child to be arranged where possible), and should be considered as central to any consultation, which was an amazing suggestion to many dyed-in-the-wool old-timers.

Most doctors talked to parents (if they talked at all) over the children's heads, never to the children, never asking their opinions or treating them as sentient beings. And as observant parents who know how to listen understand perfectly well, even three- and four-year-olds have definite opinions and, given the chance, will express them.

The Paediatric Unit, prodded hard by Sam, embraced all the Platt recommendations eagerly and most of the Sisters and senior nurses on the inpatient wards accepted it, though some rather grudgingly. It made their nice tidy wards much less tidy, of course, to clutter them up with parents, but they got used to it.

In OPD I had a ball. I threw out most of the rows of chairs that filled the dispiriting waiting room, keeping only enough for half a dozen adults. I had already organised my department's appointment system so that we never had a packed waiting room and the chairs were no loss.

For the children I filled the space with great big beanbags, boxes of toys and assorted scribbling materials, covered the cream-painted walls with posters and other things they could draw and paint on, and stood back to watch what happened.

The children loved it and so did the parents. Matron, coming on one of her few visits to our side of the massive hospital, was appalled and demanded all the mess be removed and the chairs restored forthwith. I smiled sweetly, referred her to Dr Yudkin, and knew I'd never hear another murmur from her. She came from a generation of nurses who always obeyed doctors' orders implicitly.

It was while I was standing beside Sam at yet another of his clinics, with a bunch of medical students from University College Hospital Medical School present to learn at the feet of the great paediatric guru (one was a gangling youth with red hair and a face that looked as though it had been carved out of hardwood, who could not fit into our chairs however hard he tried: his name was Jonathan Miller) that I realised something extraordinary had happened to me.

I wanted to have babies.

I had been certain for years that I would never have children, never risk inflicting on any other human being the misery I had experienced. Even when I grew old enough to understand that my parents, and notably my mother, were not wicked so much as over-burdened, ignorant and unable to cope with their own lives and needs, let alone a child's, I was of the same opinion. No babies, not ever.

So what the hell had happened to me? Was it just the effect of being with Sam Yudkin day in and day out, week after week, listen-ing to him talking about the dynamics of family life, how health and illness in children was created and how it could be managed?

Was it being with children themselves? Talking to them was always fascinating and usually amusing. Children were much more agreeable than adults – so honest and truthful, for a start – it seemed to me. But that was no reason for me to be broody! Especially after I'd seen at close hand what producing babies was really like.

I stood and looked beyond Sam at his desk and the row of medical students, and the mother and baby sitting beside him, and stared at the grimy window of the consulting room and felt tears behind my eyes. I reached into my uniform pocket for a handkerchief to blow my nose and drive the tears back where they belonged. The hand-kerchief was one I had, as usual, pinched from Des as I rushed off to work from home that morning. I never could find one of my own.

I put it to my nose and it smelled of him, and at once I was with Des. It was the most extraordinary experience, as every muscle in my back tightened and tingled. I felt dizzy and excited, and I knew at once the answer to my own question.

I didn't want babies in the abstract, or because I liked the com-pany of children, or because I knew a lot more about childcare than I once had and, indeed, had learned to be something of an expert. No. I wanted them because of Des, because I loved him, because we shared a sex life, because it was the inevitable and obvious thing to do. It was a purely sexual response and I wanted to laugh aloud at my own idiocy not to have understood sooner.

I went home that night in a quandary. We had agreed that we would not have children until we could afford them, and I cannot deny that always at the back of my mind was the thought that we'd never have enough money so that would be all right. He talked about it, said he wanted to, eventually, but I am ashamed to admit that I hadn't had the courage to tell Des that, at heart, I really didn't want any. I had always hoped he'd go off the idea.

Now I had something very different to explain. A sudden attack of wanting them very much indeed. Almost an imperative, in fact.

In the end, after privately rehearsing all sorts of approaches – the wry, the funny, the cute – all through dinner, he got it out of me as easily as pulling a cork from a bottle of wine.

'What's the matter with you?' he said.

'Mmm? Oh, I was just thinking about how to tell you I want a baby.'

I was no good then at dissembling with him and I'm still not. How I imagined I'd ever be able to be secretive about feeling like a broody hen I can't imagine.

The top, bottom and intervening line was we both agreed that we couldn't afford it. We did the sums – mortgage payments, rates, housekeeping, insurance – and that swallowed up most of it.

'Maybe I could write more articles?' I suggested. He shook his head. 'The moment you start to count on freelance income is the moment it dries up like spit in a desert,' he said. 'Trust me, I'm an actor.'

I was gloomy for a while, and then was about to say something when he said, 'Don't they say every baby brings its own luck with it? And they also say if you wait till you can afford it, you never will. So the only thing to do is go ahead and have a baby.'

1965. Adam had his tonsils out in the spring, but didn't get better afterwards. He dwindled before our eyes. It was decided he had a condition called aleukaemic leukaemia. We were devastated, fearing his death. I nursed him in the garden. And then slowly at first but with accelerating speed he simply got better. It was a lively healthy bouncer of a boy who showed off his new school uniform on the day he started school, just before his fifth birthday

Jay, aged six hours or so, taken for the cover of a book I was writing on pregnancy and birth. He looks older than a newborn as he weighed well over ten pounds at birth

Jay proved himself to be the ideal toy for his older brother and sister. Amanda sang to him, talked to him, played with him at every opportunity. Adam treated him with a slightly more lofty Big Brother authority, which resulted in Jay hero-worshipping him and doing everything Adam wanted

Adam learned early to make super bread, which encouraged Jay to be even more interested in food, if that were possible. This made Adam feel it reasonable to send Jay, aged five, very early on a Sunday, while we were still deeply asleep, to make him breakfast. Jay, stark naked, obliged, and managed to burn his hand while attempting to grill bacon. I suffered more guilt over that than Adam did . . .

My first desk all to myself (not shared with Des) was in the dining room and I had to hide all my gear to keep the room at least halfway tidy. But eventually I was able to have a whole study of my own with bookshelves I could clutter to my heart's content. And as the agony letters came rolling in and the piles of paper rose teetering on my desk, it all became necessity rather than the luxury it had been.

Signing books sounds more fun than it is. It's great if people come, not so great if it's raining whole flipping menageries of cats and dogs and no one turns up

Michael Heath

"DON'T WORRY. I'M SURE CLAIRE RAYNER WILL SOON BE ON TELEVISION AGAIN!"

I suppose I'm an easy target for cartoonists. Large, noisy and opinionated – but this one was at least a kind one. I was rather proud of it, in truth

Receiving a surprise award as 'Woman of Achievement' from *Woman's Own* in 1983 made me feel marvellous. What I didn't know was that I was supposed to be picked up for *'This Is Your Life'* on the very same day! Happily, the plans fell through. Just as well. I couldn't have coped with two such events in one day

Helping to raise money for charities is a great part of my life. Here I did it on the stage of Drury Lane with Matthew Kelly and Jack Tinker of the *Daily Mail*

Radio has always been very important to me, even on the rare occasions when I had to dress up for it. Here with, among others, Ned Sherrin, Julian Clary and Barbara Windsor in a Radio 4 pantomime of *Cinderella*

This cartoon resulted when I published a letter in the agony column from a nice lady in Ireland wanting to know if I was really a woman, since she had a friend who swore I was very much a man and that she danced with me at a Hunt Ball once . . .

NHS issues have concerned me all my working life. I sit on various NHS hospital committees, work with the Patients Association and a number of other groups, all of which means I sometimes do odd things like launch a London bus . . .

"I DO HATE THESE TV DEBATES ON THE MONARCHY."

Best Wishes of Charles Griffin

I'm very attached to this splendid cartoon which appeared after the January 2000 TV debate on the Future of the Monarchy. I'm not sure which I find most captivating, Charles' hangdog demeanour or my own ferocity, which is not natural to my nature, truly – dammit I'm a pacifist! – though I do express my views fairly robustly I suppose . . .

A bitterly cold morning and there we were, trying to get people rushing to work to stop and take an interest in Democracy Day 1992. For me the most exciting part of it was one of my fellow demonstrators, the great American journalist, Martha Gellhorn, who not only reported amazing material from all over the world but also found time to become the beloved of Ernest Hemingway

My grandson, Simon, son of Adam and Julie

My grandson, Eddie, son of Jay and Pat

Adam and Julie opted for a wedding with all the trimmings. Everyone looked utterly beautiful including my three top-hatted blokes and Amanda in her perfect summer straw. Julie, a most sympathetic daughter-in-law gave me permission to go hatless for the day. What a relief. I hate 'em . . .

This is Des' favourite picture of me, so it is here for him

This is the way we're happiest, if I can admit it without seeming anti-social. Just the pair of us, here in our garden room

Thirty-four

At first what upset me most was that I felt so stupid. Whatever other poor opinions of myself I might have held – and there have been, and remain, many – I had never considered myself stupid, and that was precisely how I felt as the months slid by and no signs of pregnancy appeared.

I had, like many people, I suppose, assumed that as long as a couple was reasonably sexually active a pregnancy would follow as dawn followed darkness. Even during my midwifery training there had been scant mention of sexual or fertility difficulties, apart from those due to infections of the tubes, so I had no reason to expect problems.

I knew I had never had any salpingitis (tube infection), so that wasn't my problem. I talked to the Sister in the obstetric unit at the hospital and discovered that she had much the same idea – that conception was a simple matter of sex without birth control – and was as puzzled by our failure to conceive immediately as we were. And I got the same reaction from Sister on the gynae ward, who, I thought, might possibly know a little more about the highways and byways of human sexual function. I realised for the first time how scant my training had been in this area. I could see far-reaching undulating mountains of ignorance all around me. I must find out more, I thought. But first, a baby—

There was little understanding of fertility problems in those days. The fact that some people had a fertility problem at all came as a surprise to many. It was far from uncommon for a married couple to be asked archly, 'No patter of little feet expected, then?' in either the sort of cutesy voice that made me want to strangle them while concurrently kicking them in their genitals, or a critical tone implying we must be too selfish to drag ourselves away from our own pleasures to become parents, which made me feel even more murderous.

The months went on. And on. I wrote like fury to keep my mind off my belly. I hated my reproductive system mightily and tapping away on Des's old typewriter really helped.

I began to branch out from the obvious nursing-journal pieces and occasional specific illness pieces ('Living with Your Haemorrhoids' and 'Take Care of Your Kidneys' and 'You and Your Baby's Bowels' and so forth), trying my hand at a sort of fiction. A Scottish company, D. C. Thompson, agreed to buy from me a series of short stories to be set in my outpatient clinics called 'The People I Meet', each featuring assorted patients and me as Sister-in-charge. Each tale had to have, they said, a twist in the tail of the O. Henry sort. O. Henry, for those who have had the misfortune to miss him, was a nineteenth- and early-twentieth-century American writer who produced very short stories with endings that always caught the reader by delighted surprise with a skill that has never been surpassed.

Each of my stories was to be eight hundred or so words long, and each featured rearranged versions of what happened to my patients, all slightly softened accounts of the truth, of course. Every item that might betray their confidentiality had to be completely and carefully excised.

Des and I used to have a story conference every so often: I would sit and chew my pen and he would march up and down. As I described the week's patients, he would suggest the twists in the tail. Some of them were impossible, like flying off in a balloon to cure a child's bellyaches, the implication being that he was as full of hot air as the balloon was. Some were charming, like having a toy bear's growl fixed so that it didn't wheeze any more and the bear sounded the same as his owner who had had *his* wheeze cured. I turned down at least half of them, but at the end of the session I had several more stories to write, all of them sentimental and gooey enough to set your teeth on edge but perfect for their market.

The company was also notorious for driving hard bargains. They paid me a fiver for every story they took but demanded world rights in them. There were about thirty tales in the end, I think, and I was well pleased with my earnings – until I was told by someone who had worked for the company that they sold the stories all over the world and made several times more from each one than I had been paid for the lot! Still, they sent me a tin of Scottish shortbread every Christmas and I have to say that at the time my cheques seemed like lots of money to me. Enough to have a baby.

And still no joy. We talked to our doctor, who showed strong signs of acute embarrassment but at least sent us to a consultant who did know about fertility and told us we were impatient. Wait a bit longer, he said. I pointed out my age: at twenty-seven nearly-eight I knew I would be considered rather long in the tooth for a first-time mother. (How times do change indeed!) He sighed and agreed to take us on, although Des's age apparently was of no concern. Nowadays fertility experts take a would-be father's age into account as well as his general health and various other factors. Then all they did was look at his sperm count.

Des was disconcerted when he discovered what was required of him to satisfy the doctor's demands for a sample but he was game and, despite my giggles and cheerleading-type behaviour outside the door as he tried to concentrate on the matter in hand, did the necessary.

For my part I submitted to a physical examination of great detail, which I hated but feared I would have to get used to. I was told to take my temperature every morning and record it on a special chart that would show whether I was producing eggs or not. Des was told that his sperm were fewer in number than they might have been (a total of twenty million was the requirement and he was a tad below. Twenty million, I thought. And I only need one of 'em . . .)

Then followed weeks of positively agitated sex. Des had to dunk his genitals in ice-cold water every day for a ten-minute bath, an activity that was supposed to increase the rate of sperm production. We bought a little kitchen pinger for him to set the time to the second for each session and he kept it in the bathroom where he did the deed. It would ensure that he would be told exactly when his time in purgatory was up and would be able to bring his frost-enhanced bits and pieces back into the warm world of the living that much sooner. Once I managed to drop the damned pinger in the loo while I was cleaning the bathroom. The works rusted and the next day Des didn't realise that fact until he'd been in the ice water for almost fifteen minutes.

That took a lot of forgiving. But he managed it, and even managed to forgive the demand that he wear boxer shorts, which he disliked intensely, instead of nice close-fitting jockeys or whatever. The idea was that the testes, in order to produce lots of healthy sperm, needed to be kept cool.

For my part, I read the thermometer feverishly and the moment the rise that indicated ovulation appeared, followed by a dip, I was after him like a mongrel after a guardsman's leg.

To add to the discomfiture, we had to have post-coital tests to see how his sperm were surviving the hazards of the ovum-hunting journey, carried out no later than eight hours after intercourse.

If the doctor had been obliging enough to hold his clinic in the mornings it would have been fine. We would just have to 'have coitus', to use his ugly language, the night before our appointment. Feeling loving in bed last thing at night was what we did best.

But he didn't. He held his clinics in the afternoon so we had to set the alarm clock for an hour earlier than usual in the morning on appointment day and try to work ourselves up into the necessary state of extreme passion. It could be done, of course, but it all felt so damned contrived and mechanical. I hated it. So did Des.

We changed doctors. We had a few rows about it all. We lost interest for a while, and that was when, by some miracle it seemed to us, I conceived. Only to miscarry a few weeks later. 'Blighted ovum,' said the doctor soothingly. 'Better a miscarriage than a sick baby, hmm?'

Of course I knew he was right but it didn't stop me feeling lousy. I must have been the proverbial bitch of a sister during those post-miscarriage weeks, once I'd been into the hospital as a patient and had the usual D and C that follows the loss of a pregnancy. I got them scrubbing everything in sight and turned the unit upside down.

Sam looked at me and said, 'Bad news?'

'I'm fine,' I said, longing to tell him all about it but too stubborn.

'Okay,' he said, and went off to leave me on my own, crying like one of the patients.

He came back just before I was due to go off duty with a small flower in a pot and pretended not to notice I'd been weeping. Every woman deserves a boss like that.

I wish I had been as kind to Des as Sam was to me. I was so wrapped up in my own disappointment that I forgot about his and took his support and encouragement for granted, somehow managing to forget he had wanted the pregnancy as much as I did. When I realised what a selfish bitch I'd been, I felt worse than ever. Why on earth had I ever said I wanted a baby and spoiled everything? I roared at myself. You bloody fool.

'You've done it once. You can do it again,' people said, and that did help a little. But when? I was now almost twenty-eight.

I did conceive again. And miscarried almost immediately. This, I decided, was getting ridiculous. I needed to do some studying on my own account. The doctors I had seen so far had been broken reeds.

I got over this disappointment by haunting the hospital library, feverishly reading, and came to the conclusion that my history of thyroid disorder could indicate an associated endocrine cause for my failure to get a successful pregnancy.

This time I acted on my own without going via a GP, a great sin in the NHS then – and, to tell the truth, the same today in many medical circles. I checked out the name of the best endocrinologist in London, who turned out to be a woman I had known at the Royal Free, which was a great beginning.

Then I made an appointment and, acting on my own initiative, I got myself a huge brown bottle from the hospital pharmacy and collected every drop of urine I produced for twenty-four hours. (Try it some time. It's a bugger!) Then I trailed up to Harley Street, knowing this was the expensive way to do it but also that it would ensure the consultant would listen to me.

I had seen this so often: a patient trying to offer his or her views on her condition and doctors freezing them off as absurd for thinking they had any understanding at all. But when it was a private patient they listened. I'll make her hear me, I thought. She'll *have* to pay attention.

She did, but not without a slightly amused *moue* when I produced my specimen.

'I thought you might want to do a 17/keto steroids,' I said firmly, 'with my endocrine history,' and plonked the huge bottle on her desk and peered round it at her.

'Well, you don't look in the least Cushingoid,' she said, using a technical term to describe a certain sort of puffy, pallid look that accompanies some adrenal disorders, which cheered me, 'so I doubt if your adrenals are affected but – well, since you've gone to all this trouble, I'll send it to lab by all means.'

And of course she didn't add, 'You are paying for the test, after all.' At the back of my mind I blessed D. C. Thompson of Scotland and their handy cheques.

A week later she telephoned me, a touch abashed, I thought. 'Well, my dear, you were right and I was wrong. There is a degree of adrenal dysfunction, according to your urine test. Come and see me, and we'll discuss putting you on a low dose of steroid and see how things go on that, hmm?'

Of course I agreed, although there were things I was worried about in using a steroid drug for any length of time. But I wanted a pregnancy more than I was worried about that so I took the prescription gladly.

It was summer, and for the first time since our Bournemouth honeymoon Des and I reckoned we had saved enough to afford a summer holiday. But I had that passport problem. How about Frinton this time?

But Des has a passion for Italy and we just had to go. He took my passport and a couple of the requisite photos and went off to Petty France and the Passport Office.

Quite what he did and said I shall never know, and he insists he can't remember now, but clearly he chatted up some official there and persuaded him or her to issue me with a shiny new passport in my married name. A shiny new passport with no rude Canadian comments written in it.

'My hero,' I told him, immensely impressed. I think he was too.

Back to the travel brochures, and he found us a moderately priced package that took us by boat and train to a tiny unheard-of village on the Adriatic coast of Italy. Now it is a huge, rollicking Costa Disgusting resort but then it was a discreet fishing village of great charm called Cattolica.

I was sick on the boat and I'm never seasick. I was bad-tempered and edgy on trips around the village and that wasn't particularly like me.

The absurd thing was that, despite the long months of trying to get pregnant, despite the six doctors we'd consulted, despite the pills I'd been taking, it didn't occur to me while we were away that I might be pregnant.

It wasn't till we got home and I'd checked my dates and observed one or two other physical signs that I could be sure. And when the photographs came back from the developer's showing us in Pisa and Florence, on beaches and on boats, on little chairs at streetside cafés, I was able to say, 'There were three of us there on holiday. Des and me and our baby.'

I sailed through the rest of the summer and autumn, growing apace and loving every moment, and often looking at the summer-holiday photographs as a sort of reassurance that 'Yes, I really am pregnant,' though by that time I had a nice round bump to prove it.

I had feared I would have problems with the pregnancy, for it is one of the great facts of hospital life that if anyone is going to have a rare and nasty disease or horrid complications it will be a doctor or a nurse. When I'd first gone to see the obstetrician, carrying my pregnancy proudly before me, he had looked at my notes, then at me and almost wailed, 'Oh, God, not another State Registered Uterus!'

But my SRN did me and my baby proud – until I began to look a bit hairy and larger than I should, pregnant or not. 'The steroids,' said the endocrinologist. 'You'd better come off them as soon as the obstetrician says the baby is a decent size in case it's a girl. The drug might have the effect of virilising her.'

So I stopped the drug as soon as I could, about six weeks before the birth. Within twenty-four hours my waters broke and I was hauled off to the hospital – the Royal Northern, of course, where I had been offered an amenity bed in the private wing – to be sedated so that the birth could be delayed as much as possible. But it refused to be slowed down and I went into labour very quickly.

I was allowed no analgesia during delivery because the baby was premature and could have been hurt by it. I was hurt instead and it really was an intense sensory experience, to put it at the lowest. The contractions were not muffled by so much as an aspirin. So I yelled a bit, howled a bit (Sister at Guy's would have been disgusted with me), and no one at the Northern minded a bit. Nice people.

Late in the evening they sent Des home; told him there'd be no news that night. Then in the small hours they phoned to tell him of the birth of his daughter on 6 January, Twelfth Night, and he wept, he told me, and went back to bed to cry himself to happy sleep.

For my part, I turned over and slept flat on my front for the first time since the autumn. I was a mother. It felt quite ridiculous.

Thirty-five

Whenever young people gaze at me in slight awe because I am of an age to have experienced that fabled gilded age of glory, the sixties, and ask me what it was like to live then, I have to disappoint them with the confession that I spent it mostly at belly level, either pregnant or dealing with small children standing well below my waist.

My only brush with sixties fashion ended in failure when I needed a maternity party dress for a special event. I went off to our local shops expecting to find something summery and shifty that would serve the purpose and all they could show me were very small mini-skirted jobs. I looked at the sales-girls in their buttock-skimming outfits and tried to explain that the trouble with a miniskirt over a sizeable pregnancy bump was that it would ride up in front and look like a galleon in full sail. Could she not find me something a little more suitable?

'Nah,' she said, staring at me as though I were potty. 'It's the *fash-ion*, see? They don't make nothin' what's not in fashion. Not nowadays.' And she threw me her pitying poor-old-woman look. I went home at once and dug out one of my tired, old dresses.

So, I ignored fashion and thought about work. I spent the sixties building a career, which I have always sworn was a gift to me from my children. Had I never managed to beat the odds and become pregnant I would, of course, have gone on working in the NHS. Perhaps I would have gone back to the idea of a medical training, perhaps got involved more in nursing politics. Either way, I would never have thought of being a writer. Amanda, almost named Olivia because of her birth on Twelfth Night (she says now she would never have forgiven us for such a label), and also Nancy in my aunt's memory, brought me the first solid basis of a career.

Before she was born I had dabbled in the world of the freelance writer, but it had been spasmodic and utterly reliant on the pressure of work at the hospital. Thus, on a good day I had a proper lunch hour during which I could write one of D. C. Thompson's 'The People I Meet' with ease. Otherwise it was a last-thing-at-night occupation, when I was too tired to write as well as I knew I could, or Sunday afternoons, which I slightly resented as that was my only really free day. Certainly the business of writing pre-Amanda was a thing of bits and pieces and quite disorganised. I had kept no records, or very few, and really hadn't a notion about what being a professional writer meant.

She made it amazingly easy for me to get my act together as both a mother and a writer. She was small, of course, weighing just five and a half pounds at birth, but like most premature babies she blossomed almost before our eyes. I swore if you stood still and listened carefully you'd hear her growing.

I wanted to feed her myself, but since she had spent her first week or so in an incubator (where, Des said, she 'looked just like a pickled walnut' the first time he saw her, a description that made me howl) I simply couldn't. She had been given her milk via a BelCroy feeder, an object with the most ferociously elongated teat. Nothing I had to offer could possibly compete in her view with that large rubbery source of all that was good and milky. She screamed and struggled, red in the face with frustrated fury at every attempt I made to provide nourishment, and settled to a bottle so quickly and so contentedly I'd have had to be a monster to persevere. So I didn't.

A pattern soon established itself between me and my baby. I

bathed her every morning. For the rest of the day I put food in at one end at regular intervals and dealt with the logical results at the other. While she slept off her lovely greedy feeds I did a bit of housework in our easy little flat – and the rest of the day stretched vast and empty in between.

It must be remembered that I had been running a big department and caring for large numbers of children and babies, as well as nurses and the administration and the teaching and the budgeting and all the rest that goes into a sister's workload. One easy-going infant hardly dented my capacity for work.

But there was another problem. Post-natal depression. There had been the usual 'three day blues', when I lay in bed at the hospital and wept bitterly, but I knew about that from my pupil-midwife days and didn't worry about it. I did, however, worry when later more depression took its place.

Sister at the hospital had offered to let me stay in with Amanda until she was deemed big enough to take home safely, a period of some three weeks. I was grateful for that, and even more so when she suggested Des take me out for my birthday and let them baby-sit for us. I couldn't have had a better offer. There was no one else with whom I would leave my tiny baby and we set off to see what I was told was a comedy.

I remember nothing of cast, plot or production. I remember only sitting in the stalls, for Des had sprung to the best seats, and while all around me howled with laughter tears rolled down my cheeks. It was horrible, and poor Des sat beside me not knowing what to do to put things right.

I had had depression before, though I hadn't known what it was. I only knew as a child that, together with the Hamlet feeling of looming disaster, I would get deep-down feelings of utter misery because I knew I was the most hateful person in the world. I knew, in addition, that I was totally useless and hideously ugly and that no one would ever want to have anything to do with me. I didn't even know why I stayed alive.

These feelings had gone hand in hand with my periods, of course;

not that I or anyone at the time was aware of the fact that pubertal children can suffer from hormonal distress and clinical depression.

I had learned then the uses of distraction. The worse I felt the more important it was to have lots of books to read, and read I did at great speed, but not missing a single word. By the end of two or three marathon sessions (all day if I could sneak off and get away with it) I would feel much better able to cope.

I did the same at home alone with Amanda. While she slept I organised a desk space for myself, and made what I called Work Books. I listed the names of articles I had written, using my memory as best I could. When I had finished I looked at the information-filled pages, which showed not just the titles of articles but the market to which they had gone, their length, the name of the contact I had dealt with and, at the end, the fee I had been paid. It made cheering reading. It encouraged me to do more. I read the papers avidly, and whenever an interesting argument was going on, I joined in.

For example, a journalist called Elizabeth Pakenham was running a column for mothers and babies in the *Sunday Times*. I read a piece in it about the Great Importance of Breastfeeding. At once I wrote a rebuttal for those of us who wanted to breastfeed but failed for whatever reason, begging for the nagging to stop, and sent it off with the usual stamped addressed envelope.

It came back a few days later, slender to my hand when I picked it up from the doormat. My spirits leaped. I'd got a sale, rather than the return of the manuscript!

That pushed my depression ever further away and in time it vanished. I had obviously had only a mild dose and I was able to give it no more thought and went on head first into this fascinating new world I had discovered where I, a chatterbox from childhood (and often punished for it), could actually earn money for chattering via words in a row on sheets of paper.

How did I know how to behave like a freelance journalist? It was a long time before I actually realised that that was what I was. I had had no training, no experience of working as a staff member on a paper or magazine, yet I taught myself the tricks of the trade.

I would telephone a newspaper or magazine and pretend to be a secretary with a lot of letters to send to the paper's senior staff, and ask for the names I needed, saying my boss would kill me because I had lost his list. Girls on switchboards would be nice and help a fellow toiler in the vineyard with the information, which was worth its weight in diamonds to me. Sending an article to someone by name and mentioning some of your earlier sales to named journals works much better than a 'Dear Sir' letter simply saying, 'Please consider my article for publication.'

I made sure all my scripts were as well typed as I could manage, properly spaced (double was best) on one side of the paper with the minimum of handwritten corrections and with each sheet numbered, marked 'mf' for 'more follows' at the bottom. If I had scripts sent back, and I often did, I would iron them carefully before putting on a new front sheet and sending them somewhere else in an apparently virginal state.

All through Amanda's first year I beavered away. When she was awake, I was all hers, but she seemed to like playing with her own things, rather than with me, especially piles of coloured beakers which she would sort into groups and then re-sort. And even before her first birthday her idea of fun was big crayons and sheets of end-of-roll wallpaper on the back of which she made fantastic drawings that pleased her greatly. She would be totally absorbed in that – so much so that I could sit beside her and read at the same time. It made excellent book-reviewing time, and book reviews then were earning me good fees from the nursing press as well as providing saleable books for Foyle's. They were always the reviewer's friend, paying one third of the cover price for each volume. They then sold them on at full price, I imagine, so they didn't get a bad deal.

And then when Amanda was about nine months old we had a fright. It seemed impossible after our previous history that it could happen again so easily and so soon, but there it was. My periods stopped. A new baby? The thought of two small ones in our tiny flat sent us almost barmy. We would have to move. We had saved a fair bit, we could get a good price for the flat, and at least the new baby wouldn't be as costly as Amanda had been. She had cost us my £750 a year salary – I had a raise by this time – a lot to us. Now I no longer earned it we didn't miss it, although my writing earnings helped to close the gap. Not to the tune of £750 per annum, I had to admit, but that was what I was aiming for.

We hunted everywhere for a house, except the one place we did not want to live. That was Wembley, a rather pleased-with-itself, slightly snobby (and, heaven knows, there was damn all there to be snobby about) North London suburb where we knew some residents and definitely did not like them. Benny Green, the music man, whom we both admired greatly and who had lived in Wembley before escaping out to Hertfordshire, said, 'Wembley isn't a place. It's a condition. Ooh, ooh, I do feel awfully Wembley this morning!'

The house we found, and could afford, was, of course, in North Wembley. It was a perfect example of Yer Actual Ancestral Semi. I didn't like it at all, but we needed the space and I reckoned Des with his talent for décor would make it better. And as long as we made every effort to move before Amanda started school, at age five, to avoid excessive upheavals for her, we could cope with living in Wembley.

And there we went, when Amanda was ten months old, not quite old enough to remember her first home. I, however, will never forget it. My little flat had been a very special little flat, the first place I could really call my own home, the first place I had ever felt I had a right to be, the place I had first shared with Des, and about which I still dream, even though it is over forty years since we left it. And I still remember with a wry grimace that I started my periods again two weeks after we moved into the Wembley semi.

Des made it marvellously handsome, that ancestral semi, with lots of colour and clever use of furniture, and Amanda blossomed in a room of her own and learned to slide down the stairs on her belly after she had laboriously climbed up them.

Des changed his job, dealing with all the advertising and PR for a huge fashion conglomerate where he earned more but would never be particularly happy. I watched him growing sadder, grieved over the acting days that were gone and felt guilty because we had married and spoiled it all, and said as much to him.

But he replied robustly, and with crystal common sense, that he hadn't been all that madly happy as an out-of-work actor, and that he had warned me when we married that he was a moody, gloomy type. I knew he had and knew what he meant, which was that he had a tendency to depression too, though not, of course, linked with his hormones. I also recalled reading somewhere that moving house was always an emotionally fraught experience and a cause of much depression. And as Des seemed contented enough, if a trifle low, I stopped fretting for that time.

I wrote more and more, throwing out articles like fireworks, using every spare moment I had, spreading my net from the medical and nursing journals to the women's magazines and most especially mother-and-baby magazines, for I felt I now had a lot more relevant experience about which I could write. I had developed, in other words, the true mantle of the freelance journalist. Everything that happened to me or mine was grist to my mill. I would write about it as long as there were editors who believed someone else would read it. I could write mainly during Amanda's daily afternoon naps, which were as precious to me as they were to her.

And I developed a vital skill. I learned to think, check facts and write *fast*. If you've always had to make the most of every second, knowing that at the first cry of 'Mummy, I'm awake!' you no longer own your own time, then speed becomes undoubtedly of the essence.

It also creates the time for you to do other stuff, of course. I found myself being invited to do more radio, following that first attempt on *Woman's Hour*, and I enjoyed that a lot, finding to my delight that I actually preferred doing discussions without a prepared script. There was a great exhilaration in thinking on one's feet.

I was asked to write my first book, to my own amazement. I was approached by a publisher, Allen and Unwin, one of whose senior partners sent me a letter in which he addressed me throughout as Miss Monica Furlong, a well-known lady who wrote on religious matters, *inter alia*. But never mind. I checked and he meant me. He'd seen my articles in the nursing press in which I had described the difference between what I had been taught as a pupil-midwife and what I had experienced as a mother, and he wanted a book about the maternity services.

One thing I had learned in my new-fledged second career was 'Never Say No'. If you say no there is no possibility whatsoever of going back and saying, 'Thought about it a bit more, I was mad, I'd love to do it, thanks,' because they'll have asked someone else even before you've cradled the phone after saying your first no.

So, of course, I cried yes, then set about teaching myself how to write a non-fiction book on the maternity services. I'd read enough books in general, I reckoned, to know what one would look like and I had, of course, all those months of experience at Guy's and the Hackney hospital. Oh, I thought, I have plenty of material. So I set to work and, to tell it the short way, it took me six months of sweat, blood, tears and any amount of interviewing people on the phone and over teacups in my kitchen.

But I got it done and managed some publicity for myself (Allen and Unwin didn't seem to think it necessary): I got myself on a TV programme called *Town and Around*, which was a local BBC evening show for the London area. That was to have considerable repercussions.

I did lots of radio as well as extra articles on the subject and became quite a guru in the field. I was the object of much appreciation from mothers who had had a bad time at the hands of tough midwives, like some I had met, and a good deal of opprobrium from nice midwives, who couldn't imagine there were any nasty ones. It's a common phenomenon that, and very hard to cope with. The good people call you a liar and the bad ones send you hate mail.

The book earned me the munificent sum of £49 17s. 11d. and had taken six months of effort. But more had come out of it than mere money – and that is another important factor for would-be writers and freelances to remember: one job should always lead to another. If it doesn't, choose another market next time.

For a start, I had had to find myself an agent, for the contract Allen and Unwin sent me was terrifying. I asked some of the friends I had picked up around magazines what to do. One of them sent me to *The Writer's and Artist's Yearbook*, a Bible for all freelances, suggested I look up literary agents therein and also mentioned a couple of names.

It took a considerable number of interviews with possible agents because it is a bit like marriage. You really have to hit it off and be happy with someone with whom you will work so closely. I suffered one humiliating turn-down by one very nasty lady who told me frankly that I would never get anywhere at all – and then I found Ursula.

Very tall, partly American and partly English aristocrat, Ursula Winant liked books and book people, and she decided to take me on because I had arrived with a book contract in my hand. 'A very good sign,' she said. 'Not a very good contract, mark you, but a good sign for the future.'

And so it was settled without any paperwork or fuss. She was my agent and would remain so until she retired. I went home by underground, feeling very posh. I was an Author with an Agent. Get me!

Life was easier now. As Amanda got older and left helpless infancy behind she became a very sweet and biddable little girl without any tendency to tantrums or terrible-twos behaviour. (She is nothing at all like that now. Strong-minded and very lively woman, my daughter.) She was clearly a happy little soul who enjoyed nothing better than toodling about in the garden and her room full of playthings, many of which Des made for her. To make life even easier, Des had done some of his sums, and said that, with the right domestic help, I could earn more than enough to cover the cost of the helper. And I hated housework, so we found Leechy.

Then it happened again. Not a handkerchief this time. Just looking at Des playing with Amanda one afternoon while we were all out there soaking up the sun.

I got the same feeling, though. Broody as hell.

Thirty-six

Des, I discovered, was as eager as I was to extend the family, but hadn't wanted to overload me, what with a lively toddler, a new house and newish career to cope with, but he had clear views on how he felt the family should be.

'One child is a child,' he opined. 'Two's a *family*.'

Five or so years later when we added a third to our collection I reminded him of his dictum. 'Yes,' he said wearily. 'And three's a bloody army.'

We had not been pursuing parenthood – no more shenanigans with temperature taking and ice-cold genital bathing – but neither had we been using contraception, which, as Des said, had to be quite the nicest way to run a sex life that he could imagine.

So a trip to the doctors made sense. I have to confess that after all these years I can't remember precisely what said doctors suggested. We had only three on our case this time, a fifty per cent reduction, so we felt we were making progress.

I do recall a certain amount of lip-pursing at my report that I had been given prednisolone to conceive Amanda but that did not surprise me.

All doctors on principle disapprove, sometimes quite violently, with the work of the doctors who saw you previously. From the start of the NHS till the present this has not changed. It is a comforting thought, is it not, that doctors have been able to maintain their certainty in their own right-thinking for so long and so thoroughly?

Whatever it was they suggested I was delighted that it was effective. I got pregnant quickly and was given an EDD* of 6 January 1963, which stunned me. To produce a sibling for Amanda on her birthday would be a bit too tidy to be normal, I thought. I already got a good deal of teasing from people who were amused to see the sort of time-saving tricks I employed to make sure I had enough writing time while not cheating Amanda of attention. Organisation to such a degree would be too much.

I would, for example, set out clothes for the morning before I went to bed. Mine, obviously, but also hers. There was to be no frantic 'oh-my-god-where-are-those-bloody-socks' in that fragile time before breakfast if I could possibly help it. Des was the first to observe the value of this practice and copied me (actually it was more a reversal to his days in the RAF as a National Serviceman).

I went further. I could never leave an unwashed dish in the sink overnight and I always set the table for breakfast before going to bed. (In time Des caught the same bug, glory be.)

Yes, I know. It sounds downright obsessive and bloody boring, doesn't it? It sounds like the behaviour of good little housewives as described in women's magazines *circa* 1935. I absolutely agree. It's a bit like being one of those geeks who work as hygiene consultants to the lavatories and wear white coats and think it makes them look clever to have a row of multi-coloured Biros in their breast pockets. The difference with what I did, however, was that it was not done to impress anyone. Only to make my life easier.

And it did that to a remarkable degree. It took a matter of moments to do these tasks the night before, and as little effort as cleaning my teeth since it was part of the bedtime ritual. Mornings with us were peaceable, on time, agreeable starts to the day. I couldn't

---

* Expected Date of Delivery.

have lived with the sort of a.m. hubbub that I know is common-place in lots of households. So it was really self-indulgence on my part that lurked behind the forward planning and the late night table-laying.

I still do it even though the children have long since left home. Habits like that are hard to break and why should I when it's always been so useful to me?

It may seem I make too much of the domestic minutiae of my life then but interest in it has always been there. Questions started early from a great many people, and by no means only women, looking for useful ideas to apply to their own lives. Men wanted to know too, although I suspected they tended to put the question with a slight sneer and a note of triumph in their voices . . . and, come to think of it, so did a few women.

'How do you manage to fit it all in? And now another baby on the way – you'll have to give up the writing and the running around doing radio and so forth, won't you?'

So this is as good a point as any to spell out the nuts and bolts of the have-it-all life which some people then and since have told me I have had and continue to enjoy. You know the sort of thing: perfect in the office, even if it's the boardroom or a TV studio, always groomed and dressed to the utmost, a household which runs as smoothly as an ocean liner and children adorable and happy from noon to night. And, of course, a tiger in bed every night sending dear spouse off to work the next day with a soppy grin on his face.

That is a dish of over-cooked and over-embellished crap the women's pages of some newspapers and magazines delight in serving up, and it always makes me steam with fury. Far from being helpful to women who have a spark of ambition to do something for themselves as well as being at home with their families, it makes it all sound much harder than it has to be.

Yes, it is possible for a woman to rear her own children and to run her own home and have a career, but with certain provisos.

I do not think it can be done without a good deal of personal sac-rifice if the woman's job involves being at the office or somewhere away from the home from crack of dawn till crash of dark. I did what I did by working the bulk of my hours at home, being therefore fully accessible to my children when any emergency arose. And, of course, emergencies are what childhood does best. So I suffered the minimum of guilt (it's never totally escapable and never think it is) and the minimum of office dramas.

The woman who goes for the full-time-plus job has to accept that she will spend a large portion of her earnings on providing a substitute for herself. Nannies cost, and their own demands and problems can double up an employer's angst even more than her children do.

I make no attempt here to offer any guidance to those single women with children who have jobs outside their homes. Women in this situation can and do build careers and care for their children. They may do it with a different sort of support system. Sometimes they get together with other single mothers and share the responsibility of childcare. Or they may lean on their mothers or their sisters or their aunts. There are as many ways of organising this life as there are mothers.

My plans always involved a spouse because there was always one there for me. And the right kind of spouse, too. A husband who is as helpless as a cat around the house and as messy as a kitten, and who takes it for granted that a wife is for clearing up after him and cooking for him is of the same degree of use to a would-be career woman as the classic bicycle is to a halibut.

If he is Galahad and King Arthur combined as well as a useless slob in domestic terms and you'd rather be with him than without him, then by all means, lady. Settle for looking after him and soothe your personal feelings by cursing his mother. But please don't imagine you can ever change things. He sees himself as your career and that's all there is to that.

I know I've been amazingly lucky. I fell for a man who shares a lot of my interests, who sees the world through the same prism I do (thank Providence! I could never love a Tory, let alone fancy one and I do hope that isn't racist) and who makes me laugh too. Furthermore he has a powerful sense of responsibility and, from the first shot of the starter's pistol, shared domestic chores and, in due course, baby-changing, bottle-feeding, bathing and shopping – whatever was domestic we did together.

When we first got together, men simply didn't behave that way. You never saw a man in the street in the fifties or even the early sixties carrying flowers home or pushing a pram, let alone shopping for groceries with a baby sleeping on his back like a papoose. Now of course such men are commonplace. I'm just glad I found an early example.

So there I am with a supportive husband, some help around the house and the beginnings of a career as a freelance journalist and one and a half babies on the scene. We're far from rich but with a bit of corner cutting we could live well enough on Des's earnings from hateful advertising alone. Why did I keep going?

I had discovered, by doing the job, that the toughest component of a career for a woman, whether she runs it from home or office, with supportive spouse or best friend, is sheer constant hard labour. You sentence yourself to chronic weariness and whatever you're doing you feel guilty because you're not doing something else and the moment the children go to sleep you yearn to wake them up and tell them how utterly gorgeous they are and how much you love them. That's the bad stuff about being a mother with a life of her own.

And then the great stuff kicks in and you know why you do it all. You get an acceptance for a piece from an up-market newspaper that you never believed would look at you, paying a ridiculous sum and wanting more.

You get a call out of the blazing clear sky from an editor who says she has heard excellent things about you and could you provide her urgently with a piece of a thousand words on the Propagation of Purple Daffodils or some such, and you think of the research and then look at the money she is offering and instantly you are filled with a hitherto totally unsuspected passion for Purple Daffodils.

Is this the birth of ambition? I truly don't know. I don't think there are many people who are not ambitious even if their ambition is no more than wanting to see their home-baked cakes rise to just the right height.

I do know that I had never believed myself to be ambitious. I recall the childish words that were put into my mouth by my pushy show-off of a mother, and that I had to learn so that I had an answer if anyone asked me what I was going to be when I grew up. 'I want to be an author and I also want to be a doctor and walk the wards at Guy's.'

But that wasn't my idea. I had no such ambition. All I knew was this was something else someone had chosen for me without asking me. Oddly, eventually it did sort of work out that way. There has to be something about childhood indoctrination.

Wasn't it the Jesuits who said, 'Give me a child until he is six and I will give you the man'?

But the truth I now had to face was that suddenly I was aware of being ambitious. I wanted things to happen to me as a writer that would make people stretch their eyes in surprise. I wanted to get inside people's heads with my words. I wanted to be *famous* as a writer.

I stopped then, embarrassed at my own thoughts. It must be the pregnancy that's doing it, I thought. I never used to think this way. It had always been fun, writing, just a way of getting a few extra bob that we needed without too much hassle. So why did I feel like this now?

It didn't go away, though I thought it might. From then on, I felt the hot core of ambition deep inside me. I wanted to do more and more. It wasn't enough any longer to dribble along with small articles for small journals, interesting though that had been and useful too, for they had taught me my craft.

Now, I wanted lots of readers, hordes of readers. I saw in a newspaper that *Woman's Own* magazine, for example, had over three million readers a week from its circulation of a million, with three readers per copy, and I thought, Yes! That's where I'll reach all the people I want to write for.

That summer was a warm one and I would take my typewriter into the garden together with sundry paperweights to keep papers safe in the breeze and work there while Amanda dug blissfully in mud, her favourite occupation. Then one afternoon the phone rang. I scooped up Amanda in case she wandered, and rushed into the house to answer the phone. It was Ursula.

I stood there with Amanda under my arm, dripping mud on the carpet and swinging her legs to drip more as she happily watched the mess grow and listened all unknowingly to the next stage of my career taking shape.

'My dear, I thought of you as soon as the publisher called me' she fluted at me. '"Perfect for Claire," I told him, "you'll adore her, so good, and always works so hard and sends impeccable copy," I told him, and now I tell you the same. He is a dear man, a most sympathetic publisher, and you'll get on madly well. It isn't difficult.' She stopped for a breath but I couldn't get a word in in time. 'Each story is about fifty to sixty thousand words long. They're immensely popular and they sell vast numbers. Do try, dear, I'm sure you'll do them very well.'

'But Ursula, I can't write fiction! Your partner told me that once, don't you remember? I'm sure she was right. I do articles and stuff in serious magazines. I mean, hospital love stories! I'd be too embarrassed, really I would, to do such stuff, truly I can't, not possibly.'

'Then use a pseudonym,' Ursula said, no longer fluting but the sensible agent again and clearly irritated by my rush of anxious prattle. 'He pays well and you can do it. I'll send you a few to read and you can let me have a synopsis and a sample chapter next week. How's the baby? And Des? Splendid, splendid,' and she hung up.

The books arrived a couple of days later, all paperbacks with pictures of sinfully handsome doctors and amazingly luscious yet clearly virtuous nurses on the covers, unlike anyone I had ever seen in any hospital I had ever been in. I cringed. I couldn't bear to write this stuff, I thought. I'd sooner try my hand at pornography if I knew any pornographers. Oh, Ursula, why are you doing this to me? I thought agents were nice to their clients.

I sat in the garden all that hot weekend with Amanda crawling over my feet, mud and all, and read the lot, all seven of them. They were written by people with names like Bess Norton and Lucilla

Andrews and I thought, Dammit, they're a doddle, about eighty per cent hospital background and twenty per cent soppy love story. I suppose I can do that and it would shut up Ursula. I'll have a go next week.

There was another big change that week. Des opted to change his job. He'd been miserable with a horrible bully of an employer, and now he felt he had to move on. But it was a scary thing to do with a baby and another on the way. But scary or not, he did it. So for both of us this was a very eventful year.

Thirty-seven

Adam was born in the middle of a patch of appalling weather, heavy snow and exceedingly thick fog of a degree that made it seem he might even have to be delivered at home, which I would have hated. In the event we got to hospital in time, which was just as well: the delivery turned out to be difficult, requiring an anaesthetic and forceps, which rather tarnished the experience.

The consultant swore I'd got my dates wrong, which infuriated me (male doctors who tell intelligent women they can't work out the dates of their own periods are the pits), because the baby, they said, patently wasn't premature, weighing six and a half pounds as he did. I maintained that he was premature and probably would have weighed at least nine pounds plus if he had gone to term. I was proven right, in due course, when they checked items like bone growth and so forth. Today he is a magnificent man of six foot two and a bit, who is, he says, the only chap he knows who can order lemonade in a pub and never get a second look.

During the pregnancy that produced him I had started writing that oh-so-embarrassing romantic fiction because Ursula had told me in her best told-you-so voice that the publisher would pay me an advance of two hundred pounds. Suddenly I wasn't quite as embarrassed. That was more money in one cheque than I had ever had as a writer, and as long as I used a false name, I thought it could do my slowly burgeoning 'respectable' name no harm, because no one would ever know.

I offered as a pseudonym my long-abandoned single name, using the second name in full. This complete change of name from girlhood to adulthood had an interesting side-effect. When I started writing novels more seriously I found many of my characters changed their names in mid story without my planning it as the author. It was very odd. It just happened and always for the best of reasons. I had offered my girlhood name as a pseudonym because it seemed suitable for the romantic touch.

When I told the editor at Corgi, Michael Legat, that I wanted to be known as Berenice Chetwynd, he almost roared his response, 'My God, no! Ghastly name. You'll have to do better than that,' then told me about a thirties writer called Ursula Bloom who had chosen as her pseudonym for romantic novels (we all succumb eventually) *Losania Prole*. He wouldn't let me be like that!

Abashed, I concocted the name Sheila Brandon, stealing my sister's first name and borrowing again the one we had so laboriously learned in Besses O' The Barn before the war. He said that would do, and I went to work on the manuscript.

I have read, over the years, more thousands of stories than I can possibly remember. And I learned a lot from all of them – except how to write a story of my own. Oh, yes, I'd had a go at school at an English teacher's behest, but that is not at all a preparation for earning the hard cash put down by a publisher as bait.

At first I wrote too much in the way of description and cut it like fury. Then I spent too long on the character's appearance. And, then to crown it all, I reached the stage in the virtuous story (all these romances had to be loving and sweet but never ever sexy) when my character, who has spurned her true love Dr Dickon (I blush over the name) in favour of a smoothie surgeon, is invited by said smoothie to – gulp – spend a weekend in Brighton with him.

In real life she would have said briskly, 'So what took you so long?' and packed her best knickers, but this was a Romance! She had to be saved in some way, without ever indicating she would have accepted or what might have happened if she had, before I ended the book on the proper upbeat note with her falling smack back into Dickon's welcoming arms, et cetera, et cetera, et cetera.

I had this brilliant idea. I made her come over all clumsy as she worked in the operating theatres so that she spilled a great dish of carbolic acid all over her legs. Cue desperate medical struggles to treat dreadful acid burns. Cue heartrending stuff in the nurses' sick bay, where she could sit for the rest of the book looking sweetly dimity in sprigged cotton and being very virginal while the men fought over her and horrid old Smoothie finally showed his real colours – the cad! All that and an Amusing Best Friend, I thought. What more can they want? And sent it off to Corgi.

And then was ashamed of myself. To tell the truth, and I hadn't been as honest with myself as I should, I had rather enjoyed my soppy Avril and her stolid boyfriend Dickon. They were thoroughly nice people, though not very sophisticated, and none the worse for that. I was pleased, if a touch startled, when they took off in some scenes and sort of wrote their own dialogue.

I didn't know then that this is the real key to writing fiction. Not until you can invent characters, set them in a scene you have worked out very carefully and therefore know well, then leave them to talk to each other and just write down what it is they say, can you be said to be a novelist. They have to take on lives and personalities of their own.

It may sound fey, but it is a very common phenomenon, I have discovered. I once talked with John Mortimer about it when we shared a platform for a BBC radio programme going out for some totally forgotten reason from the hubbub of the Ideal Home Exhibition in Olympia. I mentioned on air, a little shyly, that my characters were very masterful and pushed me around like anything, and he chimed in with delight, 'Yes! I never know what Rumpole is going to get up to next and as for She-who-must-be-obeyed – a total mystery to me. Fun, isn't it?'

I learned not to be ashamed of honest work. There is no harm in simplicity, which was what these books had. When I did the next – and, yes, the first spawned many more contracts, seven in all to my intense delight – I made the lovers as honest and real as I could, with no tricksy shutting-up in sick bays to get a heroine out of a sticky corner, and gave as accurate an account of the eighty per cent hospital background as I could make it.

I got to know the publisher, Mike Legat, very well in time and we became good friends. I still remember with great glee the day he found out that Berenice Chetwynd wasn't the invention of a fevered brow. He literally slid off the chair in which he was sitting in the corner of my sitting room after dinner one night when Des, surprised he didn't know, said something about it being my name. Lovely to see someone so discomfited for so slight a reason.

Eventually I wrote seven Sheila Brandon books for him, even allowing them out under my own name two or three decades later to prove I was cured of my nasty intellectual snobbery. I'm tickled to bits with them now and love to see them in their various languages. They have never been out of print and have been published all over the world. Mike was very generous: he allowed Ursula to sell the last of the contracted books – to be called *A Starch of Aprons* but not a romance, more a psychological study of nurses and nursing in novel form – to a hardcover publisher, which opened the door of major hardback publishing to me, something for which I shall always be grateful.

They went down like a Christmas dinner in Iceland where I think every family must have bought a set, going by the sales figures, and in the rest of Scandinavia the sales were just as satisfactory. Down Under was a great market for them too, almost reaching Icelandic proportions, which is pretty good, for the people of that country read more books than anyone else in the entire world.

Adam was a rambunctious infant. He had been so before he was born; we had nicknamed him the Duke of York because 'he marched right up to the top of the hill and marched right down again'. It was an amazing experience to lie in bed when Adam chose to go into one of his pre-birth athletic sessions. He left me exhausted, if a good deal exhilarated – it was like hanging on to the outside of a rollercoaster ride while the people in the seats kicked you. He even managed once to plant a small bruise on his father's back.

Amanda, at almost three years old, found him hugely interesting and went at once into maternal mode with him. One night at about 4 a.m. when I had had to get up to feed him and he stopped half-way through for the customary burp, his sister, whom I had thought flat out on the other side of the nursery, said sleepily, 'Good boy, Adam.' She clearly knew the importance of approval from an early age. She loved to help with his bathing and dressing and so forth though. She had a doll, specially bought so that she could do the honours with that while I or our current au pair looked after Adam, but she would have none of it. It had to be the real McCoy, and for the first few months he obliged. After that he began to bite back with his minuscule two teeth and kick with those mighty legs, and she beat a fast tactical retreat.

Those years of the sixties, whatever was going on in the world outside, tended to slide past our busyness. Who cared about the arrival of – gasp, gasp – tights when I spent most of my days in trousers and shirts? I was interested vaguely, but not really part of it all.

When the excitement about the availability of the Pill hit the media I was amused. Everyone carried on as though you could pick up a prescription anywhere, but it was as hard as it had ever been for single girls to get contraceptive help – I knew this from the articles I was constantly being asked to write for various magazines.

I do, of course, remember Kennedy's assassination. I was bathing Adam, and Birgit, our au pair, was downstairs giving Amanda her supper and she called up in a great tizz in tears and told me it had just been on the radio. I wept all down Adam's downy back. He was too young then to notice, of course, and blew bubbles, but all I could think of was that Kennedy, too, had had babies.

I started so many columns for magazines at that time that I had to work at the typewriter at least six hours a day, which was a lot with a busy family to consider. But I'd found out how to get past editors and persuade them to hire me, and it seemed a pity to turn work away. Children used up a lot of cash, we found, and however much we earned we always seemed to be saving up for something.

I'd got the running of the house down to a slightly bumpy smoothness that suited us all fine, and both children loved their afternoon naps. Amanda started going to morning nursery school when she reached three, as they were all to do. The children all called their nursery St Custard's, their version of St Cuthbert's, the church where it lived.

We both got the itch to up sticks again. We had been looking for a bigger house pretty much since we had arrived in this one, and remembering our pledge to move before Amanda was five. But we would come home from househunting expeditions and look at our Ancestral Semi and think, Well, it isn't that bad.

Des got it into his head that he could design an enlargement for it that would give us the space we needed and make it a house we'd like better. He would sit on the stairs with what I learned to call his Christopher Wren face in position and cogitate literally by the hour.

And then one day he yelled, 'I've got it! We just have to move the loo and it's a done deal.'

'We can do it,' we told each other, in the dark doubtfulness of the night when we couldn't believe we'd got our sums right, but the yearning for the extra space we would have overcame us, and we agreed it was on. Definitely on. No matter what. On.

On the day the builders came and knocked down the adjoining garage, which had to go to make room for all the new building, I had a phone call from my GP. 'Claire,' she said, in as delighted a voice as I had ever heard her use, 'that specimen you left with me – I have to tell you I was right and there are, as I've just heard from the laboratory, a couple of toads there and in a state of *great* excitement.* You are pregnant, my dear, most definitely pregnant. You did say you weren't planning another baby, didn't you? How lovely for you!'

And a house full of builders, too. How lovely for me, indeed.

---

* The Aschheim-Zondek pregnancy test then in use involved injecting a patient's urine into toads. If she was pregnant, the hormones in her urine threw the toads into a flurry of sexual activity and egg production.

Thirty-eight

I emerge from my house like a crossbow bolt to extract Adam from the pile of builder's sand that adorns our front garden and which he thinks is there entirely for his and his neighbourhood friends' entertainment. I have him kicking noisily under one arm, my glasses are perched precariously on top of my head – I'd been writing when I looked up and saw the mayhem through the dining-room window where my desk is – and I am feeling far from neighbourly.

But there she is, all neat and tidy in her hat and shiny shoes, my three-doors-away neighbour on her way to do her daily shopping. 'My,' she says, after a moment as the phone in the house starts to ring and I hear Inge-Lis, our newest au pair, screaming something urgent at Amanda, who has clearly got the cat by the tail again, 'aren't you a lucky thing? A new baby and a new house all in one year! Such extravagance! You should have spread it over a bit – so much more fun for you! Good luck with it all, anyway.' As she tittups away on her shiny shoes, I hope she finds some dog-crap to walk in, and am then ashamed of my mean-spiritedness.

She meant no harm. Just the usual neighbourly fascination mixed with a certain degree of disapproval at what we're doing.

One man even marched up the front path and when Des came to

the door said, 'Could you just let me know the cost of all this? I'm thinking of doing something similar.'

Des, startled at the man's brashness, blinked, then came up with what I believe is the perfect squelch for Nosy Neighbours. 'You tell me what you earn,' he said kindly, 'and I'll tell you whether you can afford it,' and closed the door.

I sigh deeply and haul Adam back indoors so that he can run straight out to the back garden and torment the builders there for a while. The entire house is a tip, everything is covered in layers of brick and concrete dust, and we are living on packaged cereals, fish and chips and other assorted takeaways. Adam clearly believes he is living in a three-year-old's heaven. Amanda spends as much time as she can designing the way she will have her new bedroom decorated. At six years old, at last she can have a truly girly bedroom.

And I am working my butt off. There is no point in any form of housework, apart from pulling up the beds and shoving stuff in the launderette down the road from time to time, and dear Inge-Lis can cope with that. I am able to launch on a writing jag that, frankly, we rather need.

I phone Mike Legat and put it to him. 'I could do with another little book to write, dear Mike,' I say. 'Something I can do off the top of my head without too much research and that could be worth an advance of, say, five hundred pounds.' What does he reckon? I want to know. He comes back two days later with *two* commissions in his series of mini-books, tiny texts full of wisdom that are selling nicely.

I tot up the number of books I will have written by the time the new baby arrives and the extension is finished. There are three mini-books: *Housework the Easy Way*, *Mothercraft*, and *Home Nursing and Family Health*. Then for another press, *101 Facts an Expectant Mother Should Know* and *101 Key Facts of Practical Babycare*.

What the hell was the sixth? Ah, yes, *A Parents' Guide to Sex Education*. As I had to push myself further and further away from my desk to accommodate my burgeoning front, and heard, smelled and saw my home destroyed and rebuilt around me, I hit the typewriter keys like a woman demented.

But I was also doing television for the BBC. I had never set out to work on television. We didn't own a set to start with, and somehow I never thought it as important as radio. I yearned one day to be on *Desert Island Discs* and *Any Questions?* (And, wey-hey, I was eventually offered both in the same week. I was so pleased with myself I would have exploded at the touch of a pin.)

But it was almost inevitable that any writer and/or radio broadcaster in the mid- to late-twentieth century would fetch up on TV. It was just another way of communicating, and I saw TV as a shop window in which I could demonstrate my written wares. A book talked about on TV stood a better chance of selling, so just as I had phoned every TV programme I could in order to get on when *Mothers and Midwives* was published, so I did with all my later non-fiction books.

I got the job on BBC's *Town and Around* by a mixture of cheek and accident. I had written an article for *Design* magazine about the dangers inherent in a wide range of domestic gadgetry. I was asked to come on the programme to talk about it after I'd had the supreme gall to phone up and tell them I'd be very interesting on the subject. They must have had a thin programme that night because they said, 'Yes,' and without being told to I took along some samples of lethal kitchenware, such as a most wicked German blender that wanted to eat your fingers, and a singularly vicious electric can-opener. I showed all these to the interviewer, and chattered away to him, and afterwards he said to me, 'You ought to do more of this sort of thing. You're quite good at it.'

'Really?' I said, and sat tight. It was the end of the show so they were clearing up and there was no one rushing me off.

'Yes,' he said, and seemed about to stand up.

'I'd like that,' I said, and sat even tighter.

He looked at me and grinned. 'Do you want me to talk to the producer?'

'Yes, please,' I said, riveted by now to the sofa.

He went away and came back with the boss, who was a long-time BBC man called Fletcher. Fletch to everyone.

Fletch looked at me, chewed a lip and rubbed a nose, then said, 'Well, once a month, a ten-minute slot on consumer interests like this stuff. But never show anything that could be regarded as advertising, be lively, be bright, be interesting, but *never* be controversial. Check dates with my secretary and I'll see you next month. Goodnight to you. Goodnight, Mike, see you tomorrow,' and he was gone.

'Lumme,' I said. 'Thank you so much, Mr Aspel. I didn't think it would be as quick and easy as that.'

'It'll be just as easy and just as quick to be out on your ear if you muck it up,' he said, 'but you won't. Have fun, then the viewers will. See you next month.'

Much later I did a couple of years as a regular spot on Mike's hugely popular radio show for Capital Radio where we sometimes got a little near the edge, as old friends will. One summer morning we were taking calls from parents concerned about their children's sex education. I, forgetting that Adam was not away at university but at home and working the vacation in Walls' ice-cream factory, told the tale of Adam, at three, coming in to share my Saturday-morning treat of a late bath. He stood beside the tub chatting, then suddenly leaned over, touched each of my breasts with a careful forefinger and said, 'I do like those. Did you knit them?'

Apparently a roar of approval went up at Walls' ice-cream factory where Adam was never to be free of teasing ever again. (I was mortified. I had always tried so hard not to upset them by my weird way of making a living. But he forgave me.)

Mike responded by telling me, in the interval of our chatter when he was playing a record, a charming tale of a little boy and his efforts to provide his own sex education. When we came back live to air, I insisted he repeated it for the audience. It was about a small boy who, when his father told him off while he was taking a bath, said crossly, 'I will! It's mine! And I can wash it as fast as I like!'

And then there was the time when I was caught for *This Is Your Life*, which is an extraordinary experience for anyone. By the time they got to me – after, I was told, several failed attempts – the original presenter, Eamonn Andrews, had died, but they never wasted a script. When Mike Aspel took over the programme they tried to get me again and this time succeeded. That meant he had to be a guest on his own show, because he had been written into the original Andrews version. So he interviewed himself about me. I liked that a lot. I don't know if he did.

But back to the beginning on *Town and Around*. For three years I arrived at Alexandra Palace, a.k.a. Ally Pally. It looked nothing like the BBC but like a nice old NHS hospital to me, and therefore homely.

Not that it didn't have its horrors. The thing I most loathed was that there were often no cameramen in the studio to have a little natter or giggle with between takes. Just me and a voice from above with instructions or whatever, and cameras that were controlled by remote gizmos somewhere. It was extraordinarily disconcerting to have one of these one-eyed monsters follow you around the studio. But I got used to it.

The hardest part of the job was digging out stories. Be bright, be gay, but never be controversial. I ask you! I managed it, though, and then had an idea. This was being seen only in London: how about if I offered it to a different region?

That was how I came to fall in love with what was then TWW, Television Wales and the West, and later became HTV, Harlech Television. I took my consumer slot down to Cardiff once a month so in effect I did a show every fortnight. I was also open to other offers, so some weeks included even more one-eyed monsters.

When I got pregnant I expected the BBC to fire me, and TWW to be very relaxed about it. In fact, my BBC producer Fletch said, 'Great! Do lots of pregnancy stories.' And I did – I almost had Jay on air. They came to film him when he was just two hours old. The newsreader announced us by saying, 'Well done, Claire. We all knew you had it in you.'

TWW, on the other hand, were very purse-lipped: 'Oh, Claire, no. They'll never stand for it in the valleys.' So I had to go.

And the books still came churning out . . .

It was hard work, paid peanuts, but I was learning so fast I could sometimes hear the wheels of my mind going round.

Such silly things happened that year of 1966. To start with, I didn't realise I was becoming well known. It takes years of episodic TV exposure for people to become recognisable, I had told myself. I didn't want people to recognise me. I mean, it was all right to recognise me on the screen when I was working, but not outside it. In the street I was just me, and I wanted it to stay that way.

I knew the value of anonymity and I certainly didn't intend to lose mine by decking myself in dark glasses and the fashionable fittings and fixtures of the seriously I-want-to-be-famous brigade. TV fame as compared with radio fame was much the more irritating.

For example, I made a programme called *Claire Rayner's Casebook*. There were three series of six or seven programmes each and they dealt with all sorts of anxieties, physical health, psychological illness, sex difficulties. (I was told that BBC announcers would say, 'It is 10 p.m. and time for *Come Dancing*. But if you can't, stay tuned to BBC1 and *Claire Rayner's Casebook*.' I never heard it on air myself.)

There was one programme on incest. We made it with great care, selecting participants with kid gloves, interviewing with great delicacy, avoiding the deliberately sensational as carefully as we could. We were all amazingly responsible about it. I watched it off air in my bedroom, almost hiding behind the duvet, and thought, Well, I think we got it right. I don't think we've exploited the subject in any way. But I'll have to wait for the viewers' letters to know how it really played with the audience.

In due course the letters arrived. The first one I opened read, 'Dear Claire, I watched your programme about incest last night and there is one question I must ask you. Where did you get your blouse?'

Give me radio any day.

The trouble, back at the very beginning, with working in TV was that I had never thought through the fame issue. If I'd had time to stop and think I'd have realised what was happening and deliberately stuck to words in a row, but I had all the instincts of a freelance by now. I said yes to all that came along and wriggled out if it turned out to be too rough or, worse still, to be crap. The odd judicious attack of toothache got me out of a couple of very nasty programmes. But basically I had become a media tart. Crook your finger and I'll come to you – but I don't always stay, I am proud to say.

But my memory was short. I had had a warning shot across my bows long before and had ignored it. When Amanda was still a baby I took her out in her pram wearing her new red shoes and coat. I had been on some daytime programme the day before but I didn't think anyone would watch it.

When I came out of the bank to where I had left the pram and my groceries for a few moments, I found my darling infant had poured the sugar into a pile, had smashed half a dozen eggs into it with her new shoes and was finger-painting her coat with the mixture.

I used language to that child that would have made a navvy blush, but which made her laugh delightedly.

At which point someone stopped, peered at me and said, 'Didn't I see you on telly yesterday?'

In 1966 that sort of thing began to happen more and more, and I felt worse and worse about it. At last I listened to Des, who had been telling me for some time that I was doing myself no favours by going out and about in torn tights and battered shirts and trousers. He pointed out that people would stare less if I looked the way they expected telly people to look and would leave me in peace.

He was quite right. We agreed that as soon as the new baby was born, I should have some new clothes. He would design them and have them made up by a super dressmaker. He also insisted I started to wear a little makeup during the day. 'Just in case,' he said. 'You never know what or who will turn up in the middle of a job like yours.'

Of course he was right again, and I had to give in. But I never regretted it.

Thirty-nine

It hit me between the eyes like one of those balls they use to knock down redundant buildings. I walked about feeling like my own ghost, stunned and silent as often as not or, when I did speak, getting my words tangled and confusing my already muddled mind. Except when there were strangers about or there was work to be done. Then I managed to put on an amazing show (well, it amazed me) of being the person I always used to be, who was, however dead, somewhere inside me. I felt as though I was robbing my own grave just to keep going.

It was undoubtedly the worst bout of depression I'd ever had. No amount of nice or good things happening could shift the weight of blackness on me. In later years I had learned to dissemble, as a form of self-defence, and became able to hide my misery until eventually the depression had got better by itself. It is described in the medical trade as a 'self-limiting condition'.

But not this time. With my other two babies, life had been reasonably calm at the time the baby was born. I have to admit that I had allowed the months of pregnancy before Jay's birth to be the most hectic of my life. And it wasn't just work pressure. It was the emotional struggle of trying to make sure all would be finished, clean and straight, before the baby was born. Which was stupid. By worry-ing I couldn't put a moment's speed on the project. Indeed, getting myself into a state infected the builders and that slowed them down. It was hell.

They had said they'd do it in six months, no problem. I knew better and swore to them I was at least two months more pregnant than I looked and walked all the time with my back arched until I felt I would never be able to stand straight again. Des worried over the work I was doing but I assured him that it was the one thing that kept me sane. When I was working I couldn't worry.

So, somehow we worked and lurched our way through the long summer towards the birth of our youngest child, and then heard sud-denly from the States that my brother Lionel and his wife Gloria were coming to visit. He was to take part in a university debate tour-nament all over the country for which he had been selected by the Oxford college he had attended as a postgraduate after McGill in Montréal to get an additional law degree. At McGill, the French Canadian students couldn't pronounce his name and called him 'Shitvind'. I loved that when I thought of my snobbish mother and her choices.

One of his colleagues on the team was brought to dinner one night, and bored the socks off me for he had little to say and what he did say was either painfully banal or exceedingly patronising. I put it down at the time to Oxford snobbery. Poor Jonathan Aitken. He was shy, Lionel explained, and a bit in awe of us. 'Wanna bet?' I said. He didn't.

So, Jay was born on a sizzling hot afternoon in September, the very day the builders finished at the house. I walked out of the front door in the company of my friend Peggy Montague (she had once been gorgeous Roger Moore's girlfriend, something in which all her friends took great delight), who took me to hospital. Des had had to go to the office that day and, frankly, I wanted him there: I worried about him less that way.

It was like walking down a triumphal tunnel of men, the way some brides and grooms do, only mine were sandy, sweaty, smelly builders, and very nice blokes, every one. They'd become part of my life over the previous year and I wept all the way to hospital because I was losing their company. Depression kicking in early? Maybe.

It was a long, hot labour, but quite different from the others because for the first time I was having a full-term baby. This chap weighed in at ten and a half pounds, 'And looking around for his tea, too,' Sister said, as she gave him to me. He looked at me wisely, as newborn infants tend to do, with that look of infinite knowledge that has bamboozled many a mother. Then he made the sort of facial grimace that all new babies do sometimes but one that looked amazingly like a grin.

Sister, who saw it, was stunned. 'It's like he's saying hello and thanks for your trouble,' she said, roared with laughter and called the other midwives to look, but he had gone back into inscrutable mode by that time and nothing they did in the cooing line made him unscrew the inscrutable.

I took Jay home and he settled in as though he had always been there. I said to Des, 'First babies you Bring Up, watch over and fret over constantly. Second babies you Rear and remember to keep an eye on, but third ones you just sort of hand over to their siblings and say, "Here's your brother, get on with it."'

Not that he was at all neglected. As well as the adoration of his siblings, which was real and lovely to see, we had a lovely Scottish nanny working for us now, though I felt a little embarrassed by that. I felt, perhaps, I was letting go of my family, but it was never like that. I did all the necessary things for my baby, and the older children and Isabel mucked in. From the start she was a great love object for Adam, who always had an eye for prettiness. This gorgeous redhead with the bright blue eyes was perfect for him and he fell in love immediately. We didn't understood the depth of his feeling for her until she announced two and a half years later that she was to be married to John.

'But you promised to wait for me,' he roared, and hid in his bedroom all afternoon, inconsolable till supper time. And I have to say he went on being angry with her for some time.

Lionel and Gloria arrived when Jay was ten days old, and we met them at the airport. It was odd for me, for try as I might I couldn't imagine Lionel as anything but a boy of ten all stretched tall. The man who arrived at Heathrow left me gasping with surprise. He was Lionel, of course, but he wasn't. Not this six-foot man of very Californian laid-back humanity.

But it got easier as the days went on. We were all a bit cramped for, despite the builders' efforts, we had no spare bedrooms and they had to bunk in the living room. We managed it without ever having a row, which said a lot for Lionel and me because there were a lot of hidden feelings we simply never talked about. I didn't ask about our parents; he never mentioned them. It was simpler that way. No amount of talk would change them or what they had done to us all. Talking of it would only make us angry.

But he did tell me about his career to date. He had been, he said frankly, on his way to nowhere when he did the unspeakable in Canadian middle-class terms: he joined the Army.

Maxine, by then married to Haskel, a survivor of the Treblinka concentration camp, and with a couple of children of her own, had been the one to get hold of him, lecture him at length and get him out – he was only in his late teens. She insisted he went back to school because he was a bright fellow. She had done for him what Nancy did for me, I thought. Lucky us.

By the time Lionel and Gloria left to go to Ireland, and then home to LA, I was almost on the floor with misery and at last had the sense to admit I was ill. Des was low himself, I now realise, but at the time I was too ill to pay any attention to anyone but myself, I'm afraid. I think that was the only time when our depressions marched hand in hand. Usually we managed it so that when one was down the other contrived to be up enough to haul the other back. It worked well as a rule. But not that time.

I wrote a letter to my doctor and posted it before I could change my mind. She arrived on the doorstep the next morning just after the post had been delivered at her surgery. She told me I had written a diagnostic letter and put me on Tofranil, one of the old tricyclic anti-depressants.

No counselling? people ask today, when I say what happened. No offer of a lovely talking treatment?

Indeed it was offered, and I refused it vehemently. I'd had enough of what I had learned to regard as that claptrap in the Toronto Psychiatric Hospital, thanks all the same. Give me the pills. I'll do the rest.

In time to come I was to suggest to a great many depressed and/or anxious people that they could try counselling. It does help a lot of people. But there are others like me for whom the whole process of 'talking treatment' is suspect. We know perfectly well the pressures that moulded us and made us what we are, and what happened to much of our brain chemistry.

I knew long ago, for example, that I had developed that thyroid disease as a direct effect of the emotional stress I lived with. I knew also the effects that my own hormones had on my thinking patterns and how easily they plunged me into the depths of misery. Much good talking treatments would have been for either of those problems. Wheel in the surgery. Dish up the tablets. Every time.

Medication works for me, that's the thing. Within ten days of starting on the doctor's Tofranil, during which time I slept a lot, which I desperately needed, once even falling asleep in a plate of pasta, I was me again. Not over the top, not madly rushing about, just relieved to feel normal, able to be happy and laugh, able to hug my children in a great rush of adoration and not feel guilty because I did not love them enough, able to sleep, to eat, to make love and enjoy it, to work, to stop crying. What more could I want from a therapy than that?

But I accept fully that others need to talk. Maybe they have never had to learn to think about their lives and what has happened to them. Maybe they have never dared to think some thoughts because they were so over-controlled as children by religion or conventional society. For them talking it out, learning to change the way they think and act by using cognitive therapy, which helps people to use their thoughts usefully and logically, are of immense value.

But I've been through those hoops all on my own. Also, I'm a voracious reader and people who read learn a lot on the way.

I tried hard to explain all this to Dr Anthony Clare when I was asked to be on his programme *In the Psychiatrist's Chair*. He thought I had accepted because I wanted to talk about painful past experiences, but I flatly refused to do so and stuck to my refusal even though he reduced me to a jelly for starters and finally tears.

It was a hot evening when we recorded the programme and I was exceedingly weary, but that is a feeble excuse. Some of my refusal in the end became sheer bloody-mindedness. He was so persistent, so determined that he would wear me down that he made me equally determined. I was not going to be made to talk about things I did not choose to discuss at that time, though that didn't mean I would never want to talk about it, in my own time and in my own way. (Bloody hell, I'm writing this book now, aren't I?)

Why did I accept? Partly because I was flattered (it's a flagship BBC Radio Four programme and I've already explained how I feel about the BBC) and partly because I knew him anyway and was rather fond of him. My 'nice leprechaun', I called him. Some leprechaun, I thought, after the first time he grilled me. And partly because I had already had professional dealings with him: we had worked together on some sort of 'marriage guide', I think it was, for the *Daily Mirror*, and on another occasion I was the guinea-pig for a dummy TV version of the radio programme. It never really took off and my contribution was not transmitted.

Back in 1966, when I had the post-Jay depression, there was no nagging about talking treatments, happily, and I was soon back on top, working away cheerfully, watching the kids grow and generally enjoying life. Des came out of his depression, too, without treatment, and we seemed well settled in our broad sunny uplands.

One November afternoon I was asked by Ursula to go and see an editor called Pat Lamburn, who was looking for a columnist. Now, this is a word that all freelances love. It means security. With a regular column chugging along you can be sure your bank balance will be fed regularly. It concentrates the mind wonderfully. I knew the good of columns: I already had a couple in magazines like *Babyworld* and *Mother and Baby* and, I think, *Mother* magazine. Write what you know, the wiseacres always tell would-be writers, and I listened. Oh, how I listened. I reckon by this time I was the country's leading advocate of the daffodil approach to potty training.

It goes like this. No normal child ever starts school in nappies. Given the opportunity to observe their elders and other children use the loo, all children will learn to use it by themselves. Therefore, if someone is daft enough to give a new mum a baby's potty the only thing to do is plant a daffodil in it.

So off I went to meet Ms Lamburn, who was amazingly elegant and beautiful, making me feel like a complete scruff as soon as I laid eyes on her, but she was charming and friendly and gave me tea in delicate china, which is always beguiling, and told me she wanted a mothercraft column for her new magazine, to be called *Hers*.

'It's a touch down-market, dear,' she said, 'C–Ds and below, under twenty-fives who won't bother with great chunks of copy. They need a different presentation.'

I knew at once what she meant. Magazines and newspapers know precisely who their readers are. If your tone of voice is wrong for the readers, then they won't read you. It is particularly vital to know the women who read a magazine for which you are to write and I had been given a clear description by Ms Lamburn. ('Do call me Pat, dear,' she murmured. So I did.)

C–Ds and a few below, and under twenty-fives, meant employed, if possible, young wives of unskilled or sometimes semi-skilled workers, including labourers, with a dusting of office workers among the factory production-line staff and sometimes retail shop staff. This *Hers* was not to be a glossy thick with costly fashion, uncookable but pretty dishes and concept articles that seem high-minded but always turn out to be about sex and How To Catch Your Man. It was to be a grittier, more real-life job altogether.

'Hmm,' I said. 'No solid blocks of copy. Little stories, then, about individual mums and their babies?'

Pat beamed at me approvingly for hitting her target so spot-on.

'That is exactly what I want, dear, perhaps drawn from the patients you used to look after. Ursula told me your background. Then you could be the sister in the clinic telling them how to deal with their little worries. Perhaps five stories a month with one bigger lead story. One we can illustrate with a photo. What do you think?'

It was a done deal. I went home well satisfied with my new employer, and in the train scribbled memories of about half a dozen patients I used to see in the clinics. It was perfectly ethical to use their stories, I reassured myself, as long as I did not identify them in any way. And also I was using their stories as teaching material for a readership not very well educated by and large in the psychological and modern physical care of children. That gave it an added ethical dimension for me. Oh, I was pleased with myself that afternoon.

The copy was written and delivered. Pat phoned and said it was perfect, great to have me aboard. The magazine came out, and looked rather pleasant. Honest, simple but very attractive. My column, I noted in a preening sort of way, was a full right-hand page towards the back of the magazine in a place where readers would be unlikely to miss it, and my byline was pleasingly large. More than that, in fact. It was gratifyingly large.

And then the letters started to come from the readers, and I was fascinated. Not all of them were about babies. Some were about spouses. One or two were about medical things. There were fifteen. I looked at them and thought hard, and went to the phone. 'Pat,' I said, 'I've had a flurry of readers' letters sent in to me.'

'I'm not at all surprised. The copy was very inviting.'

'Well, thanks. The thing is, now I look at the letters, I see I could use them for the column instead of struggling to remember real patients. And though it's all right to use them there is a bit of an ethical thing that worries me slightly. So, do you think I could use some of these letters if I choose carefully the right ones to put in the column? Even if they aren't only about babies?'

'Well, what a good idea, dear,' said Pat's almost beaming voice at the other end of the phone. '*Do* do that. It sounds interesting.'

By the end of three months I had a classic problem page. My byline was even more gratifying, the letters were very varied and I was ever more fascinated by them.

I worked out my own ethic for using them. Each would be shorn of any evidence of the writer's identity – no addresses, no names, no clues. I used them with great care, only choosing to publish those I thought would be of interest to a lot of readers, never those that seemed even remotely titillating or exploitative.

I answered every letter privately, including the ones that were published. It seemed the right way to do it. I suppose, right from the start, I ran the page like an outpatient's clinic, referring those who needed it to other sources of help and recommending contact with health visitors and doctors whenever necessary.

It wasn't till I began to get stuff from PR companies and invitations to events to do with family advice that it dawned on me: I'd never really read the problem pages in other publications and certainly not much since childhood, but now I did. Avidly.

And discovered that there was absolutely no doubt about it. Whatever other sort of writer I might consider myself to be, there was now no question in my mind.

I had turned into an agony aunt.

In these early days I had no idea, of course, just how *much* of an agony aunt I had become. But, right from the start, I gave a lot of thought to the job, ifs, whys and wherefores. I'm glad I did. When later I reached the thousand letters a week stage, there was little time to devote to the philosophy of the job; it just had to be done. So the early thinking time I had put in came in handy to say the least.

And the first obvious question I asked myself was, Why on earth should so many people of all ages, sexes, social backgrounds, levels of education, intelligence and any other marker you can think of, write to me about their most intimate concerns? And believe me, intimate is the word that best fitted that mailbag.

Some of the letters were frivolous, some achingly sad, many desperate, some deliberately jokey and far too many downright tragic.

But all were intimate in that the writers clearly had no compunction whatsoever about stripping themselves bare in the company of a total stranger.

Some of the intimacy involved sharing with me the most detailed of otherwise secret fantasies, sexual and otherwise (not a few would-be murderers around, at least in terms of intent), while others were physically intimate in displaying aspects of their anatomical selves they found worrying – and I do mean displaying. I received pencil sketches, both freehand and created by drawing the silhouette round the relevant part carefully placed on a sheet of paper, as well as photographs of genitalia (usually male) and, to this day, whenever I pass one of those 'photo-me' booths and see the curtain drawn, the lights on and no visible feet I know precisely what is happening and why.

The same applied to women, of course, though they usually sent pictures of breasts ('Look, they're all lopsided!') or close-ups of blackheady skin. However, quite a few sent awkwardly taken snapshots of their labia, quite terrified that they were changing sex, because their labia had started growing so big since their periods started ('I must have made things worse by keeping on touching myself down there') – a common circumlocution that meant 'I masturbate.'

And of course I was given amazingly detailed pictures of people's love affairs and marriages. What he said, what she said, what he did or didn't do in bed. The way he backed his mother against her, or she put her family before him: they formed a constant background to all the other stuff that came rolling in. Overall had I wished to set up in business as a blackmailer I could have enjoyed a substantial income. More than the column itself ever provided, that's for sure.

So to return to the question: Why? Why did they give me so much of themselves?

I can claim no special virtue that made me so attractive. The hard truth is that if anyone, anyone at all, makes it known that he or she will gladly receive letters of anguish or indeed any other kind, and will provide an answer for no cost, apart from that of the stamp on their letter, then that person will get umpteen letters a week.

When the concept of the agony column was first developed in London in the late seventeenth century, the chap who first thought of it, one John Dunton, knew at once he was on to a winner. He said he wouldn't exchange his idea for fifty guineas – a lot of cash indeed. He was right. The first advice column appeared in the *Athenian Gazette* in 1691 and there have been columns like it somewhere ever since.

And they all get umpteen letters a week to deal with.

So, there is clearly a desire in a large section of the public to pour out their fears and feelings to a total stranger in the hope of getting some sort of insight into their dilemmas.

There is also a sizeable chunk that wants information, reliable, accurate and up-to-date, and for them the public prints have always been seen as the source of such material.

So there is no mystery to it. Before printing and papers and magazines, every village no doubt had an old crone who knew a bit more about midwifery and various interesting herbs than most and who was willing to sit and listen and chat. The thousand who wrote to me every week when I was at my busiest were driven by the same needs for reliable, honest and, if possible, affectionate concern for their woes as their ancestors who wrote to the likes of Daniel Defoe, the father of the Wesley brothers, Sam Richardson the novelist and others who moonlighted as agony aunts back in the early days of the genre.

My nursing background might have added to my mailbag (remember the stereotype – Nurses Know All About Rude Things) and perhaps my willingness to use direct language contributed, having had as long as I can remember a loathing for euphemism except when it is used wittily. But beyond that, believe me, it's the people who write the letters who create agony columnists, not the other way about. John Dunton back in 1691 admitted at the time of his great idea that he got it because he needed an agony aunt himself at the time.

Anyway there I was, all ready to be launched on the newspaper world as an agony aunt, but I was still writing medical articles for magazines because I knew it was possible to provide a better service – to offer more factual information, more of a back-up service, more quality in fact – in their pages than in those of a newspaper. The difference being, for me, that in newspapers, everything is urgent, but nothing is important.

Forty

Peaceful years do not great copy make. I remember once reading that the main qualification for a writer was to have a horrible childhood and all sorts of different jobs while struggling through the adolescent and young adult years.

That had amused me then. I felt I was lucky to have had a good dollop of the necessary to make me if not into Tolstoy at least into a person capable of making a living as a writer. What I hadn't taken on board, however, was the corollary, which is that being happy and contented gives a writer absolutely nothing to write about.

We've all read those political commentators who during Parliamentary recess when nothing whatsoever is happening in the world of politics struggle to fill their 900 words. It makes you wince to go through it with them. Though some I have to admit make a handsome living writing constantly about nothing at all and do it superbly well and even make you laugh while they do it.

But if your thing is to produce useful copy for women burdened with all the anxieties and worries of their health, their inadequate finances, their children's health, their husbands' health, the price of eggs and their constant fear of some dread disease, notably cancer, you really can't do it in a posture of 'I'm so happy, why aren't you?'

Amazingly there are women's magazines that peddle the all-is-wonderful-in-this-wonderful-world attitude and we have only our matching frilled curtains and loo-seat covers to fret over. They have their readers: obviously they tend to be well off and the magazines to be glossy. I never made any attempt to write for them. I could no more imagine myself between the covers of *Harpie's Bizarre* or *House Gorgeous* than I could see myself writing usefully for the '*Canary Breeders' Gazette*.

So, when I was approached by *Woman's Own* just before Jay was born, I grabbed the job they offered. I had to struggle up three flights of stairs at Tower House to get to the editorial meeting because, of course, the lifts were out of order. And when I got there no one said a word about my vast bump – I looked at least fifteen months pregnant – or sweat-streaming face. They just gave me the job. And I knew I had found my working home.

It is easy to sneer at women's magazines, easy to look down on knitting patterns, recipes, gardening, health, childcare and housework tips all wrapped up in short stories and an occasional serial, and to regard such collections as mere fodder for feeble minds. That is the response of the patronising snobs who never read them. I just remembered something. It was partly because Jonathan Aitken made a rude remark about *Woman's Own* that I took against him so powerfully. And he a man whose sizeable family fortune was founded on peddling easy reading to the masses!

I was delighted to be on board this magazine – the undoubted market leader, I believed, though *Woman* was hot on our heels – because of what it was. A Trade Journal for people doing a complex and often frighteningly responsible job with remarkably little support and absolutely no training.

I was sure when I started at WO, which was what we all called it, that I could do a useful job, as useful as the one I had done when I was nursing.

The thing of it was, I had been missing hospital life. Home and babies were great, but no amount of typing words could supply the sort of exhilaration that dealing with real people and their needs had given me. I was a nurse all the way through to my middle and here,

I now saw, was the chance to do a sustained job of public health nursing and health education of the outpatient sister/health visitor sort.

All the writing I had done on these subjects hitherto had been unable to satisfy what WO would undoubtedly do. The magazine column would allow me to continue, week after week, month after month, dealing with the same readers and offering a structured account of health and well-being. I felt charged with a huge energy at the mere thought of it, not to say a certain amount of overweening pride. I'd show the world what a magazine like WO could do in the health field!

Of course, I was soon cut down to size. At first I didn't even get my own byline but was forced to cower behind a 'house name' – Ruth Martin was a non-existent old bag who hung over me and held me down like a late-night supper of hot cheese and cold beer. I was delighted when at last they let me have my own name on my work.

Then there was the matter of editorial control. I didn't decide what went into my column, as I had fondly imagined I would. I was told what was wanted after the week's editorial conference, to which I was not privy, and I had to deliver it to length and on time.

So: 'Claire, I want a major medical breakthrough for next Friday. Heart for choice but cancer would do.' Like I could drum up medical miracles at the snap of a forefinger.

Or: 'Claire, I want the causes and treatment of deafness in five hundred words for a three-column cut-off. By Friday.'

And: 'Claire, I want a big pullout, everything you ever needed to know about sex. Sixteen pages. By Friday.'

But it got steadily better. I worked on WO for over twenty-two years, which was a bit of a record for a freelance, seeing my way through half a dozen editors, umpteen feature writers and art editors and so forth, and loved it.

My children visited when I had to take them to work with me. Amanda fell head over ears in love with a nice layout chap in the Art Room and guess what career she ultimately chose? Jay came to crawl along the corridors, and Adam to flirt with the girls in Beauty at which he was very gifted.

We did some outrageous things on WO, pushing back the controls on what was 'suitable for nice women' as hard as we could, much preferring to offer them stuff that really mattered. Like giving away free condoms as part of the effort to help women protect themselves against both HIV and cervical cancer.

Like sticking to the covers of a whole issue (a million copies) test strips for diabetes in an attempt to track down undiagnosed cases. We only found five hundred but doctors all over the country were thrilled with us.

Like producing the first articles about the importance of fibre in the diet as a controller of weight as well as a preventer of a range of diseases, including colonic cancer.

Over those twenty-two years I hope WO, with my assistance, helped stop some mothers punishing their children when they wet their beds and using corporal punishment instead of more effective positive parenting methods, helped some men cure their impotence problems and some women to loosen up their over-controlled vaginas.

There was masses more, for twenty-two years is a long time, and I truly believe that we contributed at least as much to the huge social changes in Britain as the flower-power children did. Not that I'm competing, or that we were as obvious in our efforts. I am just glad that we are, by and large, a more relaxed nation and happier inside our own bodies, especially our sexual bodies, than we used to be.

How do I know? Because the letters I received and answered from thousands and thousands of WO readers, as well as from the agony columns, showed me what was happening. I read of unhappy homes being reshaped to make newer, happier ones. I heard also of some that couldn't stand the tide of change and crashed. And I read, too, of a growing tendency during my later years at WO towards selfishness and the to-hell-with-everyone-else and me-first-me-first attitude that reached its apogee with Mrs Thatcher.

We didn't do it alone, of course. Other magazines and programmes, notably BBC Radio's *Woman's Hour*, did a great demystifying job for women in Britain, taking them from the unfulfilling dark and dirty-minded years to the more honest open ones we have today.

And yes I know there is a small number of people in the country, and by no means all of them are old (the ultimate insult in some eyes!), who wish we hadn't helped in the liberation of women in this way.

They wish that we had left them tied unwillingly to their kitchen sinks, to uncommunicative husbands, and cowed and miserable children who had been beaten into submission by teachers and parents, just like in the Good Old Days.

But I am glad society changed, and we at WO helped change it. I saw 'ordinary' life in all its nasty detail in those Good Old Days and am delighted we were able to do as we did at WO during that hectic couple of decades, which was to help *some* women think their own way through to a better life, rather than teaching them to be obedient and biddable in the old way.

I am not for a moment suggesting that things today are perfect. Yes, we have some children running wild and some adolescents who are hell on wheels. But I deny most vehemently (and it is an accusation that has been hurled at me, and people like me, particularly those of us who were also offering guidance on child-rearing) that it was freeing women from the bonds of the past that caused that change. I'm convinced it has been far more to do with the effects of political and economic change, which has put more and more money and freedom into the hands of the rich and starved more and more of the poor, even stealing from them their sense of self-worth.

Is it any wonder that children left to rot on sink estates, to use the current cliché for stinking horrible slums, refuse to rot quietly and tidily out of sight? Too many people forget that it is we, through the political masters we choose and then tolerate no matter what they do, who must take our share of the blame for what these children and their families are driven to doing.

Of course I didn't spend all my time writing for WO and polemicising about the effects. I spent hours at home or out and about with the children, who grew like rabbits and ate like gannets.

One delicious memory: when Jay was three he was at last allowed to sit up and have late dinner on Friday, like the Big Ones, as he called them. He was delighted. He had demanded it, in fact, coming downstairs in his trailing dressing-gown after I had put him to bed to stand at the dining-room door just after we had settled down to announce, 'I got a mouf for dinner.' I couldn't refuse him, though it was supposed to be a four-year-old privilege.

From then on he was a Friday-night diner and the menu was of intense interest to him. He would ask several times on Friday after school what we were having.

One hot Friday afternoon a chapter of the book I was working on took a little longer than it should, so I had barely half an hour to plan and serve up a dinner. I opted to raid the freezer and fridge.

Tomato soup with home-made croûtons, followed by a huge salad with everything in it, as well as eggs and red peppers and lots of luscious mayonnaise, again home-made, plus big plump smoked trout served with garlic bread, and afterwards ice-cream with very thin orange biscuits sticking out of it. What more, I asked myself, could they possibly want?

Everyone was perfectly happy, except Jay. He looked at his plate and said mulishly, 'That isn't proper dinner. That's a Mummy's-late-and-what's-in-the-freezer dinner. It's not a *Friday* dinner.'

'That's as may be,' I said, 'but it's good grub for all that. *Bon appétit* and tuck in.'

'I want proper Friday dinner,' he repeated.

'This is it,' I said sunnily, and passed round the garlic bread.

After a few moments of staring furiously at his plate he got up, with all the dignity possible for a round-bellied person who could never keep his shirt tucked into his trousers, said again, 'I want a real Friday dinner,' and marched out, leaving much hilarity behind.

I gave him five minutes. This was a boy who needed his grub, he'd be back soon, and I told everyone not to tease him because, in all fairness, it *was* a freezer dinner, albeit with trimmings. Des felt a bit of paternal firmness might be in order, but I reckoned it was time to look for him and go in for a bit more discussion.

'He's been gone a long time for a hungry person,' I fretted, and we searched the house. No sign of him. After five more minutes I was getting really twitchy, when I looked out of the hall window and saw him.

He was marching up and down the pavement. He was carrying a shirt board, a sizeable square of card, which he had clipped to a coat-hanger with one of my bulldog clips from my study. On the card he had written in spiky just-learned-how-to-write letters, 'I want more diner sined Jay.'*

He was picketing the house, heaven help us. He'd always pre-ferred news on TV to silly cartoons but this was ridiculous.

The agony column was doing very well. The major problem was the answering of the letters so, at the school gates one afternoon, I said casually, 'Would anyone care to do some typing for a few weeks?'

There were lots of offers, and as the number of letters increased I took them up. I had by now been asked to take on *Rave* magazine's pre-teen readers' agony column. The editor had seen a good-looking boy in Fleet Street, asked if they could use his photo and he had said, 'Wha'?' So they had gone ahead and used it. They put it at the top of the 'Johnny Rave' column, which I dealt with. Letters came from twelve- and thirteen-year-old kids worried about spots, their emo-tions and sometimes darker things. They used to send me letters covered in lipstick kisses saying, 'I love you Johnny Rave,' and I would push another spoonful of cereal into Adam's mouth and wonder how they would feel if they could see who Johnny was.

In time I agreed to take on *Petticoat's* agony column, under pressure though, because I really felt I had enough to deal with. They nagged and coaxed and pointed out that the letters were too important to be dealt with by a journalist: they needed the care of someone who had some training in psychology and the physiology of the young.

When I read them I had to agree. Some of these older teens – up to sixteen plus – had major issues that needed advice, especially in their dealings with boys and, a few of them, men. Very worrying.

So that was another sack of letters arriving each month. I was now dealing with around twenty-five thousand a year because there were

---

* He grew up to be, among other things, an award-winning restaurant critic. Figures!

some from WO as well as the agony columns. I had to set up my tiny new study as an office so that I could provide the service that was needed.

I had to have information about referral bodies and services in a database (all this was pre-computers, of course) and I needed leaflets for readers requiring direct information. In the end I wrote most of my own, though I got some from the Marriage Guidance Council, the Family Planning Association and one or two other reputable bodies. And there we were.

I had space in my study for my and two other people's desks, although that meant the other two had to leave the room if I needed to get out for the loo. I trained myself to be a camel in the holy name of productivity.

In the end I recruited about half a dozen mothers of small children, and in holiday times the children came to our house while their mothers worked with me. They were great, Judy and Gaby and Liz and Maggy and Brenda and June, and one or two others, all of them great mates with whom to work. We ran a sort of crèche, I suppose, in an informal way. Our au pairs, especially Laura, a heavenly woman from Italy who was with us for two years, mucked in and loved the fun. Amanda, as the oldest child, got extra pocket money for helping Laura, especially when it was time to serve lunch. Sausages and beans for twelve kids – quite an undertaking!

We had lunch too, in the office – it seemed to me that it ought to be part of the recompense – and it all went very smoothly. In an emergency mothers were always there, which helped everyone feel relaxed. That was the key to the success of the operation.

We also ran flexitime. Most of the mothers worked a couple of days a week from nine to three. This freed them to work for other people too – many were their husband's secretaries, too. If they wanted to make a change for any reason they didn't ask me: they sorted it out with each other. Perfect!

It was at about this time, around 1970 or so, that I had an idea. Well, it was more than idea. It was The Idea.

I was writing novels now, having stopped the romances for Corgi and moved up a few rungs, but I was still unsatisfied as far as fiction-writing went. The novels were reasonably successful, reasonably reviewed and always made it to paperback, but I wanted to write the sort of book that would be a bestseller. I wanted to create characters that would run around in other people's minds the way Priestley's characters in *The Good Companions*, for example, ran about in mine.

I wanted to produce a *roman à fleuve*, a generational tale that would flow like a river teeming with people. That would certainly mean it had to be an historical story. I wanted to write a book about London, full of accurate detail about the city I love best.

I wanted the story to take readers behind the scenes to places they wouldn't be likely to know well. Like the theatre and hospitals, both of which I love.

I wanted to have family trees and maps, and I wanted it to be a huge book.

Better still a series, with characters appearing and reappearing in volume after volume so that you really got to know them, like the books I had adored as a child, Galsworthy's *The Forsyte Saga* or Hugh Walpole's *Rogue Herries* books.

It would be about two families, I decided, one theatrical and one medical. Their stories would start at the time of the Napoleonic wars and my two central characters, street children, would grow up to have a star-crossed love affair and found two separate families that would twine around each other over the next – how many years? Well, I thought, if I'm going to invent a hospital it'll be taken over by the NHS in 1948.

So there was the stretch of the story. How many volumes? Six. Not enough. Twelve, then. Why twelve? As many as I like! It's my story!

But now I had to find a title, and then I had to sell the idea to a publisher.

Later that night Des dug me in the ribs just as I was falling asleep. '*The Performers*. Doctors operate in theatres, actors act in 'em. All performers.'

As usual he'd found the perfect title for me. He always does.

Forty-one

The research needed for the first book in my new series was done partly by Des – he is my theatre expert, and provided me with large, carefully annotated ledgers full of every possible detail about nineteenth- and early-twentieth-century playhouses and actors I might need – partly by me, who had the medical material to collect (though a lot was in my head) and the history of London, again a subject I knew very well. The rest, politics, fashion, food, transport, amusements, was done by a super nurse-cum-wife-and-mother called Liz. She was also recruited at the school gates and produced for me the most amazing wall chart with all I might need about a particular year easily accessible. I found for myself in a junk shop a great treasure: a copy of the Meteorological Office's table of London weather from about 1790.

All of this was essential to what I considered a cornerstone for my project. I wanted a reader when he or she emerged from a day or night with one of my books to be able to say, 'Well, I've learned a lot today. It wasn't all just for pleasure.'

Heaven knows, I improved my own mind, teaching myself a great deal while writing the first book in the series, which I called *Abel and Lilith* after the two central characters. My idea was to change one character's name per book, so that readers would know precisely where they were in the series. Thus, *Abel and Lilith*, *Lilith and Jonah*, *Jonah and Celia*, and so on.

It was a busy time. The children were the happy, noisy, busy people they should be, filling every corner of the house with their presence – but not all the time. The omnipresence of infancy had given way to the bliss of schooldays. Amanda and Adam were at Big School full-time, Jay at Little School, a.k.a. St Custard's, every morning. I'd got the domestic scene organised like a battle, with people like Laura and our three-days-a-week lady keeping the place clean and orderly.

Or mostly. Mrs Garcia – who opted for no days a week, thanks, after she found one of Adam's stick insects dancing on the end of her broom – was one of the conservative sort who found us a difficult proposition.

Fortunately others did not, and I have specially good memories of Mrs Craig, who put up with amazing stuff from animal-and-insect-crazy Adam, who reared his own family of crickets in the boiler-house, a couple of axelotls (who persistently ate each other) and a pair of xenopus toads called Aschheim and Zondek beside his bed, together with his best friend, called rather sweetly, I thought, after my leading character, Lilith. She was a slowworm with a strong resemblance to a snake, but nothing fazed Mrs C. (We always said Adam's idea of perfect bliss would be to meet a beautiful girl, kiss her and have her turn into a frog. That all changed overnight when he reached fourteen or so.)

All this help meant I was able to beaver on. I spent perhaps half of each weekday on the agony columns, and on *WO* articles and sundry other jobs I was commissioned to do, but now that I had expert typists with me I could bash out my articles like mad, scribble all over them and, by some miracle, get back perfect clean editor-ready copy.

I used the end of each day to read and sign the letters typed that day, and the very early part of the morning to read and sort that day's incoming letters; urgent ones got same-day care. With the help of each day's brace of assistants, for there were never more than two a day, we kept the system running like oiled silk.

And all this planning was well worth while, because it meant I could use every precious afternoon for the book. The chapters rolled out like butter, it seemed to me. I lived, breathed, dreamed, even spoke nineteenth-century London. (Saying things like 'M'boy, you are being exceedingly tiresome, are you not?' to a somewhat bewildered Jay, who actually stopped trying to empty my stationery cupboard completely in search of the one perfect pencil and opted instead to go and do something somewhere his clearly batty mother wasn't. In fact, I walked around in a nineteenth-century haze, and enjoyed it all hugely.)

I delivered the typescript late in 1971, or it might have been very early 1972. I do know, though, that my friend Mike Legat, who was due to publish the paperback, thought I'd been a bit too influenced by Dickens here and there. 'I dare say I was,' I told him. 'How can anyone write about London life in the early nineteenth century without Dickens leaning over their shoulder?' And I pointed out that he'd find, if he checked again, the occasional homage to Thackeray and Mrs Gaskell, just as later in the series I imagined Anthony Trollope would be an influence.

'It's impossible, surely,' I said, 'to be completely new and original unless you aim for something like *Ulysses*. Even Shakespeare borrowed as well as invented new words – and, anyway, I didn't borrow for this book. It's just that everything I've ever read leaves its trails across my writing like so many snail's tracks.'

Ursula read it and said, 'Very nice, dear. I'm sure it will do very well.' My editor at Cassell's, Edwin, read it and said, 'Very nice, dear.'

And that was that. I knew the book would appear, and I knew they had sent it to the US for consideration. I had already had a couple of books published there, to muted applause, and I doubted I'd get more this time, frankly. They're a funny lot, Americans, I confided to myself, and remembered the wise words of Nicholas Montserrat, another of Ursula's clients whom I had met at her parties.

'Never look at the American versions of your books,' he advised me, during one bibulous evening. 'They don't edit books. They fillet 'em. There is only one authorised version of *The Cruel Sea* and it's the London one. Just grab the dollars and let 'em kill your books if they want to. Just remember Browning, "O, take the cash and let the credit go!"'

All I had to do now was wait for an American version of 'Very nice, dear,' I hoped, and the book would appear.

It's Friday afternoon, a dull sort of day, and I am bashing away with great difficulty at a double-page spread for *WO*, which flatly refuses to come right, however hard I try. It's all about sex for a change, which adds to the boredom of the whole thing because, as I ask the girls bitterly, 'How often can you write about the same old orgasms in new language, which is what they keep on wanting?' Suddenly I notice the time. It's almost three and I have to get to the bank to get out the housekeeping money – but, more importantly, the week's cash to pay the girls in the office. Nothing to pay in in the way of cheques this week, dammit, dammit, *dammit*.

I flee for the bank, fortunately only a three-minute walk away at the end of my road, and after the usual ten or so minutes there come gloomily home again.

I can't say we were broke. Des would never let that happen and neither would I. Together we keep track of our cash carefully as he sits on my extravagance as firmly as I prise up his occasional parsimony. But I had to admit that things were a bit tight. The cost of living at the end of the sixties and the start of the seventies was always going up – it was the time of decimalisation and the OPEC oil crisis, remember? – whereas fees for work were, by and large, not.

Our deposit account wasn't bad, but our current account – the one that kept the weeks financed between cheques – was, not to put too fine a gloss on it, slim. Not red, you understand, but with a shade of pink sort of hanging over the black.

I walked home thinking, scrag-end of lamb this week. Got to cut back somewhere, and marched crossly into my study. 'Bloody money, bloody banks, bloody hell,' I announced. 'I think I'm going to give up all this and open a restaurant. It's got to be an easier life and I bet it makes more money. Either that or I shall cut my throat.'

Judy, who is the most practical of people and who was there that day with Gaby, said sensibly, 'Well, I'd wait a bit if I were you. There was a call from New York about your new book while you were at the bank and he said he's calling right back.'

'You see?' I said bitterly. 'They don't like it and won't take it. It's always the same. Everything rotten happens at once. That stinking article just isn't working out and the bank people looked at me all pityingly and now this. I will cut my throat, you know.'

The phone rang. 'Claire, honey, is that you?'

'Yes, Peter,' I said, recognising his voice. He was my American editor from Simon and Schuster in New York, and we were good mates. He came to dinner with us whenever he was in London and, indeed, it had been something he had once told me about a series of American books about a Confederate doctor that had given me the germ of *The Performers*. 'How are you?'

He ignored that. 'Listen,' he said, 'are you sitting comfortably?'

This time I giggled and tried to hide it, for he was clearly in a portentous mood. It wasn't his fault that he had never been forced to spend all those hours as I had with the children and *Listen with Mother*.

'Yes, Peter,' I said demurely. 'You may begin.'

'Now, I want you to write down these numbers. Two, four, eight, seven, five, zero.'

I did and stared at them: 248750. 'Someone's phone number, Peter?' I tried. 'Who must I call? And why?'

'No, hon, that is dollars, d–o–l–l–a–r–s. That is what we have just agreed to take from the paperback house for the first volume of *The Performers*. We're in the Big League now, sweetheart. What do you say to that?'

I was still puzzling over the numbers. 'Is that two thousand four hundred and eighty-seven dollars and fifty cents?'

He let out a great whoop that I think even the girls heard – they were at my side by now and trying to hear what was going on.

'Try again. Try $248,750 dollars. A quarter of a million, less one thousand two hundred and fifty dollars. It's their shtick – they don't like figures that are too round or something.'

Peter chattered on in my ear and I looked at the numbers and tried to see what they meant. I began to feel rather sick.

'There's just one thing, though.'

That's it, I thought. Changed his mind already.

'They don't care for your title. They want to call it *Gower Street*, for the place where the old man Jesse takes the boy, Abel, to live, you know? What do you say?'

'What do I say?' I manage. 'Peter, they can call it the whole of the goddamned London telephone directory for that sort of dosh.'

He laughs immoderately at that, finding it a great deal funnier than I thought it was.

Then he goes all serious on me and says, 'So listen, doll, don't forget you're up in the Big League now, no more wasting your time on this and that. We'll be in touch a lot. There's the jacket and the design and the edits and, of course, there'll have to be a tour over here. They'll love you. We'll get you on all the big shows – it'll be a gas. I'll call you. All my best to Des.'

How do you come to terms with that? It's almost impossible to take in at first. More money than I'd ever heard of anyone earning. I looked again at the numbers. What did it mean? I'm not that good a writer. People who write like Tolstoy or Dickens get a quarter of a million, maybe, even a modern star like Margaret Drabble whom I so admire – but me? It can't be right. Would I ever again be able to write a word? Would I fall down dead tomorrow before the money arrived? Maybe it was all a hoax, and I called Peter back on a pretext. But it was true, every terrifying word of it. It was such an enormous sum, much bigger than the same amount would be today because of inflation.

I called Des. Told him the whole conversation, the numbers, the confusion, the whole bit.

'My God,' he said, without a moment's hesitation. 'That is a hundred thousand pounds.' I was impressed. Even after sixteen years of marriage, I didn't know he could do sums like that in his head.

I asked him if he was as pale as he sounded and he managed an 'Um, probably.' (By the time he got home he was a sort of pale green and I was the white one. It really hit both of us like a wallop from a boxer.)

I called Des again half an hour later, and said, 'I forgot to tell you – this will not change our lives in the slightest,' which seemed to cheer him a little, and then phoned Ursula, who was dumbstruck, and Edwin, who said, 'Very nice, dear. Very, *very* nice.'

I fetch the children from school, Jay, now five, at Big School at last, and Adam, still there for another few years, who quite likes to join us on the journey home sometimes.

I try to explain that something special has happened and that it is nice, and I'll tell them when Amanda gets home from her school – she is now attending a girls-only school, a choice Des and I disapproved of but, as she said, she was the one who would be going there so she should choose. We agreed, of course, because we always tried to be a reasonably democratic family and she was right, of course. Blossomed like a lily there.

Anyway, when we get them all together before dinner we tell them what has happened. They listen as they eat, then Des gives a little cough and sets out to deliver the message we already agreed on in a swift colloquy when he got home. He says, 'I want to explain something important.'

They nod solemnly and stare at him. They look a bit pale too, I decide. Are we all going to go down with a dread disease and die together because of catching something lethal from this damned cash?

'Look, we don't want you to think this means that we're so rich you won't ever have to work. You will. You have to do your school-work and your exams so that you can build your own careers and make your own money. We're young enough to be able to spend quite a lot of this money having fun ourselves and we will. There'll be great holidays for us all and nice things to do and wear, and lots of visits to the theatre and all the books you could ever want and so on, but you won't be spoiled. Privileged, maybe, but not spoiled. You mustn't ever get the idea that when we die we'll be leaving you lots of money. Because we won't.'

They seemed to take it in their stride, watched TV, played with their Lego and spilled it everywhere, had a fight or two with each other, all the nice, cosy, home things they normally did on Friday evenings after dinner with the happy weekend stretching blissfully ahead, and went to bed when suitably prodded.

Later, so did we, both a bit quiet and still stunned. To our surprise, Adam called us as we passed his and Jay's room where they had a pair of bunk beds – and a great deal more I preferred not to investigate. It was an unusual request because by this time he was generally deep in swinish slumber and would have been unwoken by the Four Horses of the Apocalypse galloping through the room.

'I need to talk to you two,' he announced, 'because Jay and I have been discussing matters and there is a question we have to ask you.'

Jay lay in his lower bunk, arms thrown up and snoring happily, but Adam didn't seem to mind in the least that his committee was *hors de combat*.

'What we want to know,' Adam said, 'Jay and me—'

'Jay and I,' said Des automatically.

'Jay and I, then,' Adam said impatiently, 'is about what you said about not leaving us any money when you die.'

'Not exactly,' I said. 'We mean we won't stop ourselves spending what we want to just to leave lots of money to you. You need to grow up and run your own lives, you see, and if there is any money left over, then you'll be welcome to it. But what matters is that you all do your own thing and don't expect windfalls. People like that turn out to be rather unhappy grown-ups, you see. Do you see?'

'That bit's all right,' Adam said impatiently. 'We understand *that*. But what we want to know is, because it's such a lot of money, are you going to have diamond coffins?'

Forty-two

I never was one to make life plans. I know of people who, almost from childhood, have made cut-out patterns for their careers and even their love lives, and managed to make them work. I have a lot of admiration for them, though they mystify me. I can't imagine being that clever.

I have had my ambitions, certainly, had my huge wishes and yearnings, and some of the former have been achieved and some of the latter have somehow come true. *But never because I willed it so.* Almost everything that has happened to me has been accidental.

I look back at myself over the years and see myself like the driver of a team of horses: a journalist, a commentator, a page editor, an agony aunt, a radio and television broadcaster, the author of over ninety books, about half and half fiction and non-fiction, and nowadays a fairly lively politicised campaigner on various issues. I watch myself pulling on the reins to keep the horses in some sort of alignment and marvel at it all. It looks so contrived, so organised, so *planned*, yet the entire equipage was built on blind accident.

All of which may help to account for the way I reacted to the vast sum of money (and it was vast in my terms) that had erupted into my life. We didn't go on a bender. We didn't throw a party, although we had lots of our friends round for meals – but then we'd always done that anyway. The only things we bought in the first week after the news came were duvets and fitted lower sheets for every bed in the house. Never again was I going to fret over bed-making.

Each child was shown the way to handle their bedding and each was solemnly assured that no adult would ever again enter their rooms without their clear permission. That meant, of course, that no one would tidy up after them, collect their laundry or change their beds. It had become their responsibility.

They seized it eagerly. A fair swap of self-care for privacy, they reckoned. A blow struck for maternal freedom, I reckoned.

And then we went on as usual. We had already decided to buy a small second car, to use when possible instead of the big family-sized job we already had in order to save petrol: the world was struggling with the OPEC oil crisis at the time. We went on saving hard and not spending as much as we might have liked to because prices were high and rising, partly due to said oil crisis and partly due, everyone was convinced, to the impact of decimalisation a few months back.

As for the money itself, the accountants wanted me to invest in property, riding high in London in particular just then, but I bridled furiously. I, with my East End background where landlords were people you hid from behind the front door on a Friday? I, who considered 'landlord' a swear word to be hurled at a nasty man? Not a chance.

They tried to get me to invest it overseas and, although I am not normally a nationalistic type, I bridled again and said that I had earned the money here and I'd pay the bloody taxes due here at home.

The accountants, now fully aware they were dealing with a raving lunatic, said that left only the stock market, and I grudgingly said yes, but only if it was invested in ethical companies and gave them a list of those I could not possibly countenance, like RTZ and Barclays Bank and Nestlé and tobacco and booze companies. It didn't leave them much leeway, they said gloomily, and at last went away.

So we reverted to our contented selves again and I would make supper every evening as I listened to the radio news just as I always had. The difference was that now I listened to the bit of the news that featured the FTSE index, which in the past I had always ignored. And week by week the numbers drooped and dwindled until I reckoned there was barely a scrap left of our entire investment that hadn't gone down the tubes. And laughed. Truly laughed. It all seemed so ludicrous that I, of all people, should be concerned about the FTSE index.

I remembered my younger self back in the forties when I had the wherewithal to buy either knickers or a bra. FTSE index, indeed! It had to be funny, and I said as much to Des, with a cheerful, 'Well, easy come, easy go!' He didn't find it quite so funny, I must admit.

And then we did make a change. A big one. The accountant came again and this time told us that my earnings, quite apart from the American Biggie, were sufficient to provide all our needs, which put Des into a higher tax bracket. 'If you love your job and don't mind handing over most of what you earn to the Inland Revenue then stay as you are. But it'll cost you money if you do.'

We talked half the night after that. Des had been miserable in advertising for years and I had always felt lousy about it when what I was doing was so much fun. My lovely clever actor who should have been having a glorious actorish life, stuck in an advertising office! But he was very much a man of his background and times, and every atom of him rebelled against not bringing home the bread and letting his wife do it.

I understood how he felt: how could I not? I remembered all too well how his feelings about being unable to earn as he believed a husband should had nearly scuppered us before we began. He had tried to end our relationship because of his poverty – but my poverty had matched his then, so glory, glory, love won the day.

But the feelings were still there, of course. That was when I really understood the effects of the baggage a person brings into a relationship with him or her. That I was now earning so much made them even more painful.

I was not, of course, suggesting we should swap roles: there had been talk of 'house-husbands' in the press, but that wasn't for us. I had no notion of relinquishing my control of our household (I was as old-fashioned as Des, in my own way) and, anyway, I'd got the house and childcare business licked. I was at home more than I wasn't and with my super au pairs and daily helps it all ran very well. And the children weren't babies any more. That made a big difference.

'Why not,' I ventured, 'go back to theatre? You're older, more characterful than you were. You always said you were too young at the time. Well, maybe now – why not go for it?'

He shook his head firmly on that one. 'Two bites at that cherry? No way.' He sank back into thinking mode.

'Painting?' I tried then. 'You always wanted to do more. And you're good.'

Silence this time. This was an advance because, so far, all I had suggested had been rejected. I pushed harder: 'Look, I spend a lot of potential writing time fiddling with the bank and the bookkeeping, and all the details about contracts and so forth are always having to be chased up – and they've just brought in this new Value Added Tax that's going to add to the work in that area. Couldn't— Would you act as my manager part of the time, and paint the rest of the time, and see if you can't start a new career there?'

And then I got hyper-emotional. 'The only reason I've got to the point I'm at is because you kept me all these years so that I could try and learn how to do it. You've worked bloody hard for every penny I've earned and it's your turn now. If you'll take it. You could try. It worked for me. It could work for you. Can't you be generous and agree it's your turn now?'

It took time, but in the end that was what we agreed. And for the next few months, as Des settled into all the changes inherent in being at home and working in the dining room, which became his studio, and running the financial side of life, he swung from contentment to attacks of depression, which both of us had known were a possible outcome of this change in lifestyle.

It wasn't an easy time but I knew we'd get through it, and we did, in spite of unpleasant public comments from some fellow journalists in gossip columns who had got hold of the news of our changed lifestyle. People we had even considered friends made cracks about 'men who live off their wives', using our names, and Des was bitterly hurt by it. But we got through that too.

And he made some great paintings. I remember asking him why he didn't try an abstract and he did, to please me, working as he usually did in gouache, which has a texture I love to look at.

And when I saw it, I flipped. It wasn't at all what I had expected. This was an elegantly controlled design of classic art-deco shapes lit by the most intense colours. I loved it at sight and wanted to hang it in the living room.

'It's for sale,' he said firmly, and into the portfolio it went. It was the first of a very successful series of art-deco images in perfect colours, which he mixed himself with meticulous care.

Since then he has produced some amazing collections of paintings. There were seventy based on the art-deco buildings of New York where we went so that he could do on-site research. This was a project in gouache, oils and mixed media that broke very new ground for him: although the paintings were still design-based and not representational, he has a gift for arranging the design elements in the painting so that the original building is easily recognised. His painting of the Chrysler building, for example, had more colours than the rainbow and all the charm and cheekiness of the day it was built. That one sold almost before the paint was dry.

The New York exhibition happened at the Barbican, the first to use its concourse, and was consequently very glitzy. We had the American ambassador to launch it and the BBC to make a programme about it and about us. Des sold over half of the pictures in the first few weeks.

There was a similar project for London, which sold equally well, and 'Art Deco in Egypt', a collection that was all in rich earth colours like the Egyptian desert, and the 'North American Indians' group, which did very well too.

His paintings can be found now in homes and galleries all over the world. There is a sizeable collection hanging at home, to which he adds from time to time and which we show at private views.

I'm very proud of what he has done and grateful too.

Shortly after all that excitement something new: I was offered two television jobs at the same time.

Decision time. Thames TV wanted me to present their afternoon show one afternoon a week. But two days later, before I had a chance to keep my appointment with the producer, I had another offer. Would I care to do a regular letter spot on BBC1's upcoming lunchtime show out of Birmingham every day? I would be wanted one day a week and would pretty well run my own spot.

A local show, asking the questions, or a national one, answering the questions. No contest. I chose the BBC and thereafter spent every Thursday during term-time for three years at Pebble Mill studio in Birmingham. Even the holidays were better with the BBC!

It was the right decision. In no time I had a sense of belonging, of being an intrinsic part of the show and very much part of the audience's awareness. The letters people sent were serious as well as funny sometimes, and answering them was an important part of each Thursday: I dictated answers *sotto voce* into a hand recorder on the train going home.

I met amazing people and made lifelong friends of those I sat beside in Makeup, like Marian Montgomery and Cleo Laine. Lunchtime BBC TV had good stuff to offer in those years!

One fact I had to face now, though, was that the fame thing was getting bigger. Now, as well as invitations to lush, lollipop-type affairs, I received genuine requests from charity groups wanting help. I liked that, and took on as many as I could where I thought I might be useful.

I've accepted invitations to be Supporter or Patron or Vice or full President so often that I have to admit I now have a list of over sixty (gulp). I do my best for all of them, but I never feel it's enough. There just aren't enough days in the year to fit it all in.

Now I'm older and less committed to writing columns it's rather nice to have the time for them that I lacked before. It's why I turned into a campaigner.

The dates I remember best are those that coincide with family birthdays. So on 22 January 1974, my forty-third birthday, I was looking forward to meeting Des in town later that evening to celebrate.

The phone rang. The caller was the woman's page editor of the *Sun*. The editor, she told me, would like to discuss the newspaper's agony column with me. When could I come in? This afternoon, perhaps? It was important. Would I care to make an appointment?

I sat there in the grip of very confused feelings. Normally I would have said a haughty, 'No thank you,' claiming the freelance's perogative to be picky. It's one of the few benefits we have over staff members on papers. The thing was, I hated what the paper was doing. It had been the old *Daily Herald*, a lovely, honest, working-class paper, keen on left-wing politics. Now that it had been transmogrified into a cheap nudge-nudge leer-leer scandal sheet it really was the pits. The titillation of the famous page-three girls didn't bother me so much as its dishonesty. I have no hang-ups about nudity. Bare flesh is great stuff. But the pictures in the *Sun* weren't bare flesh: they had been tweaked and twiddled till the girls looked like Kewpie dolls on a fairground stall.

But I had a bone to pick and it was a big one. Just after the publicity about *Gower Street*, the new name of *Abel and Lilith*, I had gone to a lunch put on by the Marriage Guidance Council, now Relate, for agony aunts. It was a convivial affair, we all exchanged notes and, as usual, there was a good speaker.

At the lunch after the publicity first exploded I turned up as usual and was greeted with congratulations by lots of friends and generally made to feel good.

Except by one. Her name was Wendy Greengross. She was a GP and had been on the BBC programme *So You Think You Have Problems* for years. Now she was working for the *Sun*. All over town, buses bore huge streamer adverts: 'Write to Dr Wendy!'

'Well,' she said, 'hello. You know, my husband was saying to me only this morning at breakfast, "Now, here's this chap giving up his own job to stay at home and be kept by his wife writing rubbishy books. Why can't you write some rubbish for me?"' She laughed. 'So I told him I simply don't know how to write rubbish so he'd have to keep on working.'

It was breathtakingly rude and all I could do was be equally rude back. 'Hardly rubbish. Not for a quarter of a million. Anyway, tell me, Wendy, have you started to do the *Sun* job properly yet?'

'I beg your pardon?'

'It's just that Priscilla, who has to write your copy, poor girl, tells me you refuse to answer letters.'

She stared at me, then shrugged. 'You don't think I take those letters seriously, do you? They're barely literate, those people!' She turned her back and went on talking to someone else.

Now, sitting with my phone at my ear, I saw a way to get my own back. I made a date to come in at four. I'd tell them what I thought of their agony column.

I dressed to the nines and looked, I must say, as terrific as I could.

They were very direct, the three editors who interviewed me. The main editor, Larry Lamb, had been held up somewhere, they said apologetically. Get me, I thought. Apologies!

'We like your column in *Petticoat*. We think you could beat Marge into a cocked hat.'

Ah, I thought, the old rivalry. Marge Proops was on their hated competitor, the *Daily Mirror*.

'Will you do it?'

My moment at last. I drew myself up to my full five feet ten and said, with huge hauteur, 'I wouldn't dream of writing a column that did not answer every single reader's letter. So of course I will not.'

'But we know that's what you do! We checked! It's what we want. A top column with top answers written by someone who really knows her stuff. We're the *Sun*, the biggest newspaper in the country – and most of the world, come to that. Nothing but the best for our readers. Every single letter matters.'

'Expensive!' I managed. 'I employ my own letter staff and they have to be well paid. And if you're bigger than the *Mirror*, and Marge reckons to get a thousand letters a week—'

'No problem. When can you start?'

'What about Dr Wendy?'

It was my moment then. One of them looked up at the ceiling with a highly expressive 'oh-my-God' sort of look, another giggled and the third just shook his head. 'Not a problem,' he said. 'I'll deal with her.'

'One favour,' I said. 'If I do agree to take over, will you tell her I'm the reason she's being sacked?'

It was the only time in my life, I swear, that I had ever been so catty and so vindictive. It really is not my style. But she and her even more hateful husband with his insults about Des had had it coming to them.

It wasn't till I reached the end of Bouverie Street and stood staring out at the bustle of Fleet Street that I realised what I had let myself in for. I'd never meant to. All I really wanted was to get my own back on someone who had been hateful to me and mine. And now I'd gone and got myself involved in another bloody accident.

Forty-three

It was like life on a rollercoaster. Not only was I getting great piles of letters from viewers of *Pebble Mill at One*, *WO*, *Petticoat* and various other assorted publications, for which I wrote from time to time, now the *Sun* began to add its pile.

I organised the office to the utmost and the girls, as we were all known – it wasn't insulting in those days, and we quite liked the label: it made us feel positively skittish – mucked in magnificently.

Whenever we received more than a dozen letters on a subject I wrote a leaflet about it and offered it in the paper. There were always vast numbers of requests so we knew we were filling a real need. I also gathered information leaflets from all sorts of other sources, such as the illness organisations and support groups for everything from miscarriage to depression, tranquilliser addiction and so on.

They weren't added to the databank on the nod: each had to be checked by one of us to make sure it was *bona fide*. To help with that I added a new member to our working group, a researcher, to find out info for me for articles, keep up the databank of contacts readers might need, and read, clip and file all of the medical journals as well as many others to ensure I stayed bang up to date on everything. It became our proud boast that no matter where in the country a reader lived we could find them the best sort of counsellor or support needed. On a Rotodex, of course, as it was still pre-computer times.

One of the best ways of checking an organisation's value, or the truth of new piece of information, was to confer with the other agony aunts because between us we had a huge well of knowledge of the services offered by statutory and other bodies all over the UK.

The weekly mailbag in those first months hovered between seven hundred and fifteen hundred a week. If there had been an interesting leaflet offer it could lift the total to thousands. I remember most of all a leaflet I did on premature ejaculation – 'trigger trouble', they call it in the trade – which is no fun for the afflicted chap and worse for his partner, who usually feels guilty (women tend to be exceedingly good at self-blame).

At last I met Larry Lamb, the man with the most oxymoronic name I met in all my life, who was never cuddly, never curly, never kind, never sweet and, as far as I knew, never gambolled, but who was the gifted editor of the *Sun*. He had taken it from a dying scrap of Fleet Street history to a bouncing, highly successful piece of brashness fired by the motto 'A nipple a day keeps the *Mirror* away'.

He told me to be very careful. 'My *Sun*,' he said in his flat Yorkshire voice, 'is a man's paper. A working-man's paper. I want none of this nerdy stuff about finding their inner selves, no rubbish like that. That'll do for the women, that will. It's the women you're here to write for. Nor do I want any suggestion ever that the Great British Working Man has sex problems apart from not getting enough. Right? I want no suggestion that he can't get it up, neither.'

I think I was meant to be intimidated by this display of rampant (ever-so) masculinity in all its throbbing power and fearless use of robust language but I wasn't in the least. Not after almost twelve years of nursing, dammit, with surgeons like the Arse Angel, who could swear from the North Pole to the equator before lunch and go back in the afternoon.

I assured Mr Lamb in my most 'there-there' of Sisterly voices that I would keep all he had said firmly in mind but that, of course, the only true guiding light of the column wouldn't be either of us but the readers.

I promised him I would take every possible care to select letters for publication that truly reflected the overall balance of the mailbag, and would always be sure to reflect exactly what the readers said, for that was the only truthful way for an honest paper to be, wasn't it? But I would, of course, always remember Mr Lamb's advice about the GBWM and of course the GBWW, for her letters would be most interesting too, I was sure.

With which I smiled sweetly and left him growling. He wasn't used to people – well, women, anyway – who had opinions of their own and expressed them (not many of the men on the staff did either).

Also, we had totally different visions of what my page was about. I saw it as an extension of my nursing career, a chance to do useful and interesting, I hoped, even amusing sometimes, health and social-welfare education exactly as I had done on *WO*. I rather saw my readers as patients attending a clinic. Their welfare was paramount and I would battle for it against, well, anything. Editors included. Just as I had fought when necessary with doctors.

Larry, on the other hand, saw my page, I am sure, as a money-maker that would sell papers to women and allow him to run adverts at inflated prices on mine as well as the opposite page. It would keep women happy while the readership that really mattered, the GBWM, devoted itself to good old manly pursuits like goggling at page three.

I knew I had won when I managed to get a particular letter on the page that was typical of a great many I had received. The chaps who couldn't make their loving last . . .

Despite the editor's well-known views on the GBWM and his ever potent member the subs had let the letter through when some-one else was editor of the day as Larry was away. Sub-editors are very powerful people, and I used to suck up to them shamelessly, get-ting to know the residents on the subs' desk much more quickly than anyone else. I wanted them to know I had a genuine respect for what they did and to get them on my side.

It worked this time. The sub on my page let the letter through. I explained in my answer that premature ejaculation is a common problem and susceptible to self-treatment. 'Send me a large SAE, marking your outer envelope PE to help me sort them, and aid will be on its way to you in the form of a detailed leaflet,' I promised.

We got eighteen thousand requests in the next ten days. Most came from individuals, but a surprising number from offices, garages or factories where groups of chaps had got together to ask for dozens of copies. I realised that perhaps they preferred to get their leaflets at work. Nothing displayed more clearly the commonest cause of marital distress – failure to communicate adequately, if at all, on issues of vital importance to both partners – than the use of accommodation addresses for obtaining information on sexual matters.

The incoming mail had to be sent up to my office from the paper by van (I usually dragged the week's mail home in a bulging briefcase) and it kept coming in for weeks, until we topped, I am sure, the twenty thousand mark. The local printers' shop where we had the leaflets run off in bulk went nearly potty. All the girls mucked in with envelope-stuffing, doing overtime day after day, which we needed even though we had added a post clerk to our force. But with a big push like this even the children had to help. Sack after sack after sack . . .

I passed Larry in the corridor a couple of weeks later and stopped to tell him the numbers. From the paper's point of view it was a triumph, of course. We had hit a sensitive nail on the head and it proved we were on the right track – or, at least, my column was. Perhaps it created a refuge from all that steaming, sweating masculinity everywhere else in the paper, I thought.

I don't think he ever forgave me for defying his rule. He kept me on because I was getting the results with the readers, but there was never any rapprochement between us.

He would take me out for lunch from time to time as he did with all his columnists (it was a ritual) at the Savoy Grill, which he loved, or Robert Carrier's, and would so arrange himself that when the bill came I could not help but see how much he was spending on me. I was appalled at the over-consumption and indulgence he displayed. Display being the key word, I often thought, as Larry made his little flourishes with the bill and watched me from beneath his lashes. I used to think that sort of swanking should be spelled the honest way.

Once or twice I nearly suggested to him that instead of expensive, indigestible lunches I'd rather have a pay-rise. I only found out by accident (again) that I was paid a good deal less than other journalists who were not columnists, and when Des had worked out what it should be we were not at all happy.

One thing I was adamant about: the letter-answering should never be run at a profit. Every letter and leaflet was paid for by the paper, but at cost, which Des worked out meticulously. There was no profit margin at all.

And we found that we were providing the cheapest answer per letter in all Fleet Street. But I didn't mind: I could sleep better that way. I didn't mind being well paid for what I did, indeed I expected it, but the letter service was precisely that: a service. It never did make a profit, and I'm proud of that. I had to lose my temper pretty spectacularly when one of the accountant types at the *Sun* tried to add the costs of the letter-answering service to my fee and say it was all my fee. It most certainly was not, and both he and the editorial staff came quickly to understand that.

But no rise was forthcoming for me, they told me, because of the current pay freeze, so we simply soldiered on. I was doing quite well in other jobs and I can't pretend we were poor. It was only the *Sun* and its attitudes that made me feel angry and exploited. Time will sort it out one day, I thought. And remembered Grandma. This, too, will pass.

I just got on with answering the letters as best I could, and it was far from easy. Yes, there were routine ones, such as 'I have acne', 'I blush a lot', 'I've got spots on my private parts' – I'm afraid, ribald as we were, we labelled those the 'spotted dick' letters, but of course the readers never knew that. Then there was 'My breasts are too small, their label was 'tiny tits corner', too big, lopsided, of different sizes.' I have a particularly affectionate memory of the girl who was perfectly literate but had only a shaky grasp of letter formations: she told me, 'My nibbles never stick out except when I'm cold.'

It wasn't just young women who fretted over their physical selves. 'I get the impression sometimes,' I told the girls one day despairingly, as the letters I was sorting and reading dealt with the same anxiety over and over again, 'that half the male population of these islands is born clutching a ruler in his hot little hand. And they send us all the evidence. Look at these,' and I threw across photographs clearly taken in one of those photo-booths you see in railways stations.

I felt guilty sometimes about being amused by all this. The problem was desperately important to the boys – and men – who wrote, and I answered as constructively as I could, referring them to the best sort of counselling where necessary and telling them always that true dwarfism of the genitalia is not common, and whatever size the resting penis, the erect one is always big enough for its purpose – most fellas just need reassurance.

But it did help the girls and me to laugh sometimes in the middle of all the misery. And there was plenty of it. Real agony, in fact. I could do so little to help, and I knew it. I couldn't cure cancer, make a horridly behaving teenager revert to the cuddly, easy baby he once was, stop an alcoholic husband beating the woman he loved, or help the beaten woman who insisted she couldn't leave him because she loved him.

Nor could I do much for the self-flagellator who wallowed in misery because he or she hadn't a scrap of self-esteem, the gay boy living in a remote Irish village where he would be sent to hell in a handcart if he came out and tried to live like a normal gay person. There were alcoholics and drug-abusers, over-eaters and self-starvers, potential suicides, men with rapist fantasies they were beginning to fear they could no longer control, people struggling with debt and all the terror that brings, adulterers desperate to dump their girlfriends and save their family lives but being bullied and often blackmailed by said girlfriends, foolish men and sometimes women who thought they could live double lives with no one finding out or being hurt. The list was enormous.

People used to ask me if I was ever shocked. I had to say I wasn't. Human needs and human responses are what they are, and to be shocked by them implies a disapproving judgement of them, and I tried not be judgemental if I could help it.

I know it is impossible to be non-judgemental – the very stance of being non-judging means you are agreeing with or condoning the action. What I tried to do was be matter-of-fact to help the letter-writer understand what was going on in his/her life and thoughts so that they could sort out their own confusion and find a better way to handle their dilemmas. I also suggested ways in which they could stop being destructive and become constructive.

I maintain that I have never solved another person's problems for them. I helped them untangle their confusion, perhaps, pointed out facts they might not have mentioned outright but which were there between the lines of their letters (like unspoken resentment of in-laws – a common breaking-point in marriages), suggested remedies other than those they had considered, passed on leaflets of useful information, addresses of caring support organisations and encouragement to see a doctor because, yes, they were entitled to – they were not well and needed medical help.

And I would give praise for hard efforts already made, good sense and kindness of heart displayed. People need the encouragement of recognition of these things.

But sometimes I was robust in criticism of selfishness, cruelty and downright wrongdoing, like hitting a woman and beating a child, and abandoned my non-judgemental efforts. Some things deserve to be judged and I took it upon myself in these letters to do some judging. It is what nurses do, you see. Look at the evidence, make a diagnosis, consult with other healthcare experts, consider the family and social background, then come up with the best possible solution.

I became deeply embroiled in the problems of my readers, and therefore in the reasons for their problems. Therefore the job politi-cised me even more than those early forays into the pages of John Stuart Mill and Thomas Paine had. It soon became evident to me that while many of the miseries people suffered were, to an extent, self-inflicted (like a lot of illness, come to that), even more were caused by faults in the way the State was run, with built-in injustice to the poor and helpless, and that the only remedy for such ills was a political one. If it could be found and promulgated, of course.

Thus in answering individual letters I was able to campaign for freedom of choice over abortion for women; free access to contraception for all who needed it, married or not; free access to sex education at all ages; the ending of all physical punishment of children, which always brutalises and never disciplines them; tolerance of different ways of living as, for example, homosexuals or unmarried parents (still relatively uncommon when I started the job); and tolerance of difference such as religious, political (in dealing with readers from Northern Ireland, I never forgot that they were the same thing) and race.

I continued to distribute a great deal of reading material from helpful organisations such as the Samaritans, Relate, the Family Planning Association and other educational sources including the Government's own Health Education Unit.

Some anti-sex moralists, such as Mary Whitehouse, and Valerie Riches, of the self-styled Responsible Society, disapproved vehemently. (Indeed, Whitehouse had complained about my being given the *Pebble Mill* job even before I started it because she feared I was going to pollute the BBC. She was never one to wait for evidence to complain, not if there was rumour to act on.) And not because I was writing for the *Sun*. It was because of information I had offered *Petticoat* readers.

They had spotted a letter on my page asking, 'What is wanking? And what did boys mean when they talked about it?' I had had so many letters like it that it was obviously right to put it on the page, and I did, explaining that masturbation is a normal experience, very much so when growing up but also throughout a lifetime. I added that it was an excellent and enjoyable way to get to know one's own body.

Whitehouse *et al* were in full cry after me for that. How dare I tell these innocent children about masturbation about which, of course, they would never have heard, let alone tried, if I had not written about it? I was filthy, disgusting, perverted and, in one of Whitehouse's more telling phrases, 'the Anti-Christ'.

One thing that gave me and my editors (who, I must say, were with me all the way) a good deal of ironic amusement was that I was dealing with exactly the same sort of questions for *Sun* readers, many of whom were of the same age or younger than *Petticoat*'s, but neither of the moralists, Whitehouse or Riches, gave a damn about them, for they never mentioned them. But, then, they were just working-class kids reading a working-class paper. *Petticoat*'s readers were 'naice' middle-class gels. The hypocrisy was sickening then and it still is, but the campaign run against us did neither me nor the journals for which I wrote any harm. The reverse, in fact. More sensible people noticed what we were doing and why, and joined in the debate, which was great.

What right did I have to do the job? None, I suppose, except being asked to do it, and finding that more and more people wanted me to. I never marched up to a stranger and said sternly, 'I am here to solve your problems.' I was just there in newspapers and magazines if I was wanted. And it seemed I was. I got one letter addressed 'To the lady who cares, London'. It was delivered to me and the letter inside started 'Dear Claire'. I have also had a large number of touching thank-you letters, bits of crumbly wedding cake and babies named after me, so I shan't apologise for doing the job for so many years, even though I got into it by accident.

Of course, despite all the high endeavour laughter crept in. There was the sad lady who wrote anonymously to say she knew sex should do something for her – she'd seen all the movies where the waves came rushing up the beach and cobwebs trembled – but the great climactic experience had eluded her. In spite of *much* effort, she pointed out. She had had three husbands and umpteen lovers and, she then wrote, and I could almost feel her frustration with her: 'Once I even bought a vibrator but the batteries ran out.'

There were other moments of joy:

'We'd never met, of course, but I saw her one day in the town when I was out shopping and I went up to her and told her in a very nice way that the baby in my pram was her husband's.'

'The story you are about to hear is true, but only my side.'

'We have some plans to marry – I have, he hasn't.'

'My boyfriend has been having trouble with premature ejaculation and I am afraid this is coming between us.'

'I am having trouble reaching a climax though I never used to. My husband is very good – he goes on and on trying to make me come but I am afraid this is causing friction between us.'

'To cut it short – I should have done – there he was with another woman.'

'I am a second wife. My problem is his mother worshipped the water his first wife walked on.'

'I know he's been taking other women out – I keep finding foot-prints on the inside windows of the car.' (I told Bob Monkhouse this one. He adored it so much that, I was told, he put it into his act.)

If you hear any of these from other comics you'll know where they found them.

Forty-four

In 1976 we started house-hunting again, recalling the old promise to ourselves that we would move by the time Amanda was five.

Well, she was sixteen now, tall, willowy and taking up her fair share of space. The boys, Adam at thirteen and Jay at nine, were even more sturdy. We needed space badly, despite all the extensions, including the second kitchen development and the lengthening of the living room.

Such a hot summer, 1976. We all fried and tried to save water, and the boys looked like hot buttered toast as the sun tanned their skins and bleached the hair on it golden, and Amanda spent all her time in a large shady hat, which she even wore to breakfast 'because it suits me', and it did.

I had been working extra hard at television for some time doing extra bits and bobs, as well as turning out the two books a year that had become the norm for me – I know, a glutton for hard labour. But, truly, it was fun and now the office was so superbly womaned and run I could do it. So why not? I kept the columns going, though I had dropped some as time had gone on, and did a bit of radio – as much as I could get, actually, for it was and still is my favourite medium of all. I had finished my three years on *Pebble Mill at One*, which I had enjoyed but didn't miss when my time was up, but it was soon replaced by other requests for appearances. As is so often the case the best years of any show are the early ones and I had the best, I think. It was all great fun, anyway, even being almost swamped by Wombles on one memorable occasion.

I had also had a lot of pleasure with a series for Thames TV called *Kitchen Garden* in which Keith Fordyce, who had been a disc jockey, made a graceful segue to being a TV presenter. Ostensibly he grew the vegetables and fruit that I cooked. It was unbelievably hard work because I actually did the cooking, inventing recipes, writing a trio of cookery books to go with them, the lot. And Keith gladly admits he never grew so much as a radish. We ran three series of that over three successive summers. The smell of blackberry jam boiling over will always bring *Kitchen Garden* back to me. I still have the burn scars as an *aide-mémoire*.

That had been enjoyable, and so had a number of other odds and ends of TV I fitted in, some serious and some amazingly ridiculous with titles I can't now remember and which I would never have thought of doing normally. Shows like *The Pyramid Game* and *Tell the Truth* and, heaven help us all, *Blankety Blank*. It was my adoration for the brilliant Les Dawson that got me on that. Why did I do the rest of them? I used to explain it to people like this: they send a comfortable car to get you. They give you a dressing room for your gear and then you go and giggle with your friends, old and new, and then it's costume and makeup with lots of nice pampering. Then more giggling and gossiping as you run through the show in a sort of mad rehearsal, and everyone moans they can't do it, and then it's curly sandwiches and chicken legs, and then you're dragged away to do the show and usually once again you laugh a lot. And then when it's all over there's a party in the hostility – hospitality suite and you have a nice drink or two, and then you're driven home to get a fat cheque in a few weeks or so.

The only drawback is that they will insist on transmitting the bloody programme.

The newest TV job I was offered, however, was not frivolous. It was a BBC series about childbirth and I was asked to be the resident guru to answer viewers' questions and also to write the book that would accompany the series. It was to be filmed in Bristol so there would be a fair amount of travelling.

I also agreed to do a regular series for LBC radio. It was to be a weekly afternoon show from around 1 p.m. till 5, which meant being in the studio all day to prepare in the morning for that afternoon's guests, all of whom had to be found in the morning. It was a panicky and exciting idea, and I jumped at the challenge. I love those.

But as well as all this there was the house business to get through. I adored the house we found half-way up the other side of the hill at the foot of which we had lived for seventeen years. It was square, red-brick and Georgian in style, although it had been built in 1907, and had lots of art-nouveau and art-deco touches. I fell in love with it at once. It was also dilapidated and in need of a total makeover. I wanted it so badly it hurt. I knew it was my house and that it had been waiting for me all my life.

Des was less sanguine. It was so *big*: nine assorted bedrooms on three floors, only one bathroom, although there was a loo on every floor, minimal central heating, a need for rewiring, replumbing – re-everything, really.

The main staircase was what I fell for hardest. The hall was tiled in black and white, which I have always liked, and at the far end of it the stairs rose in the middle to form a half-landing under a massive window that looked out to the south. The stairs then split into two flights that rose on each side to an even larger upstairs hall. 'It looks a wow for parties,' I told Des, and he looked more dubious than ever.

But there was a room with a north light on that floor that he could have for a studio, which would be perfect for him. I watched his resolve crumble and began to think about curtains. And carpets. And extra furniture . . .

It took six months to get us into the house, and we were well into spring 1977 before we could see how it was all going to happen. But it did, and Des stopped all his own work, except for the financial stuff and bookkeeping, to act as clerk of the works for six months.

On the April day we moved in the garden looked bare and dreary, but a couple of weeks later it was a drift of colour: the bluebells came, then pink and white fruit blossom, and every other colour you can think of when the honeysuckle and roses started. There were raspberries and strawberries, and red, white and black currants too.

Adam immediately installed a pair of geese, a grey mother and her small white gosling, and put up, with Des's help, a house and run for them beyond the raspberries to keep the smell of them as far away from the house as possible. (Geese crap like dogs and smell worse.) The house was called 'Sozzle and Pizzle's Hilton Hozzell', which they seemed to like.

Their scent brought the foxes, who came down from the church-yard on the Hill, where they lived, just to sit and stare at them in their secure home. Four years later when Adam, at eighteen, was off to university, we had a problem. Who was to care for and give food to the surviving gander, Pizzle? His mum had flown off to Goose Valhalla a couple of years ago, which seemed to have left him free to display a temper like an anaconda with a hiss to match. He hated me almost as much as I loathed him and it was a problem to find some-one to feed him and care for him. Adam's siblings and father had more sense than to take on the job.

The night before Adam left home the foxes finally got into the contained area and did for poor old Pizzle. Even I felt a little sad. All there was to see was a hulk of bloodied white feathers for the foxes had gutted him and left the carcass.

I fretted for Adam, but he was surprisingly insouciant. He looked a little sad, and then he said, 'Ah well, that's the way of it, then,' and set to clearing up the mess.

Was he heartbroken? Not a bit of it. A biologist on every level, was Adam.

'That's what Nature's all about, love,' he said when I expressed dis-tress. 'Bloody in tooth and thingy, as you well know. I must say, I think the old devil of a fox timed it great, didn't he? Stopped all your worries.'

The men who put in the terrazzo floor in the kitchen offered us a bargain bundle of huge terrazzo slabs – left over from flooring the terminal, they said, at Heathrow – for a terrace, so we added that, complete with a magnificent pond for Adam's frogs and newts. Des designed so many things as well as the terrace – cupboards, units, fittings of all sorts. His drawing-board was red hot with it all.

Another memory of those garden-fixing days: Adam standing in the front garden staring up into the massive horse-chestnut tree that grows there and which is listed so we're not allowed to cut a branch from it without council permission. He gazed deep into the branches where the conkers sat plumping in their prickly green cases and sighed deeply. 'All my life,' he said mournfully, 'I've longed to have my own conker tree. And now I have one, I'm too old.'

Oh, the tragedy of being fifteen rising sixteen. But his brother was still young enough to wallow in the tree's riches and, indeed, he made a great thing of conker games that autumn.

But it was a temporary sense of well-being. There is no experience as likely to cause stress as moving house.

We fought, we two who hardly ever had more than the sort of short-lived spats all couples have, and fought bitterly. I was worn out and so was he. We needed security and comfort and home cooking, and all we had was the stink of paint, dusty clothes and beds, and food from the local takeaway shops, which had declared a bonanza when we moved into the area. The kids thought it fun. We loathed it and took it out on each other.

Every hateful thought I had ever had about his family I poured out. It was vitriolic and, even as I let it happen, I hated myself.

He gave as good as he got, but Des is less resilient than I am, and all of the fuss, effort and, I fear, my own explosions threw him head first into as bad an attack of depression as he had ever had. Those were tough months and I worried myself sick over him, as he sat silent and sad and had to be coaxed to work. Once I could get him to go to his studio it got better. As the day progressed his mood would lighten, and he would paint and turn out good work (though some of it reflected the depth of his depression). So we went on, day by day, until at last he began to come out of it.

There had been previous attacks of this horrible illness, when he had been treated with psychotherapy, and also anti-depressants. The latter worked much better for him than the former. Indeed, some of my doubts about the value of 'talking treatments' come from having lived so closely with Des through all the years he was seeing a psychotherapist at regular intervals. Far too often he would set off for a session relaxed and comfortable to return in a tense, agitated state, sometimes in floods of painful tears.

It seemed to me as an onlooker that when he was at home enjoying distraction from his darkest thoughts and painful memories, with entertainment and the ordinary company of family and friends, he would emerge from his depression, begin to sleep and to eat better – he became painfully thin with each illness episode – and enter an altogether more comfortable state, even showing interest in the world beyond home, reading the papers, wanting to go to a film or a play, behaving like himself again.

But then he would have another psychotherapy session and be pushed right back down again as the scabs were pulled off old wounds. So while I agree that TT can be of immense value for people who have never been able to talk about themselves, for others it can just be a way of prolonging distress.

In some of the episodes of depression that Des has suffered he got so ill that he was suicidal and I was scared witless. Trying to be with him and watch him constantly, without behaving like a prison warder or a nanny, was horrid for me as his wife, made him feel wretched and did neither of us any good.

It was a relief when his psychiatrist recommended hospitalisation where he could have ECT, another much-maligned therapy, to get him out of his terrifying suicidal state.

Most people see ECT as it was shown in a seventies film *One Flew Over the Cuckoo's Nest*, an account of the lives of psychiatric patients in a *fifties* hospital in a backward southern state of America. It's like getting agitated over having an operation on a broken leg because you once read an account of one in a novel by Charles Dickens. The good news is that, used in the modern way under a light general anaesthetic, it is safe, it does not damage long-term memory (indeed, the illness of depression itself causes more memory loss than ECT) and it works. Des describes the effect: 'I feel I'm in a deep, dark tunnel, and then slowly I start to rise and I go up and up and it gets lighter and lighter, and then suddenly there I am and I feel like a person again.'

ECT shortens episodes of suicidal and therefore dangerous depression, and I for two – Des agrees totally on this – plead for its critics to stop trying to get it banned. It needs to be one of many therapies available to every patient, for they all have different needs. I may not think very highly of 'talking treatments' but I don't seek to ban them.

With Des well again and the children emerging from school to go to university, we finished off the seventies and entered the eighties in pretty good shape.

I was now about eight titles into the series of *The Performers* and I needed a change. The idea I came up with would be such a challenge. It was an ambitious project: a story of the Jewish diaspora covering almost the whole world, the way fleeing, persecuted Jews had done over two thousand years. I was settling down to what proved the biggest job of my career.

Forty-five

It was not until 1980 that I finally lost my temper with Larry Lamb and decided to listen to the friendly overtures that had been coming my way from the Mirror Group for some time.

I wish I could say I had been noble and chosen to give him a flea in his ear about the way his newspaper was sliding ever further down-market and ever closer to the political right. That would be something I could boast about, because his enthusiastic adoption of the repellent Margaret Thatcher, a woman I had despised ever since her education secretary days when she had deprived children of school milk – I knew from my letters that it was a vital part of the diet of a great many poor children – led directly to her success in the general election of 1979.

When the *Sun* embraced her and told its readers to do the same, so winning the election for her, I was sickened. But it was Lamb's behaviour to me personally that finally made me go. All I can say in my own defence is, first, that the *Sun* was the highest soapbox in the marketplace and since I felt I had messages to send it was the best place from which to send them, but also that I have a deep dislike, amounting almost to a fear, of change.

It's a sort of freelance neurosis. Once I'm settled in a job I fear to let it go thinking, probably foolishly, that trying to change what I dislike about the job is the better option. And, of course, it is not vital to share the views of a journal to work for it.

Anyway, the day Lamb scribbled '10%' in large figures on my application for an increase in my fees, which would bring me parity with the other journalists when the chapel – the union – had asked for and been given something like 35 per cent, I wrote a sharp letter of resignation to end a seven-year stint. And in what I regarded as an electric-light-bulb-over-the-head-bright-idea moment I addressed the letter to Mr Larry Lamb, even though Thatcher had announced his pay for his election services: his knighthood. He had immediately changed the sign on his office door to 'Sir Larry Lamb' in bright silver.

I checked with *Debrett* and found, to my glee, that my electric light had been right. He could not use the title until he had been to the Palace and been dubbed, and there had not yet been an investiture.

I was told by his secretary that when he got my letter addressed to Mr Larry Lamb he 'walked up one wall of the office, over the ceiling and down the other side in his rage'. She also told me that one of the reasons he loathed me as much as I loathed him was that I had been invited to take part in the BBC's *Any Questions?* and he never had.

They made a big fuss of me at the *Mirror*. I had been scared to be even considered for a job there because I had always seen the daily as a really important paper, as important as *The Times*, in its own niche, whereas the *Sun* had seemed less so. Admittedly I had been wrong about the power of the *Sun*, but that didn't alter the way I felt about the *Mirror*. It was special to me. Even joining the Sunday rather than the daily made me feel I was taking a real step upwards – perhaps because I had learned to read from it back in the 1930s.

It was very different at the *Mirror*. The *Sun* had been pushy, noisy and, above all, go-getting, especially in its efforts to go-get the *Mirror*. The *Mirror*, on the other hand, made itself comfortable. The place was full of journalists who seemed never to get a word into the paper, which puzzled me. There were also lots of assorted bodies who seemed just to wander around from coffee-machine to coffee-machine. I could have been misled, of course, by the fact that I was now on a Sunday paper rather than a daily where, of course, the pressure was constant but even so . . .

Then someone told me that the Group on the whole was seen by its staff as a sort of 'velvet coffin'. You could lie there and rot in well-paid comfort for years if that was all you wanted out of life. Or you could be like a girl I soon noticed who was clearly fizzing with energy, drive and not a few hormones, called Anne Robinson. She was clearly on her way to somewhere wonderful.

I soon sussed it. There were two kinds of *Mirror* people. The job-for-life ones – Marge Proops was one – and the I'm-on-my-way lot exemplified by Anne.

For my part I just wanted to get my column neatly into the paper each Sunday – I soon found the best sub to work with – and no more than that. No extra articles for a while, if I could avoid them, because I still had my *WO* input to get through each week, and I wanted to concentrate on my new book as much as possible, and, of course, there were still the readers' letters, now running at a pretty steady thousand a week. (I wondered if they would decrease on the *Sunday Mirror*. They did not, heaven help me.) All this as well as the new book.

If there was a small cloud on the horizon it was Marge Proops. She was then about seventy, although she never admitted to her age. I only knew this because one of my secretaries, Judy, whom I'd met at the school gates all those years ago, had turned out to be Marge's only niece and she told me.

I was informed quietly by the managing director of Mirror Newspapers that I was there as a lady-in-waiting. 'I'm sure Marge will want to retire soon. And when she does you will take over on the daily. But we won't hurry her, of course, although we do think she's past the normal retirement age, but she's Marge, so . . .' His voice dwindled away rather helplessly.

I soon found that she was indeed the Queen. What she said must happen happened, and not only on the daily. Her influence spread to us. I did wonder, for example, why I so rarely had a poster promotion advertising my Sunday column outside newsagents. These were the norm everywhere. I had always been promoted like this on the *Sun*, but here, somehow, it rarely happened. Although it did sometimes, and then I discovered something interesting.

It was only when Marge was away from the paper on holiday that her guard was down and they managed to slip in a poster for me. In all fairness she gave up on that when the publicity unit decided to put a huge pair of pictures on the side of the building that looked down High Holborn. There was one of each of us with Marge's picture a tad the larger. After that there were no more poster problems.

I thought it all rather funny. She would take me out to lunch on occasion and always to places where the staff knew her well and almost fawned on her. The trouble was that once they knew me too they fawned again – as I arrived the prescribed two paces behind. After that she always had her secretary check that I had not been to the restaurant of her choice. It was all silly and almost schoolgirlish but I managed to keep myself in second place until one rather unfortunate day. Because I was on TV so much more than she was, I was rapidly recognised. One afternoon, outside the Gay Hussar in Greek Street, a man stopped me and held out his autograph book. I duly signed and then, in the usual way, handed the book to Marge so that she could sign too.

The punter snatched it back. 'I only want famous people,' he said and flounced off. I wanted to die. Oddly enough she was amazingly nice about it, seeming to enjoy my discomfiture more than she was upset by the insult.

She won in the end, of course. I had long since left the Mirror Group and, indeed, given up being an agony aunt by the time she died, still in harness, at the age of, I think, eighty-six or -seven. One of my old mates at the *Mirror* called me to tell me the news and then said, 'I reckon it was you who kept her alive all those years. She was damned if she'd let you step into her shoes.'

Which was great, because truly I had never wanted them. I was perfectly happy in my own.

Forty-six

Once I had become a *Mirror* lady, the attitudes that other people in the media showed towards me changed in a way that underlined my own feelings about being on the paper. People took me more seriously. The *Mirror* was just as far down the market as the *Sun* but it had behind it a long and distinguished history as a working-class paper devoted to its readers, the Labour Party and its principles but, above all, to the values of the ordinary British family and its right to be heard and respected.

I began to be invited to take part in conferences, seminars, Think Tank sessions and similar activities to speak as 'the ordinary person'. The thinking was that since I read the readers' letters all the time, I was an obvious amplifier of their voices. For the same reason I was invited to take on more charity work. I did all I could – it was worth doing and, anyway, I liked the other people involved.

I was happy to do it, but it did chew holes in my working days although many of the meetings were held over lunch, in the evening, or latterly over breakfast, in the American fashion. All the members of the groups were busy people. That meant I could plan whole well-filled days in town and save a minimum of three writing days a week.

The book plodded on and on. I had bitten off a vast piece of history to cover but it was running almost as well as the title – *The Running Years*. I stopped worrying about the delivery date I'd promised and let time flow round me. I packed it as tightly with work as I ever had, but as the children were now almost adults it was easier. They did make me feel old. Though as someone said to me, 'You make a date with a fella and the next thing you know you've got a kitchen full of blue-jeaned asses.' She sighed. 'And then they're all gone and you wonder why you minded.'

Actually I didn't. The constant parade of friends and hangers-on that wandered in and out of my kitchen and regularly hoovered up the contents of my fridge added flavour to life, although Des sometimes muttered about it being a bit more flavour than he wanted, thank you very much. 'Marmite people,' he called some of them. 'Too much spoils the flavour and a little goes a *very* long way.'

We gave parties of our own in which I revelled: I enjoyed doing the catering as well as seeing lots of friends, while Des collected a couple of his special mates and they would find a corner in which to gossip in peace. I was always the more sociable of the two of us but he let me have my head over parties for eighty or so, which turned his life upside down for a weekend. As long as we also had the small dinners for half a dozen he was happy.

In the early eighties I was asked to join TV-am to do a weekly appearance for seven weeks, and stayed for eight years until the station closed down in 1992. I had been unwilling to do this because I had already cut my teeth on BBC breakfast TV, which was serious, stuffy, self-important and, worst of all, dull. I only stuck it for a few months, and I was so relieved the day I quit I swore I would never again get up at 5 a.m. for a TV programme.

But I was beguiled into giving a TV-am a try, and found a different world: lively, fast with news, cheeky with features and well ahead of the BBC's game. One special effort was in the field of health education and I really came into my own here. We sent out vast amounts of material about cancer of the breast and I think I was the first presenter ever to show bare breasts at breakfast time – outside the porn channels, that is. I did so to demonstrate to viewers how to identify

potential cancers by self-examination, and had a flurry of grateful letters from women who, using the programme as a guide, had found a
breast lump, which they had taken to their doctors, found out it was
malignant, had it treated, and were now clear. If that wasn't worth
getting up at 5 a.m. for I don't know what is.

We did items about unspeakable things like incontinence and gut
disorders. One cameraman told me cheerfully I was the most disgusting thing in his life and I regularly made his day.

When it came to the vital issue of cancer of the cervix killing far
too many women every day, I pulled out all the stops. I had wanted
to put up a big cut-out of a naked man with a big placard over his
genitals reading 'These may seriously damage your health,' but that
got a firm no-no from nervous cameramen and others of their gender.
Instead, I demonstrated the use of condoms on the programme to
remind women that they needed to protect themselves against the
risk of infections that could lead to cervical cancer and waxed if not
lyrical very graphically about penile warts and genital herpes. I also
tried to reassure men as best I could by pointing out that the lovely
shimmer of the latex 'would enhance any man's beauty'.

(A sudden memory: I was asked around this time to appear with
Kenny Everett on Gloria Hunniford's show with both of us reporting
on films and shows she had sent us to see. We saw, *inter alia*,
Schwarzenegger in a body-building epic of some kind. Asked for my
opinion of the attractiveness of the mighty Arnold I said I found him
frankly unappetising and that I couldn't possibly fancy a man who
fancied himself so much more than I ever could. Then Kenny was
asked for his reaction. He thought for a moment and said reflec-
tively, 'He looked like a condom full of walnuts.')

From then on they called me the Condom Queen because of my
TV displays of them, and I didn't mind a bit. I always had some in my
briefcase for cheeky taxi-drivers and bus-conductors, and once threw
handfuls into the audience at a charity show. I gave them to all sorts
of visitors to the programme and sent them in their hundreds to
Ireland and Eire, in plain envelopes on request. Even my boys at
home were being asked by schoolmates if I could provide some for

them as they were now almost sixth-formers, after all, and wanted to be responsible chaps.

I had ample supplies. The manufacturers were charmed to keep sending me great boxes full of the things so that I could go on pushing them in my one-woman health campaign. As far as they were concerned I was valuable advertising because this was a product that could not then be shown on TV in a paid advertisement.

It was not only condoms that were considered too disgusting to be advertised. So were sanitary towels, and for years I had supported a campaign started and run by Thames TV to allow such advertising so that women could lobby for the VAT on them to be removed. They are not luxury products, except in the eyes of the Inland Revenue, was our cry. Come up to date and stop this secret tax against women! So, getting them advertised on TV, as well as in women's magazines, was the first step.

At last the campaign was heard and at last it was agreed: TV advertising was permitted but would be carefully watched for signs of offensiveness. I was called by Saatchi and Saatchi and asked to front an ad for Johnson & Johnson's Vespré Silhouette. I accepted with alacrity. Another blow I could strike for the Sisterhood of Women!

I think mine was the first or perhaps second to hit the screens of Britain but either way it was the first of its kind. There were to be no nymphs in lacy dresses flowing by in slow motion. Nor would there be immensely sporty, immensely energetic girls leaping out of planes on to motorbikes with nary a stain to be seen. No, the new Vespré Silhouette was to be displayed on a simple to-camera discussion with real women (i.e., not paid actresses) on the pros and cons of the towels and the nice things about them. Saatchi and Saatchi collected a sort of stadium full of women with me as the interviewer, then chose the most positive comments about the product to put to air.

My role then was to show the pack, and say, 'Now with wings,' because this towel was of a new design that incorporated side flaps to increase protection. Any and every woman who had ever had to throw away otherwise pretty but utterly ruined knickers because of the lack of wings in the design was going to whoop and yell, 'YESSS! What took them so long?'

There was one other detail in the ad. Liquid is poured from a jug on to the pad to show its absorbency. Blue liquid. I protested. Couldn't we be honest and show scarlet? Not real blood, as that would be tricky, but stagy old Kensington Gore. It wouldn't fool anyone but at least it would be an approximation of the truth.

No, they said. The TV people will never allow it. Nor will the client.

So, what's left? Yellow? Pus is yellow. So is pee.

Brown? Too close to the nappy and, in fact, too excretory alto-gether.

Green? Pus again. And mildew. Not a nice image.

Black, dammit! We think not, they said, looking contemptuous, and please don't mention white on account of it can't be seen.

'I never thought of that, of course,' I said, all mock-humility. 'Blue it is, then. Nice, medical, clean, washing-day blue.'

When *Spitting Image* decided to add me to their repertoire by making a model that looked like the Witch of Endor or her sister and, worse still, had a bust made of balloons filled with water to make them floppy, which I took as a mighty personal insult but admired for its cleverness, they had me responding to a reader on the show one night. 'This little girl,' purred my model, 'tells me she started her periods last night and she's very worried – *they aren't blue.*'

I *told* them to use Kensington Gore . . .

Not long after my first 'appearance' as one of Roger Fluck's cre-ations I was invited to do a programme for Gloria Hunniford. I arrived to find lots of mates, but especially Ronnie Barker for whom I have always had a great affection.

'Ah, Claire,' he mumbled, when he saw me. 'Um – you mustn't be upset, dear.'

'Upset? Seeing you? It's always a pleasure,' I said, laying it on thick because I really do like him.

He ignored the thick. 'It's just that – we'll be nice, of course.

Nothing nasty or unkind, I do promise you, just a little friendly – all very kind, I do promise.'

'Ronnie, please explain. I don't understand.' Thick is useless; clear and to-the-point is better. 'What are you talking about?'

'We're doing you, you see, Ronnie and I. He'll be Marge on the piano and I'll be singing a song about you as you – but it won't be nasty.'

I was enchanted by the idea. 'Ronnie, that's wonderful! I'm honoured, really. Can I loan you a long skirt because I never wear short ones? And would you like to borrow a lorgnette because I always wear one? Oh, this is great!'

He went on as though I hadn't spoken, apologising, reassuring me, looking so sweet and worried, and suddenly I heard myself saying, 'Truly, Ronnie, I'd much rather be Barkered than Flucked – don't *worry*.'

He looked puzzled. 'Hmm?' he said. Obviously he had never heard of Fluck and Law of *Spitting Image*. It was my best gag ever and I can never use it ever again anywhere. And the man it was aimed at didn't understand. No wonder Woody Allen looks so miserable all the time.

Once the ad had gone out I thought that would be the end of any activity involving me. I'd done my bit. Was I wrong!

The whole country, it seemed, exploded with disgusted wrath. The client, Johnson's, got masses of hate letters for this revolting ad – although they also got a great many congratulating them warmly on the new wings design and sales shot up by twelve per cent. Every paper and every TV and radio call-in programme claimed to be besieged by infuriated people, mostly women.

I got a couple of hundred letters, some of them abusive. I remember one lady in particular who consigned me to hell then and for ever for 'revealing to those horrible men our monthly bleeding secret. How could you, as a woman, take part in such filth?'

Some of the letters were also sweet and supportive, and thanked me for doing the right thing for women.

In the middle of it all I remembered the day I started my own periods, without a word of warning from my mother or anyone else. She told me first 'never bring a bastard to me' – I had no idea what she meant – and, second, that I had to be clean and decent all the time because if ever a boy saw any blood on me like a dress stain or, God forbid, a discarded towel my face would turn yellow and stay that way for ever.

I asked how my face would know to turn yellow if I didn't know a boy had seen a stain, and all she did was slosh me, a good deal harder than usual (my cheek was bruised next morning), and made it clear in other ways that she wasn't at all pleased about my starting my periods. She wouldn't sit at a meal table with me during a period, which I know now from my own reading is an interesting piece of atavistic behaviour. She certainly felt threatened by it, and I now remember she had already stopped her own periods, having had the hysterectomy long before my menarche. She told me she thought it was disgusting having periods at my age – eleven – as though it had been my choice! Poor creature. She was a mess, one way and another.

Anyway, I was asked to appear on any number of TV programmes to explain my filthy self. I was interviewed to a thread, written about and commented on to an amazing degree. And all I can say now is what I said then.

What on earth was wrong with a country where a normal female physiological experience was regarded as so foul that it could never be mentioned, except among women speaking in secret?

What was so awful about women and their bodies that this ordinary product, required for their care, could not be honestly advertised?

What is wrong with all of us, of both sexes, that so many of us are such stupid prudes? Because I still get complaints about that ad.

Well, that was then, in the eighties. Now, in the early noughties, no one seems to care any more. No one would put down an early-day motion in the House of Commons about an ad for sanitary towels. No one would thunder disapproval from the pulpit – a couple of churchmen had a lovely time, I was told.

Nowadays the ITC lets through amazingly sexually explicit ads, as well as some of the nudge-nudge hinting kind, and no one turns a hair. Like the one for a chocolate bar given a sexy female voice and beseeching a man to eat her: 'Lick my ripples! Bite me. Bite me.' My sanitary towel ads were very chaste in comparison. These ads are part of life, just as periods are.

I suppose, though, I can take some pride in helping to take the covers off.

Or, of course, blame, if that is the way you feel.

Forty-seven

We began to travel more. When the children had been young it would have been no fun to go away for long periods without them, for I would have missed them too much, though Des had insisted we take some short breaks of a week or less as they got older. But now they were grown up, as near as dammit, we were much more free and I felt less guilt if I went away. After all, they had plenty to do with their own friends.

I had done some lone journeys purely for work over the years, like lecturing on ergonomic design in Prague – very sad, it was just after the death of Dubček and the country was in shock. I had joined noisy debates on abortion in the Channel Islands, where an illicit abortion, as recently as the eighties, could send a woman to prison for life, and had gone to Italy to meet and interview the man who discovered the dangers of dietary cholesterol. But now we flexed our passports and set off to travel for fun.

We spent breaks in the Mediterranean, notably the island of Corsica, which we loved – we went there for ten years on the trot, so it clearly had something very special – but also Mallorca, which is still unspoiled if you know where to look, and Ibiza before the pop stars found it, and Cyprus. But there was also North Africa –

Morocco and Tunisia – and wonderful Greece, and Italy and Spain and Portugal, so we covered a lot of ground.

The special thing about all these holidays was that it was just the two of us. Dearly as we love our children, just being together is our favourite thing.

Sometimes the travelling involved work. We went to the USA and searched for and found ourselves a new USA agent, a lovely chap called Aaron Priest. I would have gone for him on the grounds of his name alone but he had other qualities, like a gift for persuading publishers to do good things for their authors. He found me troublesome, though, for I could not get along with US editing style, and kept altering their editorial corrections to what I preferred.

This bloody-mindedness of mine about wanting proper English in my books and not what I regarded as a sort of wishy-washy mid-Atlantic compromise for American readers made me very much *persona non grata* in the US publishing world, although oddly enough my books published in the UK have always done well in US public libraries. I believed US publishers insulted their readers by assuming that they wouldn't cope with UK English.

This was why after that first great coup with *Gower Street* I never again made a huge advance. One US publisher had assured me she could turn me into the new Danielle Steele/Judy Krantz and I would make shedloads of cash if I just let her edit me US-style, but I ignored Nicholas Montserrat's advice and did it my own way. That means I refused, preferring to stay just the same old me rather than become a feeble copy of a local US product.

As a result, Aaron told me gloomily, my name was what he called *ashenblott*, a good Yiddish word, which in this case meant dust and ashes in the mouths of the USA publishing fraternity. I have no regrets and I can swear to that. We had quite enough money for our needs, and more would only have been something else to worry about. I feel I kept my integrity as a British storyteller, such as it was, and can hold up my head because I wouldn't let anyone transmogrify me.

When *The Running Years* came out I was delighted to find I had a UK bestseller and that the US also wanted it. They had to change something, of course: in this case it was the title. They thought that the word 'running', which refers in the book to the fleeing over two thousand years of the people in the story and also to the inexorable rolling by of the years, would make US readers expect a book on jogging. So they called it *The Enduring Years*, which wasn't a bad approximation I suppose.

To market it they dragged Des and me all over the States, where I gave lectures, appeared on TV and radio, signed books in shops and generally went through flames to achieve the results the publishers wanted.

I made a similar book trip to Australia, this time with a non-fiction epic called *Claire Rayner's Marriage Guide*. The *Sunday Mirror* made a big thing of it, labelling me, despite my painful blushes, their 'Cuddles Ambassador'. The idea was that I carried messages from families in the UK to Aussie emigrants and would bring back their messages, including cuddles all round. I feared for my ribs, but Des would be there so I hoped it wouldn't be too difficult.

It wasn't difficult so much as exhausting. I must have done six or seven gigs a day for three weeks, what with TV, radio, newspaper interviews, public appearances and signings. At the end of it they apologised that my exposure had been a bit limited but, of course, it was 1984, Olympics year . . .

The toughest part of the trip, though, was our bear-leader, given to us by the publishers to look after us. 'I don't want to piss in your pocket,' he said cheerfully, 'but I do want to take care of you.' He spent most of his time running a most fiery affair with the young woman who had also been sent by the publisher as general bag-carrier. The chap's wife found out what he was up to around Adelaide (the most boring city in the world) and thereafter spent a lot of time talking to me on the phone about what bastards men were, especially the one she had married. Served me right for writing the book, I suppose.

One day in Sydney we were in a car in a traffic jam listening to the radio: I had made a recording in a radio station outside the city and we wanted to hear it on the way to the next broadcast.

But it wasn't on yet and we sat in the traffic on that great coat-hanger of a bridge, looking down into the glorious July glitter of the bay around the 'scrum of nuns', as the locals fondly call their opera house, listening to the last few moments of the *Health and Welfare* phone-in programme that had to end before mine came on.

A caller-in said, 'I went to a naturopath? And he told me I needed high colonic lavage? A washout right the way up to my middle? That can't be healthy, can it? It doesn't sound normal?'

The respondent was herself a naturopath with a flatter than usual Australian voice. 'Oh, yes, dear, you needn't worry? It's entirely normal? I can tell you there is a breed of West African storks and they have very long thin bills? And they suck up water out of puddles into their very long thin bills and then they insert their very thin bills into the anuses of their friends and squirt in the water they sucked up to help their friends by washing out their parasites? So you see, it's totally normal?'

There was a short silence in the car and then Des and I started to laugh, a huge down-to-our-boots laugh that we couldn't contain. I tried to bleat something about the BBC having a lot to learn from Australian radio and about the way I'd been clobbered just for mentioning periods on TV, and here was a lady on radio talking about anuses and parasites. It was wonderful stuff, and I laughed harder and harder.

Until I saw our bear-leader's face. He looked like a thunderstorm about to happen. I sobered quickly and explained to him it wasn't Australian radio I was laughing at but the BBC because it would be too prudish to allow on air a lovely open-natured and sensible lady like the one we had just heard.

He calmed down, saying he'd make allowances for us because he was born in West Ham and knew what a handicap it was to be a Pom.

One of the lollipops of my work was an invitation by Cunard to sail the Med on the *QEII* and lecture to the passengers. The trip, for both of us, was the reward for the lectures, which had to be entertaining, of course. And I must believe they were, because we were invited back lots of times. Eventually we went to New York and back on that lovely ship with which I am totally besotted. Magic it was to come into NY harbour early on a sunshiny morning and watch the Lady grow from a tiny figure to the Statue of Liberty in all her massive glory as the Staten Island ferry nipped between us and we could see the traffic bustling across the avenues as we were slowly jockeyed into our berth.

Later we went in another Cunarder through the Baltic as far as St Petersburg where they put on a special ballet performance at the Mariensky Theatre inside the Hermitage museum. Magic, all of it, and all in exchange for doing what I like best: talking a lot.

Every one of those trips was so enjoyable that eventually we chose to be ordinary ticket-buying passengers instead of lecture-giving types and booked ourselves rather posh accommodation on Cunard's *Seabourn Sun* to go to the Caribbean for a little November sunshine.

The result was one of the most horrendous experiences of our shared life: on that trip, Des came as close as he has ever been to dying. On our amazingly safe return home I wrote it all up as a diary entry for a newspaper.

3 December 1999: 0100 hours

Am standing in a bathroom that is rocking vigorously as I hold my husband's head while he throws up, thinking frantically, This isn't happening. We are in the middle of the Atlantic Ocean, hundreds of miles from anywhere, and Des is filling the cabin washbasin with the reddest of red blood and *this isn't happening.*

But it is, and I get him back to bed, and phone the ship's hospital, trying to keep my terror and my demeanour under tight control. Within minutes the ship's doctor and a nurse arrive, take one look at the state of the bathroom and tell us urgent hospitalisation is necessary. Des must be taken into the bowels of the ship to be looked after there by the nurses, while the doctor talks to the Captain on the Bridge about turning round the *Seabourn Sun*, currently on her inaugural voyage, and returning her to the Azores. We had called there two days previously, found them closed, and sailed on our way to Barbados.

It becomes very clear that we will not be seeing Barbados on this cruise. Not that I care: all I can think of is the cause of the bleed, the risk of a second possibly catastrophic one, and the huge distance we are from home and British doctors in a British hospital. Illness and fear bring out the latent xenophobia in us all.

The ship, we are told, *is* returning to the Azores, and our guilt about discommoding other passengers is eased when we hear that we are the second medical emergency of the night: another passenger has fractured her hip and needs hospitalisation. I do sympathise with Mrs H, but am grateful to her for sharing the burden of blame.

I see Des settled in hospital with intravenous drip *in situ*, and insist on sitting with him all night. I am still a nurse, however long it is since I was in clinical practice, and I want to watch my precious patient myself. Cunard's doctor and nurses understand, take no umbrage and accommodate me.

3 December: 0630 hours

The worst night of my life becomes morning. I have held Des's hand, as far as he is concerned, throughout. In truth I have had one finger on his pulse, watching for early signs of more internal bleeding. Dr R and I discuss possible causes of the bleed. A drug side-effect? Des has had some non-steroidal anti-inflammatory drugs recently for severe migraine, and they are notorious for damaging stomach linings. However, he took another protective drug to avoid that. A cancer? A gastric ulcer? He has shown no signs of other ill-health and is very fit and well: non-smoker/drinker, with normal blood pressure, works out at gym three times a week, swims half a mile every morning. Severe disease seems unlikely.

Dr R says diplomatically no point in trying to second-guess the endoscopy Des will have in Azorean hospital. I know he is right so try to stop making scenarios in my head. This is not easy.

I am told ship is to be met by a Portuguese Air Force helicopter, which will take us to the Azores. It will arrive at 1700 hours. I have all day to pack. Since Des seems safe at present, I return to cabin to alert our insurers: the ship has excellent ship-to-shore communication, even this far out in the Atlantic.

I also call younger son. I hate to upset offspring but there are still bad scenarios in my head. Am to be v. glad I did. He alerts whole family and all three work wonders, dealing with UK doctor appointments, collecting vital info, and phoning regularly thus making us better able to cope with crisis. Gratitude for great kids to overwhelm me often in days to come.

3 December: 0800 hours

Message from the Bridge. The helicopter will arrive sooner than expected: in one hour to be precise. Swirl of busyness as I dress (am freezing cold, and realise that spending the night barefoot in flimsy robe and nothing else was not wise). Stewardess Jessica arrives to offer help with packing and proceeds to do it all, a wonderful woman in every respect, as I deal with flurry of calls from insurance people in London, Purser sorting out passports, money, Cunard agent's phone number in Azores and similar. Feeling of numbness and disbelief has replaced bad scenarios. When I am told helicopter won't actually land on ship but will winch us up on a cable, numbness becomes complete. THIS IS NOT HAPPENING.

3 December: 1100 hours

We assemble on deck, which is pitching hard under a bright blue sky. Other passengers kept away by large numbers of crew thronging deck with us, but staring agog through windows. I watch Des, in icy horror, as on red-blanketed stretcher he is hauled on absurdly fine cable up into unbelievably loud helicopter hovering over ship. He swings in the airstreams and I want to scream, but do not. Am impressed by own self-control.

My turn. Only fact Des already up there persuades me to go.

Amazingly beautiful young man with legs and bottom of a ballet
dancer encased in black wetsuit throws his arms about me, attaches
delicate-looking hammock across my back, tugs on cable (which
Des describes later with total accuracy as looking like a thread of
cotton with a safety-pin on the end) and suddenly I am in mid-air
after violent blow to one knee as it hits the rail of the deck as the
ship pitches again. Breathing is exceedingly painful, the sea reels
away beneath me, the helicopter roars over my head and I yelp like
a puppy all the way up. Sudden thought slides into my mind: Is
Portugal in NATO? If not, by God, they ought to be: this young
airman is A HERO. Am startled by own thought processes.

Journey seems hours. Des often sick and out of my reach to help
him. The terror of another bleed returns. My leg hurts like hell. This
definitely not happening . . .

3 December: 1700 hours

Dr T, now looking after Des, is amazing man. The hospital far from
handsome, few trimmings, but staff top rate, nurses caring and generous, and all v. sympathetic. Dr T knows I am a nurse, invites me to
endoscopy suite to watch. Superb communication despite lack of
shared language. See for myself patch of damaged stomach lining,
probably caused by NSAID as suspected and that bleeding has
stopped. With right drugs, as available here at Hospital de Santo
Espirito de Angra Do Heroisme as in UK, he will do fine. May need
blood transfusion, but no need to worry: standards of blood safety as
stringent in Portugal as in UK.

Nasty scenarios banished at last, and I repair to a bed-and-
breakfast establishment (a *quinta*, in Portuguese) found for me by
ever-solicitous nurses. There is an international sister- and brother-
hood in my old profession and I feel very cared for. They even phone
a retired nurse who speaks perfect English, since she trained in the
UK, to come in to make sure we understand all that is happening and
that they understand all our needs. Are we as caring of foreign
nationals in UK? I hope so, but have some doubts.

Speak to younger son and find he has wrought great telephonic deeds all day. Has spoken to ship's doctor, to Cunard in Southampton, to travel insurers and also to hospital doctor here, despite language difficulties. How? Sitting at his desk in his office at home in Brixton, he realised he needed fluent Portuguese speaker who also understood medicalese. Ah, he thought, I'll just pop next door, then . . . Neighbour is a GP married to a Portuguese wife. Our lines indeed fall in pleasant places.

Son able to tell me where we are, hitherto a mystery. There are nine Azores islands, and we are on Terceira, which is the home of the Portuguese Air Force helicopter. That figures.

6 December: 0900 hours

After a long weekend minus food, and the drip still up, Des showing clear signs of recovery, being hungry, fed up and deeply bored. Am elated at this progress. Have spent all day every day with him, learning to admire Dr T and his staff more each day, and hope to take Des this afternoon to the Quinta San Carlos, which is charming and well worth coming back to for a proper holiday one day. Maybe. In fact, have to wait another night – he does need a transfusion.

7 December: 1100 hours

Calloo, callay, Des better. The transfusion has restored his energy and he is determined to get what can be got out of remains of holiday. We hire a taxi and tour the pretty island, though I disgrace myself when we are taken to seaside village with amazing volcanic rock pools when I read its name on a signpost and immediately translate it from my memory of schoolgirl Latin and French into something very coarse indeed. Biscoitos* may sound like a cookie, but it isn't.

---

* It means double-fucked if you haven't managed to work it out!

We eat at local restaurants – great fish and an amazing fish soup served in whole crusty loaf – take in the local air and general peacefulness, and frequently hug each other with gratitude for just being together.

10 December: 1030 hours

Our plane to London via Lisbon leaves on time. We will come back to the Azores one day. It's a very safe place to be, medically speaking, though we can't speak for the volcano crater, which smokes contentedly on Terceira.

13 December: 1100 hours

I collect Des from hospital near home where a follow-up endoscopy shows he is fully healed. He had a mild Mallory-Weiss tear of the oesophageal-gastric junction (science time) and, yes, a small area of inflammation due to NSAIDs. The whole episode lasted just ten days, and has left us even closer than we were and grateful to be so, with the highest possible regard for Cunard, our insurers (PPP), everything Portuguese, especially handsome lads in wetsuits, and a story to dine out on. What more can travellers want?

Late in the eighties I left the *Sunday Mirror* to go to *Today* newspaper. I wasn't sure I wanted to be on a Maxwell paper any longer – it was a while since he'd taken over the Mirror Group – although I personally had had no trouble with him.

If Maxwell shouted at me I shouted back – it only happened once – and if he was rude I was too. He kept me waiting fifteen minutes for a prebooked appointment so I ignored the message of regret I was given by his secretary and walked out. He never kept me waiting again.

But there was something so disagreeable about the atmosphere in the building, with people running about looking pinched and fearful, and some fawning over him. Marge did that – she flirted with him, an awesome sight. Even Anthony Jay, once HM Government's ambassador to the USA, became an 'aide', reduced to sorting out people's parking rights.

Also, the *Sunday Mirror* got a new editor, whom I had known for many years. I had great hopes that this meant the paper would change its old-fashioned and boring tits-and-ass style, but that didn't happen. In some ways, it seemed to me, the paper got even more sex-oriented, with demands coming to me for 'sexier letters'.

Which at once put my back up. In all the years I had done this work, I had never let anyone use letters addressed to me as titillating fillers for a sexy page. I wasn't going to start now. The letter-writers were my patients, and no one was going to get their hands on them for the wrong reasons. I received all the letters at home, directly from the post office, so they were safe. But the pressure on me to provide more access to them was considerable and tedious, so I reckoned it was time to go.

I called my old friend Jane Reed, a brilliant editor, now the kingpin of Rupert Murdoch's empire to which *Today* belonged. I chose it because, on balance, I thought I'd as soon work for Murdoch as Maxwell, I didn't fancy approaching either the *Mail* or the *Express*, and there was nowhere else.

At least the number of letters diminished at *Today* as it was a smaller paper, though I still got masses from TV-am, of course, and lots of *Mirror* readers sent stuff to me at the new paper. But working life wasn't too tough, although I was working as hard as ever filming my own *Casebook* series for the BBC, and doing extra articles for dear old *WO*, where my favourite editor Joan Chapman kept me hard at work.

'You're doing too much, Claire,' she would say. 'Ease up! Take life a bit easier!' And then, in the next breath, 'I need a six page pull-out this week on leukaemia and all the causes and treatments – you know the sort of thing – and next week we're doing a blinder on sex in the first year of a relationship so you'll need to get your head down.'

She was the best and most delightful editor I ever worked with and a great friend. I miss her dreadfully, for she died far too young.

The children were all thriving. Amanda had taken her degree at Chelsea School of Art and in due course joined a magazine on the art desk. She soon discovered her *métier* was promotions and events organising and took to it like the proverbial duck – in her case I think swan – to water and has continued with it ever since.

Adam was all set for life as an ecologist or marine biologist of some sort after the University of East Anglia. He dubbed it, rather bitterly, the University of Extreme Apathy, and got more involved with music, in which he has worked ever since. He is a remarkably well-known journalist in his own special sphere.

Jay weathered a classic adolescent crisis, in his own phlegmatic way, gained a string of good A-level grades, and went to Leeds University, where he still was.

Des was well again, working hard in the studio, selling his paintings, having exhibitions, and being generally productive.

The only fly in the ointment was me. I had not consulted a doctor for years and didn't want to, thank you. I knew perfectly well that I should because something wasn't right about my internal economy. I had pain and all sorts of other tiresome symptoms.

I tried to persuade myself to go, talking to myself like a reader, but of course paid no attention, until I woke in the small hours one morning with appalling chest pains. I thought maybe it was my turn to have a heart-attack, but was certain that in fact it was to do with my guts.

I was right, which was small comfort. It wasn't a heart problem at all. It was a combination of things: a section of the roof of my stomach had, I discovered, been tucked into my diaphragm ever since I was born and, to make digestive life even more uncomfortable, I also had a hiatus hernia, in which a section of the stomach rides up into the chest.

The resulting pain was really horrid, and at last I was persuaded to consider surgery. Anything to get rid of the way I felt, I thought.

In all my years of observing the NHS, commenting on it more or less acidly and in general acting as a health educator to a larger than average captive audience, I had obviously closely watched the behaviour of doctors and nurses in my old stamping-ground. I knew of the amazing developments there had been in maternity care, of the baby lives salvaged that in my time would have been considered no more than miscarried foetuses, of the extraordinary intra-uterine surgery that was now possible to ensure a live birth of a baby we would once have regarded as lost, of the many amazing new techniques available to lengthen and improve human life. Now I was going to have a look at the story from the other side of the counterpane.

I was, of course, shit-scared. I pretended not to be to keep the family happy, putting on a show of insouciance of which I am proud to this day. But my nights were scarred with bad dreams.

I was scared because the access the surgeon would have to use was via my chest, and the thought of having it cracked, to use theatre jargon, was very nasty indeed. I was also deeply uncertain of what they would find when they really started digging around. It was not that I was particularly concerned with the possibility of cancer – indeed, I never gave that a thought because both the consultants I had seen had assured me that this was not an issue. What I feared was a number of things, none of them above the others, but all together creating a pall that hung over my head, from beneath which it was not easy to see clearly. One fear was of so much damage to my digestion that I would never again be able to eat properly. I had nursed patients who, after extensive stomach and gut surgery, had had to live on puréed food and vitamin supplements, and that was a bleak prospect.

Which makes me sound dreadfully greedy, but there was more to my fear than loss of my own eating pleasure (although, yes, I am moderately greedy, and extra specially so when offered really good Chinese food). It was that one of the major pleasures in my life has been to cook for then share meals with people I love. To gossip with friends and family over a littered table while replete and happy is a special delight, and to find new restaurants in foreign parts and share new food experiences with someone you love – these are life-enhancing in a way that sucking fluids through a straw for mere life sustenance could never be. And I agree with Dr

Johnson, who said that a man who does not mind his belly will hardly mind anything else.

Above all, I loathe general anaesthetics. I know that modern ones are amazingly safe. I know they no longer cause the horrible days of vomiting afterwards that used to be the norm, and that I went through in the past after that thyroid operation and also some later ones. But I hate the loss of control that comes with the blackness of anaesthesia. It feels like a little death to me. It might be better if one dreamed, even bad dreams.

I made the waiting for the operation easier for myself by being extra busy, with lots of writing, lecturing and TV, including the totally unexpected (of course) experience of being captured for *This Is Your Life*. The most amazing thing about it all was discovering that Des and the children could lie like Ananias to me so successfully and for such a long time.

I can't pretend I enjoyed doing the programme. I like TV best when I'm doing useful things or talking about useful things and not when I am the centre of attention. That makes me feel like a real lummox, all awkward and odd. I have seen the tape of the show a couple of times since and each time I shudder with embarrassment because I look so stupid.

However, it did take my mind off what was coming, and also reminded me happily of when I appeared on stage at the London Palladium in the *Night of a Hundred Stars* shows. People were coerced and bullied by the producer Barry Mishon, known fondly as Mishon Impossible, to do things they normally never would. He once got me to sing (Me? Sing? I sing like a corncrake, so I spoke the song instead) Fats Waller's 'Gonna Sit Right Down and Write Myself a Letter' with suitably rewritten lyrics for an agony aunt, and appear as Sophie Tucker, wandering my uncertain way through 'Some of These Days'. Both were pretty awful, I thought.

The one thing I did in a *Hundred Stars* show that I was not too ashamed of was with tiny Jack Tinker, a brilliant theatre critic who died much too young, and very tall Matthew Kelly. With our very differing physiques we made an absurd trio, especially when we were dressed up in gymslips with sprung plaits under battered straw boaters, well-drawn freckles on our noses and battered hockey-sticks. We sang 'Triplets', and I had a marvellous time. Seeing them again in all the gear on *This Is Your Life* was a great moment.

And then there was nothing to do but submit myself to the surgeon, which I did, I cannot deny, with a very ill grace.

Forty-eight

Once the operation was over and done with, I was filled with a surge of extra energy that made Des and the children quail. I hadn't felt so well for years. I even took on a new TV series for a channel I had never seen and, indeed, barely heard of. I thought it might be a little something to help me get back to normal but it turned out to be a colossal contract for Sky TV to be used for its launch. I hadn't realised how colossal until I signed up. I had understood I was to be booked for thirteen weeks for a weekly half-hour of problem discussion and health education.

When we got to signature, it turned out that the plan was actually for twenty-six weeks with five half-hours a week. A total of 130 programmes, all to be made in a rather battered studio fashioned out of an old church in St John's Wood where there was no air-conditioning (and it was a horrendously hot summer in 1988) and the dressing-room-cum-hospitality-green-room was a battered Winnebago.

I had to have a special medical examination for insurance since it was so big a contract, which worried me, but the doctor was quite blithe about the surgery I'd had just six weeks ago. He passed me as fit, so I signed a contract promising to do nothing dangerous or to be ill, if I could avoid it, for the ensuing six months.

And then Des and I went on my 'convalescence' holiday to Barbados where I was successfully tempted to go up on one of those wonderful parasails. It was bliss, hanging in an amazing silence, with just the wind whispering in my ropes a little, between a brilliant rainbowed sky and a sea surface that looked like an elephant's skin. All I was able to think was that I had signed a contract promising I would do nothing dangerous. Whoops!

When the series finished filming, and I got my Thursdays back (we had taped five half-hour shows in one day over the twenty-six weeks of the contract), it was good to return to my normal working week. Which upset the family a bit.

'You're always going like the clappers,' Des said. 'You're almost into your sixties now. Isn't it time you thought about relaxing instead of rushing around like a lunatic all over the place?' This is his favourite phrase when he is particularly annoyed with me for over-doing things, which I can't deny I do.

I have a particular penchant for packing days as tightly as a sardine tin. I'll book myself in for a working-breakfast-cum-press-conference in a hotel in town, then go on to the paper or the magazine I happen to be working with at the time, then possibly to a meeting with a publisher before a working lunch with someone important like a magazine editor or, better still, with a mate. I'm likely to end up at an evening reception for a book or a charity, perhaps, after spending the intervening couple of hours with my feet up at the Royal Society of Medicine, of which I have been a Fellow for some thirty or more years and which is a great club.

I think this intense use of time is a leftover from not only my nursing days when I had to be able to do two or three things at the same time, but also the children's infancy when the only chance I had to write was while they slept or were at nursery school. I learned to use time like a miser uses pennies, and it is a habit hard to break.

The reason for packing so much into a day is that I want to spend the other days at my desk doing solid writing. It's only by making sure I limit my acceptances for outside things to just two days a week at most that I can get everything done. As it is, I don't suppose I'm able to accept as many as one in twenty-five invitations or worse. It's a pity because lots of them sound fun as well as very interesting.

I was temporarily stopped in my tracks again by illness, to my fury, in late 1989. I developed an acute infection of the gall-bladder and had to get rid of it as an emergency. This time I had a scar encircling my ribs from the right, almost meeting last year's scar, which encircled my ribs from the left. Amanda looked and said drily, 'Take care not to let anyone step on your foot,' an image that made total sense. I really did feel like a garbage can.

It was all very tedious, but there was one moment I will always cherish from that experience. When they brought me back to my room from the special-care unit I had been in post-operatively the TV was on. I blinked at it, then told myself woozily, 'Rayner, you have very high-class hallucinations, yes, you do. You ought to be pleased with yourself, being so political when you feel so lousy – hee-hee! They're pulling down the Berlin Wall! Must tell Des.'

I was quite crestfallen when I heard it wasn't my imagination, and then, of course, hugely elated.

But things change. By this time – the late eighties and early nineties – I was beginning to feel that the time for my agony aunting was ending. I had always known it was not for ever and it had lasted many years longer than I could have expected. The arrival of any number of aid agencies able to advertise widely was a sign that more and more people would be able to find the information they wanted by direct access to sources of help. They wouldn't need to use my databank or even my leaflets and literature.

Furthermore, subjects considered unmentionable when I started the job, such as oral sex – I had to call it 'Inventive Kissing' in a WO article way back when – were now covered in a whole range of new books, telling readers all they ever needed to know and possibly a lot more besides. All available in high-street shops and even, in some cases, supermarkets.

Then, although the computer age was still very young, I would have had to be a complete idiot not to realise that, in time, people would be able to get from the burgeoning Internet all the detail they could possibly need or want on any subject at all, however esoteric, however embarrassing. They would certainly no longer need the sort of agony aunt I had always been.

I say 'my sort' because I always tried to lead people to the solutions of their own problems rather than be the hander-down of edicts. I hope I'm not pushing this point too hard but modern aunts, I think, with a few exceptions, are expected by their editors and, I suppose, their readers to be sex writers and little else. I would hate to be painted with even a few strokes of those colours.

I was also sick and tired of trying to cope for my readers with the anguish caused by political actions. Whether it was Thatcher herself who said it, or one of her morons, the dictum 'Some unemployment is the price we have to pay for a stable economy' cut deep into family life in the UK.

Poverty and family happiness are rare bedfellows, and too many of the letters I had to try to answer were from people directly hurt by Thatcher's 'Greed Is Good' policies. Some people got rich with her – dammit, I was one of them, up to a point, because of the low level of tax she demanded from high earners as I was in those days. And I resented it bitterly.

I wrote to her at Number Ten asking why she left so much money in the pockets of people like me when other citizens were virtually starving for want of extra benefits from the State. The message I got back was that I should 'give my excess to charity'. Her only answer to poverty was Lady Bountifulism, which I have always hated. It is, of course, a very different thing from real charitable effort, which means putting yourself out to aid others in whatever form they want it. Lady Bountifulism is much more a case of glorifying the giver. Anyway, in a civilised fair society no one should have to rely on handouts to survive. And state benefits are not handouts, but a citizen's just dues. Without such a structure, we are little more than anarchists.

Then there was Norman Tebbit's advice to the unemployed, which clearly the Cabinet approved, to 'get on yer bike' and seek work elsewhere in the country. Many did and the result was a huge increase in my mailbag from desperately lonely, frightened wives afraid that their working-away spouses were having affairs because of their loss of home comforts. They knew perfectly well that together-ness is everything in a relationship. It takes a very special sort of couple to survive prolonged separation.

And it wasn't just the wives who wrote to me. Many men were, indeed, caught in the trap of sexual flings because of the loneliness of being away from home all week, the weariness of the prolonged jour-neys on occasional weekends – and, of course, the stress that built in them as they feared their wives might find out and break up the marriage and home.

The children of those families, inevitably, were caught in the crossfire and showed their misery in their own ways, which added to the pressures on the mother alone.

The same applied to unemployed people who did not get on their bikes but who tried to make a go of things while keeping their fam-ilies together. Their depression, anger and resentment, often complicated by the use of alcohol, could and did split hitherto happy families wide open.

I found it more and more distressing to be under the control of a government that had no notion of what real life was like for the majority of people in the UK. And on top of all of it I felt so bloody *useless*. At least in the early days of trying to advise people I could offer some help – a new idea, a thought they had never before con-sidered, some information to enhance their chance of making good choices.

Now, what could I do, faced by the sort of misery with which these letters were packed? I suppose I felt I had been tolerably useful so far in helping people to mop up the puddles in their lives, but what was needed now was an effort made to mend the plumbing. That was the only long-term answer.

So, my restlessness increased and I wasn't sure what to do about it.

I was also getting restless on the magazine. I had moved from *WO* to *Woman* to write their medical articles when my good friend Joan Chapman, the Deputy Editor of the magazine, had left because she found the new form the magazine was taking was one with which she was unhappy.

I was accustomed to careful fact-checking, of fretting over the style of what we published, concern over whether we had been fair to an interviewee or inadvertently held her up to ridicule. We – the regular staff, who were, I suppose, the old-timers – were not into, and never had been, hostile spin. The new way, however, was to use whatever was 'fun', just as the tabloid newspapers did. And never a hint of remorse when challenged.

I couldn't believe that the magazine for which I had been so proud to work for so long had changed so quickly. Always in the old days it had been 'Is this article fair, factually correct, honest in spirit, interesting and of value to the reader?' It had to be all those to see the light of day.

Now the only question that seemed to be asked was 'Can we get away with this?'

That was why I moved to *Woman* magazine.But after four or so years there I was getting restless again. The space for major feature articles like mine had been cut brutally until a five-hundred-word piece was regarded as an epic. 'It's getting more and more like an old-fashioned draper's shop window,' I complained to the editor, an old colleague from *WO* days. 'Lots of bits and pieces but nothing solid.'

'That's what they want upstairs,' he said cheerfully. 'They say the mag has to go downmarket to compete.'

I stuck with *Woman* but I brooded, working extra hard at TV-am, going to Romania for them in 1991 to film babies with Aids as soon as it was discovered what Ceauşescu had been doing to that desperate country. It was a gut-wrenching assignment, but I'm proud and glad I did it. One of the most powerful memories I have is of a battle-hardened cameraman, who had been everywhere and seen everything, bursting into tears after spending half an hour filming these babies, all of whom we knew were just waiting to die.

We came home on the day the Gulf War broke out and that meant a horrendous journey via Moscow: shorter routes were closed to us. Fiona, the producer, and I were dead on our feet when we did get back – and I found myself up to my ears in a load of frantic letters from war-terrified people everywhere.

And then I got a letter from Virginia Bottomley. We knew each other by sight, having attended the same press and parliamentary events over many years. When she was appointed Secretary of State for Health I thought she might feel somewhat torn: she had been a psychiatric social worker and, like many people who work in the NHS, had, I suspected, developed an affection for it. How would she cope with having to do the awful things Thatcher was planning for it?

The creation of self-governing trusts out of UK hospitals, with all of them being responsible even more than they already were for their expenditure and now also for their income, was Thatcher's Great Idea. She had stolen it from America via an economist guru whose opinion she apparently treated as gospel. The trusts were to 'market' themselves, like supermarkets or suchlike, to local GPs so that they sent them more patients needing operations than they did to other hospitals. Each trust had to make every patient and family doctor consider it the best and consequently to take their business there in what was labelled an 'internal market'.

The trouble with that, in my opinion, is that the ethics of the marketplace, be it internal or external, never put people at their core unless there is money to be made from doing so. It was not the sort of stance the NHS and its staff were accustomed to. For us it had always been, and still is, patients first, second and always.

It was even worse than the old pre-NHS days, because then, at least, all hospitals did their own work and raised their own cash. They didn't feel it was incumbent upon them to undercut other hospitals by reducing their charges to do down 'competitors' – other hospitals. Yet that was precisely what the new system meant. Contracts would be made with the Government via local health bodies, which would set the price of an operation or a treatment, and that was that. Heaven help the patient who had expensive complications! The trust was stuck with the debt. Or, of course, found a way not to treat and saved their money.

Changes in the GP system added further complications. Some were made fund-holders so they could 'buy' care for their patients directly from any hospital of their choice. Others were not, so their patients languished on ever-growing waiting lists while fund-holding GP patients cheerfully barged ahead in the queues. It was a dog's dinner of a plan, a recipe for injustice and as stupid a piece of 'thinking' as any I had ever met.

It seemed to me to make a nonsense of the whole concept of a National Health Service. If hospitals were to be money-minded trusts, who would worry about national quality standards, about fairness to patients north and south? (The North has always had the dirty end of the health-service stick, a shameful thing to admit, but true.) No one, that was who.

I wrote several articles complaining robustly about the scheme, pointing out what I believed were the risks to patients and seething over it all.

And then I got this letter from Virginia. Would I, she asked, accept a post as non-executive director at my local hospital? It would take up to four days a month out of my working life, or more if I was interested enough to get involved in various things. I would be paid five thousand pounds a year for doing it and she would be glad to have me on board, et cetera, et cetera.

Amazement wasn't in it. And then indecision. Was I to stand at the hospital gates and wave banners that screamed 'Down with Trusts'? Or get in and meddle? It took some ten minutes to decide. I'd get in and meddle. Like fury.

Des, of course, worried over the workload. I assured him I could cope, and pointed out that I had been thinking of ending the agony-aunt job at *Today*, though I'd like to stay with TV-am. That would be easier with the reduction of letters from *Today*, and *Woman*, which I'd also like to let go.

He lit up like a lamp at that. But I was a bit concerned. The thing was, could we afford it? To drop such large slices of income would make a considerable difference – even now that the children were all grown-up and almost self-sufficient.

And Des came into his own magnificently. I really had no idea how much we had. I was too interested in doing my own writing thing, and hated arithmetic in all its manifestations. But he had watched our finances ceaselessly and had done it so successfully that he could assure me immediately that there was not the slightest reason why I should not cut back on earning work and do something else if I wanted.

'At just past sixty,' he said, 'you're too young to retire, but if you're ready for something new, fancy going in for a bit of self-reinvention, well, why not? And there are still the books, remember.'

He was right, of course. I was still writing novels at that point, and many were still in print and earning their keep.

'And the odd and sods won't go away,' Des said. 'If you aren't in *Woman* and *Today* every week it'll be noticed and other editors will pop up with ideas. Just you wait and see. Go for it, girl. Turn yourself into an E of the T. They need an Elder of the Tribe over at that hospital. Their A and E's a horror.' He stopped. 'Mind you, if you end up working harder than ever, all bets are off. I'll be after you with a whip and a whistle and get you back to your keyboard.'

'That's a deal, then,' I said. And so it was. I became a non-executive director of Northwick Park Hospital in Harrow.

Forty-nine

I have now almost reached the 'here' from which I started this volume, having gone back to the 'there' where it all began. I've truly tried hard to be honest as I retraced the series of sometimes awkward and painful (as well as thoroughly enjoyable) steps that made up the journey. But I feel I have come full circle from scared cadet in a cap she can't pin on properly to one of the guv'nors running a hospital and calling the shots. It is to me a considerable circle, one to be finally cemented when I am asked, a few years later, to sit on the Royal Commission on the Care of the Elderly.

It is clear to me now that my whole adult life has been centred on one thing: seeking out, then dealing with people in pain and trying to bring them some relief. Why? I wish I knew. And sometimes I wish it weren't so. I see people walk past street beggars without noticing them, hear some abuse those who have to sleep on the streets for want of a better bed, and I cannot, however hard I try, understand them.

Others' misery is to me so potent an arouser of the need to take action that its failure to have the same effect on others mystifies me. When those others assure me that the people I am so upset about are afflicted with 'self-induced damage', I'm amazed that they can't see that people who drink or drug themselves into such misery are sick and not merely wilful.

I suspect that there are some inherent tendencies in people like me to behave so and, of course, I've met plenty in my own profession and outside it who are as distressed as I am by others' pain and feel the drive to try to alleviate it. When Professor Anthony Clare interviewed me for *In the Psychiatrist's Chair* he suggested that this was the case for many doctors and nurses. And the more I think about it, the more I believe that it is so. Some of it may be due to personal experience of pain in childhood but the rest of it, I think, is hardwired into us: we have an extra strand or so of human altruism DNA.

And never forget, of course, that human altruism pays off. It brings benefit to those who dispense it as well as those who receive it, so don't fall into the trap of thinking that such people are special. They're not. They're just made that way and, anyway, they almost certainly gain as much from their own altruistic behaviour as those at whom it is aimed. The sense of warmth, relief and peace of mind that comes from making an effort on behalf of someone in need is very rewarding.

It took me a good while to uncover my own altruism DNA. I have always maintained my life was unplanned and followed accidental pathways. I became a nurse 'by accident' while seeking an escape from an intolerable home life. I became a health educator and writer 'by accident', while looking for something interesting and remunerative to do while my baby was asleep. I turned into an agony aunt 'by accident' because a clever editor pushed me that way.

And that has truly been the way I perceived it. But writing a book like this does more than offer some entertainment (I hope!) and elucidation of a life to others. It's shown me a hell of a lot too.

It's shown me that one of the facts I have learned in a long and busy life applies just as much to me as it does to anyone else. *And that fact is that accidents are uncommon.* It is almost always possible to identify the contributing causes. A series of the same accident is as rare as hens' teeth. Such series imply intent and/or need of some kind whether the person involved knows it or not.

For example, I have told many a sad woman who has written to me about, say, a series of disastrous marriages that she has to understand they don't happen by accident but because she keeps making the same bad choices, even though she doesn't realise she's doing it.

If that is true for the wife of a series of difficult men then it is just as true for me. Her 'accidents' have a function and a meaning. So do mine.

But do I want to know what that meaning is? The beaten wife most definitely does, if she is to escape her next crop of bruises, broken bones and misery. But my neuroses, as a much-loved old friend once told me, I have used to my advantage rather than letting them ruin my life. That being so, would I have been any better off without them?

My friend, a sagacious and highly experienced practitioner, thought most definitely not. And so do I.

It was this that I tried so hard to get across to Professor Anthony Clare fourteen years ago when he first interviewed me, and which I repeated on the second occasion. Whatever foul mud might lie at the bottom of my private pond, it supports some healthy and useful growths. Why stir up the roots at risk of spoiling them? I think I also spoke of using past pain as a philosopher's stone to convert base metal into gold. A bit fancy, that idea, but it goes hand in hand with the notion of altruism. You take on a disagreeable task and out of it comes great satisfaction, not only for the person you helped but for you too. It's one of the great lessons taught by folk stories. Remember *Beauty and the Beast*?

The issue of pain and its effect as a driver in a person's life is trickier. The definition, for a start, is almost impossible. I could write you an exceedingly academic paper on the pain pathways involved in headache and you'd still be none the wiser about headache. Is yours the same as mine? Is mine at all like yours? Pain is the great indescribable, and what one person shrugs off as a gnat's bite another will brood over for the whole of his life as the worst experience a person could have had.

One child can be beaten black and blue and half starved yet

emerge as a tolerably well-adjusted adult, who accepts that some-times things work out badly but never so badly he can't cope. Another can have had two parents who loved him but loved each other more, something for which he can never forgive them; he claims he was neglected and blames them for all his adult shortcom-ings (and, yes, I know both of these people). The first has found his philosopher's stone; the other wouldn't know what it was if it was shoved up his nose. Obviously I regard myself as belonging to the first category.

There are other things about myself I have discovered on my jour-ney from there to here that I did not know, and one embarrasses me deeply: I have a taste for power. That is an admission that shames me because all my political-thinking life I thought what I cared about was the powerless people who needed help to be powerful in their own right. I imagined that in a really fair society no one person would need to try to rob or hurt another, or to exercise their own power at the expense of others. I also believed I wanted no power for myself: just the sense of a job properly done would satisfy me nicely, thanks. Naïve? Of course.

But now I go further and admit the way I enjoyed the frisson of self-satisfaction that I experienced when, on the Northwick Park board, I managed to get something pushed through against the apathy of others. It wasn't due just to the fact that I truly believed that what I had pushed was a better action than the one the other people might have wanted. I just enjoyed the success for its own sake. And that is an embarrassing admission.

Perhaps my frisson came as much from the pleasure of working in a group of people after forty or so years as a freelance, working mainly alone. Whatever the reason, I now know that I have a tendency on which I keep a close eye. It would never do at my time of life to let it run away with me.

I am pleased to say, however, that there is one form of power I have never tried to exercise over others and have managed to resist when others have tried to exercise it over me. And that is the insid-ious power used by the beautiful and the thin to make others less beautiful and less thin feel abject self-hatred. I used to succumb to it, long ago. Those ever-repeated comments 'My, you're a big girl' used to make some part of my guts seem to shrivel inside me. As I got older and watched the way the crowd gathered around the beautiful and the thin, the sense of loneliness and the conviction that I would be lonely all my life filled me with desolation.

I learned to laugh at jokes about my height, like 'It must be bloody freezing up there!', at comments shouted down to me by builders on rooftops like 'You won't get many of those to the pound!' aimed at my breasts, which were always bountiful. At jokes about wearing the boxes shoes come in because no one could possibly sell shoes big enough for my size-eight feet. And all the time pretending not to notice the giggles of other girls who observed my discomfiture and loved it, and who were, of course, beautiful and thin.

But then, when I started work at Epsom and found how much patients appreciated a strong arm to hold them when they were trying to sit up, how many liked having an ample front to lean on when they were feeling sick and I was holding their foreheads, and how many liked to have me alongside to oversee a first post-operative tottering walk to the loo, I began to take pride in the person I was and my size. (Interestingly, it was at the same time that the hateful Problem that had so stained my young years finally vanished. A little self-esteem goes a long way.)

And then when Des turned up and made me stop wearing flattie shoes to diminish my height and great bundled dirndl skirts meant to hide my ample hips, the last hint of the power of the beautiful and thin to hurt my feelings finally trickled away.

As a result I have not weighed myself for years (not interested in numbers) and don't give a damn what size is written on a garment's label as long as it fits. I only show my teeth in a growl when doctors try to bully me into what I regard as sick dieting behaviour. I eat a healthy Mediterranean diet, don't use alcohol and am still the size I am. So bloody what?

Of course there are some hazards to being big, but there are to being thin. For example, I have fine strong bones – no need to fear osteoporosis: that kills as many women as fatness does. Surely we were never designed to look as though we were all squeezed out of the same tube of toothpaste? I always maintain that my relatives and I (a lot of them, both distant and near, match my physique) descend from a long line of winter survivors.

I have said I am now at the end of the journey I set out on, from 'there' to 'here', but not quite. I have said I reinvented myself to a degree when I stopped agony-aunting and gave up the regular columns that had dominated my working life for years. Did my re-invention succeed?

I hope so. I do know that my life is as busy as it ever was, with all my time accounted for and Des still complaining that I run around like a lunatic. Only now I sit on umpteen committees for all sorts of things. Sometimes it's Hospital Food, sometimes it's a Whistleblowers Charter scheme at a hospital, sometimes it's a special project about one or other aspect of NHS business, from ward design to blood trans-fusion policy to the screening for cervical and breast cancer systems, sometimes it's a Funeral Care Forum and so on and on. Always I am there as the Voice of the Patient.

There are also a great many conferences at which I either speak or act as chair, and *ad hoc* symposia, at which I am again the Voice of the Patient. This is because I am now, and have been for many years, involved with the Patients Association, a very hard-working and active pressure group for which I served, long ago, as a vice president, for a short time as chair and now as president.

Latest of all, I have become more active in politics and intend to do even more, if they'll let me. And no, not for the Labour Party.

As far as I am concerned Tony Blair broke this lifelong Labour supporter's heart over the years since 1997 when so many of us believed that at last the political sun had risen and would shine on everyone everywhere.

He has failed us appallingly. His government's stance on such matters as education, transport (!), the environment, the NHS (even more!!), the treatment meted out to refugees, the unpleasant sleaze scandals that have covered his government's reputation in slime and, above all, their disgusting neglect of the care of elderly people leaves me ashamed to be a citizen.

I am now a Liberal Democrat and will do all I can to support them. This is not just because of their stance on the matter dearest to my heart, which is care of the aged. It has been ever since that year I spent at the table in the shabby room over the bingo hall at the Elephant and Castle with the other Royal Commissioners, beavering away and not realising we were being shafted by New Labour even as we worked. It is also because they have other plans in their manifesto worth working for and because, as far as I can tell, they are honest. It's a refreshing experience to be with them, after my dealings with the current incumbents of Westminster.

There is one other political activity in which I take part. It's been a lot more obvious during the weeks I have been writing this text because of the death of the old Queen Mother and the jubilee of the present monarch. I have been interviewed and quoted on the subject rather a lot.

I have tried to explain to all who will listen properly that my views about the monarchy are entirely political. I hold no personal animosity against the present incumbent of the throne, though I have to admit that I reckon the family are a pretty ramshackle bunch. But, then, what family doesn't have its ramshackle sections? I only have to contemplate my own past to know that.

I just want to see this country freed from an atavistic system that makes no sense today: the use of the absurd hereditary principle in our government. I want us rid of the hereditary monarch and the hereditary peers, all at once, please, to be replaced with an elected head of state and an elected second House of Parliament. There are a lot of good political reasons for ridding ourselves of the monarchy, and those who are interested will find them well documented in many places so I shan't offer them here.

My views have attracted a good deal of opprobrium, which is exactly as it should be. A dreadful world it would be if not. Disagreement keeps us alive. Some attackers have wanted to know why I have an OBE. I am happy to explain. John Major's government offered it to me, which was funny, for a start, but it cited me for 'Services to women and to health care', which was cheering. I was glad they'd noticed. I have no objection whatsoever to getting a tick from Teacher, as it were, for a job well done.

Every country has its system of gongs for respected citizens. France has the légion d'honneur and is a republic, as is the USA with its Congressional Medal of Honour. Both meritocracies, yet both have a system for honouring citizens of whom they are proud.

What I object to in the UK is that the gong system is firmly tied not only to the monarch but also, heaven help us, the empire, that defunct and shameful relic of an exploitative and imperial past. Because of this I was going to refuse it but the family bore down on me from a great height, pointing out all that the charities I work with might find it handy to have a gong hanging on the name of their patron or president. And then Adam said thoughtfully, 'You could be called the Old Bag Extraordinaire.'

So I gave in as I was not well at the time (convalescing from yet another knee operation). But I was adamant that no power on earth would get me to the Palace. I don't think my friends believed me but I meant every word. When the summons came I phoned and told the frightfully well-spoken person in the Lord Chancellor's Office that I wouldn't be there. She assumed I wanted it to be given to me by my lord lieutenant, whoever he might be, but I said it meant nothing to me, and if she wanted she could just pop it in the post. Or not bother. Either way was fine.

She popped it in the post two days later. It lives somewhere in a dusty drawer, but don't ask me which. Which is a pity. I could have taken pride in a gong from the Republic of Great Britain, almost as much as I take from two pieces of London-centred notoriety. In 1981 I got the freedom of the City of London. Ten years later I slipped into rhyming slang. Streetwise kids now refer to their trainers as 'a nice pair of Claire's.' Now that *is* an honour!

Fifty

As I sit here in my garden with my feet up on a gentle July afternoon in 2001, 'resting', under direct familial instructions, I look back over the past six weeks, which have been extraordinary for me. Right now, I feel well, I'm told I look well, and I'm happy as Larry – not what you'd expect, perhaps, just six weeks after having both breasts removed because of cancer.

Well before I was diagnosed with breast cancer, I knew I'd taken a gamble that might cause it in me. I was a prime candidate; I'm big and I wasn't able to breastfeed my first child, Amanda, because she was premature. Then, out of perhaps a misguided sense of wanting to treat all my children the same, I didn't feed her two brothers either.

At fifty, I went on hormone replacement therapy (HRT) because I was having very unpleasant flushes and rushes of adrenaline. The evidence *at that time* was that there was a slightly increased risk of breast cancer with HRT, though a reduced risk of heart-attack and stroke, and I thought I'd rather not have a heart-attack and I'd certainly not like a stroke, but I'd take a chance on breast cancer because it's much more treatable.

You meet your body again on holiday getting in and out of swimsuits, and in April we went to Cyprus where I discovered a thickening in my left breast. I thought it was just my boobs going southwards as I got older but it was enough of a change for me to go to my GP when I got back. She referred me to a consultant.

I wanted to see someone at Bart's in the City of London because I'm an associate non-executive director there. Every NHS patient who goes to Bart's with a query lump gets an immediate examination, a needle biopsy if necessary, a mammogram and ultrasound.

When I saw the ultrasound I thought, There's something there, but, even so, I still wasn't that concerned. I was sure I was one of the lucky ninety per cent for whom the lump or thickening is benign.

So it came as bad news when my consultant came back and said, 'I'm afraid you've got breast cancer.' I think I said, 'Oh, bugger!' and after that had a bit of a cry.

My consultant is a wonderful, good, tactile man, who gave me a huge hug and said, 'Don't worry, we'll get you through this.'

I said, 'You'd better or I'll have your guts for garters.'

I was due back for a liver and bone scan the following week, and that weekend was rough. I got really spooked on the Sunday and rang a close friend, who is also a consultant at Bart's. He assured me I'd get the results as soon as possible.

The scan itself was a long, drawn-out and pretty grim business: I knew if I had secondaries I wouldn't do terribly well. But then I was told it was clear, clear, clear, and I was as high as a kite.

I had decided I wanted the whole breast off, not just a lumpectomy, but then two days before I was due to be admitted into hospital I rang my consultant and said, 'I've been thinking and I'd like you to take the other breast as well.'

I was quite a busty wench and I knew from the bone scan that I had some bulging discs: having a heavy breast on one side and a prosthesis on the other can disarrange your back. Also, I knew I'd have no peace of mind as long as I still had the other breast.

I was also worried about a condition called lymphoedema, which can occur when the lymph nodes under the arm are removed. It's a procedure to prevent the cancer spreading but the trouble is that when you take out all the lymph nodes you're also destroying the drainage system, which can make the arm very swollen and uncomfortable.

Luckily, my consultant told me there was a new system they were trying in which they identify and remove the sentinel node plus the immediate ones around it, while leaving enough to continue draining. I decided to opt for that treatment. The risk I was taking was that they'd find the sentinel lymph node was affected with cancer and I'd have to have another operation to remove the rest of the glands.

I was euphoric when I was told on the Tuesday after surgery that the lymph nodes were clear. Also, tests on my other breast revealed that although there was no growth yet, there were early changes in some cells to indicate that there was a high risk of cancer developing. All this meant that I needed no radiotherapy or chemotherapy, though I was offered tamoxifen, which clears the body of any leftover oestrogen that might trigger a return of the cancer. I've got about as good a prognosis as you could have.

Now I have two very neat lambswool falsies. I rather like them. Everyone thinks I should be grieving over my lost breasts, but I'd had them sixty years and they weren't the pretty things they had once been. If I were younger, of course, it would have been different, but I'm a fairly grown-up person and what I value about myself is from the neck up rather than the neck down.

Dammit, I'm past seventy: I'd had them a long time. Des and I celebrated our forty-fourth wedding anniversary last weekend and I knew he wouldn't be heartbroken. It's like old friends: you miss them, but it's not the end of the world.

There have been some faint regrets. On a lovely day when I'm driving along beside Des and the girls are out in their little skimpy sweaters and their boobs are bouncing along . . . I've thought, Ahh . . . But I'm not grieving over the loss of my breasts: I'm grieving for the years that have gone by so dreadfully quickly.

Occasionally, I've been tearful but that's a post-operative anaesthetic effect. It takes very little to reduce me to tears. It made me cry receiving all the flowers and so many letters and cards – three hundred in all. One lady told me she'd meant to write in the late eighties when I managed to get bare boobs on to TV-am to show women how to examine themselves. She said she'd found a lump, that she did have cancer, it had been treated, and she'd never looked back. 'I meant to say thank you then but I'm saying it now,' she wrote. That was a real choker.

I only had one disconcerting reaction when someone I didn't know terribly well phoned me four days post-op to ask, with a sort of avidity in her voice, 'What does it feel like to have no breasts?' I think my answer was 'Interesting' – it's a useful word, covers everything.

I've coped because I'm phlegmatic. The first fifteen to twenty years of my life were pretty grotty, as these pages have shown, but once I'd escaped from the awfulness of my childhood, I had nowhere to go but up, and up I went like a cork. I married someone who is my best friend as well as my lover, and my offspring have been wonderful too. They are some people, that half-dozen – and I say half-dozen because my three children's partners are as good as they are.

My daughter is obviously a little concerned now because there may be a genetic link. My much-loved auntie Nancy, whose name she bears, died of breast cancer in her forties, and I was told by her solicitor, some time in the eighties, that my mother had had both breasts off before she died of ovarian cancer in her seventies (a year before my father died of liver disease). Then my younger sister Maxine died of breast cancer in the early nineties. This means that Amanda, my sister Sheila and her daughter Debbie will have to consider having genetic tests to find out how big the risk is for them.

I had the surgery in a private hospital. I feel ambivalent about having had part of my medical care in the private sector, but I did it only because I wanted to have a room on my own. I didn't do it because I thought that the care was better or even to jump the queue – though inevitably it has that effect. I don't share my bedroom with strangers when I'm well and there's no way I will when I am ill, if I can possibly avoid it.

And, yes, I do feel angry, ashamed and guilty that that choice isn't available to all other women – in an ideal world it would be. But I hate the way some people have picked this fact up and given it a negative twist by turning it into criticism of the NHS. This drip, drip, drip of criticism that comes from certain areas of the tabloid press and goes straight back into the NHS is desperately destructive and desperately unjustified. Of course there are problems, but the successes far outweigh the failures.

There was always a risk of certain papers finding something mean and nasty to say about me. There are tabloids that only feed on malice. So I went public about my breast cancer for three reasons.

First, it was going to get out anyway and I'd rather try to control the coverage if possible.

Second, I was diagnosed on the day the general election was announced and I was gearing myself up to write articles about a Mori poll I'd helped set up to find out what people's voting intentions were when it came to care of the elderly, since the Government had refused in 1999 to implement the most important part of our recommendations regarding nursing care and many of us had been seething about it ever since.

The results were spectacular. An average of forty-three per cent of respondents were prepared to change their vote on the issue. The *News of the World* said that if I'd give it the story of my own disease it would campaign for the elderly for the next three weeks. And I said, 'It's a deal.'

I'm grateful that the cancer turned into a staircase that got me to the top of the highest soapbox in the world: whatever you may think of the *News of the Screws* as a serious newspaper it has a huge readership, and in that context it's powerful.

The third reason I went public was that I've been a lifelong health educator. It seemed wrong to keep my own breast cancer secret when I'd been telling people for years that it's only another disease so let's talk about it. A result of talking about my own disease is that I've been told I'm brave, but I know I'm not particularly.

It bothers me that we've developed a culture that denies mortality and that so many are terrified of the end of life. Death is inevitable, but we wriggle and wriggle and wriggle. I don't want anyone to struggle to keep me alive if I become very ill. That's why Des and I have written living wills. I've made it quite clear that if I have a terminal illness I don't want heroic treatment. I share Woody Allen's feeling: I'm not scared of being dead – I just don't want to be there when it happens.

The tyranny of positive thinking also bothers me. People will use this terrible language about being strong, and fighting cancer by visualising the growth. But you don't tell someone with a broken leg to visualise the bone healing. We all have a certain amount of control over our thinking patterns, and it's well worth thinking intelligently and positively about what's happened to you, but don't get swept away on a tide of mumbo-jumbo.

To get over cancer you need good doctors, good nurses, good food, plenty of rest, the right sort of exercise and people to love you. I'm lucky because I've had the lot. So I think I'll be around for a while yet, making a noise about things that matter and enjoying what life has to offer now that I'm *here*, a contented grandmother of two little boys, Simon, born in 1995, and Eddie, born in 1999, rather than *there*, back in the Bad Old Days.

Epilogue

The Royal Commission on the Longterm Care of the Elderly left the dreary, dusty, sweaty room over the bingo hall at the Elephant and Castle around March 2000. We had worked mightily over our report, which was called *With Respect to Old Age*. (A moment of showing off here: Stuart Sutherland, our chairman, offered a bottle of champagne for the best title any of us could devise. I won the champagne, and even drank a little.)

We knew, of course, that one of our number had written a dissenting report: he had been hell-bent on doing so from the start, but the rest of us stood firm behind *With Respect to Old Age*.

We had made many recommendations, some of which the Government eventually accepted, albeit in a watered-down form. But the core issue, the one that ten of the commissioners held to with a passionate certainty, was not accepted.

It was and remains our firm conviction that those people who cannot, because of age- and illness-associated frailty, wash, feed themselves and deal with their own lavatory needs (especially if they suffer from incontinence) are entitled to free care of those needs on the NHS.

The Government denies that such care is real nursing and decided it should be categorised as personal care and therefore bracketed with social care. This sort of care means the provision of a roof over a person's head, full board, lodging and laundry services in a warm and clean environment. And this, says the Government, a person should pay for according to his or her means, even if that requires selling the family home to realise assets.

The result of this is that if an old person has a brain tumour he goes to hospital where, if he needs feeding, washing and care for his incontinence, he will get it free on the NHS.

If he gets Alzheimer's disease, which also causes inability to feed, wash or clean himself, there is no NHS bed provided: he will have to go into a care home and pay for his feeding and washing.

It is this basic injustice that we are still fighting, via a national campaign called 'The Right to Care'. I seem to pop up on platforms all over the country pleading the cause, and will go on doing so as long as the Government remains intransigent on the issue.

Even though it's not as easy to get about as it was. For our fortieth wedding anniversary we pushed the boat out and went to Hong Kong, China and Bali for the holiday of all times. On the train that took us from Canton city in the Pearl river valley in southern China to Kowloon in Hong Kong we ate in the restaurant car. There, we noticed, with fascination, that diners with bits of bone and skin in their mouths disposed of them by simply spitting them out. On the floor or wherever.

And as we got up to leave the carriage, in a train doing a rocketing hundred miles plus an hour, I forgot the crud was there, slipped on it and went base over apex to land on my knees.

This not only mucked up our holiday, but has mucked up the past four or five years and still causes trouble. When I returned to London I had two or three of those pop-a-light-in-and-look-around operations on the right knee where the pain was worst, but eventually needed a total knee replacement. It is usually a successful operation, but not for me. After several months of continuing pain it was discovered that the wretched thing was loose and had to be replaced again. No fun at all.

Six months later my left knee, worn out with the effort of being the only supporting member, packed up. So, knee replacement number three.

That worked perfectly. To this day it gives me no trouble at all. The only worry is that knee number two on the right – no prizes for correct guesses – is causing lots of pain because it is loose. So, in a month or two I shall be setting out on the journey to collect my fourth new knee.*

Not bad for a biped, I suppose.

All this has meant that my relationships with walking-sticks, wheelchairs in airports, Shopmobility in shopping centres (this is one of the great services of all times, long may it prosper) have become deep and intimate. I am excluded from so much, though, in spite of these aids. I can't use the London underground – all those stairs and miles to walk when changing trains – and have a lot of problems with main-line train services too. I spend far more than I like on taxis, but I'm damned if I'm staying at home to sink into slipperdom. Not when there is work to be done and fun to be had.

At least all this orthopaedic misery has given me extra clout as president of the Patients Association, for which I also campaign and work whenever I can.

I still write – how could I not? – but not as much. It all depends on what I'm asked to do and the sort of ideas that come my way. There is still radio, glory be, though I turn down a great deal of TV because most of it seems to me to be . . . well, let me be generous: not really worth the effort that has to go into it.

For the rest of it Des and I rattle round in our big house from which no power on earth will move me. I love it so, and it fills, from time to time, with assorted offspring and their offspring, and also with my nieces and nephews from Canada and the States. One of them, Josh, who is Lionel's second son, can be seen reporting on

---

* It has been done! In October 2002 my fourth artificial knee was put in place and, at the time of writing, the pain has gone.

baseball on Channel Five: he is an Olympic player, which impresses me greatly. His brother, Mike, is a journalist in the USA after a stint on the *South China Times* and that is impressive too.

I am enchanted by my daughters-in-law, Pat and Julie, who spoil me rotten. As does Colin, Amanda's partner. And as for the little ones – both of them are perfect in every way, of course!

My sister Sheila and her family live a peaceful life in Toronto and two of Maxine's children live and work in Europe. Lionel thrives in Hollywood. To my Leftie embarrassment, he is a member of President Bush's Committee on the Arts and Humanities, and spends a lot of time at the Oval Office, but then our politics have always been poles apart.

I offer all this Happy Families information not in any spirit of showing off – well, perhaps a little – but to prove that it is surprising what can be salvaged from a life, however inauspiciously it begins.

And to warn those who had my sort of inauspicious start or worse that you can't spend your adult life grieving for the child you once were: it is wasteful and pointless, and obliterates the present, which is meant to be your time to live happily.

That child who was you is long gone, dead in fact, and the best you can do for him or her is to make the best of the life that you have now.

I'll never forget the day a dozen transvestites came to tea. They arrived in ones and twos, a group of slightly uneasy men and women clutching bags of clothes and asking for somewhere to change. Quickly they scattered to the four corners of the house only to re-appear ten minutes later, relaxed and happy in their gender of choice. I sat on the stairs and watched, fascinated as men went in and women came out. I was ten years old. So Mother was working late again. This time she was making a BBC radio documentary on transvestism. The contributors had said they'd feel more comfortable talking in domestic surroundings. It was only natural they should converge on Rayner Towers in north-west London. I loved every minute of it.

Being Claire Rayner's son, the youngest child of the famous agony aunt, sometimes had about it the air of a spectator sport, a grand carnival during which almost anything could happen. Because she has always worked from home we never knew what or who would come through the door next.

There was a man who sent Mother a highly detailed, lifesize wooden carving of his erect penis 'just so she could see what it was like'. It got passed around the breakfast table for examination. Then there was the chap who telephoned her one morning and asked very politely whether she would mind listening while, in his own words, he had a wank. 'If you need to,' she said, ever willing to please. Then she put the receiver down on her desk and left him at it for a few minutes until he had finished. These were the stories that filled our mealtimes.

The revelations about Marge Proops's marital strife, published in 1992, may have given the impression that the family life of an agony aunt is destined to be a battlefield. Such emotional problems have nothing to do with the job, and everything to do with the people involved. For the record, my parents have remained blissfully, joyously, ridiculously, happily married for more than forty-five years. My childhood was deeply happy and secure.

It was not, however, ordinary. For one, the pocket money jobs were different. Regularly, Claire would invite the readers of her problem page, first in the *Sun*, later in the *Sunday Mirror* and *Today*, to send in for leaflets on a number of common problems, and my elder brother and sister and I would be the ones to dispatch them.

I would always read them first. When I was ten I could recognise the symptoms of the menopause from fifty paces. By the time I was eleven I knew half a dozen remedies for thrush. I still cannot look at a tub of natural yoghurt without blushing.

Sex education was another recurring theme. Well, it came with the territory, didn't it? When I was three I told my mother I wanted to write a book about where babies came from. My sister Amanda, then ten, did the words. I did the illustrations, or at least some of them. I was good at drawing what I called squirms. Twee but true.

Later, when the era of safe sex dawned, our home took on a more practical role in the field of sex education. Beneath the large oak desk in Claire's cluttered office were hundreds of free condoms, given to her by the manufacturers to distribute: every colour of the rainbow was represented. Every shape, strength and flavour. We were invited to help ourselves. Our friends were invited to help themselves. The household became Condom Fun City.

As funny as life could sometimes be there were also irritations. We all knew that the bottom line to Claire's job was that the thousand or so letters that came through the door every week were from desperately unhappy people. There was nothing more annoying than people nudging you at school and saying, 'But they're all made up, aren't they, those letters?' Of course they bloody aren't.

There were also the people who would say, 'Do you go to her with your problems?' thinking they were the first to ask. The answer was, in the main, no. She may be an agony aunt but she is also my mother. At certain delicate points in my adolescence she was the last person I was going to talk to.

Then came the point, when I was sixteen, when I could not avoid going to her with a problem, when I managed to put the word 'agony' into 'agony aunt'. As well as being an advice columnist, she is also a prolific novelist and broadcaster, constantly in the public eye. We always knew that if any of us screwed up badly, people would notice. I screwed up badly. People noticed.

One evening, at an after-school play party, I smoked cannabis. The school found out and, along with a dozen others, I was suspended. The press had a field day, I was on page three of the *Daily Mail*, the *Evening Standard* twice, the front page of our local papers and many national diary columns. I was talked about on Radio 4. I was the Problem Son of Agony Aunt, a drug-crazed youth walking on the wild side. Hell, I was famous. (Journalists need not look for the cuttings. I nicked them from newspaper libraries many years ago.)

Claire and my father, Des, handled it beautifully. They told the press I was a bright kid who had been experimenting and learned my lesson. They told me I was a bloody fool and admonished me for taking risks with my health. They have always disapproved of any of us smoking even tobacco.

My mother did not, however, clamber on to any moral high ground. It was never her way. When, as the storm was dissipating, I turned to her and said, 'I may have got into trouble but the party where it all happened was bloody wild,' she nodded slowly and said simply, 'I bet it was.'

Jay Rayner, The Guardian, 1993

Bibliography

Fiction

The Final Year*
The Cottage Hospital
The Children's Ward*
Shilling a Pound A Pears
The Lonely One*
The House on the Fen
The Doctors of Downlands*
Lady Mislaid
Death on the Table
The Meddlers
The Private Wing*
Nurse in the Sun*
A Time to Heal
The Burning Summer
Gower Street (Book 1 of The Performers)
The Haymarket (Book 2 of The Performers)
Paddington Green (Book 3 of The Performers)
Soho Square (Book 4 of The Performers)
Bedford Row (Book 5 of The Performers)
Long Acre (Book 6 of The Performers)
Sisters
Charing Cross (Book 7 of The Performers)

---

* as Sheila Brandon

The Strand (Book 8 of The Performers)
Reprise
The Running Years
Chelsea Reach (Book 9 of The Performers)
Shaftesbury Avenue (Book 10 of The Performers)
Family Chorus
Piccadilly (Book 11 of The Performers)
The Virus Man
Seven Dials (Book 12 of The Performers)
Lunching at Laura's
Jubilee (Book 1 of The Poppy Chronicles)
Maddie
Flanders (Book 2 of The Poppy Chronicles)
Clinical Judgements
Flapper (Book 3 of The Poppy Chronicles)
Blitz (Book 4 of The Poppy Chronicles)
Postscripts
Festival (Book 5 of The Poppy Chronicles)
Sixties (Book 6 of The Poppy Chronicles)
Dangerous Things
First Blood
London Lodgings (Book 1 of The Quentin Quartet)
Second Opinion
Paying Guests (Book 2 of The Quentin Quartet)
Third Degree
Fourth Attempt
Fifth Member

Non-Fiction

Mothers and Midwives
What Happens in Hospital
The Calendar of Childhood
Your Baby
Careers with Children
Essentials of Out-Patient Nursing
For Children

Shall I be A Nurse?
101 Facts an Expectant Mother Should Know
101 Key Facts of Practical Baby Care
Housework – The Easy Way
Home Nursing and Family Health
Mothercraft[†]
A Parent's Guide to Sex Education
People in Love (Published as About Sex by Fontana)
Protecting your Baby
Woman's Medical Dictionary
When to Call the Doctor – What to do Whilst Waiting
The Shy Person's Book
Childcare made Simple
Where do I Come From?
Atlas of the Body and Mind (Contributing Editor)
Kitchen Garden (with Keith Fordyce)
The Body Book
Related to Sex
Greenhouse Gardening (with Keith Fordyce)
Everything Your Doctor Would Tell You If He Had The Time
Claire Rayner's Lifeguide
Baby and Young Child Care
Growing Pains
Claire Rayner's Marriage Guide
The Getting Better Book
Woman
When I Grow Up
Safe Sex
The Don't Spoil Your Body Book
Life and Love and Everything

[†] as Ann Lynton